"What makes a writer? What makes a radical? After reading *The Outspoken and the Incendiary* the answer is clear: a heaping of joy, dollops of dreams of a better world, and a soupçon of strange. Terry Bisson, himself an agile and at-a-slant writer, here guides us deep into the hearts, minds, and eyebrow-raising origins of PM's Outspoken Authors—some of the most subversive, sharp, and wickedly funny cultural producers of our time. What changes the world? Story. And these are people doing it."
—Nicola Griffith, author of *Menewood*

"This superb book represents nothing less than a group portrait of the radical mind in conversation with itself. The interviews are illuminating and entertaining in equal measure, as some of the great speculative writers of our time expound upon what has propelled them on their artistic journeys. The book is also a tribute to the late Terry Bisson, literary provocateur, writer extraordinaire, and—as evidenced here—genius interviewer."
—JJ Amaworo Wilson, author of *Nazaré*

"These interviews read like blazing samizdat missives on the last half century of the culture, mainstream, and underground, conducted by a man who witnessed much of it and is interested in all of it."
—Andrew Nette, coeditor of *Dangerous Visions and New Worlds: Radical Science Fiction, 1960 to 1975*

"I've come to think of PM Press's Outspoken Authors series, which has by now been going on for some thirteen years under the editorship of Terry Bisson, as my favorite collection of author hangouts. These modest collections of fiction, essays, bibliographies, and interviews have ranged from legendary authors like Le Guin and Delany to newer voices like Meg Elison and Vandana Singh, and each one feels like spending a fascinating evening with the subject."
—Gary K. Wolfe, *Locus*

"Terry's been an outspoken writer for a very long time, and that he thought what I had to say was important enough to be heard is a lovely thing."
—Nalo Hopkinson

"Fluent and moral and wry, and very much a writer dominated by aftermath issues and emotions, Bisson will continue to be read with great intensity by those who hope to recognize the version of the Matter of America whose complex stories he told, and so wisely and wryly cherished."
—*The Encyclopedia of Science Fiction*

"Terry Bisson was a man of the left—the far left (as his novel *Fire on the Mountain* makes abundantly clear)—and one of his great contributions to SF was his editorship of the Outspoken Authors series."
—Rich Horton, editor of The Year's Best Science Fiction and Fantasy series

The OUTSPOKEN and the INCENDIARY

OUTSPOKEN AUTHORS SERIES with Terry Bisson

1. *The Left Left Behind*
   Terry Bisson
2. *The Lucky Strike*
   Kim Stanley Robinson
3. *The Underbelly*
   Gary Phillips
4. *Mammoths of the Great Plains*
   Eleanor Arnason
5. *Modem Times 2.0*
   Michael Moorcock
6. *The Wild Girls*
   Ursula K. Le Guin
7. *Surfing the Gnarl*
   Rudy Rucker
8. *The Great Big Beautiful Tomorrow*
   Cory Doctorow
9. *Report from Planet Midnight*
   Nalo Hopkinson
10. *The Human Front*
    Ken MacLeod
11. *New Taboos*
    John Shirley
12. *The Science of Herself*
    Karen Joy Fowler
13. *Raising Hell*
    Norman Spinrad
14. *Patty Hearst & The Twinkie Murders: A Tale of Two Trials*
    Paul Krassner
15. *My Life, My Body*
    Marge Piercy
16. *Gypsy*
    Carter Scholz
17. *Miracles Ain't What They Used to Be*
    Joe R. Lansdale
18. *Fire.*
    Elizabeth Hand
19. *Totalitopia*
    John Crowley
20. *The Atheist in the Attic*
    Samuel R. Delany

21. *Thoreau's Microscope*
    Michael Blumlein
22. *The Beatrix Gates*
    Rachel Pollack
23. *A City Made of Words*
    Paul Park
24. *Talk like a Man*
    Nisi Shawl
25. *Big Girl*
    Meg Elison
26. *The Planetbreaker's Son*
    Nick Mamatas
27. *The First Law of Thermodynamics*
    James Patrick Kelly
28. *Utopias of the Third Kind*
    Vandana Singh
29. *Night Shift*
    Eileen Gunn
30. *The Collapsing Frontier*
    Jonathan Lethem
31. *The Presidential Papers*
    John Kessel
32. *The Last Coward on Earth*
    Cara Hoffman

OUTSPOKEN AUTHORS SERIES with Nisi Shawl and Nick Mamatas

33. *Not What I Intended*
    Nancy Kress
34. *She Is Here*
    Nicola Griffith
35. *Veni Vidi Venti*
    Ian Shoales
36. *The Tongue I Dream In*
    Sheree Renée Thomas
37. *FLUME*
    Brian Evenson
38. *The History of the Decline and Fall of the Galactic Empire*
    Toh EnJoe

The
OUTSPOKEN
and the
INCENDIARY

Interviews with Radical Speculative Fiction Writers

Terry Bisson

PM PRESS | 2025

The Outspoken and the Incendiary: Interviews with Radical Speculative Fiction Writers
Terry Bisson © 2025
This edition © PM Press

ISBN (paperback): 979-8-88744-121-4
ISBN (ebook): 979-8-88744-124-5
LCCN: 2025931281

Cover design by John Yates/www.stealworks.com
Insides by Jonathan Rowland

10 9 8 7 6 5 4 3 2 1

Printed in the USA

CONTENTS

Foreword: Outspeaking in Our Field   xi
Nisi Shawl

Introduction   1
Jonathan Lethem

"At the Edge of the Future"   3
Eleanor Arnason

"Fried Green Tomatoes"   23
Terry Bisson Interview by T.B. Calhoun

"A Babe in the Woods"   35
Michael Blumlein

"I Did Crash a Few Parties"   45
John Crowley

"Discourse in an Older Sense"   57
Samuel R. Delany

"Look for the Lake"   67
Cory Doctorow

"Sprawling into the Unknown"   77
Meg Elison

"More Exuberant Than Is Strictly Tasteful"   85
Karen Joy Fowler

"I Did, and I Didn't, and I Won't"   95
Eileen Gunn

"Flying Squirrels in the Rafters"   103
Elizabeth Hand

"Who Does the Work in a Utopia?"   117
Cara Hoffman

"Correcting the Balance"   127
Nalo Hopkinson

"Encounter with a Gadget Guy"   149
James Patrick Kelly

"I Planned to Be an Astronomer"   161
John Kessel

Reflections of a Realist   171
Paul Krassner

"That's How You Clean a Squirrel" Joe R. Lansdale	183
"A Lovely Art" Ursula K. Le Guin	193
"Rooms Full of Old Books Are Immortal Enough for Me" Jonathan Lethem	201
"Working the Wet End" Ken MacLeod	211
"Put Your Twist in the Middle" Nick Mamatas	221
"Get the Music Right" Michael Moorcock	229
"Punctuality, Basic Hygiene, Gun Safety" Paul Park	251
"But I'm Gonna Put a Cat on You" Gary Phillips Interviewed by Denise Hamilton	259
"Living off the Grid" Marge Piercy	271
"Radical, Sacred, Hopefully Magical" Rachel Pollack	281
"A Real Joy to Be Had" Kim Stanley Robinson	289
"Load On the Miracles and Keep a Straight Face" Rudy Rucker	311
"Gear. Food. Rocks." Carter Scholz	327
"The Fly in the Sugar Bowl" Nisi Shawl	335
"Pro Is for Professional" John Shirley	345
"A Source of Immense Richness" Vandana Singh	359
"No Regrets, No Retreat, No Surrender" Norman Spinrad	367
Afterword: For Terry Nalo Hopkinson	375
Elegy Rudy Rucker	379
Elegy Peter Coyote	383
About the Authors	387

Foreword: Outspeaking in Our Field
Nisi Shawl

From low-hanging humor to highfalutin flights of wit wearing fancy-minded velvets, these interviews fill a real void. What void? The void that exists between the words of our stories and the worlds of our lives. Outspoken Authors really want to say what needs to be said. Our stories and essays do that very thing, which is why editor emeritus Terry Bisson picked them for the Outspoken Authors series. But the interviews he included in every OA volume also gave us another chance to tell yet more of the truth and be what we all love to be: heard.

Did you know that Eleanor Arnason's first home was in the past's version of the future? Did you know that Samuel R. Delany received the exact same amount as an advance for the novels he got published in 1961 and 2012? Or that Vandana Singh's New England home is haunted by mountain spirits? Or that Karen Joy Fowler's first published story was judged wanting by Schrodinger's L. Ron Hubbard?

Learn these and other fascinating facts as you pore through this book's pages. Who I took a shit with at the Rainbow Family Festival in 1977. Which one of us found creative inspiration in bloody surgical photos and Brecht revivals. Ponder how such factors could have influenced our stances as stirrers-up of change.

Terry asked us so many questions during these interviews. Sometimes those questions were surprising. Sometimes they pissed us off, and sometimes they gave us low-flying haircuts. We just answered them the best we could.

One of Terry's final acts as editor of PM Press's Outspoken Authors series was to name me as his successor. Such a hard act to follow. I've been lining up a list of appropriate writers and hoping that, with the help of my coeditor Nick Mamatas and the support of the PM's staff, this transition will be wonderfully smooth. Maybe even seamless? Maybe I can ask interview questions Terry would have wished he had ever dared to think of asking?

Or maybe something else. Maybe Nick and I will find some other way to get us authors out here speaking the truth in our extremely verisimilitudinous field. We'll see.

Introduction
Jonathan Lethem

SOMETIMES WHEN I'M PREPARING to write something especially challenging or meaningful I find myself forced to wait until I begin dreaming about the project in question. Typically, this is something that happens to me with novels, projects I've anticipated for years, and which, once begun, will take further years to complete. Occasionally this is true of something briefer, even a piece of writing that seems, when I first agree to do it, to be a simple matter, something easily accomplished.

Last night I dreamt that I was listening to myself on some sort of broadcast or podcast, but what I heard instead of my own voice was Terry Bisson's.

I took it as a sign that it might be time to attempt this quietly challenging introduction to the collected interviews from the thirty-two volumes in his Outspoken Authors series.

Although it might strike some as unnerving or even sinister, the dream of Terry's voice coming out of my mouth was the absolute opposite of those things. It was consoling and embracing. "Oh, do I sound like that to people?" I dreamed myself thinking. "Just like Terry Bisson? That's wonderful." This plainly indulged some sort of wish-fulfillment on my part. I'd be so glad to imagine I could have the effect on listeners that I associate with Terry's voice—glad that I could somehow simultaneously embody avuncular warmth, rigorous skepticism of all received notions, a teasing, even at times needling quality of humor, and a continuous deep engagement with the person or persons in front of me—among other things, Terry's was a *listening* voice. It was also unique in its timbre and tone, the honeyed scratchiness, the equivalent of a mellow bourbon whiskey.

Needless to say, my voice isn't Terry's. Yet when I awoke from this dream, I didn't feel disappointment, but a kind of cheer, as if I'd spent some time with him without even realizing it. I liked thinking that if Terry's voice was so deeply encoded in my brain that I could listen to it in a dream, then it wasn't going anywhere too soon—it was still with us. And it is. A writer with Terry's gifts remains audible on the page for as long as he's read, and Terry will be read for a long time. But in Terry's case I think there's an insinuating, affectionate vocal quality that will keep people hallucinating his actual living presence among us as well. I doubt I'm the only one.

Terry wrote superb novels. *Any Day Now* and *Fire on the Mountain* are my two favorites. Yet it is the title of his first, *Talking Man*, that is most appropriate to the nature of Terry's gifts. So many readers will associate him not only with novels but with a handful of delightful short stories, like "Bears Discover Fire" and "They're Made out of Meat." These are works that encode the grain of his voice, that quality of casual, insouciant surrealism, which is cherished by anyone who knew him. That quality also propagates in the two immediately posthumous books we've been so lucky to get from him: *Tomorrowing*, which collects his miniature short stories published in a column in *Locus* magazine, and this one, which assembles his beguiling and utterly singular conversations with the writers he honored by selecting them for the Outspoken Authors series. In my humble opinion these two little assemblages go straight to the top of the Bisson shelf, and both allow us all to tune him in like a radio station that's still playing somewhere—to dream in his imperishable voice, to sip him like whiskey.

"At the Edge of the Future"
Eleanor Arnason

What in your own background prepared you for being a writer of speculative fiction? Did living in an experimental dream house help?

I did grow up in an experimental house, built in 1947 to be a house of the future—the utopia that was going to happen, now that the Depression and the war were over. We had a garbage disposal, electric heat, and central air, when these were futuristic. The furniture was cutting-edge modern, designed by Charles and Ray Eames, Isamu Noguchi, Alvar Aalto, and so on.

It had been built by the Walker Art Center. When my father became director of the Walker in 1951, we moved into the house, which was right behind the museum. So I grew up in a design project house next to a contemporary art museum, and I grew up around artists. My father loved contemporary art, architecture, and design, and he genuinely liked artists, which is not always true of art historians. He knew a lot of them, as well as designers like Charles and Ray Eames and at least one engineer, Buckminster Fuller.

I came home from school one day and found Fuller holding court in the living room, surrounded by young college students. The Walker was building a geodesic dome at the time. Kids always figure their life is the way life is. It never occurred to me that there was anything unusual or wonderful about finding Bucky Fuller in the living room.

So I grew up around people who were avant-gardists, which means—I guess—they lived at the edge of the future. That was one reason I became an SF writer.

Another was my mother, who was a feminist and a socialist. Like avant-gardists, socialists believe in the future. Her parents were missionaries, and my mother grew up in a missionary community in Western China. I don't think her parents were typical missionaries, since they seem to have been motivated by a belief in social justice and a genuine liking for the Chinese people. I got the impression from my mother that many of their fellow missionaries were bigots and lunatics. In any case, my mother always thought of China as her real home. She never had a bad word to say about the Chinese Revolution. As far as she was concerned, anything that alleviated the terrible, evil poverty she saw as a child was okay.

Chou En-lai was once asked his opinion of the French Revolution. He said he was waiting to see how it turned out. That is my opinion of the Chinese Revolution. But I never saw the poverty my mother did.

My father's parents were from Iceland, which was primitive and desperately poor in the nineteenth and early twentieth century. He grew up in an immigrant community in Canada and somehow became an art historian fascinated by avant-garde culture.

What does this have to do with writing SF? Well, both my parents moved from insular, premodern communities—the Icelandic immigrant community in Winnipeg, the missionary community in far western China—into modern America. For some reason they felt at home in the most progressive and avant-garde parts of American society. I think you could say they were travelers in time as well as space.

So I was raised by time travelers in a house of the future.

Finally, I fell in love with science fiction the first time I encountered it in the TV show *Captain Video* when I was eight or nine. I grew up reading SF. I think I liked it partly because it told me there was more to life than the claustrophobic, white-bread society of Minnesota and partly because it was so realistic. I was living through the McCarthy period and through the period when there were fallout shelters and nuclear war drills in schools. Young children expected to die in a nuclear holocaust. That was their reality. And popular culture was stuff like *Father Knows Best* and *I Love Lucy*. SF talked about radioactive wastelands, and it talked about an American police state. It seemed true to life.

At what point did you decide to become a writer? How long was it between that and your first (or next) success?

I told stories to my kid brother before I was able to write. They were my stories, made up by me. After I learned to write, I wrote my stories down. That continued through high school and college. There was a period in my twenties when I mostly wrote poetry. Then in my late twenties I went back to fiction. I made my first short story sale to *New Worlds*, the legendary English New Wave science fiction magazine edited by Michael Moorcock. In its last or almost-last incarnation *New Worlds* was an original anthology, edited by Charles Platt and published in the US by Avon Books. I sold to this *New Worlds*, which was still a good publication.

I tend to think winning the Tiptree Award in 1992 was my first success. But this is not entirely true. My second published story, "The Warlord of Saturn's Moons," was a Nebula finalist, and the critic John Clute said kind things about my first novel. Maybe it would be more true to say I *felt* obscure until the Tiptree Award. It made a big difference to me.

How come an award for "feminist" SF is named after a guy?
Well, the Tiptree Award is named in honor of Alice Sheldon, who used the pen name of James Tiptree Jr. Sheldon did more than use a pen name. She posed as a man in her correspondence with many SF writers, editors, and fans. She was finally outed by one of her correspondents, who was able to use the information in her letters to figure out her real-life identity. Tiptree was never as comfortable in the SF community after she stopped being a man, and many people think her writing, which had been fabulous, declined in quality.

The award is for gender-bending speculative fiction. Tiptree seemed like the perfect person to honor. It's also a bit of a joke: the first SF award named after a woman is named after a woman who used a man's name.

Were you politically active in the '60s? In what way?
Yes, though I hung out with people who were far more serious than I was. I was in the Student Peace Union during the "Ban the Bomb" period, before Vietnam became a serious issue. I remember riding down to Washington for a demonstration during the Cuban Missile Crisis, when we all thought we were going to die in a nuclear war. We were having a really depressing conversation. Someone finally said, "We have to stop talking about this. Has anyone seen a good movie lately?"

I said, *Hiroshima Mon Amour*.

I went on the 1963 March on Washington with my mother, a college friend, and the college friend's mother. I didn't hear the famous "I Have a Dream" speech, because I convinced my mother to go to the National Gallery. I always finished demonstrations in Washington with a trip to a museum, or tried to.

My college was outside Philly, a short ride by commuter train, and I hung out with political activists in Philly. For the most part, they were members of the Young People's Socialist League, the youth group of the Socialist Party. They left the YPSL in the mid-'60s to form the American Socialist Organizing Committee, which had a brief life. After I moved to Detroit in 1968, I hung out with followers of C.L.R. James, a remarkable man and a wonderful writer. His best-known book is *The Black Jacobins*, a history of the slave revolution in Haiti that took place at the same time as the French Revolution.

My favorite book by him is *Mariners, Renegades, and Castaways: The Story of Herman Melville and the World We Live In*. James wrote most of it while being deported from the US as an undesirable. I read *Moby-Dick* as a result of James. His vision of the *Pequod* as an ocean-going factory, full of workers from all over the world, was compelling.

I knew members of the New Left, but they weren't my people. My friends—who were mostly in their twenties—came out of Old Left traditions and were still—in the 1960s—condemning Lenin and Trotsky for the way the new Soviet government treated sailors at the Kronstadt naval base in 1921. In 1917, the Kronstadt sailors had been heroes of the Revolution. In 1921, sailors at the base made what look to me like perfectly reasonable demands for a more democratic society and one less dominated by the Bolshevik Party. Lenin and Trotsky sent in the Red Army to crush them.

I can understand that Lenin and Trotsky were in serious trouble after the failure of revolution in the West. The isolated revolution in Russia, threatened by foreign armies and civil war, must have felt very precarious. But they shouldn't have been crushing revolutionary sailors. Power to the people!

I worked on a campaign for a third-party candidate who was running for city council in New York. That was in 1963. A lot of the work was gathering signatures to get the candidate on the ballot. Because I was shy and reluctant to ask strangers for a signature, I was given the job of office manager at the campaign headquarters on 125th Street in Harlem. I have a vivid memory of the night I couldn't get the door to lock. There I was on 125th Street. It was pitch black, and I couldn't leave the office unlocked. A couple of kind passersby got the door locked for me.

I was part of a group of college kids who gathered supplies for striking coal miners and ran the supplies down to eastern Kentucky. As with Harlem, what I mostly remember is how difficult it was for me to communicate with people I admired. The hills are their own world.

Mostly I read books and listened to people argue political theory. I was more comfortable with words and ideas.

The '60s were long ago. Have you been politically active since then?
On and off. Mostly, I have been active where I lived and worked—I was a shop steward in an art museum and a hat factory, a local and national official in the National Writers Union, in DFL precinct politics when Patrick and I owned a house.

I should mention that the DFL is the Democratic–Farmer–Labor Party, the Minnesota version of the Democratic Party. It was formed by a merger of the Farmer–Labor Party and the Democratic Party in 1944. This is a quote from Floyd B. Olson, Farmer–Labor governor of Minnesota, speaking on the steps of the state capitol in 1933:

> I am making a last appeal to the Legislature. If the Senate does not make provision for the sufferers in the State and the Federal Government refuses to aid, I shall invoke the powers I hold and shall declare martial law. . . . A lot of people who are now fighting [relief] measures because they happen to possess considerable wealth will be brought in by provost guard and be obliged to give up more than they would now. There is not going to be misery in this State if I can humanly prevent it . . . Unless the Federal and State governments act to insure against recurrence of the present situation, I hope the present system of government goes right down to hell.

And this is from Wikipedia:

During his three terms as governor, Olson proposed, and the legislature passed, bills that instituted a progressive income tax, created a social security program for the elderly, expanded the state's environmental conservation programs, guaranteed equal pay for women and the right to collective bargaining, and instituted a minimum wage and a system of unemployment insurance.

Mostly, the DFL is another Democratic Party. But there something left from the Farmer–Labor party—how much I am never sure. The progressive wing of the DFL remembers the party's Farmer–Labor roots.

Did your artistic side propel you into politics or was it the other way around?
Given my background, the two went hand in hand.

Like Hansel and Gretel?
Yes, though I don't remember leaving a trail of breadcrumbs. I don't like leaving tracks.

How would you describe your education? What were your most productive (not favorite) fields of study?
My formal education was the University of Minnesota's experimental grade school and high school, plus Swarthmore College and grad school at the University of Minnesota. My undergrad and grad major was art history. I like art history, because it positions art in a historical context. Art doesn't float above the real world like a Platonic form. It is rooted in a specific age and society and social class.

But my real education came from my parents, the activists I knew in the 1960s, and the people I worked with in office jobs in Detroit.

I started writing seriously in Detroit. After I moved back to Minneapolis, I continued to work office jobs, along with some rather nice warehouse jobs, and I kept writing, though always slowly.

I gradually acquired a skill—full charge bookkeeping—and got better jobs, which took more time and energy. For about ten years I wrote very little. I'm trying to get back to writing, now that I am unemployed.

And with undiminished artistry it seems. **Mammoths of the Great Plains** *is a story within a story, told by one character to another. Is that structure a departure for you?* I like embedded stories. But I have never done anything exactly like *Mammoths*, where the whole story is being told with quote marks, so the reader never forgets the frame setting in Fort Yates on the Standing Rock Reservation.

A lot of real history is told to us, how our parents grew up, what they did during the war. And Native Americans really respect oral tradition. I didn't plan this—in fact, I just thought of it—but I am describing a classic form of Native American learning, a kid listening to an elder, who is likely to be an elder relative.

In Ring of Swords *and* A Woman of the Iron People *we see alien cultures through the eyes of scientists or diplomats from Earth. I find the society they left behind as mysterious and wonderful as the one they are investigating. You suggest utopian elements that remind me of Marge Piercy's* Woman on the Edge of Time. *What a peculiar, and wonderful, way to construct a utopia, almost as if it is seen in peripheral vision. Can you talk a little about the Earth your far travelers leave behind?*
I'm not sure about the Earth in *A Woman of the Iron People*. My travelers have been on a starship for two hundred years, and Earth has changed a lot during this period. I suspect society there has moved past socialism to something post-socialist, maybe a communist utopia, though the people on the ship think the new society back home is more than a little nuts.

I'm working on a sequel to *Ring of Swords*, which begins on Earth, and it is making me crazy, because I have to describe the society on Earth, and I am stuck with what I wrote in *Ring of Swords*. Earth has nine billion people, and it is still a class society. But it hasn't fallen apart, which I suspect it would have. Instead, people are trucking along, doing the best they can, dealing with the environmental mess we left them. My current theory is, the rich have moved to space colonies where they live surrounded by their middle-class servants: doctors, lawyers, artists, scientists, and hairstylists.

(They don't have all the professionals, but they have the ones who are into serious luxury. Earth is a place of rules and limitations. It has to be, in order to keep nine billion people fed and housed and living okay lives.)

The rich are left alone, because it's too much trouble to destroy the space colonies. I assume they have some power, but I don't know how much. I think the Earth in this novel is something like a Scandinavian social democracy, though maybe with less money.

The novel is set about 150 years in the future. The decisions we make now will determine that future, which means my idea of the future keeps shifting as I watch contemporary politics. If global warming continues along its current route, Africa is going to be arid and deeply impoverished. An official from Senegal at the Copenhagen Climate Summit said the behavior of the rich countries—refusing to deal with global warming and letting the nations of Africa face death by starvation and war—was like the Holocaust. The rich countries were outraged, of course: How dare this person compare what's happening to Africa to the Holocaust? The Holocaust was a real tragedy and crime.

Anyway, one of the important characters in the novel is from Harare. So I need to think about her Africa.

Can you explain why you favored this indirect approach to world-building?
Maybe because I'm habitually oblique. I can write a straightforward story, I suppose. But in most of my writing, I use indirection to find direction out.

As mentioned above, it's hard to figure what our future will be and how we will get there. It's easier to do an end run around the problem.

In Woman of the Iron People *you describe a world with no cities and no wars. Is that a utopia? Most of your books have happy endings. Is that a political position or an artistic propensity, or both?*
No wars would be great. It certainly looks utopian from here. I like cities, but I think they need to be smaller or at least much more compact than contemporary American cities. Right now, we need to preserve every bit of arable land we have, so we can use it for farming. This probably means very dense urban areas. But we are also going to have to stop relying on long-distance shipping. So maybe we will have small, dense cities that can live off the surrounding land. Or bigger cities with lots of gardens.

I am in favor of happy endings in fiction and real life. I think people need to believe that life can be better than it is right now.

Do you have a regimen or routine for writing? Do you like doing first drafts or revisions most? (Or dislike one of these least?)
I am trying to create a routine, in order to up production. Right now, I tend to write when I feel like it, which is not often enough.

In general, I like writing the first draft, because that's when I find out what the story is about.

I used to do three drafts: the first handwritten, the second typed with handwritten revisions all over it, and the third a clean typewritten manuscript which I could send out.

Now, I mostly work on a computer and revise as I write, so there are no longer three distinct drafts. I write a few pages, print them out, revise by hand, input the revisions, and continue. If I don't do this, I begin each session at the computer by revising the last section I wrote, then continuing. It's back and forth, like sewing with a lock stitch.

After I have a complete story, I run it though my workshop. They suggest changes. I input most of their changes and maybe a few of my own. Then the almost final version of the story goes to my agent, who may suggest a few more changes.

Your novels are unusual in that the characters take time out to pee. Would your mother approve?
My family loved food and eating. What goes in must come out in some form sooner or later. I think my mother was realistic enough to know that. And I got my love of American plumbing from somewhere. I wouldn't be surprised if it came from my mother, who grew up without it.

There was talk of a sequel to Ring of Swords. *Where is that now? Does it have a title?*
Hearth World.
It's set on Earth and on the alien home world—two hearths for two different species.

I'm revising it and going crazy trying to figure out the Earth society. Also, the novel is too dark right now. I have to make it happier.

What writers were most influential in getting you underway? Who are the most influential today?
The writers I remember from my childhood are William Tenn, Philip K. Dick, Cyril Kornbluth, Frederik Pohl, Avram Davidson, Fritz Leiber, Robert Sheckley, Leigh Brackett... The New Wave writers were important later, then the women writers of the 1970s. I read Samuel R. Delany and very much admired his work, also the people published in *New Worlds*. I especially liked John Sladek, who was from my part of the country, though he lived in England for years. John was a brilliant and brilliantly funny writer who died too young. I read Suzy McKee Charnas and Joanna Russ, Octavia Butler, James Tiptree Jr. and all the women writers who began publishing in the 1960s and '70s. Ursula K. Le Guin has been the most important influence. When people ask me what my writing is like, I say it's like Le Guin.

As the first winner of the Tiptree Award, you have been deeply involved in the feminist movement in SF. Can you give us an idea of that and how it developed?
I wasn't active in the feminist movement in fandom in the really hot period, during the late 1960s and early '70s. I was out of touch with the science fiction community at the time. However, my fiction is feminist, and I have done a lot of panels at cons, starting in the mid-1970s when I moved back to Minneapolis and reconnected with science fiction fandom. A lot of panels have been about women's issues, gay and lesbian issues, race and racism in science fiction, class issues in science fiction.

I guess you could say a lot of my political activity since the late 1970s has been talking politics in the science fiction community.

When I went to my first science fiction convention in 1961, fandom was entirely white and 80 percent male. Women were marginalized as "femfans." Gay people were in the closet. The history of the community since then has been the painful assimilation of women, GLBT people, people of color...

If science fiction is going to be a real community—and a real literature that matters to the real world—it has to deal with prejudice and class.

There is an anthropological bent to most of your SF. Is that from your own original inclinations, or does it reflect the influence of Le Guin? Or both?

I've certainly been influenced by Le Guin, also by Marx and Engels in *The German Ideology*, where they argue that people

> are the producers of their conceptions, ideas, etc.—real, active [people], as they are conditioned by a definite development of their productive forces and of the intercourse corresponding to these, up to its furthest forms. Consciousness can never be anything else than conscious existence; and the existence of [people] is their actual life-process. physically do in the concrete universe. . . . Life is not determined by consciousness, but consciousness by life.

In other words, I am interested in the relationship between ideology, technology and the organization of everyday life.

I'm also interested in alienation and disjuncture—the people who don't fit in, the moments in history when tradition is not adequate to deal with new realities.

I think all of this is anthropology, though it isn't the study of unchanging, traditional societies; rather it is the study of societies on the move.

A critic once described you as a poet of "the beautiful and the loony." Was this a friendly comment?
Yes.

There is a lot of humor in your work, but it's unannounced (i.e., dry). There's no laugh track. As you say in Mammoths, *you are not going to point out the jokes. Is this because you are sneaky, or just classy?*
I didn't realize I was telegraphing my humor technique in *Mammoths*. But yes, you are right, that line tells the reader exactly what I do.

Part of this is my habitual sneakiness. The other part is Scandinavian and Scandinavian-American humor, which is often deadpan.

Tell me something about the Rivendell group. How come Minneapolis has such an active SF/fantasy community? Is it the weather?
If it's the weather, we are in trouble, because the weather is getting warmer.

Rivendell happened and continues to happen because of David Lenander. He has done most of the work. David also maintains websites for several local authors and critics, including one for me. I am very grateful to him for this.

The local science fiction semipro zine *Tales of the Unanticipated* is due to Eric Heideman, though Eric has had help over the years. *TOTU*'s poetry editors—Terry Garey and Rebecca Korvo—have been excellent. Eric is also responsible for a lot of the serious literary programming at local science fiction cons.

Ruth Berman and I started the oldest local SF fiction-writing group in the 1970s, and it was really hard to get it going. There were far fewer writers and aspiring writers in the Twin Cities then.

Other writing groups appeared later. I am in two at the moment, one for poetry and one for fiction.

Then there are all the people who worked on Minicon, back when Eric and I were active on the con committee, and who split off to form new conventions. Once you have an environment where writing is taken seriously, more writers begin to appear. Fandom is always full of people who love science fiction and dream of writing it.

Isn't Rivendell more fantasy than SF? Or do you make those distinctions? How does the Mythopoeic Society fit in? Do you feel at home in SF today?

I read and write both fantasy and science fiction. There are obvious differences between the two, but the writers I grew up with wrote both. American fantasy has two roots, I think: Tolkien and science fiction. Like science fiction, it builds worlds that are more or less logical, given the premises. I suppose you could call it pedestrian, one-foot-after-another fantasy, as opposed to the wild flights of surrealism and magic realism. When it doesn't work, American fantasy plods. When it does work, it has many of the pleasures of science fiction.

David Lenander, the guy responsible for Rivendell, is an old friend of mine, and other old friends belong. So I feel very much at home there.

I feel at home with the people at the WisCon science fiction convention, which bills itself as the only feminist SF convention in the world, and with much of the Twin Cities science fiction community, especially the people who split off from Minicon during the Big Blowup. I was involved in an extended struggle within the Minicon con comm in the 1980s. The struggle was between people who wanted to open the con up and create a more diverse local fandom, and the people who wanted to keep local fandom the way it was: white, straight, male–dominated and hostile to media fans.

The people who split off formed three new conventions, all of which welcome diversity, and all of which are rolling along quite nicely. Minicon has shrunk from three thousand attendees to about four hundred. It has survived thus far, though it's been a struggle. I told them years ago they weren't going to last if they relied on aging, straight, white fans. Mortality gets you every time. I have mixed feelings about the SF community outside the Upper Midwest. Sometimes I feel close to it, and sometimes it ticks me off.

How come?
Boy, a hard question. Partly, I often feel out-of-place in the larger science fiction community. I don't like going out to dinner with forty other people. I'd sooner have breakfast with a couple of people, especially at WisCon.

I like the SF community when it is open-minded and open to the world—liberal in the oldest sense, with the same root as liberation and liberty. I like it when it deals with serious questions, such as the nature of our current society and our future, if any. It can do this through humor and satire. Many of the best SF writers are very funny.

I don't like the science fiction community when it's narrow and closed-in and trivial.

How come so many of your characters are furry or hairy (including the mammoths of the Great Plains)? Is it because St. Paul is so cold?
I am trying to use more scales and feathers, because readers confuse my various furry aliens. I grew up with cats, and I love the furry little critters. I think my love of fur comes from them.

There's more than one way to skin a cat.
I would never even think of skinning a cat. It sounds horrible. But I have more mittens than I need already.

Your first book had a dragon in it, I believe. Does that mean you started as a fantasy author? It was a small one.
As I remember, there is no magic in *The Sword Smith*. The dragons are intelligent therapod dinosaurs, and the trolls are hominids of some kind, maybe Neanderthals. So that book was science fiction disguised as fantasy. My third novel—*Daughter of the Bear King*—was fantasy, but the editor labeled it as science fiction on the spine, because "it felt like science fiction" to him.

I write both quite happily and like stories that mix science fiction with fantasy.

Do you do hack work or media work in addition to SF? Have you done comics, kids' books, other peripheral SF genre stuff?
No. I might enjoy doing some of this, but I write too slowly.

Any movie options? A Woman of the Iron People *would make a great road movie.*
Nope. Nothing of mine has ever been optioned. I understand the money for the option is great, but actually getting a movie made can be painful.

There are references in your work to poets such as John Donne and Gerard Manley Hopkins. What poets do you read for fun? Do you write poetry? Do you do readings?
Right now I am reading Bill Holm, the wonderful Icelandic American poet who just died. I'm also reading Freya Manfred, another Minnesota poet, and Louis Jenkins, yet another Minnesota poet. I very much like the North Dakotan Thomas McGrath, who was a great twentieth-century American poet, I think, who has been undervalued because of his politics. Tom was an unreconstructed Stalinist. He once almost ripped my head off because I said something nice about Trotsky. But he loved "no war but the class war," which is a line Trotsky wrote. I didn't tell him this.

I do write poetry, and I belong to a poetry workshop, which does performances at cons under the name "Lady Poetesses from Hell." (The group includes two men, but women are the majority.) We are working—very slowly—on an anthology. The people in the group are *good* poets.

You refer in Woman of the Iron People *to the Finland Station. Is this in Moscow, Leningrad, or Outer Space?*

In the novel it's a space station. Obviously, it's a joke—and a reference to the train station in Petrograd where Lenin arrived at the start of the Bolshevik Revolution. He had been in exile in Switzerland. Trotsky was in Brooklyn when the revolution began, a fact I love.

In an interview you once expressed annoyance with far future novels that are based on today's science, and your works are often set in the near (or an alternate near) future. Does that make you part of the "Mundane" movement in SF?

I don't think so. My irritation is with the hard science fiction writers, who take so much pride in having their science right, even though it's twentieth-century science and their story is set thousands of years in the future. Most of these writers are guys, and their societies are often quite traditional. The characters have Anglo-Saxon names, like the characters in 1940s pulp science fiction stories. The society they live in is like our society now or like American society in the 1950s. This is ridiculous.

All human societies change. You can see this in changing stone tools during the Paleolithic. You can see it in art and architecture from the Neolithic on. How do you think art historians date most art? By the technology and techniques used and by the style, all of which change.

I have nothing against far future SF and off-the-wall, almost-magical SF. Just realize that technology changes society, and weird technologies are going to create weird societies.

Also realize that real science in the far future is going to involve ideas and machines we can't imagine, any more than sixteenth-century scientists could imagine Relativity and the Large Hadron Collider.

I haven't liked the term "Mundane science fiction" since Geoff Ryman almost made me crazy a few years back by saying that nanotechnology is impossible and not worth writing about. All nanotechnology means is "very small technology," and it's happening right now. Scientists are designing machines made from molecules and atoms, and they are doing things with viruses and genes that are changing the world.

Most of us may remain human, because gene mod might well be expensive. But I don't think the rich are going to be human in the future, and if they need modified servants, they will get them.

I tend to stick to the next couple of hundred years, because I don't want to twist my brain into knots trying to figure out where science and society are going to be in the far future.

If you could read in any language other than English, what would it be?
I already read French, though not so well, and Icelandic with a dictionary in hand. I'd like to be able to read Icelandic fluently, so I could read the sagas in the original, also modern Icelandic poetry. I'd like to read Chinese poetry in the original, but I understand classical Chinese poetry is insanely difficult, even if you are fluent in the language.

Why?
Chinese because China was my mother's home, and I love Chinese poetry in translation, and because it's a really different language.

Icelandic because it was the language of my father's ancestors, and I love the Icelandic sagas. I took medieval Icelandic in graduate school. It's a Germanic language, as is English, which makes it a lot easier than many languages. One of my plans for retirement is to settle down with a dictionary and the *Grettis saga Ásmundarsonar* in normalized Old Norse and keep translating till I can read Icelandic easily. Of course, the Icelandic I will be able to read is thirteenth-century Icelandic. I will then have to learn the modern vocabulary.

Have you traveled a lot as an SF author? Where to? Have you ever been to Iceland?
No. I traveled a lot as a kid with my parents. Now I stick to trips around the Upper Midwest and visits to New England and the Bay Area, where I have relatives. I've been to Iceland twice. I'm interested in Latin America—Costa Rica for the birding, Venezuela and Bolivia for the politics, Cuba because it's supposed to have a sustainable economy, the only one in the world. I hear Cuban music is awesome.

A lot of your work has to do with aliens and alienated people, in other cultures than their own. Yet you live in the same city where you were born and raised. Explain.
I was born in New York. As a kid, I lived in New York, Chicago, Washington, DC, London, Paris, Chicago again, St. Paul, Minneapolis, Paris again, Minneapolis

again, Honolulu, and Minneapolis again. Some of these stays were only a few months. Others were years.

I spent six weeks in Kabul as a kid, which is not long enough to say I lived in Afghanistan. But it shows up in my writing. A beautiful, utterly amazing country. As an adult, I went to college in the Philly area, then moved back to Minneapolis, then to New York, then to Detroit, then back to Minneapolis. I now live in St. Paul. So, I did a fair amount of traveling before I was thirty-three and very little since then, except around the Upper Midwest. There's a lot in the Upper Midwest. I figure you can know only a few places well.

But I should travel more. That's on the to-do list. The plus side of my upbringing is—I learned to dislike prejudice and believe in justice, to love art and take joy in the range of human cultures, above all the range of human food. My family ate its way around the world in 1959 and enjoyed every bite. The downside is, I didn't fit into the very white, midwestern culture of Minnesota in the 1950s.

That sense of not belonging is still with me. I have never thought that I understood Americans as a group. (I am not entirely sure they are a group. Minnesota has more in common with Manitoba than it does with the southern half of the US.) But I am in many ways a product of Minnesota and of this part of North America. I guess you could say I am both rooted and alienated.

Rosa in *Mammoths* is like this.

Why am I still in the Twin Cities? They are more affordable than New York and safer than Detroit. The weather's better than Seattle. The greater metro area sprawls way too much, but the two core cities are reasonably sized. There are three good art museums, two good orchestras, a perfectly adequate opera company, two good city park systems, and a lot of good regional parks. There are many theaters and lakes. Bald eagles nest along the Mississippi in the metro area. I see wild turkeys now and then, along with lots of hawks and herons. I understand Minnesotans as well as I understand anyone, and my friends are here.

Do you read mostly fiction or nonfiction? What sort of fiction do you read?
It's fifty-fifty. I read science fiction, fantasy, and detective novels. Very little "literary" fiction, unless it is fantastic. My nonfiction is science and politics. I love books about biology, evolution, and dinosaurs.

Do you have any hobbies? I hope not.
Bird-watching. I became a bird-watcher after I discovered birds are descended from dinosaurs and can be called living dinosaurs. The love of my youth was returned to me—smaller and able to fly. I am not a fanatic. I do not keep lists. But looking for birds makes me notice my environment more, and I do love having dinosaurs around.

What kind of car do you drive? There are not many guns or machines in your work. How come?
I don't drive, which is weird and hard to explain. The household car is a Saturn SL1 with 170,000 miles on it.

I don't like guns. When I lived in Detroit, lots of people were armed, and the murder rate was eight hundred a year. I didn't see that the guns made life better.

Fiction is a way for people to think about their lives and imagine ways to change their lives. Most of the violence in science fiction isn't helpful. It doesn't work as an example of how to change the world.

I am not sure that violence is always a mistake. But you had better be very careful how you use it. It can easily lead to really dire consequences.

If there is kind of violence I feel comfortable with, it's the kind used historically by working people: tossing a sabot into the gearing or a spanner in the works.

Obviously, working-class violence can go beyond this. The father of one my friends in college was a CP thug in the 1930s. He and his buddies would beat up fascists in New York City. Was this wrong? I leave it to you to decide. Fascists are very dangerous. And I remember being told that you can't run an unarmed picket line in eastern Kentucky. Still and all, workers are more likely to rely on fists, bricks, bottles, and sabotage. The bosses do most of the shooting and killing. I can think of outright labor wars: the famous war between mine bosses and the Western Federation of Miners in Colorado early in the twentieth century. But it seems most of the violence—especially the violence directed toward people—came from the bosses and the state government.

I don't have a lot of machines in my fiction because I don't understand machinery well enough to imagine future machines. I do have a dragon flush toilet in my first novel, and there's a fair amount of plumbing in my fiction. The modern American bathroom is a wonder, though it wastes far too much water.

Do you go to a lot of movies?
No, though I like some anime, especially Miyazaki, and the Aardman movies, especially *Chicken Run*, which is the best socialist chicken movie I have ever seen. I love *WALL-E*.

Going to more movies is on my to-do list, along with going to more plays and museums and traveling more.

What do you think of Al Franken? Barack Obama? Sharon Olds?
I like Al Franken and have hope for him. He might turn out to be a good progressive. Though this might not be adequate. I am starting to think the country may well swing either far right or far left. If far right, Al may end up like his friend Paul Wellstone. If far left, he may turn out to be too much of a centrist.

My opinion of Barack Obama is not fit for a family publication.

Sharon Olds the poet? I don't know her work, though I will now look it up. She turned down an invitation to the White House. Everyone should. It's not a decent place to visit.

Do you believe in life after death? During? Before?
I believe in life during life. Death seems real and may be useful. I began to like mortality, when I realized it was the only way to get rid of the leaders of the American union movement. But I don't like personal mortality and would like to live long enough to see how this century turns out.

"Fried Green Tomatoes"
Terry Bisson Interview by T.B. Calhoun

Is writing a political project for you or an artistic project?
I reject the distinction, at least for fiction. Though I have done a lot of straight propaganda writing. For several years I helped write and edit the newspaper of the John Brown Anti-Klan Committee. For me propaganda is about One Thing, in that case trying to encourage, indeed to build, an antiracist resistance among white people. Everything was bent to that end. Fiction writing is by definition about complexity.

How did you get into writing? Was it something you always wanted to do?
Ever since I was a teen. I was seduced by the Beat Generation back in the 1950s. They were in *Life* magazine and they were so cool. I wanted to get away, out of the South, out of the suburbs, indeed out of '50s America where I was born and raised.

I was always a reader but now I wanted to be Jack Kerouac. I even subscribed to the *Village Voice*.

I'm pretty sure I was the only subscriber in Owensboro, Kentucky.

What is your personal background?
Pretty conventional, middle-class, small-town Upper South but a liberal family. I was raised in the suburbs but my mother was one generation off the farm. I'm old enough to remember coal stoves and squirrel suppers, but I was raised in the new postwar suburbs, two cars and skinny trees. My father came from the North (Illinois). I was a TVA baby.

My Kentucky family was (and is) pretty liberal, from the days when the "Solid South" was still Democratic. FDR brought them electric lights and concrete roads. Once in my twenties, home from New York, I tried (probably foolishly) to explain to a favorite aunt why I was a radical, a Marxist, an all-round antiwar hippie rebel. She nodded and said, "You are still a Democrat, though?"

I said sure.

Did you go to college?
English major. Very conventional. But committed. Literature was my thing by then. I ended up in New York, trying to sell a Kerouacian novel which never sold, and ended up working for romance magazines, softcore porn mags, astrology and western pulps, *Enquirer* type tabloids, low-end publishing in general. And discovered I liked it.

No science fiction?
SF was my first literature but I outgrew it, or so I thought. I wanted to be a serious novelist. I was working on a "serious" novel called *Eats Corpse for Rare Coin*, based on my experiences in the tabloids. The problem was, it kept getting short instead of longer. It was '68 and things were busting loose all over. I quit trying to write and joined up with the hippie movement in the Southwest.

No politics?
We were all political in those days, or so we thought. I went to all the antiwar demos, but I wasn't part of the organized left. That came later. I spent a lot of time in hippie communes in the Southwest and later back in Kentucky.

I didn't become actively political, in a real way, until the later '70s. I was one of those who got organized by the Weather Underground, by Prairie Fire, and by the groups they organized after they broke up. My wife and I moved to New York and did a lot of work about Puerto Rican independence. Then the John Brown Anti-Klan Committee. At the same time, I started writing again. And it turned out to be science fiction!

Go figure.

Ever write for comics?

My first paying freelance stories were for *Creepy* and *Eerie*. I edited a comic mag for a while, *Web of Horror*, and even wrote a series for DC. But I never liked the superhero stuff and never passed the "Marvel test."

(Don't ask.) A couple of years ago I worked on a project with Stan Lee himself, but it came to naught.

Where did you get the idea for The Left Left Behind?
From France. A French writer and critic, Patrice Duvic, suggested that we work together on a book in which the world is a better place after the Rapture, minus all the Born-Agains. I thought it was a cool idea. Patrice had cancer and died before he could do much on the project, but the idea and the inspiration was all his.

I swiped the beginning of the story, the encounter with the prophet in Israel and the disappearances on the airliner, straight out of the *Left Behind* movie, then made up the rest. The ending, by the way, the scene on the train, is swiped almost word for word from R.A. Lafferty's wonderful utopian story "The Interurban Queen." Find it if you can.

Did you see the movie The Rapture? *Did you like it?*
Several times. A lot. It was written and directed by the great Michael Tolkin (who also wrote *The Player*). Mimi Rogers and David Duchovny, and a great ending. But much much darker than mine because it takes the idea seriously. See it!

You wrote a novel about John Brown, Fire on the Mountain. *Did that come out of your work in the John Brown Anti-Klan Committee.*
Totally. I became fascinated with the old man, and visited Harper's Ferry and Kansas, where he fought a guerrilla war that prevented Kansas from entering the union as a slave state. Brown was not a nut, as the right would have it, or a martyr (as much of the left sees him) who sacrificed his life for a just cause. He was in my view a seasoned and effective fighter who might have succeeded. My novel is about what if he had. And the nation of Nova Africa in my novel was inspired by the Republic of New Africa (the RNA), revolutionary Black nationalists dedicated to liberating the Deep South.

And there's yet another connection between the John Brown Committee and the John Brown book. I wrote the first two chapters while I was in federal prison.

For fighting the Klan?
For refusing to testify before a grand jury. The feds were looking for some folks who were still underground. Several of us in John Brown were subpoenaed and were jailed for contempt when we refused to talk. Not that we knew anything. We had a principle of noncollaboration—following the lead of the Puerto Ricans who had refused to "cooperate" with the search for the FALN. I only did three months, and several others did more. It gave me a start on the book, which was the most complicated thing I had done so far. I had to read a lot of history and make up a lot more.

So it's not exactly a science fiction novel.
Sure it is. It's an alternate history, a what-if.
Plus I threw in a lot of wonky technology and even a trip to Mars. I even swiped a device from SF's famous alternate history, Philip K. Dick's *The Man in the High Castle*, which is about a post-WWII America occupied by Germany and Japan. Dick has a novel in his novel about what might have happened if America had won the war. I have a novel in my novel, a right-wing fantasy in which capitalism gets a new lease on life and America becomes a world power. A tragedy.
Alternate history has a long and respectable tradition in SF. Much of it is dystopian: The south wins the Civil War, the Nazis conquer England, etc.
Philip Roth wrote a cool one, *The Plot Against America*, in which Lindbergh and not FDR is elected president and the US becomes an antisemitic fascist state. He didn't even know he was writing SF!

After that you ran a business called Jacobin Books.
Back in the '80s. My wife and comrade Judy and I ran a mail-order business that catered mostly to prisoners. We would buy revolutionary books in English from Africa, Ireland, the Caribbean, and here in the US, and mail them to prisoners. Political prisoners like David Gilbert and Mumia Abu-Jamal wrote reviews for

our catalog. In those days prisoners had access to a little spending money, so it was a break-even operation. Not so easy today. The prisons are tighter than ever, and I doubt we'd even get the books in past the mail room.

All political books?
Mostly. Though Charles Mingus's *Beneath the Underdog* was a big seller. Assata's bio was big. Our bestseller was *Settlers: The Myth of the White Proletariat*. Every student of labor history should find and read that classic.

Have you ever been a union member?
I tried the National Writers Union (NWU) once. But alas, freelance scribblers are independent contractors, including myself.

Do you miss your time as an activist and organizer?
Not so much. I was never good at mass work. I finally had to face the fact that I am, in fact, a petit bourgeois intellectual and make the most of it.

Have you written any traditional SF? You know, with a rocket ship on the cover?
Absolutely. Time travel, first contact, little shop stories, space travel. Even a robot or two. My latest novel, *Planet of Mystery* is about the first landing on Venus. I believe in knowing and respecting the conventions and traditions of your field, whatever it is. I think every rock band should be required to work up a version of "Johnny B. Goode."

As a matter of fact, my next book after *Fire on the Mountain* had a *big* rocket on the cover. *Voyage to the Red Planet* is pretty standard space travel stuff with some elements of political satire, I suppose. In it, the first trip to Mars is financed by Hollywood.

Do you work on a regular schedule?
I try to, mornings. My novels have never made enough so I have always had to do pickup writing and editing on the side. What I call afternoon work. I wrote a bunch of novelizations (making a film script into a book, which is sort of a backward project) and packaged a goofy series called *The No-Frills Books*. I did a car book with Click and Clack, the Tappet Brothers (NPR). Working with

them was fun. They hired me because I had mechanic experience and because I had once played in a bluegrass band, the Allen County Jumper Cables. I also wrote a biography of Nat Turner for "young adults," whatever that means. I'm still fond of that book, which is found in most libraries.

And you wrote a biography of Mumia Abu-Jamal.
On a Move. Mumia's title. That was a labor of love, though it paid well too. I was lucky enough to meet Mumia back in the '80s, through a friend who was in prison with him. I visited, and we became friends. I helped him get his first book, *Live from Death Row* published. We still are friends, though I have seen him only once since I moved to California. He wrote the introduction to the new edition of *Fire on the Mountain* which PM is bringing out. He has been in solitary confinement for over twenty years. Yet he continues, though his radio work and his writing, to be the "voice of the voiceless."

And he is innocent.
And they know it. That's the most shameful part.

Perhaps your most widely read story is "They're Made out of Meat." It's often found on the internet.
That's cool. I like writing all-dialogue stories. I have done several. They tend to be short, although one of them, "macs," was longer. There is something about stories in which everything is revealed in dialogue that appeals to me.

Like a radio play?
Exactly. I have done several radio plays, and even got one produced at Radio City. But it's way too hard to get anything produced on the radio. It's a perfect venue for SF, but it seems all anyone wants to do is jokey retro stuff like Garrison Keillor's "noir" detective. It's a drag.

You worked as a mechanic. Was that a stretch for a literary guy?
Not at all. I have always loved cars, even big evil American cars, and I got back into working on them when I lived in the communes. There are always plenty of cars to fix. When my wife and I left the Southwest and moved back to Kentucky

(she's from Tennessee), I found myself working as a tractor mechanic, and then as a transmission man. I still do it but not enough. I miss the problem solving involved. It's more intellectual than writing, which is a lot of guesswork.

Did your parents read to you?
Never. They were middle-class but not bookish. There were no books around our house. I read to myself from an early age. I was lucky. I was taught to read before I went to school by a "colored" babysitter, Lily Mae, who helped me work out the words in Captain Marvel. Shazam—it made sense immediately. I went straight from comics into the *Oz* books, all thirty-some-odd of them, then on to science fiction, which was easy to find on the drugstore racks. I remember getting a chill reading "Surface Tension" by Blish, probably my first genuine literary experience.

I still think *On the Road* is a great novel. Other early influences were James Ramsey Ullman and his biography of Rimbaud. A teacher gave me *Walden* and another turned me on to Beckett. All this was like honey to a sixteen-year-old in Kentucky.

Do you still regard yourself as a southern writer?
Not really. Some of my early work was set in the South, particularly *Talking Man*, which is about a hillbilly wizard, and "Bears Discover Fire," a sweet little tale set in Bowling Green that won me my only Hugo. I still love and identify with the South, particularly the Upper Redneck NASCAR South.

Darrel Waltrip and Jeremy Mayfield are both from my home town. But I can't stand the "fried green tomatoes" sort of folksy hometown southmouth crap.

Where do your ideas come from?
From my butt. If I sit on it long enough in front of a word processor, I usually come up with something.

Have you ever written for movies?
I've done scripts. An independent producer hired me to write a film about Mumia, which is still being shipped around but with no success. The media is

afraid of Mumia. I recently scripted a biopic of Paul Robeson, which is still in play but has never been produced. I would love to see that film done. Robeson is the forgotten man of the civil rights movement. He was totally cast aside because of his politics—he was an unapologetic red and a steadfast friend of the Soviet Union at a time when that was verboten. They were careful not to include him in the March on Washington.

Is your interest in Robeson the source of your play Special Relativity?
No, the play was done long before the screenplay. My agent suggested I write something about Hoover's long-time harassment and hatred of Einstein. What I came up with was a comedy, sort of. I'm not sure Robeson would approve. I know Hoover wouldn't.

SF critic Nick Gevers once called you a satirist, and you insisted you are not. Who's right?
Gevers, probably. *The Left Left Behind* is certainly satire, and rather broad at that. So is "The Old Rugged Cross," though less broad. It's about a guy on death row who gets religion and insists on being crucified. But usually the satirical elements are secondary. I regard myself as a realist, really. Humor and satire are part of reality.
    Aren't they?

Do you have favorite short story writers?
R.A. Lafferty, the late great SF writer, was a huge influence, though as writers we are very different. He's a singer; I'm a talker. Thom Jones is I think the best short story writer wiring in America today. Molly Gloss runs a close second. Another favorite is David Sedaris who doesn't call his work short stories, though they are. He is sneaky.

You have hosted several SF reading series. How did that come about?
Luck, mainly. A good friend in NY, Mark Jacobson, a high-powered journalist (*New York* magazine, *Village Voice*) put together a casual "nonfiction" reading series for his fellow journalists who, unlike poets and the literati, rarely get to read in public. Mark pulled me in to help and it was fun. We got big names like

David Remnick (before he took over the *New Yorker*) and Jimmy Breslin and Jack Newfield, plus real-life pornsters, rock critics and wild punk gonzos. Mark knew everybody. Even Steve Earle came and read! We had a regular slot at KGB, a downtown literary bar. Alice Turner, my editor at *Playboy*, and I decided to try to same thing with fiction, and we teamed up SF writers with "straight" writers, and since Alice also knew everybody, we got Joyce Carol Oates reading with Lucius Shepard, Michael Cunningham with Rachel Pollack, Jonathan Lethem with Brett Easton Ellis. When Alice dropped out I teamed with Ellen Datlow, the premier SF editor, and we ran it as straight SF. Once a month, big names and small. When I moved to California in 2002 I teamed up with Adam Cornford, a poet and professor at New College. Then New College folded and now the program, SFinSF, is sponsored by Tachyon Books. I get to be the "host," and that's fun as ever.

What's your advice to a wannabe writer?
The same advice Gary Snyder once gave to wannabe poets. Learn a trade. Plumber, carpenter, cook, mechanic. Learn how things fit together.

You have some experience teaching writing. Do you really think good writing can be taught?
Writing can be taught. The conventions of fiction: dialogue, point of view, timeline. Every writer should learn the baseline conventions. What can be taught about writing can be learned in a few months. Good writing is a different matter. It can be learned but not taught.

Peter Coyote gave you lots of credit for editing his memoir, Sleeping Where I Fall. *How did you get that job?*
Peter and I are old friends. We met in college and remained friends through the hippie commune Digger days, though we ran in different crowds. I was never part of the West Coast scene. Peter is a fine writer, had already won a Pushcart Prize for a piece of the book, and only wanted another (colder) eye on how to shape the thing. That was me. It worked out well. I tried to get him to change the title, but Peter rejected all my bad ideas.

You also worked on Walter Miller's sequel to A Canticle for Leibowitz.
Alice Turner recommended me for the job. Miller had worked for years on the sequel to his classic bestseller, but he was depressed and old and alcoholic besides, and he wanted somebody to finish the book according to his instructions. It was all there. All I had to do was land the thing, and the wheels were already down and it was lined up with the runway. I never got to meet Miller. He killed himself before *St. Leibowitz and the Wild Horse Woman* was finished.

Are these different skills—editing and writing?
Absolutely. The trick in editing is to stay out of the way. The editor should be invisible. I have edited several memoirs since Coyote's, mostly of old political comrades and friends. I edited Diana Block's book about being underground, *Arm the Spirit*. That was a pleasure. Also political prisoner David Gilbert's memoir. And I edited a serious nonfiction book, Dan Berger's history of the Weather Underground, *Outlaws of America*.

Does this mean you approve of the Weather Underground?
Very much. I came to know them late but I dug them from the beginning. Like the Panthers, they were young and foolish, and like the Panthers they restored militant internationalism to the American left. The first time I saw them running through the crowd at the March on the Pentagon carrying a "Vietcong" flag, I thought, "Of course!"

How do you feel about anarchism?
As an idea I like it. But I am a big government guy. I'm a TVA baby. Still a Democrat.

Why are you raising your hand?
I thought of another satire. I wrote a story called "Pirates of the Somali Cast" a few years ago. I did it to make fun of all the people who thought pirates were cool (the Johnny Depp syndrome). I was unfair to the actual Somali pirates, though. In my satire I made them very cruel and, in fact, they are not, at least so far, or so it seems. Nothing to rival Guantánamo.

What do you think of hip-hop?
I think it's sad. To me it's a minstrel show. Saddest of all are the Black intellectuals who celebrate it because it's "authentic." Lots of stuff is authentic.

How come there are no pirates in Pirates of the Universe?
Pirates are boring. The universe, on the other hand, is interesting.

You have written several books for young readers. Do you enjoy writing kid's books?
Not particularly. I still get fan letters for my Boba Fett books though they were a nightmare to write, since Lucas had to approve everything. I did a YA series about stock car racing that was even worse: NASCAR was trying to go mainstream and they killed all the hillbilly and redneck jokes. My adult characters couldn't even chew tobacco or say "ain't." This was before NASCAR got hip and allowed *Talladega Nights,* the second-funniest movie ever made.

What's the funniest?
Spinal Tap. Everybody knows that.

Other than Lucas and NASCAR, have you had any encounters with censorship?
Very few. SF is generally under the radar, which is one of the advantages to not being taken seriously by the media. I did have a hard time placing *The Left Left Behind,* and I suspect that's because it satirizes Israeli militarism. Christian fundamentalism is fair game but Israel is not.

You've been writing for some thirty-odd years. If you had it to do over, what would you do?
Work harder. Learn to touch type. I still hunt and peck which is maybe why I am such a stingy writer. I always write short. My last two novels are novellas. This is not a career plan in SF.

Do you like fried green tomatoes?
Of course. Bourbon even better.

"A Babe in the Woods"
Michael Blumlein

What's the story behind "Paul and Me"? The dedication suggests one.
The Paul Bunyan stories were favorites of mine when I was a kid. I remember a drawing of him: short, dark beard, rolled-up sleeves, lumberjack pants. Except for his size, he could have been one of the Village People. The dedication is to my friend and fellow SF writer, Terry Parkinson, who died in the epidemic. RIP, Terry.

What did you become first, a doctor or a writer?
I longed to be a doctor from a very early age. I adored my pediatrician, who wore a bow tie, carried a black leather bag, and made home visits. In high school I pored over color photographs of bloody surgeries and worked in one of the early genetics labs.

At about the same time, I fell in love with theater. It sparked me in an entirely different way. Seeing Brecht's *Caucasian Chalk Circle* in 1965 was an epiphany. I wanted to do something that mesmerizing and charged.

I acted in college. After college I went to med school and started playing in a rock 'n' roll band.

My guitar chops were no match for my inner fantasy life, which was overpowering. I wrote my first story during my internship, after making a nearly fatal mistake on a patient. Fantasy is useful when you feel like shit. It's alchemical.

Who is Vladimir Vitkin? What's the story behind X,Y, *the movie?*
X,Y (based on my novel of the same name, directed by Vladimir Vitkin) is a cult classic. The cult is not big, nor is it particularly vocal. The lucky few who saw it at Slamdance and other film festivals when it was first released obviously want to

keep the secret to themselves. Because of postproduction difficulties, of which I am largely ignorant, the film disappeared. Rumor has it that a handful of copies exist in private hands, deep underground, carefully guarded.

What writer inspired (or compelled, or condemned) you to write SF and fantasy?
My own damn self condemned me to write this stuff. I was prone to nightmares, loved puzzles, and was insatiably curious as a kid. In sixth grade I asked our wonderfully urbane and delightful history teacher, who was waxing poetic on the Renaissance, if Michelangelo could cut a diamond. This stopped him cold. My classmates ridiculed me. But I was undeterred, then as now. "What if?" I asked. "What if he could?"

Inspirations? Writers came later; books were first. *Harold and the Purple Crayon*, by Crockett Johnson. I devoured that book. Still a great read. *One Thousand and One Arabian Nights. The Phantom Tollbooth*, by Norton Juster. Richard Halliburton's *Book of Marvels. The Wonders of Life on Earth*, a sprawling, coffee-table-sized bonanza of a book, published by *Life* magazine in 1960. *The Mathematical Magpie*, compiled by Clifton Fadiman. DC Comics, as shepherded by Julius Schwartz. Of the New Wave writers, Zelazny in particular struck a nerve. And J.G. Ballard showed me what was possible.

You were twenty in 1968. Where were you? What were you up to?
In '68 I auditioned for the SF Mime Troupe. They were blowing people away. I didn't get in and went back to Yale. Pre-med, but only by a thread. Did some theater, picked up a guitar, bought a camera, a Pentax, and started shooting film. Industrial stuff mostly. Black and white. Cinéma vérité. Started writing poetry and hanging out with filmmakers and poets. Weekends in NYC. Hitchhiked that summer across the country with my girlfriend, a trip that turned into a highlight reel of fun and misadventure. She was an activist, an organizer, and a radical feminist. The second wave was just breaking. I got swept up in it.

Your first published SF story, "Tissue Ablation and Variant Regeneration: A Case Report," is about presidential politics. Isn't it?
What is this? HUAC? Homeland Security? I demand to speak to the ACLU.

Doesn't space travel interest you at all?
Living things are my first love. Space travel interests me mostly as a means to get from here to there. But not exclusively. I love the questions it raises about time and cosmology, and to a lesser extent, its effect on living passengers. But loving it doesn't mean I understand it enough to write about it. If only.

As for the space ships, the stations, the portals, and the travel itself? The nuts and bolts? Gimme a cup of coffee, and I'm hooked.

You have been dubbed by some a "language writer." Could you explain what this means?
In college I wrote poetry. I ran with a bunch of poets who kept writing it after college. Gradually, it got more abstract and experimental. Headier. To people like me, harder to understand. These writers formed the nucleus for what became known as "language poetry."

I never wrote the stuff. My mind doesn't work that way. When I read it, what appeals to me is its apparent spontaneity, and the challenge to understand its meaning. But most of the time I don't understand, which is why I rarely read it.

Language writing? Not sure what this means. If it's the prose equivalent of language poetry, I plead innocent. If it means caring about words and phrases and sentences, saying them aloud, working and reworking them, striving for something, being way too OCD, I plead guilty. Count me in!

What was your first interaction with the SF community. Did it provoke scorn or terror?
Two experiences stand out. Can't remember which was first. Both involved individuals.

One was a woman who'd advertised (can't remember where) about starting a SF writers' group. I met her at her house, a big Victorian, might even have been a mansion—dark wood walls, poorly lit, kind of creepy. I was the only one who came. The whole thing seemed weird, and after five minutes it became clear we were on completely different wavelengths.

The other experience happened at Fantasy, Etc. in San Francisco, a great little bookstore in the Tenderloin. A guy was browsing the shelves, and we got to talking. He was smart, opinionated, acid-tongued, and funny. He knew the field much better than me, and he became something of a mentor. This was Terry Parkinson, whom I mentioned earlier. For a while we were inseparable. Terry was never afraid of dreaming big.

My first convention, I believe, was a SerCon at the Claremont Hotel in Oakland in the '80s. My reaction to it: about equal parts terror and scorn. You hit the nail on the head. I was a babe in the woods.

Ever do a writing course or workshop? Do you have a method?
I taught writing briefly. I used the workshop method I'd read about and participated in at Sycamore Hill. I didn't last long, mainly because I spent more time providing written comments to stories (1–2 pages, single spaced) than the writers spent writing them. No time left for anything else. Fortunately, I had a fallback job, so I stopped.

You were sixty in 2008. Where were you? What were you up to?
My father died in 2008 at the age of eighty-nine. That summer my beautiful California became an inferno, forest fires raging up and down the state. I wrote a story called "California Burning" about my dad and his cremation. Fire is a prominent theme. Also aliens, who somehow snuck their way in.

We did a staged reading of the story, harking back to my theater days. Big fun. You played one of the aliens, Terry. Remember? Everyone thought you were Terry Bisson, but we knew better.

The story's been optioned for a movie. My advice to you: stay by the phone.

Each in one sentence, please: Arthur C. Clarke, Molly Gloss, Atul Gawande.
Clarke: He had me at *2001*. But deep-sea diving? A life underwater? The space elevator?!

Gloss: Stunning. Soulful. Not a wasted word.

Gawande: I haven't read him. I know, I know . . . and I do read widely in the field, but almost exclusively in professional journals.

You wrote a play, No Fast Dancing. *Was it performed?*
I was commissioned to write a play for an evening of Grand Guignol theater. *No Fast Dancing* was the result. Was it ever performed? I wish I knew. I've had

work performed on stage, including short stories, that I only found out about afterward.

You wrote a screenplay, Decodings. *Was it produced?*
Decodings is a groundbreaking independent film of found footage. Michael Wallin, the filmmaker, asked me to write the script, which I did. The film received a number of awards, including the Special Jury Award of the San Francisco Film Festival. It was also selected by the Whitney Museum for its biennial exhibit of American art.

What aspect of medicine interests you the most? Of writing?
Of medicine: our body's extraordinary and ongoing balancing act, its nearly flawless internal communication network, its deep ecology and multiple layers of consciousness. In the office, the most interesting stuff, not to mention the highest high, comes face to face, when a patient and I connect.

Of writing: rewriting. Digging.

A lot of writers deal with pain, psychological, spiritual, existential. You work deals with it as a medical event. You even suggest that it has a therapeutic function. Is this a scientific or a literary device?
Pain is universal. Every creature on Earth reacts to it. It teaches us human creatures what to avoid. Internally, it alerts us that something's not right. Without pain we wouldn't survive.

In conditions where pain is blunted or absent, like diabetes, leprosy, and drug and alcohol overdoses, injuries go unnoticed and can lead to infections that also go unnoticed, and these can lead to loss of limb, or worse.

For several years in the 1950s, prefrontal lobotomy was used for intractable pain. Cancer pain, for example. A last resort. The procedure involves severing the nerves that transmit pain from the lower to the upper brain. A funny thing happens when you do this. The patient continues to be aware of the pain but is no longer bothered by it. One is conscious but unperturbed.

This advanced the thinking about pain. A distinction was made between pain and suffering. The two could be detached, severed as it were.

Therapeutically, this can be useful. People can be triaged. This one to physical therapy, that one to psychological or emotional therapy. Some people benefit from both.

Pain is a fact of life. We've all experienced it, each of us in our own unique, self-defined way. I'm tempted to say the same about suffering, but I'm less sure. Personally, I've suffered, and professionally I've seen my share of it. But then I'll come across a patient who by all rights should be suffering terribly but isn't. Suffering somehow isn't in their DNA.

There's a saying I've heard, a kind of teaching: pain is inevitable, but suffering is optional. I think I understand what this is driving at, and it may be true. Or the truth may be more complicated, because our brains are complicated and only rarely severed.

True or not, it's a pretty high bar, if you ask me. But who doesn't like a person who meets adversity with pluck and courage?

Literature is full of such characters, including some of my own. They're among my favorites.

Anything new coming out?
All I Ever Dreamed, a collection of all my stories and novellas since the ones that appeared in *The Brains of Rats*, from Valancourt Books.

A new novella, entitled *Longer*, about everything under the sun. Under *my* sun, that is: love, sex, gender, betrayal, forgiveness, a mysterious life form, weird experiments, life after death and death after life, space travel, olfactory suspense, and more. The usual stuff, in other words. Lots of fun.

What kind of car do you drive? I ask this of everyone. Actually you can ignore this question, since I know you drive a car that initiates little discussion, which is perhaps its signal virtue.
Little discussion, save from my kids, who ridicule it mercilessly. Smelly and ugly, dented and scratched. But as it ages, so do they, and with age comes wisdom. In their case, an appreciation of the fact that the more they laugh, the less likely I am to trade it in.

Your work is concerned a lot with ethical dilemmas. Is this a feature of medicine or of science in general?

Science is amoral. You can't pick and choose. Or you can, but then you run a big risk. It's like free speech.

Medicine is not inherently ethical, any more than an individual is, or an institution is, or society is. All of them have an opinion and a say, not to mention a stake, in what is right and wrong.

Personally, I never *stop* thinking about ethical behavior. After I wrote my Reagan story, a man noted for his casual disregard for the sick and needy, I asked myself: if he were shot and came to me for help, would I give it? More to the point, could I refuse?

In practice, medicine should—and mostly does—make ethical decisions. But beware of unintended consequences.

Recently, under sustained pressure from PETA and other groups, the last medical school still using animals to train students stopped the practice. This was a victory, not just for the animals, not just for the animal rights activists, but for all of us who believe that life is precious, life of all kinds, that it's wrong to unnecessarily kill other species. Ethically, this represented a step forward. No more animals sacrificed for the benefit of budding surgeons. Now these surgeons will do their practicing on people.

If you have money, you'll go to a surgeon with experience. If not, you'll get one of the others, who, in the absence of a dog or a sheep, will do their learning on you.

You say much of your medical practice is with the underserved. How does this work in the real world?
Except for one year in private practice, I've spent my whole career working in public, not-for-profit institutions, doing primary care. For four years I worked in a federally funded clinic in the Mission District of San Francisco, caring for immigrants, refugees, and the very poor.

For fifteen years after that I worked in an acute care clinic at UCSF, caring for roughly that same population.

My Jeopardy *item—I provide the answer, you provide the question. Answer: Gender.* Question: Do you have time for this? Medicine called to me from an early age. Later, theater called, then music, then writing.

Somewhere between my first published story and my second, a memory called. I was holding the latest *Superman* comic in my hands. I was twelve or thirteen. The cover showed a big chunk of red kryptonite, which did weird and unexpected things to Superman, unlike green kryptonite, which was lethal. The red kryptonite issues were my favorites, and from my very first glance I knew this one would be my favorite of all time. Something really weird happened to Superman in this one. Really bizarre.

He turned into a woman.

I remember little else. I know he found a way to get rid of the red kryptonite, because he always did.

The question to me: why not, just this once, keep it around?

I started cross-dressing by accident. I was on a cruise with my best friend. We were thirteen or fourteen, the only boys on the ship. There was a costume party, and a fun-loving French newlywed decided she needed two female consorts. She dolled us up. I remember being titillated and nervous. When I look at the photo now, I am struck by how happy and natural I look.

I didn't dress up again for many years. When I did, it wasn't easy. Nothing fit. I wasn't into shopping yet, and my roommate's dresses were too small. When I tried them on, the seams ripped. Later on, I moved into an apartment of my own and became friends with the woman upstairs, who was extra-large. I had the key to her back door and would sometimes let myself in when she was at work. Her knee-high leather boots fit perfectly. This was a revelation, and a turning point, for me.

The cross-dressers I met in person, like the incredible Charles Ludlum, or on screen, like the beautiful and utterly convincing Harlow in *The Queen*, were gay. I wasn't gay. I wasn't precisely hetero, but those were the choices back then. When gay men came on to me, which happened with regularity, I was apologetic, while feeling misunderstood. When I later learned that the majority of cross-dressing men are heterosexual, I understood myself better.

As a transvestite I was lucky in all sorts of ways. I never judged myself harshly for who I was, or what I did, or fantasized doing. I was comfortable in my body and my skin. I liked dressing up. I liked having sex and saw nothing wrong having it in whatever way was fun. I was never hurt, and I never hurt anyone else.

Actually, I was hurt once, but not badly. I prostituted myself, not for money but for the experience. It was intense. I don't regret doing it, but I'm glad I didn't do it a second time.

I was a shy TV and kept to the shadows. After a while I got up the nerve to appear in public: it was the first and last time I did. That embarrassing.

I chose Halloween, which in San Francisco, if you weren't a flamboyant queen but instead a shrinking violet like me, was the night to come out of the closet. Come out I did.

I made two mistakes. One, I unwittingly chose to reveal myself at a hetero ball, *the* hetero Halloween ball, where women and men were dressed to the nines and looking for action, hetero action exclusively. This was a time of low awareness, not to mention tolerance, for hybrid creatures. Plus, I wasn't there for action. All I wanted was to be seen.

Two, I did my own hair, makeup, and clothes. Fine in the privacy of one's home. Inadvisable, as any fashion magazine will tell you, for galas, soirees, and coming-out parties.

I doubt I fooled anyone, though mercifully it was dark. Mostly, I was ignored, which was a blessing. At the end of the evening a kind woman took pity on me and handed me a long-stemmed rose, as you might to a sad, pathetic homeless person. I felt brave for having gone and for having stayed, but in the moment mostly what I felt was awful.

It could have been so much worse, but as I said, I was lucky. I was lucky to live in the city I did. I was lucky in having friends who understood, or at least humored me. I was (and am) lucky for having a wife who, after the initial shock, was all in.

I was lucky not to get AIDS. I was lucky to live to the twenty-first century and a time when gender identity is understood to be not one thing, not fixed, but fluid and freewheeling, as it most certainly is.

"I Did Crash a Few Parties"
John Crowley

You received the World Fantasy Award for Life Achievement in 2006, yet you are still with us. What went wrong?

Mario Puzo once remarked, after getting a $400,000 advance on *The Godfather*, that an amount of money like that (it was worth lots more at the time) was like finding out you don't have to die. I'm wondering if you can win a lifetime achievement award over and over without end.

Like many ambitious, eager, overly self-confident wannabes from the provinces (I'm one myself), you bolted for New York as soon as you graduated to long pants. What party were you hoping to crash? Any luck?

I went to New York from Indiana. There were two directions ambitious artistic/literary types could go then, to New York or to Los Angeles. I wanted to make movies, not write fiction (I'd done that), but I chose New York. The films made in New York were "underground" movies, and I saw a lot of them. I wrote what are now called pitches, also scripts, with an old Indiana chum—Lance Bird, who was more passionate about filmmaking than I was—and in the end I did work in film, but in documentary—historical docs made from old film, a job I loved. I did crash a few parties, too. At that time it was nearly impossible for anyone living in certain neighborhoods or going to certain bars (Max's Kansas City) not to brush up against famous people or people once famous or about to become famous.

Ever cross paths with the Warhol crowd in those days?

My first New York job was as a photographer's assistant to a big fashion/advertising studio photographer of a kind that hardly exists any longer. He shot fashion spreads for *Life* magazine, and the *Life* fashion editor thought that a shoot using underground movies as backgrounds would be cool. So as the resident young hip person I was sent up to the Factory to collect the reels from Paul Morrissey, who was about to become a filmmaker in his own right. I had tried to explain that Warhol's films were stunningly boring (that was the point, of course) and that Jack Smith's *Flaming Creatures* or the Kuchar brothers' *Sins of the Fleshapoids* would be better, but *Life* mostly used Warhol's *Empire* and *Sleep*. At a party afterward one of the editorial women told me she was going to "get" Andy. I listened as she told him a story about the famous Art Market show where the paintings were set up as in a grocery store (including Wayne Thiebaud's cakes and Andy's Campbell's Soup). Buyers took away their purchases in grocery-store shopping bags. She'd got one—they were signed by Warhol—and her son, she said, had thought it was just a paper bag and took it to school with his books in it!

Warhol, po-faced as always, murmured, "Oh, that's wonderful." The woman was a little put off by this, and said, "But here's the thing—the bag fell apart on the way! It was a lousy bag!" Warhol was almost thrilled. "Oh, that's so wonderful. Is that really true? Oh, you must tell that story to Henry [Geldzahler, the critic, who was at the party]," and he pulled her over to meet him. Andy was un-beardable.

Unlike many of your Grub Street colleagues, you are a member of the prestigious American Academy of Arts and Letters. Is the food any good?
At the one luncheon I was invited to, it was quite nice. Jackie Kennedy, Philip Roth, and others were there. I have never been asked back. I'm not a member, or a fellow, or whatever. I was given an award in literature that year along with Roth and the wonderful Vicki Hearne (*Adam's Task*). There was real money attached. Harold Bloom was on the prizes committee that year. I was quite poor. The name has changed, and now you must say The American Academy and Institute of Arts and Letters.

What's the deal with The Girlhood of Shakespeare's Heroines *(which is rather hard to find)? What's its relationship to the nineteenth-century classic by Mary Cowden Clarke?*

It was published by a small press (Subterranean) as a limited edition, and reprinted in the famed "New Weird" issue of *Conjunctions*, the Bard College literary magazine. How hard to find can that be? Actually I'm hoping to make it easier to find soon—I'm working on a book of my uncollected stories, and this is one. Mary Cowden Clarke's book, which I have, and have looked into, was described to me by John Hollander as a "very common romance type of the late nineteenth century," though he didn't describe the type further. It tells made-up (i.e., baseless) tales of the, yes, childhoods of Shakespeare's heroines—how Beatrice won over a gang of robbers, how Juliet's mother came into possession of the poison that later Juliet uses, and so forth. The language is sort-of-Shakespearean. The book's long. In my piece (which originally was simply called "Avon") the title is used to describe an aspiring teenage actress who contracts polio and is a heroine in several senses. She and the boy in love with her come upon the book in the library of a small town in Indiana, where there is (though there really wasn't) a Shakespeare festival in the 1960s.

You wrote the "Easy Chair" column in Harper's *for a while. How did that come about? Do you have a different discipline and approach for fiction and nonfiction?*
Christopher Beha, who was then coeditor of the magazine, liked my novels, wrote a fine review in *Bookforum* about them. When I was asked to do a reading at the 92nd St. Y in New York I was told I needed an introducer, and I asked Chris. *Harper's* later published a lecture I did about Utopia in the front matter of the magazine, and a review of a biography of Madame Blavatsky (very fun). When I found I needed an operation on a failing heart valve and would lose a semester's teaching (and the accompanying income), I called Chris and asked if maybe I could submit some article ideas, and—to my astonishment—he asked if I wanted to do the "Easy Chair" every other month. Saved my ass, in effect. He didn't know about the operation and just thought I'd be good at it.

I don't know about a different discipline. My fiction often depends on an authorial voice telling things—not only stories but facts and thoughts—to the reader. A lot of it is drawn out of research on all kinds of things. So are the columns. I felt a great freedom, and at the same time a fear: were these subjects and their treatment really interesting to anybody? Why did I think I had a claim on readers' attention? Chris (who, sadly for me but not for him, is no longer at the magazine) was uniformly encouraging.

What are the Least Trumps?
If you think I am going to allow myself a cheap joke in answer to this ("the ones he hides in his hairpiece") you mistake me. The Least Trumps—that is, a deck of cards with mystic or allegorical pictures having connections to the story—appeared in my first novel, *The Deep*. The images and mottoes on the cards were inspired by Renaissance magic images described by Frances Yates in her book *The Art of Memory*. The deck that various persons in *Little, Big* lay out has picture cards that are more like the Greater Trumps of the Tarot deck than the Renaissance images. Great-aunt Cloud—the character in the book who uses them most—calls them the Least Trumps because all they seem to answer are questions about small events of daily life—whether it will rain on a picnic or if a cold will get worse—though in the end they are discovered to be Great after all. Charles Williams's 1932 mystic novel is called *The Greater Trumps*.

Why are there so many John Crowleys in IMDb? Which one are you?
I recently went to see the fine film *Brooklyn* and at the end was pleasantly disoriented at seeing my name loom up amid the titles, all alone and about nine feet long. If only. Of course he is the Irish film and stage director, living the life I should have had instead of this one as an ink-stained wretch.

Another John Crowley (with middle initial W, inverting my own middle M) teaches American history at Syracuse. When we communicated once to untangle a confusion that had arisen about which of us wrote what—our bibliographies had gotten mixed together in Wikipedia—he told me that he'd had a student who went to Syracuse specifically to study with John Crowley, that is with me. Sorry I missed him.

My filmography is long but most of it wouldn't be on IMDb.

Perhaps your best-known documentary film has a definite science fiction feel, The World of Tomorrow. *Who is Lance Bird?*
Lance Bird (yes, his real name, though in an [unpublished] *roman à clef* about the movie scene in NYC in the 1970s the author gave him the name Blaise

Falcon.) The real Bird's middle name is Evan, which allowed me to make the neat and similarly absurdly romantic anagram Nic Ravenblade. Lance and I were at Indiana University together. We both wanted to make films, but he had already worked on a microbudget horror film that was finished and exhibited in a couple of theaters. We both took photography classes (on the principle that the lenses and the film were the same) and set out to make an underground film (this term is getting too constant here) with the IU photography department's windup Bolex 16mm camera. It was never finished but was to be called *Tigers in Lavender*—I had read somewhere that tigers respond to lavender plants the same way cats respond to catnip. Lance moved to NYC too and spent his time trying to get scripts read and deals made; I collaborated on the scripts. That never happened, but Lance began working with a partner, Tom Johnson, on documentaries about auto racing, beginning with stock cars and then Le Mans–style endurance racing. I wrote narration for some of these, despite the fact that I had not learned to drive and had never had a license (and me a Hoosier, sort of!).

In the late 1970s the NEH began giving away lots of money for work in TV, and the three of us made a documentary that started as a study of Walker Evans and became a story of the whole Depression. And then *The World of Tomorrow*, about the 1939 World's Fair, which is a weird kind of masterpiece (my wife calls it my "secret fiction film"). Working with Lance and Tom I acquired my love of archival film and the strange metaphysics of making movies with dead people walking and talking, sometimes about the world to come.

The famed critic Harold Bloom dragged you from the Den of Obscurity that is the birthright of every SF/fantasy author. Have you forgiven him?
I'm not sure how much less obscure I am. But I owe Harold Bloom much. The connection had an odd beginning: I had never read his criticism, though I knew his name and fame, and once in the library I picked up his book *Agon*, which has a long essay in it on what he calls heroic fantasy. It was so illuminating and interesting that I wrote him a letter—I'd never written to an academic critic—and sent along a book of mine that I thought reflected his views (it was *Engine Summer*). Pretty soon he wrote back and said he'd read it, was moved by it, and had gone to the library and picked up some other books of mine and read them too. *Little, Big* was the one that touched him most, and he has never ceased to

praise it to anyone nearby. His sponsorship got me the half-time teaching job at Yale I still hold.

Like many SF/fantasy authors, you teach writing. Do you actually have a method or are you winging it?
Isn't winging it a method? I talk mostly about the shapes and forms of fiction, the machinery that generates all kinds of stories. I don't instruct them as to what *sort* of fiction I think is good or not good; I try my best to discover what they want to achieve and try to help. I have one great advantage at Yale—creative writing classes require applications with writing samples, and from thirty to fifty applications I can choose a class of twelve. So I get not only good or promising writers but ones I think I can help. I had no idea when I began how much I would enjoy teaching—mostly for the chance to be with young people and know their thoughts. I know more about how a certain (but broad) class of twenty-year-olds thinks than a great majority of people my age. Next spring, 2018, will be my last semester.

Bloom praised your "superb and sustained elusiveness," and I join him in that. But I sometimes wonder, commercially, is it a feature or a fault?
Oh jeez. There is a nearly ontological difficulty here. I think I am elusive sometimes, but I also think I lay tracks (though sometimes I brush them away). I really want readers to follow, to play the game I'm setting up. At the same time I understand that a large percentage of the general reading public has little interest in such agonistic labor or pleasure. And I also want many many readers, both to enhance my self-esteem and make me money to live on. And (again) I want my work to please me in its multiplicity and its interconnections, formed sometimes by the repetition of a single word in differing circumstances. I keep believing that I have written a book *this* time that everyone can like, or at least millions can like, and it will make me honored and rich, and I keep on queering the deal by my usual elusiveness, peculiarity, literariness (by which I mean that the secret subtext of my works is always *this is a book*), and general self-pleasing. Oh well.

What's the deal with The Chemical Wedding*?*

The Chemical Wedding, by Christian Rosenkreutz (the actual author was a German theology student named Johann Valentin Andreae) is a sort of romance written in 1616 about a self-doubting and anxious but essentially good man who receives an invitation to a wedding in a magic castle. It's usually regarded as some sort of allegory, maybe of the alchemical process (a lot of alchemical sort of stuff goes on in it, and some of the characters could stand for alchemical stages), but at bottom I think it's a mad sort of novel, using the farthest-out technologies and sciences of the time. It might also be a parody of those sciences and technologies. I have loved it for years, and I did a new version (not a translation) that I hoped would make it more accessible to readers. In trying to describe what sort of thing it is, I unintentionally created something of a stir by describing it as a candidate for the first science fiction novel. Complaints were made that the "science" in it was unscientific (Kepler and Galileo were the real scientists of the time) and that you can't have science fiction based on bogus guesswork science. I imagine such critics hadn't read much early SF.

You once spoke in an interview of your "compassion for characters in novels—who live in a world that has a shape that they don't know and can't finally alter." Hmmm. Equally true for Little, Big *and for* Four Freedoms? *Is it a feature of The Novel in general?*
I think it is a feature. Just as we ignore unwelcome or difficult facts in our actual lives—personal and public and universal facts—we ignore the absolute fact that the characters in the novels we read have made all their decisions, errors, triumphs, before we start to read the book. The end that they will come to, which determines all that they will do in the story, is fixed—the book's in print! Of course writers can fall in love with a character in the course of the writing and find themselves unwilling finally to subject them to the endings planned for them—but even so, the endings are the endings and can't be changed when the book's done.

Little, Big and *Four Freedoms* seem to differ in that in the first there's a tale being told whose shape is finally revealed, which all the human characters learn they have been enacting all along, and who exit that tale as the book ends. In the second, nothing seems fixed, and characters come upon new openings and new turnings they can't have imagined; nevertheless they come to an ending in which they are as fixed as the archetypes they embody on the last page. If you'd like to read more of my thoughts on the subject you could go to *Harper's* magazine and look for my "Easy Chair" essay called "A Ring-Formed World" (https://harpers.org/archive/2015/11/a-ring-formed-world/).

Ever get a bad review? One that helped?
I've actually had very few bad reviews. I've wondered if this is because reviewers who are among the small band of committed readers of my books somehow manage to get the review copies and submit positive reviews. The vast number of bad reviews I seem to collect on Amazon (along with vast numbers of moderate, disappointed, confused, ecstatic, and unintelligible ones) suggests something of the kind. The worst review I ever got was in *The New York Times*, when they used to run short "also noticed" reviews. It was for *Dæmonomania*, the third volume of a four-volume novel, and the reviewer was apparently unaware of this fact. He was puzzled and annoyed and found the book both silly and tortured.

Reviews that helped? Long ones, like Chris Beha's that I mentioned, or James Hynes's in the *Boston Review*. If for nothing but to learn if what I wrote was intelligible, if my general purpose was understood.

Do you still write for film? Ever try a narrative (fiction) feature? How is writing for documentaries different?
I have been working with Laurie Block, who is my wife, on a biography of Helen Keller for *American Masters* (PBS). It's been in the works now for a long time, but there are signs it may soon be headed for completion. I cowrote the script (it was a heavily scripted show, much of it based on Keller's writings, spoken by the great Cherry Jones—not portraying Keller but giving us Keller's written words). I've long since given up trying to write fiction films. It's easier to write a novel of a movie idea—at least you have *something* in the end. None of my novels have been sold to the movies, though there was some interest in a couple. Now I'm looking into the possibility of *Little, Big* being a "premium TV" project with multiple seasons. More on that in some possible future where there is more.

Most documentaries have minimal writing; when I began writing those historical docs in the 1970s I took as my model the 1930s–40s docs like *The*

River and *The Plow That Broke the Plains* and *Night Mail* (with narration by W.H. Auden!). Since sound recording was so clumsy then, most of the work of explication came through an intimate, characterized voice, sometimes even speaking in a (manufactured) present tense—that's how I wrote *The World of Tomorrow*, with Jason Robards in effect playing a character. Today all of that is unnecessary (as you can shoot a nice doc with your smartphone) and unwanted.

One sentence on each, please: Trollope, Lovecraft, Western Mass.
I have read almost no Trollope; my mother was delighted by him, but the conventionality of his writing and the kinds of things his innumerable books are concerned with are largely uninteresting to me.

I have read almost no Lovecraft. High school nerds I knew were delighted by him, and some people I know admire and cherish him, but the absurd extravagance of his writing, and his inability despite that extravagance to convey actual human feeling in extremity, make him uninteresting and in fact repellent to me.

I love Western Massachusetts, where my children were born, to which I fled from a decaying New York City in 1977. I now live in a house forty minutes from where my conscious life began seventy years ago in southern Vermont, and where I live among all kinds of people, rich and poor, back-to-the-landers and never-left-the-landers, pickup drivers and Prius drivers—about as close to a practical utopia as it's possible to get and still live in the ordinary.

*You often (*Little, Big *and* Ægypt*) write about arcane and conspiratorial religious orders that secretly control not only our lives but our realities. Do you know something that we don't?*
There is much that I know, Terry. Actually, not so much. I can't say why I am so attracted to stories and circumstances where thought and notions have power over the human realm and the natural order. It's noticeable, though, how few real believers in the kinds of Gnostic mythologies I retail are interested in my writing, and how the few I have met that are attracted to it get it wrong. The best example of what I attempt is in the fabulously long *Ægypt Cycle*: through three volumes the Gnostic realm both of hope and terror continually grows, the world

is posited as being labile and able to undergo shifts of reality that human souls can influence. In the last volume the final shift or change is into the common world that the non-Gnostics among us (in fact all of us) actually live in: "the Great Instauration of everything that had all along been the case." It occasioned some disappointment, though this conclusion was implicit in everything that went before.

You write about poets (Lord Byron); do you write poetry? Do you read it for fun? What about James Merrill (who blurbed one of your books)?
I assembled a personal anthology of poets and poems in my early years and it's basically lasted the rest of my life. Small additions have been made over time (I like John Ashbery very much, and James Merrill, yes). I wrote my last poem somewhere around 1975, and there weren't many in the previous decade—though masses of it in my teens and early twenties, most of it now well lost. But I don't read much modern poetry at all. I wrote a novel about a poet (*The Translator*) in part because a poet—Thomas M. Disch, my friend Tom—said that a poet would make a great hero for a bestseller. Americans, he averred, *love* poets even though they don't read poetry. I loved writing the book—and writing the poems in it, mostly the early poems of my heroine, and the translations she makes of the supposedly Nobel-worthy poems in Russian of her mentor. That was great fun. (It's another Gnostic-gods-and-angels novel that puzzled people and came nowhere near being a bestseller.)

At Yale you teach a course in utopias, yet you've never attempted one. Or have you?
I think *Four Freedoms*, my World War II home front novel, is a sort of ambiguous utopia. The gigantic (imagined) factory, the care for the workers at all levels, the welcome to women, people of color, Native Americans; the money spent and the effort expended to make workplaces healthy and safe (they were neither by modern standards, but the effort was real); the provision of nurseries, clinics, information, recreation—well, I probably exaggerate all that, as utopias tend to do. At a point late in the book a woman who has won a management job in the factory wonders why the model provided by this factory, and by the astonishing productivity of industry in war, couldn't be simply continued in peacetime, producing cars and refrigerators and radios for everyone. She imagines

something like a nationwide telephone tree that would let the government know who needed what.

In my essay "Totalitopia" I present a glimpse of a socialist utopia with a world government, a distribution system like Amazon's but owned by the world, and all people siblings. Lewis Lapham, the publisher of the quarterly where the article appeared, couldn't decide if I was kidding. Neither can I. I recently read somebody saying that all utopias are dystopias in disguise. I reject that, though examples are legion.

What's next?
I have a new novel coming out from Saga in fall 2017. It was deliberately conceived to sell lots of copies, and because it's a frank fantasy I'm hoping it will win back the fantasy-fan readership I seem to have partly lost with the last couple of books. (To be clear, many readers of fantasy fiction also happily read books of other kinds, like mine.) The book is called *KA: Dar Oakley in the Ruin of Ymr*. Dar Oakley is a crow, born some two thousand years ago, who becomes involved with the human world and its otherworlds, and by mistake comes to possess a sort of immortality—he dies over and over but always comes back. He travels from somewhere in Celtic Europe to the American continent and lives in various societies through the centuries, up until sometime in the future. Dar Oakley learns to speak with various humans in many times and places, including one in near-future America who writes down his story. I've wanted to write a book about crows for years—for reasons obvious and not so—and here it is, or soon will be. I consider this my last full-dress novel—I'm very nearly as old as you—but my agent insists I never say that, so mum's the word.

What kind of car do you drive? I ask this of everyone.
My first car, acquired when I was thirty-six or so (I only learned to drive at that age), was an old American Motors Ambassador, a boat but a beaut. Next was a VW Dasher. A few others of indifferent lineage. Now a New England Hilltown Liberal Subaru.

The fairies in Little, Big *forget the past but remember the future. Were you remembering that Ted Chiang was someday going to be developing that idea for Hollywood?*

It's inappropriate for an interviewer to ask wittier questions than the subject can come up with answers for. Ted Chiang is much smarter than I am. His original story "Story of Your Life" is a marvel of syntactical invention which the movie based on it, *Arrival*, wonderful as it is, can't match.

"Discourse in an Older Sense"
Samuel R. Delany

You recently completed a novel, Through the Valley of the Nest of Spiders, *almost as long, every bit as challenging, and seemingly as ambitious as* Dhalgren. *What's it about? Isn't the "Great American Novel" a young writer's game?*

Well, it was published on my seventieth birthday and, yes, was celebrated with a conference, Delany at 70, at the University of Maryland. But—paradoxically—it was published by a very small press (Donald Weise's Magnus Books) that never seemed to have copies available over the next few years. Thus are the paradoxes of achieving age and what may (or may not) be artistic maturity (or the old-age dodderings of an artist who has gone on babbling long past the time he might have done better to shut up because he's only destroying his—or her—own reputation: which are certainly many of us) in a marginal genre in this age.

It's about two working-class garbagemen, one from the area, one transplanted from the big city in Atlanta, who meet, become lovers, and live and work on the Georgia coast together for the rest of their lives.

It's got a lot of what I learned about relationships from the twenty years I'd been with Dennis, and the eight years I'd been with Frank Romeo—and even the thirteen years I'd been with Marilyn Hacker.

As well, I got the same thousand-dollar advance for this 804-page novel as I got for my first 148-page book, *The Jewels of Aptor*, back in 1961. Now, consider the inflation over those fifty years. Or the fact that this was the first novel I'd called "science fiction" in thirty years, though I'd published a number—including *Hogg*, *The Mad Man*, and the series Return to Nevèrÿon that a number of critics think is my best work (its actual worth I don't know and can't know, even if you try to tell me)—in between time that had made me more money, certainly.

You dedicated your Paris Review *interview to the late Joanna Russ (1937–2011). Were you friends? Why was she, is she, important to you? (I'm writing this query on her birthday.)*

She was a brilliant writer at the sentence level. She was a brilliant thinker at the social level—and she was a great believer in doing everything from an oppositional stance, as well. Yes, we had a great deal of simpatico from the first time we met at Terry Carr's for dinner, during which she didn't tell me she had just finished a novel that I would receive in galleys in only a few weeks: *Picnic on Paradise* (a.k.a. *Picnic in Paradise*, Russ's original title). Friends? Well, we never saw a great deal of one another, but for more than a decade we had a correspondence that reached Victorian proportions. Yes, I think of her as my friend, though there were moments when I strained that friendship.

What's the source of "The Atheist in the Attic"? I know you are a scholar of literary history, but this seems a little off that grid.

Not really (my answer to both implied statements: I'm "not a scholar" and it's "off the grid" only in terms of which grid you mean). Spinoza is the philosopher whose name lurks behind *Through the Valley of the Nest of Spiders*. Eric struggles with reading him, there on the coast of Georgia, for many years. (I remember rereading *Ethica* in my doctor's office for an in-office procedure where a microwave generator was shoved up my butt to take care of my enlarged prostate, a couple of years before I came down with actual prostate cancer.) I struggled too, though I had a whole library of auxiliary readings to help me. From that auxiliary reading, the Nadler and the Bennett and the Stuart Hampshire, and the various anthologies that were once in my very threatened library along with Wiki online—I managed to put together that very small and slight novella, during a very fraught time in my life, just before my library was finally lost . . . or at any rate mostly rendered inaccessible.

I used my own struggles with the text over several years as the fictive basis for Eric's on the Georgia coast—with the difference that I had not promised any transgender Black seminarian that I would persevere through three readings the way Eric did in order to hook him on the experience. "Did I succeed in creating a believable fiction?" and "For what percentage of my readers?" are questions I will never know the answers to.

Kim Stanley Robinson often compares historical fiction with fantasy and SF, in that in both you have to create as well as populate a world. Do you find similarities in the two genres as well?
Yes. And the further away in time you get in both cases, the more the discursive differences have to be faked. These are genres in which nothing can be real except by accident, though reality it still the aesthetic effect you are trying for.

You are considered one of the members of SF's "New Wave." Were you ever part of the London crowd?
On a couple of occasions, in the mid-1960s: for my first visit to Europe, which ended with a trip to London, and my second trip over the subsequent Christmas and New Year's, to stay with John Brunner; and then again in the 1970s, when I actually moved to London for a couple of years, when my daughter was born in Queen Charlotte's Maternity Hospital in Hammersmith, where I was a more or less interested visitor, and where I did my last rewrite of *Dhalgren* and wrote *Trouble on Triton*, before coming home pretty much permanently for many years. But paradoxically, I never considered myself a part of the London SF crowd. I was there because my wife had asked me to come, and her own relation to that crowd was somewhat problematic.

Your debut novel, The Jewels of Aptor, *was postapocalyptic and also ecclesiastical in its way. Was* A Canticle for Leibowitz *an influence? Or was atomic disaster just in the air in those days?*
From Hiroshima through the Cuban Missile Crisis and beyond, atomic war was a pervasive fear in this country. It was what the "Cold War" was about. (Full disclosure: I always found *A Canticle for Leibowitz* all but unreadable.)

Many people now assume it's under control, though some of the reported behavior of our current popular minority president makes it seem still a possibility. Often, it's only after the fact that we know for sure when such crises (have) happen(ed).

You wrote a critical appreciation of SF, The Jewel-Hinged Jaw. *I wrote the cover copy (!) on the first edition back in the 1970s, but I can't recall what the title signified.*
Not the first hardcover edition, but the first paperback edition (David's own very small company, Dragon Press, published a hardcover edition before you got to it at Berkley Books)—and I remember it well. It was the smartest cover copy I'd yet had on a paperback book, and I told David Hartwell to thank you personally for it. For one thing, you'd read the book. That put you notably ahead of most paperback copywriters, at least those who had anything to do with science fiction.

I remember when you came out of the back office and we first said hello to each other, in the office.

The title was not explained in the book. You just had to recognize it. It was from a line in Thomas M. Disch's *Camp Concentration*: from Sacchetti's poem, "The Hierodule," when Disch describes the black idol of language/knowledge/art, which is presumably supposed to speak the truth:

> Behold! Behold the black, ungrainèd flesh,
> The jaw's jeweled hinge that we can barely glimpse . . .

So, no, you probably didn't and don't recall what the title signified, unless you've been rereading Disch's novel with your literary antennae alert to explaining precisely that conundrum.

In the standard bildungsroman, the young artist lights out from the provinces for London or Paris. You took a subway to Washington Square and Greenwich Village, and then moved into the Lower East Side (alphabet city and the East Village) because the Village proper was too expensive. What was the appeal?
When I was thirteen or fourteen and not sure whether I was going to be a writer or a musician, or even what kind of musician—a folk singer or a composer of serious, avant-garde music—I was drawn to the Village like so many others, as a place where it would be easier to experiment with art and sexuality both.

Washington Square looked entirely different. The fountain and the layout of the park and the restrooms were entirely other from what they are today, and kids came down to the square on the weekend. There was already a bohemian tradition associated with the area, and had been one since the whole thing was an ethnic Italian neighborhood, with its coffee shops and New York University and bookstores and experimental off-off-Broadway theaters.

So did Tompkins Square.

You and the poet Marilyn Hacker have had a lifelong relationship. How did that begin?
We met on our very first day of high school, at the Bronx High School of Science Annex Building, at the other end of the city. We were friends from then on. My parents had sent me to the Dalton School (and before that Horace Mann–Lincoln) in the center of the city on the east side. But soon we were on that axis that ran through the city—and Marilyn had gotten an early admission into NYU and hadn't liked it; so I went to City College, after my father died and I had managed to graduate from Bronx Science without showing up for my high school graduation.

Like any other life, it was a combination of personal forces, neighborhood forces, and larger forces that are always easier to read after the fact than before.

I had a condition that I didn't even have word for until my wife discovered it in an article when we were both twenty-one: dyslexia.

The dyslexia is part of a larger condition that my daughter—who is a doctor—only explained to me some months ago: Adult Attention Deficit Disorder (AADD). There are drugs for it that I've never tried because I never knew I had it until relatively recently. I spoke to a good friend who has a form of the latter and discovered that he'd tried the drug—which is speed—and hadn't liked the effect, so he'd discontinued it. Since I am twenty years older than he is, would I have the same reaction? I simply don't know.

In the Imaginary Index to Delany, *published by Tyndale House in 2011, there is no entry for Dr. Johnson. What's your beef with the Old Tory?*
First, I've never heard of Tyndale House's *Imaginary Index to Delany*—so I imagine you're making a joke.

Let's just say that I imagined that I was. I was interested in your opinion of Samuel Johnson. Your opinion of his opinions.

I've written about Johnson and recently prepared an essay for a new collection (or rather a letter-essay), where I discussed him and his refutation of Bishop Berkeley, by—rather notoriously—kicking a rock. One of the things I have written, however, is that there is so much knowledge available today that there can be no such thing anymore as a classical education that we can expect more than a relatively few people to share.

Some people's information is other people's misinformation and even disinformation. That is pretty much the contemporary condition. When we say that the same forces that put Obama in office also put Trump in office, eight years later, but at work on a very differently structured political field, what exactly are we saying?

Larry McCaffrey and other critics claim that your Return to Nevèrÿon *series "undercut[s] the premises" of the genre [sword and sorcery]. That sounds sort of sneaky. What about your more academic treatises and lectures?*
They become less and less academic as I get older: I try to write as clearly as I can. But I roam through genres, letters, lectures, interviews, journals, Facebook posts, and various kinds of fictions.

You won a Hugo for an early memoir, The Motion of Light in Water, *about your time as a young, gay writer in the East Village. Then there was your novel,* Dark Reflections, *about an older gay writer walking the same streets. Anything of interest happen in between?*
Interesting to me? Or interesting to readers? Presumably it was interesting enough for me to make whatever effort I needed to write it. The interest of readers—which is the one that finally counts—lies *with* readers. So they're the ones you have to ask.

I believe the éminence grise who excoriated you (and Zelazny) at the '68 Nebula Awards banquet has long since been identified. Can you name names?
Yes, it was Frederik Pohl. And, as I said, shortly he actually *read* the work in question that had inspired him to such ire, and decided—to his surprise, I gather—that he rather liked it in spite of Lester Del Ray's fulminating against it, which is what had convinced him to bad-mouth it sight unseen. (This is

supposition on my part. We never discussed it directly.) He started assigning me cover stories—which was a mixed blessing. But they made me a few hundred dollars when it was money I needed. Both "Cage of Brass" and "High Weir" were Pohl cover stories for *If*, the most experimental of what were then known as the Galaxy Combine. A cover story, which is something that almost never happens in the magazines these days, is where the editor has brought one or a number of covers before the story is written, and then shows the cover to the writer and says, okay, write a story to go with this.

A few years after that, Pohl was the editor who bought and published *Dhalgren*. Which is to say, he managed to do a 180-degree turn when it came to judging my work. But the whole SF community was smaller, younger, and things like that could happen.

You are one of the few literary academics in the US without a doctorate. Has that been an impediment or an asset?
To the extent it represents a lot of experiences with the university system I never had, it was an impediment. (I not only don't have a PhD, I never finished more than a term of college. I made two stabs at completing my second term—and couldn't hack it. I wasn't organized enough. That's the ADD that encompassed my dyslexia.) Perhaps to some, it made me look a little more interesting; but then—as I said—you'll have to ask them, not me.

One sentence on each, please: Alan Ansen, George Eliot, Junot Díaz.
Impossible question! But here goes, though I might try for a small paragraph.

Alan Ansen was nice, civilized, and in his capacity as Auden's secretary, an interesting writer; after we met at a table outside a Plaka Kafeneion, he allowed Gregory Corso to invite me on the spur of the moment to his house in Kolonaki for lunch the next day, back during my first trip to Greece, in 1966 I think it was—the only time I ever saw him. (How would we get through these one-sentence restrictions without the semicolon?) In his kitchen I ate Gregory's very hot rice, peppers, and sausage concoction ("Aw, man—you guys don't have to eat this shit," was his own verdict on what he'd made, but Ansen and I both did; I had come in a tie, slacks, and sports jacket: Greg was in jeans and some kind of short-sleeved shirt); and there were original Cocteau drawings framed and hung on the walls, I remember. I only saw him on two consecutive afternoons, both times with Corso, whom I only ran into about five times—four times in Greece, and once a few years later in the Lower East Side.

Later, I remember learning that his home was where Chester Kallman was staying when, years later, he drank himself to death once his older partner, Auden, had passed away.

George Eliot was a great English novelist whom C.L.R. James ranked with Melville, when James was writing *Mariners, Renegades & Castaways*. *Moby-Dick* and *Middlemarch* were his two nominees for the great mid-nineteenth-century English-language masterpieces. I can't argue.

Junot Díaz: an extremely hardworking writer, who puts immense amounts of effort into the Pulitzer work he does on the prize committee every year, and his own political work, as well as his own writing, of which there is far too little, though what there is is beautiful and exquisitely crafted: *Drown* is an amazing book, and the concluding novella, "Negocios," took my head off when I first read it; it still holds up well. And I'll say the same for his novel *The Brief Wondrous Life of Oscar Wao*. He is also a wondrously patient and loyal friend to an often confused older fellow.

You often speak of writing as "discourse." With yourself? With the reader? Is it the same for fiction and nonfiction?
I'm using "discourse" in an older sense: discourse as response, understanding, discourse as structure both conscious and unconscious: not dialogue, but what impels and structures dialogue: not the "discourse between . . ." but the "discourse of . . ."

My son (formerly of Tenth and A) tells me that hipsters are moving back to the Lower East Side because it's more affordable than Brooklyn. Is this a good thing?
My understanding of the mysteries of gentrification or of what happens inside or around it is just not that great. I don't know the neighborhood anymore, nor have I been there for years. We'll let that one sit.

You had a long relationship with the late, lamented David Hartwell, SF's Maxwell Perkins. How did that come about?

It began as the friendship between two young men who both liked science fiction, both liked poetry, both liked music. David was a year my senior, and in the first years I knew him, he did get his PhD and worked very hard on a poetry magazine called *The Little Magazine*, of whose voluntary staff I was a member. How we actually met I don't recall, but I believe it revolved around Paul Williams, creator of an extremely successful music fanzine that became the first serious rock 'n' roll magazine, which I got to write for, named *Crawdaddy*. At the time, Paul was going with Trina Robbins, who was about five or six years older than he was and was then a dress designer. She made Marilyn's dress that she wore to the Nebula Awards (which I attended not only with an unhappy Marilyn—she'd only agreed to come because I assured her I hadn't won—but with my mother and sister and an albino friend named Whit Whitman, who came in a black denim suit, and with whom I had been to bed a couple of times and was a friend of Marilyn's from the Old Reliable, while I wore a black tuxedo and a silver lamé turtleneck), the night Fred delivered his jeremiad—and I won my second and third Nebula Awards (a total surprise to me) in one evening.

Even after *Nova* was written, I was still not sure if I was going to be a musician or a writer. David was often my best friend and on more than one occasion saved my ass. But the absurdity of trying to capture a long friendship in a paragraph . . . What can I say? I'm glad it happened and I miss that I'll never get to go out to lunch with him again, down near where he worked at Tor Books, in the Fuller Building (better known as the Flatiron) on Twenty-Third and Fifth. The history of science fiction tends to be the history of its editors, and David was the most important of those editors since the crop in the 1950s, Campbell, Gold, Boucher, Cele Goldsmith, and the Furmans, Joe and Ed.

I was lucky to be as close to him as I was. At his death, we had physically drifted apart, even as we'd come to appreciate and respect each other—at least on my side—more and more. His sudden and unexpected death startled us all. There were a lot of young editors, both at Tor and at other places, whom he'd trained. We'll see what kind of job they do.

After all, he was the editor who pretty much discovered you, wasn't he?

Yes, he was—and I'm glad I got (and took) the chance to thank him for my career that time we were all at Williams College together. The last time I saw him. But enough about me. What's next for Samuel R. Delany?

Probably I need to get some lunch, which is about as far ahead as I can see right now. I hope some of this was of interest. But we all live our lives from the inside of our bodies out, not from the outside in. Which is why fiction has the texture that it does.

Thanks for the questions, Terry.

"Look for the Lake"
Cory Doctorow

Let's see if I can make this work. Across a sea and a continent. Oakland to London via Skype. Seems appropriate.

Hey, Cory. I've met you in several of your incarnations: coeditor of Boing Boing, *the hottest site on the web; award winning SF writer;* New York Times *best-selling YA author. Which one am I talking to?*
Any or all of the above. I've been lucky, it's true. But it's complicated. It reminds me of when my grandmother called me up from Florida and said, "My friends want to know what you do for a living. They don't really understand it." I have that problem every time I fly into the UK and have to fill in a landing card and get it all in eleven letters. Writer, blogger, editor, professor, speaker, hacker, journalist, and so on.

So let's start with Boing Boing. *The first time I checked out that amazing site, I thought, this is all new! And yet (I'm an old-school '60s guy, as you know) it was strangely familiar. Then it came to me: It's the* Whole Earth Catalog.
Absolutely. Access to tools and ideas. I opened up one of my old *Whole Earth Catalogs* a few years ago and I was like: These are the layouts we use. And here's something else that blew my mind: I was yard-saleing in Burbank and I found a replica of a nineteenth-century Sears catalog and it reads like *Boing Boing*.

So the Whole Earth Catalog *was the Sears catalog for the '60s?*
Yeah, and *Boing Boing* is the electronic version that can change to keep up with shit as it happens. I kind of had a watershed experience in my professional and intellectual life when a friend of mine slipped me a copy of *Whole Earth Review*, which grew out of the original catalog. "The body is obsolete" was the theme of

that issue, with articles by a bunch of early transhumanists, and it completely revolutionized my outlook.

I went from there to *Co-evolution Quarterly* to *Mondo2000* to the first issues of *Wired* to downloading Bruce Sterling's article on the best software developers being not well-rounded but being thoroughly spiked. And it's like a straight line, like an arrow, from the day I got that issue of the *Whole Earth Review* to the day I dropped out of university to program for Voyager in New York.

It looks to me like that's what you might call the agenda of your fiction, the project. You're trying to give readers that same kick.
And of my nonfiction as well.

I write fiction because I find it aesthetically pleasing and because I find it artistically satisfying. I like the way the sentences sound and the way the people come to life in my head and on the page. I like to tell stories.

Blogging has a whole different aesthetic. One thing that blogging does for me that nothing else ever did—it creates those synthetic moments when a bunch of things that are seemingly disparate snap together. When you write up material for public consumption, you have to clarify it in your own head, and doing that often makes it connect in new ways. I have a lot of those *aha* moments. Maybe I have five disparate things to write about, and I find this sixth one, and I'm like, "Aha, so this is how they're all related!" And then I rush off and write a book or a short story or an essay about it.

So in a sense *Boing Boing* is the *Whole Earth Catalog*, arming folks for action and understanding. But it's also a cognitive prosthesis for me, without which I wouldn't be able to write the stuff that I write.

So you're saying Boing Boing *serves as a writer's notebook?*
Even better. You can't cheat a blog the way you can cheat a writer's notebook. I have notebooks that are filled with notes to myself that I wrote in such haste that I can't remember what I meant anymore. You can't do that with a blog.

You were pretty well established as a SF writer when you sort of veered into YA (young adult). How did that come about?

I wouldn't call it veered. It started with Kathe Koja. I'm a big fan of her books, and she was like "country before country was cool." She started doing

YA before there was a boom and before it was profitable. I ran into her at a con and she told me about the level of engagement she got from her readers, about how she was meeting up with kids who explicitly read to find out how the world worked. To me, that struck a chord. It reminded me of why I read, not just SF but *everything*. I was one of those reader kids, as you probably were too. And reading was a lot about figuring out about how the world worked. I remember having these *aha* moments, especially reading older SF. "Oh, so *that's* who Woodrow Wilson was. Oh, so that's what the Great Depression was all about!" I was also hanging out with Scott Westerfeld and Justine Larbalestier and Charlie Stross at that same con.

You know how you meet people that you just *click* with, and you form a little rat-packy group and end up going to all your meals together? Scott talked about this too, this level of engagement with younger readers. Someone else (I thought it was Garth Nix, but he tells me it wasn't) told me that a YA story had all this dramatic potential because when you're young you do a bunch of stuff for the first time. It's like you're jumping off a cliff, over and over. Cliff after cliff. That all resonated with me in a big way.

So you wrote Little Brother.
It cohered in my head, like, overnight. And then literally from that night to the day I finished the first draft was eight weeks.

That velocity certainly carried over. I heard you read from Little Brother *at SFinSF and was jealous as hell. What I liked best was the way you defined the character through the information he carried. You never say what he looks like, but you know all about him because of what he knows and what he wants to tell you. Through info dumps!*
Well *Little Brother* is deliberately expository in that Heinleinian way, and in that sense it's a rule-breaking book. I'm sure you've heard Stan Robinson complain about the Turkey City Lexicon—"no info dumps," "show and don't tell," and so forth. Useful rules for writers, but fun to break as well. Sometimes the most efficient way to get something into the head of your reader is "tell and don't show."

There is an admirable fleetness in taking info that might drag out an otherwise dramatic scene, and just dumping it on the reader; saying, "Got it? Good. Let's go!" Heinlein did that so well in his juvies!

These days a lot of SF writers (and others!) are moving into YA because it's more profitable. But it seems to me that you also have a political agenda. Can say anything about that?

That goes back to what you said earlier, about having a project. I don't have a name for it, but it's about technology and liberation. Those are the words I'd use. My work is all in service to it—the blog, the YA fiction, the technological advocacy, the standards work, the lobbying. All of that stuff is part of a bigger project.

Where YA comes in, I guess, is that kids are never part of the status quo. They are outlaws by hereditary design. Plus they are tuned into technology. And technology always favors the attacker, not the defender.

Cool. So you're arming a constituency that's interested in changing things. You're passing out weapons to the kids.

That's a lovely way to put it. I'm sure that'll read great on my indictment sheet. But it does seem a little like that. The weapons of course are ideas and information. I've thought a lot about what it's like to be an activist in the era of Google. I think it's less important to know facts than it is to know keywords. Keywords are capabilities: if you know something can be done, you can figure out how to do it.

What do you think of WikiLeaks?

That's funny, because the novella I just finished is kind of a WikiLeaks story and I didn't mean for it to be. So that tells me that I have a strong opinion about it.

I think it's important to disambiguate whatever you think about Julian Assange from WikiLeaks. I don't know Julian, I know him only peripherally through some friends. But the story of Julian has taken on a life of its own.

The real story of WikiLeaks is what it is—the total open release of former state secrets. That part is really interesting. I believe that it's meaningful and substantial and game-changing for us to know for a fact, with citable information, some of the nastiness, arm-twisting, and corruption—and there's no word for it except *corporatism*—that takes place behind (formerly) closed doors.

Many of us grow up thinking that we live in a society where governments and corporations more or less behave themselves. But this is so visibly untrue when you go through WikiLeaks! What looks like democracy is really corporations shopping for "the best government that money can buy." Over and over again, our best interests are set aside and auctioned off. WikiLeaks reveals the ways in which our society is corporatist. Maybe not every policy that gets made and maybe not everything is corrupt, but at the end of the day this is the society we live in. This truth is unequivocally powerful.

So on the whole, I think WikiLeaks is generally a force for good. On the other hand, the notion of everything being leaked, everything being leakable, is one we have not yet come to grips with. What happens when it gets personal, not just for the rich and powerful, but for everybody? All the things that are embarrassing or humiliating, all that stuff is just going to start oozing out onto the internet linked with your name.

So transparency turns into its opposite. An enemy of personal freedom.
It could happen. It could also not happen.

We've had telescopes for a long time but we don't have an epidemic, at least not that I know of, of people using them to spy on their neighbors. There are creepy people who do it, but they're creepy, right? It didn't turn into a social norm that if you haven't put your blinds down you deserve to be peeped. Instead we somehow managed to cling to the idea that you're a dick if you're looking through my window.

That's a morality, an ethic that I hope we can maintain in this surveillance culture. And I do think there's a major difference between exposing the wrongdoings of governments and elected representatives, and governments and elected representatives spying on us, using technology to control us better. Those aren't the same thing.

You went to that Singularity Conference back in 2006. What do you think about the Singularity? The idea that at some point (and soon!) our machines will be smarter than we are?
You know what's funny about that question? I had the first lines of a short story this morning that I tweeted because I didn't know what else to do with it. Let me see if I can find it. It was a very "Bears Discover Fire" first line, if I do say so myself. Here it is:

"Honey, the Singularity is at the door. He says everything is different now."

"Tell him we don't want anything now."

"He's very insistent."

I love it. What happens next?
That's the problem, isn't it? I think the Singularity is a literary device (and also a spiritual belief system) that naturally arises from people who try to imagine a world in which everything gets better and, at the same time, run up against the limits of their imagination in trying to imagine a boundary condition for progress.

What happens when you reach the end of progress? Well the end of progress, when it all bursts, is the Singularity. Predicting it is one thing, describing it another. It's like when our species developed a theory of mind. I think that someone who has a theory of mind and someone who doesn't probably don't have much to say to each other. But we're trying. Charlie Stross and I are writing a book right now called *The Rapture of the Nerds*. We stole the title from Ken MacLeod.

I hope I'll still be able to read it when it comes out. Do you go to lots of SF conventions?
I always go to Worldcon. But the con thing is fading, empirically. The numbers are down at almost every con, and the fans who go are getting older. I was a con-going baby fan. When I was fifteen I volunteered at the local convention and slept in the gopher hole, and that was my entre to SF fandom. That was Ad Astra in Toronto, and when I was going, there were like two thousand people, and now there's four or five hundred, and the younger people who are turning up are basically my generation; there's no one behind us. In contrast, the gaming and anime conventions are so orgasmically huge! The interesting thing about them is that almost without exception they were founded by con-going SF fans.

ComicCon, the huge San Diego comics gathering, was started by people like you and me. We would recognize them instantly as part of the tribe. They hit 275,000 before the San Diego fire marshal made them limit memberships. So cons are running, but not our kind of cons. Not the traditional science fiction fan con.

Why do you think that is?
My Tor editor, Patrick Nielsen Hayden, who knows more about this stuff than I ever will, traces the decline back to a conscious decision to exclude a certain kind of celebrity and commerciality from SF cons. In the 1980s, everyone was worried about the Star Trek conventions turning into a kind of velvet-rope deal, with the guests emerging from the green room to see the public, then retreating back into it. And there'd be the good party and the bad party, and you can see why SF, being the literature of outcasts, rejected that. You wouldn't want your thing where everyone belonged to turn into a thing where once again you were sitting at the uncool kids' table.

What happened was that the cons that were run by fans who were willing to integrate a little of that glitzy stuff, like the ComicCon founders, just kind of took off; and the cons that stayed the way they were, didn't.

You went from fan to pro pretty quick, with Down and Out in the Magic Kingdom. *I know you went to Clarion, the famous SF workshop. Do you still workshop stuff, pass it by others before it's published?*
I don't workshop anymore, because I travel too much. I miss it. When my daughter gets a little older, I'm going to go back to my summer workshop, the one we do in Toronto every year. Some of us went to Clarion together, others just got invited in because we knew their work and taste. You bring a story and you write a story and you workshop them all. You learn to look at your work through the eyes of others.

I really like the process but I can't do the weeklong workshops. I have too many projects going at once.

Sounds like a good problem to have. How do you keep up with it all?
I set a word target and I just hit it every day. When I hit that word target I stop. Period. I stop in the middle of a sentence, so I can start the next day without having to think of anything. I don't remember who told me that trick, but I swear to God if there was just one thing I could teach other writers, it would be that.

Wasn't it Hemingway who said that if you stop in the middle, you always start up easy?

Might have been Hemingway. I wouldn't be surprised if it were a Babylonian scribe. It's one of those things that, once you learn it, just feels right. But until you do it, it seems crazy.

What if there were two things?
If there were two things I could teach people, the second would be to write every day. It's the one thing I wish I'd started doing ten years earlier. I always thought, "Every damn day? What are you talking about? I have to lure the muse into the room, how can I write every day?"

But writing every day was transformative. Now it's at the top of my to-do list. I sit down. I put my bum in my chair and I write. When I'm super, super busy or traveling, my target might be as little as 200–250 words a day, which is peanuts. I type 70–80 words a minute. I've got twenty-four hours to think about what those words are going to be. I can write them. So I do.

That was Trollope's method.
So, you see?

How do you keep the plot in mind?
Usually I work from a treatment instead of a plot outline. I know the kind of things that are going to happen, and maybe a few set pieces, but I don't always know how to get from A to B. My rule of thumb, my heuristic for getting from A to B, is to use what I call The Lake. I always try to have the character trying and failing to solve his (or her) problem and for the problems to always be getting worse. It's an Algis Budrys (the SF writer) type of thing. So long as the attempts to solve the problem are intelligent, there's always a reason to turn the page. Because you want to see people who are intelligent trying to solve problems and you can't look away when they're failing and things are getting worse. I think that's almost a pocket definition of dramatic tension.

What the hell does that have to do with a lake?
I grew up in Toronto, which is in a lake basin. The lake is south, so downhill is always south. You can't get lost. Wherever there's a junction, if you just go downhill eventually you get to the lake. And if you just make things get worse

for your characters, eventually you get to the end. They solve the problem and the novel ends. There are probably more compact ways of getting there, but you can always get there if things are always getting worse. So you can always get to the lake, if that's where you're trying to go.

Back to Boing Boing. You cover an awfully wide and wonderfully eclectic variety of stuff. How do you decide what to keep up with? (Not to mention, how do you do it?)
With a little help from my friends. As a culture, we have gone from a deterministic method of consumption of media to a probabilistic one.

For example, the old SF fans still talk about how you could read the whole field, back in the day. You could read every novel, every magazine, and if you missed something, someone would tell you about it. Deterministic.

Now what happens is that I can't even read all my RSS feeds or e-mails or tweets, much less the novels or events they are about. But the good stuff bubbles up anyway because of reblogging, retweeting, whatever you want to call it. That's what I mean by probabilistic.

Some folks—like the people at *The New York Times* or the *Advertising Age* resident curmudgeon, or that guy at the Columbia School of Journalism who hates my guts—dismiss retweeting, reblogging and such as "parasitic." They don't get it. It is the only way we can have an adequate navigational apparatus for negotiating the sheer volume of material available to us. Without it, there would be no movement from inside your first orbit of social and cultural contacts, no line to the millions who know a million others from a million different walks of life, the cross-pollinators who gets a little bit of information from here and send it there, and connect us all. Without them, the conversation would die. These are the people who are essentially making sure that whatever is locally good for you bubbles up to the top of your pile. They are as important to the future fecundity of media as bees are to the future fecundity of plants.

There is one question I ask everybody. What kind of car do you drive?
I've only owned one car in my life. I owned it for one year, the year I lived in Los Angeles. It was a Hyundai Elantra. A friend who is a car geek told me: "Find a car that's never been in a wreck, that's below its bluebook, and then sell it at the end of the year. It'll be cheaper than leasing." And he was right, I sold it for

exactly what I paid it. I covered everything in it in sheepskin as an experiment. Sheepskin steering wheel cover, sheepskin seat covers, and it was like it just oozed lanolin everywhere. I got a horn that played "Low Rider." So that was LA. Now I have an RFID key that gets me a short-hire bicycle. They're all over London, and that's how I get around.

So, back to my original question. When you look in the mirror these days, who looks back? A science fiction writer, a journalist, a teacher, a blogger, an activist?
Depends on the day, or maybe the time of day. I don't spend a lot of time looking in the mirror. I don't sweat that stuff anymore. It reminds me of when we were all generic subculture kids trying on identities. Are you a cow punk? Are you a crusty punk? A hardcore punk? A straight-edge punk? Worrying about what niche you're in is a little too much like high school.

Let's just say you're a Cory Doctorow sort of guy.

"Sprawling into the Unknown"
Meg Elison

It's EELison, right?
It is. Every time I get asked if I'm Harlan's daughter, I wonder if there would have been any advantage in it.

Where are you from? Where are you headed?
I'm from everywhere; I grew up an army brat and got evicted a lot, and nowhere feels like home. The good thing about growing up like that is that I've always been able to say I'm headed somewhere better, and it's always been true. I'd like to think that I'm headed home, but I'll have to let you know when I've seen it.

Philip K. Dick Award! I'd say you hit the ground running. Was The Book of the Unnamed Midwife *your first try at a novel?*
I definitely did not expect to win an award with my debut novel. I hit the ground stunned, but running. This was, however, not my first novel. I wrote a truly execrable short novel when I was twenty-two that's like a shit salad with mortification for dressing. It will never see the light of day.

The unnamed midwife is pretty good with a gun. Are you?
I learned to shoot rifles when I was quite young. Picked up handguns as an adult. I'm not sure we should be allowed to own them, but for as long as we can I want to be good at it. So I practice with a secret lesbian gun collective and stay sharp.

Did the PKD change things for you?

It's hard to say. I know things would have been different if I hadn't won. Most indie books get very little press and make hardly any sales. I did it backward; I didn't have any short stories out before I published a novel. I didn't know the genre at all. I didn't know I was eligible for the Campbell/Astounding award until my eligibility had passed. I learned everything on the fly with an award-winning book on the market, without an agent or a Clarion class or a clue. But I snatched a brass ring with my very first piece of published fiction. I know that the award opened doors for me, that it made the career I have now possible. I don't know where I'd be now without it. It changed my life.

In San Francisco are you an immigrant or a native?
I wish I came from here. I meet people from here who are effortlessly cool, with an innate sense of the topography and always knowing what neighborhood everything is in: upper and lower, inner and outer, right down to the block where the Tenderloin becomes the Tenderknob. I think of San Francisco as a very beautiful woman who is completely out of my league. I follow her around, and I know everything about her that she'll let me know. But she'll never love me back. We'll never be intimate. I can't afford her, and she knows it. There's a poet named Nazelah Jamison who wrote a poem about who Oakland is as a person, how accepting and chaotic and kind she is. Oakland isn't my city, either. But at least she's always glad to see me.

You are pretty prolific with short stories. Does that mean they are easy for you? Or just that there are lots of markets?
Short stories are easy for me. I get ideas for them all the time, typically knock them out in a single sitting, and I keep a couple of spreadsheets to track my submissions and publications. I love them as an art form: they can do one thing perfectly. I grew up reading short story authors like O. Henry and Shirley Jackson and Stephen King and yourself and Joan Didion, and I studied what they did, how they encapsulated a whole world in just a few pages. I wanted to do that, too.

But lots of markets? There are very few markets and they fold all the time. The word gets passed that *Playboy* and the *Atlantic* are buying fiction again, and I watch writers lick their chops thinking about paying the cell phone bill with a short story. They're challenging to write well, selling them is highly competitive, and at ten cents a word I'm barely beating Jo March in the nineteenth century. I must really love the form—there's no other compelling reason to go on.

Was getting published an ambition or a byproduct?
Getting published was the supreme ambition of my existence. I have terrible flight anxiety and it's gotten a lot better since I've been able to think to myself, *At least I've been published, so it's okay if I die.* It happened sooner and easier than I expected, and I ended up sprawling into the unknown as if I was pushing against a stuck door and it suddenly flung open. Once you've achieved your life goal, what do you do then? Publish more, I guess. Set your cap for various lists and prizes and benchmarks. I wanted to see my name on covers, my book on library shelves, and reviews of my boiling brains in the papers. I got everything I wanted. I have been trying to aim higher ever since.

Do you think writers have a special responsibility? To whom or what?
There's this artist who works in mixed media, a Mexican named Jorge Méndez Blake. He created this piece of art that shows the impact of a book by jamming a copy of Kafka's *The Castle* into the first row of bricks in a wall. The book does not conform to brick shape, and the entire wall is warped around it. There's a ripple to its structure, and it's a powerful visual metaphor for the work that a book can do.

Throughout our history, books have done what kings and legislators and even the Bomb fail to do: they make people see things in a way they hadn't seen them before. That's an awesome power, and that must come with some responsibility. We are all responsible to the societies we inhabit; we make up the tenor and pace of life to the people around us. However, I don't think that a writer's responsibility is any greater than that of a pipefitter or a president. We are all bound to each other and are all capable of callous cruelty or kindness. Books are uniquely powerful—all art is. But writers are simply human. We are responsible for our work and ourselves. By the time our books are a brick in the wall, most of us are as dead as Kafka. And maybe half as well understood.

You are being deported from the USA. You are handed an envelope welcoming you to another country. What country are you hoping it's from?

The most practical choice for me is Germany. I speak the language, I am prepared to be a good part of a socialist society, and I've always felt quite welcome there. As much as I've always wanted to be a Brit, they've got a hell of a mess going over there right now. I loved my time in Mexico, and my Spanish is pretty good, but I could never get over the way men look right past me to speak only to my male companion. Germans are terribly polite. I could settle there quite well.

One sentence on each please: Rudy Rucker, Uber, Nell Zink.
I met Rudy at a party and I was struck by how vital and wry he is. He won the PKD the year I was born. I'm banned for life from Uber for writing about the CEO being less than honorable when I was a college journalist. Nell Zink's *Mislaid* is a hell of a book, and I'd like to make her a cocktail sometime.

Cliterary Salon. Okay, I get it. But what's the deal?
Some friends of mine (Louis Evans, Lauren Parker, Maggie Tokuda-Hall) wanted to do a San Francisco LitQuake event that nobody else was doing, so we put together a feminist reading called ClitQuake. We packed the house two times in a row and decided to make it a monthly show, highlighting voices that don't always get to speak into a mic. We've been doing it for a couple of years now and it feels like pure glory. We make enough to pay the writers who perform. This city is rich with literary events, and I shine with pride that we get to be part of that.

After two years at a college that nobody has ever heard of, you transferred to one that nobody has never heard of. What did Berkeley do for you?
That college that nobody has heard of had some of the best professors I've ever studied with and set me up for success in ways I can't ever pay back. They peened my logic and argumentation until I could write clearly, concisely, and reason my way through anything. I hope to someday make a large gesture of some benevolent kind to Mt. San Jacinto College. They deserve a lot of recognition.

After I was properly prepared to receive, Berkeley gave me everything. A million doors opened up to me that I couldn't even have seen from where I was standing. MSJC taught me to write, but Berkeley taught me to read. I'd never had instruction in close and engaged reading like I got at Cal, and I had my nose forced back to the page like it hadn't been since I learned to sound words out. Learning to write was important, but there's nothing you can do with it until you've learned to take a story apart and see how it works. I published my first book within a month of graduating. It was jet fuel on the fire of my voice.

What's hardest about being big?
Fitting in a fucking airline seat. I feel great, and I climb pyramids and dance all night. I get all the attention I can handle. All I want in this world are things that fit my body. Clothes. Chairs. Bathtubs.

Where did you meet your husband?
My husband and I both dated the same girl in high school! She was a dragon-clawed goth queen, and I couldn't stand that he had her attention. Other things I couldn't stand: his highlights, his attitude, his letterman's jacket, his Mormonism. Things have changed a little since then.

Did you ever want to be small?
If I had it my way, I'd be much, much bigger. My true form is fifty feet tall and made of gold, shrieking like Godzilla and eating entire oyster beds.

You have been nominated for the Tiptree Award but now will never, ever win it. What went wrong?
Without in any way condoning the killing of a disabled spouse, I was troubled by the name change on the Tiptree. Sure, the tide is turning, and people are beginning to realize that there are no heroes, just people. But I couldn't help but notice that it takes a lot of high-profile agitating and protesting and insisting that we remove the name of a dead man from an award. Tiptree's legacy was as fragile as the legacies of women and queer people always are. We have to be perfect. Campbell had to be a fascist to get blowback. Lovecraft had to be a monster. Asimov's reckoning is never going to come, and he was a serial public assaulter. Women and queer people are almost always footnotes in science fiction history. Tiptree was imperfect and did a terrible thing. But now even the footnote that name held has gotten smaller.

What can you tell me about Layla?
Find Layla is the most deeply personal thing I've ever written. I grew up very poor and with criminally bad parents. I don't talk about it much, but I decided to work some of it out in fiction. Layla is the culmination of a lot of my worst stories. Also she swears like a sailor and does small crimes like I did as a kid. I feel naked looking at that book.

Like Hemingway, you often use simplicity as an ornament. Do you share his background in journalism?
I became obsessed with Hemingway when I was at Berkeley. I had this incredible professor, the late Ron Loewinsohn, who taught us *The Sun Also Rises*, and I got time alone with him in office hours. I asked him if the woman in the book, Brett, was meant to be read as barren as a foil to Ernie's ever-castrated heroes. It's the 1920s, she's fucking a nineteen-year-old bullfighter, and pregnancy never comes up. Loewinsohn blinked at me and told me he'd never thought about it. It was a seed for my first book.

From there, he taught me how to pick apart Hemingway's simplicity. The way he lays short phrases over one another like a net. The way he lets an image carry the scene without getting between the reader and what he wants the reader to see. Emerson's transparent eyeball. I had been working as a journalist for a year at that point, and I knew that's where Hemingway had cut his teeth, too. But factualism as a style is more than that. It doesn't just tell you the who/what/when; it puts you in the middle of it. Like anything great, it looks easy until you try to do it.

If you could read one other language fluently, what would it be?
Whatever the hell the Voynich manuscript is written in. That thing drives me crazy. For everything else, there's Google Translate.

Is humor a sauce in your fiction, or an entrée?
Humor is a sauce. I'm not funny enough to make it the entrée. For that matter, I'm not smart enough to make science fiction the entrée, or romantic enough to make love the entrée. The story is always the main dish; I bought a whole

chicken. I'm gonna slather it with something I like the taste of and serve it up hot.

My Jeopardy *answer: Five. You provide the question, please.*
I read this to my husband and he reminded me that I was knocked out of the *Jeopardy* qualifying rounds because I declined to study state capitals like he suggested. He further suggested I write up a question about state capitals to go with this answer. Once again, I decline.

What do you read for fun? And don't ask me what I mean by "fun." I ask the questions.
McSweeney's online stuff always makes me laugh or makes me think clever thoughts. I read *F&SF* every month with great joy and ceremony, in the bath with my phone shut off. I love John Scalzi and always find his work fun. Seanan McGuire is fun until she rips my heart out and makes me eat it. I love reading old joke books on Project Gutenberg and trying to figure out how humor and language change over time. And Carmen Maria Machado has skill and whimsical control that makes me scream—it's pleasurable, it's maddening, it's deep and connected to popular culture and transcends genre. I can't keep quiet when I read her. I huff and I wheeze and I cheer. And N.K. Jemisin once wrote a fight scene (in *The City Born Great*) that made me stop in the middle of the financial district in San Francisco at 8:30 a.m. and howl like a wolf in my office clothes.

Have you ever been attacked by self-driving cars?
Not attacked, but late one night in San Francisco I saw a fleet of them being tested, silently gliding like black sharks through the night.

What kind of car do you drive? I ask this of everyone.
I drive a 2015 Nissan Versa that's covered in vinyls and quotes from Neil Gaiman's Sandman graphic novels. It gets me some of the oddest questions around town.

We met at a Locus Christmas party. I missed it this year (2019). How was it? How's 2020 shaping up for you?

We actually met at SF in SF, and I was blown away to see you there. One of your stories ("They're Made of Meat") gave me an out-of-body experience when I was fifteen and set the course of my career. But I was just another adoring fan, and you were very gracious and had no reason to know who I was at the time.

I love the Locus Christmas party, particularly for the reason that I meet people like you there. This year's was no exception. I had a long talk with Isaac Fellman and flirted abominably with Ellen Klages, who is a genius, and I'm not fit to touch the hem of her garment. Almost nothing I dreamed would be true about becoming a real writer turned out to be true; most of it was out of movies like *Romancing the Stone* or *Misery*. But the parties are every bit as grand, as sophisticated, as electrifying as I ever wildly fantasized. I party with the gods.

This year, 2020, is shaping up to be great and terrible, as only an election year can be. But I've got two books coming out, and three more in the chamber. It's good to be alive.

What question do you wish I had asked?
I'm just relieved you didn't ask me one of the four questions I always get. Terry, you're a treasure to the genre, and it is a great honor in my life to have you ask me about my car.

"More Exuberant Than Is Strictly Tasteful"
Karen Joy Fowler

Do they really put chopped nuts in sushi in Santa Cruz?
It's one of the town's many charms.

There is a rumor that L. Ron Hubbard played a role in your development as a writer. Explain.
My story "Recalling Cinderella" was published in *Writers of the Future*, an anthology funded by Scientology. This was my first publication, though not my first sale; the Scientologists proved more efficient than Ed Ferman, editor of *Fantasy & Science Fiction*. The anthology was made up of winners in a quarterly contest. I did not even place. But Algis Budrys, who edited the volume, liked my story enough to include it. So I would say that Algis Budrys had an impact on my career but that L. Ron Hubbard found me wanting.

This all happened in that particular period in which L. Ron Hubbard was maybe dead or maybe not dead. There was an extravagant launch party in LA where I met many science fiction writers of whom I was in breathless admiration. The party and my thirty-fifth birthday were on the same day, so I hardly minded turning thirty-five. Many days of sorrow would have been avoided if the Scientologists had also thrown me a big party when I turned forty.

Several of your works I would describe as historicals. Certainly The Sweetheart Season, Sarah Canary, *and* Sister Noon. *Does the research come before or after the idea?*
The research begins long before the writing, years before, but continues throughout. Initially, I just free-read through the period, looking for things I can use,

elements that will shape and adorn the story. If I find an interesting setting, well described, I will steer my story into that space for a scene or two. I make decisions about the story I'll tell based on the things I've been able to find.

Later I have specific needs. I might want to know what the residents of the Steilacoom insane asylum ate or what chewing gum looked like in 1871 or how radioactive the atomic ring you could buy from the back of the magazines actually was.

There was a time when approaching the desk of the research librarians at UC Davis was like Norm entering Cheers. "Where everybody knows your name..."

How often do you go to the movies?
About once a week. That's in the winter; we go less in the summer. One of the things that drew me initially to my husband was that we both believed seeing a bad movie was better than seeing no movie at all. Now we're old and cranky and have changed our minds about that—but we both changed our minds together, which is how a marriage must work when the initial contract is so substantially altered.

And suddenly, these days, television is better than the movies—more interesting, more original, more compelling. What science fiction writer saw *that* one coming?

The title of your newest novel is We Are All Completely Beside Ourselves. *Why completely? Why, for that matter, all? The title seems to be saying more than simply nonplussed.*
All is, of course, necessary, because, though I am the one raising the issue here, it is most certainly not just me. Not just my narrator and me. Though she has lived an extreme version of being beside herself, still, it affects us all.

Completely addresses the magnitude of the situation. Everywhere we go, there we are. Surrounded. Us to the right of us, us to the left. Nowhere we are not once we've gotten there.

The line between us and not-us is a blurry one: that's what the title is trying to say. This is partly because we are incapable of seeing anything that isn't transformed into us by the mere act of seeing it. And partly because we are all part of Darwin's world.

Does that clear things up? Surely it must. Nonplussed is the least important part.

Many of your works have what I would call an exemplary aspect. Is this to add an old-fashioned patina, or is it a natural ingredient of SF? Or do you just think people need fixing?
People need so much fixing. It's exhausting, honestly. And unappreciated.

"Hey! You there! Shape up!"

See what I mean? I hardly have time to be interviewed, there is so much fixing to be done.

You were one of the founders of the famously feminist James Tiptree Award. Why is it named after a guy?
Technically the Tiptree is not a feminist award. In theory it could go to a work of severe antifeminism as long as the antifeminism was interesting, innovative, and original, and not the same old tired claptrap. But little is new in the world of antifeminism. I can't help but feel they are phoning it in.

So feminist works usually end up winning the award.

It's named after SF writer Alice Sheldon, who made up a man, James Tiptree Jr., to write her science fiction stories for her.

"The Pelican Bar" is pretty scary. Where'd that idea come from? Guantánamo?
Definitely Guantánamo. Also Abu Ghraib. But even more directly, from the chain of overseas schools run by the World Wide Association of Specialty Programs and Schools (WWASPS), particularly the notorious Tranquility Bay in Jamaica and High Impact in Mexico. I read online a statement that we shouldn't be surprised that Americans are okay with torturing foreign prisoners, because apparently we are okay with the torturing of American children, as long as it happens overseas. That statement was the seed of my story.

What kind of car do you drive? I already know but am required to ask.
Like everyone else in Santa Cruz, I drive a silver Prius. I take it downtown to pick up my sushi with nuts.

In What I Didn't See, *your short story collection from Small Beer Press, a narrator declares, "The older I get, the more I want a happy ending." Is that a promise or a threat?*
It's a plea.

You have success in both short and long form, stories and novels. Do you go at them differently?
I love writing short stories best. They are so manageable. By the time I finish one, I know how it works, how it's been put together. I feel like a clockmaker.

Novels are just a mess. I never have a sense of the whole; I never am sure what I've achieved or what I've failed to achieve. But I do like spending more time with my characters, which a novel affords. I miss my characters when I finish a novel. I don't miss the ones from my short stories.

Ever been attacked by drones?
No, but they stalk me. I see them out of the corners of my eyes.

Maxwell Lane, your imaginary imaginary [sic] detective in Wit's End, *recommends asking at least one question that won't be answered. What would that be for you?*
What happened to Beverly in my story "What I Didn't See"?

What's the deal with all the apes? I was a little surprised when one didn't show up in The Jane Austen Book Club. *I didn't say disappointed.*
You do understand that you and I are apes? Great apes, which takes the sting out.

So both of us have apes galore, only your stories have more bears. Even just articulating that makes me suddenly feel all competitive. Note to self: write more stories with bears. Don't cede the bears to Bisson.

Here's my Jeopardy *question: I provide the answer, you provide the question. A: Small boys with big ideas.*
Q: What's even scarier than drones?

If you weren't a writer what would you be, as in do?

I would go on anthropological digs and find amazing pottery shards. I would study cave paintings and also elephants in the wild. I would restore old books, damaged by weather and fire. I would sail around the world. I would be such a valuable member of society that you would hardly recognize me.

Is it true that Sarah Canary *was originally titled* Sister from Another Planet?
Something should be titled *Sister from Another Planet*. It would be nice if I didn't have to write it myself, but I am here, waiting and eager to read it. Doesn't this seem like a job for Eleanor Arnason? I think she might be just the woman for it. I would read *Sister from Another Planet* by Eleanor Arnason in a heartbeat.

What do you think California will look like in 150 years?
More salt water, less fresh. Water wars all up and down the state. It's Chinatown, Jake.

One of your favorite plot devices is "nice girl gets falling-down drunk." Did you steal that or make it up?
It's a standard romcom trope. See *The Philadelphia Story*, *The Sure Thing*, *The Cutting Edge*, countless others. The woman cannot admit her true feelings until she gets drunk. Because these are movies and not life, the man refuses to take advantage of the situation. Sometimes the woman is angry about this refusal and true love is delayed yet again as a result.

So I've just taken this same trope and am using it in non-romcoms. No one is in love. No one is learning anything about their true feelings through the magic of alcohol. In my books, people are simply getting drunk. I am subverting the genre. It's possible I'm drinking heavily as I do so.

Have you ever been arrested? Were you eventually released?
By the time I joined the revolution, the police had stopped arresting us. It was seen as pointless since the courts just released us again back into the wild first chance they got. So the police were beating us up instead and skipping the arresting part. I've never been arrested, but I've been beaten up.

I've also been rescued by the police in other contexts. It's all been very confusing.

But I *am* clear now that my constitutional rights are not meant to be actually, you know, exercised.

What are you reading this week?
Snapper by Brian Kimberling. So recommended!

Your thoughts on each in one sentence, please: John Crowley, Agnes Smedley, David Sedaris, Molly Gloss, Evelyn Waugh.
I can name that tune in one word. Brilliant, inspiring, hilarious, impeccable, eternal. You can pretty much rotate the adjectives, give them a spin, as they apply equally to all of the above.

Do you have a regular drill as a writer? Ever work in longhand?
I can't work in longhand. I get too involved with penmanship. I become a monk with an illuminated manuscript.

My regular drill is to intend to write and then spend the day sitting at my computer doing my e-mail and browsing my favorite sites instead. Watching some TED talks. I love TED talks. They are the only place where I find hope for the future. But then I spoil the mood by scoping out the political scene. All the while filled with a faint but ineffective self-loathing because I'm not writing.

Why do drivers wait so long to start moving when the light changes?
They're on the phone.

You have a solid reputation in genre (SF) and in mainstream as well. Does that ever make for a conflict?
Do I? A *solid* reputation? Are you sure? It seems to me that the question of whether I write genre fiction at all has dogged me my whole career. I was very pleased when *Locus* publisher Charles Brown told me years ago that of course I was a science fiction writer. It didn't matter *what* I wrote, he said, because I *thought* like a science fiction writer.

I do love genre fiction. I also love mainstream literary fiction. As a reader sometimes I want one and sometimes I want the other. There is no reason not to read both.

As a writer, sometimes I want to write one and sometimes the other, but this has been trickier. When I began publishing, NY believed that either people read science fiction and nothing else, or they never read science fiction. Scrupulous attention was paid to my positioning and though it never seemed like a problem to me, I was aware that it seemed like a problem to others.

It probably was a problem. It has been my great good fortune not to have to spend much time thinking about it.

The social world of science fiction has been extremely welcoming to me. I do truly want someday to repay that kindness by writing a book in the genre for those steadfast friends and readers. But guess what? Genre fiction is very hard to write well.

What do you like doing best, first draft or revisions?
I hate the first, fumbling, dispiriting draft. Team Revision all the way.

Tarantino, as in the name of the film director, originally meant citizen of Tarentum, the ancient Greek city in Southern Italy. Did you know that?
I know it now.

You teach in lots of writing workshops, and with some apparent success. What's your emphasis there? What do writers leave with that they came without?
How would you measure success as a workshop teacher? I try first to do no harm. I make my best possible effort to see the story the writer is trying to tell and help them achieve that. I try very hard not to confuse their story with the story I would be telling, given that same material. Sometimes I fail at that, but not for lack of effort.

I believe that the learning in workshops happens to the critiquer not the critiqued. So I do demand that my students put careful attention into their responses as readers. As writers I caution them not to make changes based on the critiques they get unless they see clearly how that will improve the story they want to tell.

And I also provide such craft tips as have worked for me over the years. It's been a bit strange, or was at first, to look closely my own process, because most of it was happening unconsciously. In order to teach, I've had to observe myself at work. It's not always a pretty sight.

Who do you think would win in a fight, Dr. Johnson or Jane Austen? A footrace?
Austen would refuse to compete. Johnson would win, but he would look such a fool for having done so.

Ever do any hack work? What sort?
Nothing literary, but I once spent a summer sorting tomatoes for Hunt and Wesson. I was not good at this. The potential for advancement to catsup labels was always there and always out of reach. I turned out to be too picky about the tomatoes I wanted in my tomato sauce. I was also pregnant at the time and suffering from morning sickness. I couldn't eat tomatoes for years.

Even now, the smell of mountains of off-peak tomatoes streaming past on conveyor belts haunts my dreams.

Do you read on the Kindle?
I read on the iPad, but only when I travel. I persist in liking books on paper best. I've learned that the sense of how close to the end of a book I am, which no electronic version can recreate for me in quite that same physical way, is an important component of my reading experience.

Carter Scholz claims he had a role in the development of The Jane Austen Book Club. *Is this true, or just another of his tall tales?*
There would be no *Jane Austen Book Club* without Carter Scholz. That's the plain and simple truth of the matter. I was at a bookstore with Carter when I misread the sign that gave me the title.

You spent your early youth in Indiana. Do you like James Whitcomb Riley?
I was kept away from the great Hoosier poet as a child. My parents surely had their reasons and I never developed a taste for him and his homespun dialect. The Hoosier poet my parents did approve of was Samuel Yellen, and they read to me often from his book *In the House and Out*. Especially at bedtime. "It's time to take your place in Cassiopeia's Chair." This was a line from a poem ["Lullaby"] about the constellations, very beautiful and starry. Put me right to sleep.

What authors do you think have had the most influence on your work?
T.H. White, by a mile. Author of *The Once and Future King*. T.H. White is why I have never believed that I had to follow the rules or consider anything resembling a "contract with the reader." T.H. White is why I never believed that I had to pick a single genre or a single tone or choose between comedy and tragedy, between historical and contemporary, between realistic and fantastical. No reason not to do them all and all the time, either piece by piece or within the same work or within the same paragraph. T.H. White taught me that writing can be more exuberant than is strictly tasteful, and I like exuberance best, though I'm not sure I often achieve it.

Do you read poetry for fun?
I do. For fun and for fuel. The innovative use of language is inspiring to me. It makes me want to write, which is a helpful first step in writing.

I understand that you are the only science fiction writer in the Baseball Hall of Fame. Is that fair?
Nothing in baseball is fair or foul but thinking makes it so. Actually, I'm not *in* the Baseball Hall of Fame. I merely have my own key to the door. They gave it to me because my novel *The Sweetheart Season* was about a women's baseball team. At least in part.

What did you think of the film of The Jane Austen Book Club? *You are allowed to dissemble on this one.*
There are parts of the movie I think work really, really well. Some of those parts come straight from my book, but many do not.

There are also parts I don't care for. I don't believe reading Austen aloud can save a marriage. I don't believe a high school teacher should sit in the car necking with a student no matter how poorly she was mothered. My characters would never behave so badly.

And it is tiring to have people approach, as they quite often do, to tell me what they loved about my book, only to realize they are talking about the movie. If I persuade the people reading this of one thing, let it be that. The writer is going to know if you pretend to have read the book when you've only seen the movie. Don't even try.

But all in all, I like the movie. It's not my book, but it's smart and entertaining and there is a scene (not in my book) in which a nice woman gets falling-down drunk, which is, as already established, the mark of great storytelling.

What will your memorial bench say?
Hey! You, there! Shape up!

"I Did, and I Didn't, and I Won't"
Eileen Gunn

Who are you? Why are you here?
I'm a writer. I write short stories and essays, and this is my third collection. I've also written a few essays about people and ideas and what science fiction is good for. I am probably best known for my story "Stable Strategies for Middle Management," which describes the evolutionary strategies deployed in an unusual corporate ecosystem. From 2002 to 2008, I published and edited the online science-fiction magazine *The Infinite Matrix*. Just before that, for a year or two, from an attic in Brooklyn, I edited the world's largest outdoor recreation website, publishing articles that covered, in heart-stopping detail, everything from hiking in Tierra del Fuego to fishing in a public park off Interstate 5. I also had a career in the advertising and marketing of technology products that began in 1968 and ran in parallel with the development of microcomputers, the commercial internet, and the World Wide Web.

Why am I here? What must I do to justify my existence? When I was younger, the answer to that question was "write a novel." Now, with the self-knowledge that comes from having matured, I can tell you the answer is "Finish the novel."

Did you wander into science fiction or did you fall?
Familiar story. I started on *Peter Pan* and *Alice in Wonderland* and soon moved on to the hard stuff. I grew up in a rural suburb of Boston in which a tiny drugstore was the only source of *Mad* magazine, science fiction, and the rest of literature. When I was a teenager, I babysat for several people who liked science fiction, and I read my way through their paperbacks, while their kids raised hell. I also read Salinger and Nabokov and my grandmother's Reader's

Digest Condensed Books, anything I could get out of the library, laundry lists, etc.

I could have grown up to be a writer of laundry lists, but when I was in college, my creative writing teacher forbade me to write science fiction, and I've been writing it all these years out of sheer orneriness.

You worked at Microsoft early. What was that like?
Ninety-hour weeks, on salary. (A meager salary.) A sense of adventure, because if you saw something that needed doing, you just did it, and suddenly it became part of your job. A modest amount of terror, because the computer industry morphed every three months into something new and strange, and so did all our products and strategies. There was a certain amount of anything-goes.

My favorite cultural moment at Microsoft occurred when I was newly arrived. I passed, in a hallway, a Microsoft tech escorting two customers from IBM. It was an unusually hot summer day, but the IBM fellows were wearing crisp gray suits, white shirts, and ties. The Microsoft guy was wearing dungaree cutoffs, and nothing else. I caught a snatch of what he was saying: "Oh, yes, we have a dress code. You have to."

Was The Infinite Matrix *a luxury car, a pharmaceutical, or the first respectable online SF magazine?*
It was a bit of each: a not-very-respectable luxury pharmaceutical. Its origin was a glorious acid trip, in which I'd been hired by a tech company to create a fabulous online SF magazine and was given the budget to do so. I built it from the ground up during the Web's adolescence, before the adults got involved, with the help of a small raft of programmers and the underground artists Paul Mavrides and Jay Kinney.

It had, over the course of its six years of existence, a daily blog from Bruce Sterling, nonfiction by William Gibson and Howard Waldrop, literary criticism by John Clute, and publishing news and gossip from David Langford. It had new fiction by Ursula Le Guin, Pat Cadigan, Nisi Shawl, Rudy Rucker, Cory Doctorow, Richard Kadrey, Michael Swanwick, and everyone else you've ever heard of. And it had a strange, smart daily feature, "Today in History," by one

Terry Bisson, which documented history that hadn't happened yet. He writes it still for *Locus* magazine.

The Infinite Matrix was conceived of and originally funded by Matrix.net because they loved science fiction and thought that all the best UNIX programmers did too. It was rescued by a generous and anonymous donor, and later by auctions and fundraising events. It never learned to provide for itself properly, but it was always free to readers and paid good money to contributors, and when its time was up, it left a lovely corpse: an archive of almost all its content at www.infinitematrix.net.

You often, more than most, collaborate with other writers. How does that work?
Sometimes it works well, and sometimes it doesn't. It works best, I think, when one writer has an idea or a beginning that they don't know what to do with, and another writer sees a way of moving it forward. It can fail when one writer has a vision of what the whole story should be but can't communicate that to the other writer.

The most fun story I ever collaborated on was written with Michael Swanwick, Pat Murphy, and Andy Duncan, and we sketched the story out in advance, leaving room for surprises. In fact, we made surprises mandatory. Or maybe the most fun story was the one I wrote with Rudy Rucker in which, at the end, the two main characters fucked the entire Earth alive. Or maybe it was the one I wrote with Swanwick with the evil elves and the monster that turned into Dick Cheney. Or the one with Leslie What about the high school for psychic teenagers and the criminally insane.

I would never have written any of those stories if left to my own devices.

Why Seattle?
I moved to Seattle for love and economics. It turned out to be a smart move in each case. But sometimes, when I'm driving around the city, my car radio will boom out "This is KUOW, Seattle," and I'll think, "Seattle? What am I doing in Seattle?"

What is Ted Chiang really like?
I could tell you, Terry, but if I did I'd have to exile you to a parallel universe.

What music do you listen to most often?
I asked my iTunes app, and it replied that the music I listen to most often is reggae by the Abyssinians, followed closely by accordionist Adam Trehan, a Cajun musician who recorded four sides for Columbia in 1928 and then left music forever. I think iTunes must be wrong about this. I have long been a fan of the Holy Modal Rounders, the Fugs, the Clamtones, the Pogues, Delta blues, and Elizabethan lute music, but the musician I listen to most often right now is probably singer/songwriter Warren Zevon, who's been dead for nearly twenty years and to whom I rarely listened when he was alive.

I used to play guitar and lute, so I listen to a lot of guitar and lute music. I can't write while listening to music, however, so I have had to make hard choices.

Jeopardy *question: I provide the answer, you come up with the question. Originality not a requirement.*
Okay, Terry, here's the question: What is reality?

You started out as a copywriter (so did I). Was that a lucky break or a hitch?
Both. It was a lucky break because my first real copywriting job was at a small agency run by funny, talented lefties who did clever campaigns for high-tech clients. They taught me how to understand subjects I'd never studied and how to work with capitalists without becoming one.

Writing ads was a hitch in my fiction career because I got really good at short, snappy sentences and never mastered the long, loopingly graceful writing you need to write novels. Twitter is my ideal length, and it's all advertising's fault.

One sentence on each, please: John Clute, Lord Buckley, Jean Auel.
I have always liked Jean Auel, because her name is pronounced Gene Owl, and I like owls and genes. I have always wondered how Lord Buckley, an American, came to be a vassal of the King. It's been nearly thirty years, but I'm still grateful to John Clute for sitting me down in his favorite chair, handing me a cup of hot black coffee, and playing directly into my jet-lagged brain the newly released track of Bob Dylan singing "Blind Willie McTell."

What kind of car do you drive? It seems I ask this of everyone.
Right now? A copper-colored 2015 Fiat 500. Why?

If you could take Oscar Wilde out for a drink in Seattle, where would you go? What would you order?
Either Canlis, the most expensive restaurant in the city, or one of the rougher bars down by the waterfront, if any of them are still there. I'd let him make the call. I would order Death in the Afternoon, a cocktail invented, they say, by Ernest Hemingway, consisting of a decent iced champagne poured over a shot of absinthe until it turns the color of a mossy pearl.

If Clarion and WisCon had a child, who would it be?
Quvenzhané Wallis, both the actress and her brave, independent character in *Beasts of the Southern Wild*.

The Clarion and Clarion West workshops, held for aspiring writers of speculative fiction, are about individuals venturing out into the unknown, often at an early age and with no clear destination. I attended the Clarion Workshop in 1976, and it improved both my fiction and my reality. I later joined the board of the Clarion West workshop, a similar six-week convocation, which exists to empower women and BIPOC+LGBTQ writers of speculative fiction, and I occasionally teach a week.

WisCon is an annual convention, held in May. It celebrates and furthers speculative fiction that reflects the richness and diversity of the human imagination. I have attended it frequently over the past thirty years, as its interests moved from feminism to issues of race and gender and cultural appropriation. In addition to being about politics and books, WisCon is about diligently examining who you are, what you mean, and how you affect others. Sometimes that's fun and sometimes it's threatening to one's self-esteem, but it's always been worth the effort. As I write this, WisCon has been in pandemic hiatus for the past two years, but I expect it to reopen stronger than ever. Check it out.

What poetry do you read for fun?
All poetry, really. Never had a job in which I was obliged to read poetry.

The book of poetry that I've had the most fun with lately is *Dictator*, by the Oulipian poet Philip Terry, which is a re-creation of the Epic of Gilgamesh using the 1,500-word vocabulary of Globish, a sort of pidgin created for use in business communications by nonnative English speakers. Oulipian writers use constraints on their writing to force themselves into new ways of thinking and expressing their thoughts. *Dictator* is a wondrous work that transcends the limits of time and translation: it channels the imagined voice and psyche of a Bronze Age storyteller in ways that conventional translations do not. Also, it makes me laugh out loud and demand that people listen to me read especially wonderful passages. The one in which the trapper is explaining to the harlot how to seduce Enkidu is my favorite.

I am also very much drawn to the poems of JT Stewart, a remarkable poet and teacher, a Black woman who has had a strong presence in the Seattle poetry and literary scenes over the past forty years. Her poems are very immediate, grounded in the now, even when they speak in the voices of people who died centuries ago. My partner, the book designer John D. Berry, is working with JT to put together *Our Bones Sing of Salt*, a collection of all her published poems.

There are lots more, but that's enough. Philip Terry and JT Stewart are both visceral poets: their poems engage with a rush of sound and meaning. That is pure poetry.

You attended a Catholic college. How come?
I made a deal with God: I would attend eight years of Catholic schooling, and if I still didn't believe in Him at the end of it, I wouldn't have to believe and would not be expected to repent on my death bed. I did, and I didn't, and I won't, and I am not planning to.

What do you read for pleasure these days?
The book that has given me the most delight in the past month is the newly released collection of comic strips by Shary Flenniken, *Trots and Bonnie*. First published in the *National Lampoon* in the 1970s and '80s, they are exquisitely inked with an elegant Art Deco aesthetic and an incongruously filthy sense of the ridiculous.

What role does humor play in SF—feature, bug, ornament?
Terry, that's like asking what role garlic plays in dinner. Humor is hard to get a handle on, because it's entirely subjective: what's funny to me is not necessarily funny to you. But I know from your writing that what's funny to *you* is pretty damn funny to me.

What is the Difference Dictionary?
The Difference Dictionary is Dr. Gunn's Patented History Restorer, intended for SF readers who have had their understanding of the nineteenth century scrambled by William Gibson and Bruce Sterling's novel *The Difference Engine*. Properly administered, the dictionary will restore the hairy details of the history of our time stub, and the hapless reader will no longer think of Lord Bryon as a radical politician, Texas as an independent country, and computers as giant clockworks made of rosewood and brass. I wrote the dictionary in 1990 as a sort of review of the novel, and in 1997, while learning to code in HTML, I coded it and posted it on the Web. A few hours later, it was declared Cool Site of the Day, I guess because it was sort of a single-sourced Wikipedia, but Wikipedia didn't exist yet. You can find its dry bones (untouched for a decade or more) at eileengunn.com/difference-dictionary.

Why isn't science fiction taken seriously as literature?
It's true that the marketing category known as science fiction is often not taken seriously, but what marketing category is? Romance novels? Bestsellers? Big fat fantasy novels? Jane Austen wrote romance novels. Charles Dickens wrote bestsellers. Mary Shelley wrote science fiction. I don't think that the writer or reader has to transcend genre for a book to be taken seriously—I think the academy has to.

Ever fish?
I fished when I was a kid. Another kid taught me to fish. I had a reel and line and had been jumping around from rock to rock, wondering what to do. He caught a grasshopper, baited the hook, told me where he'd recently seen a legal-sized trout, waited with me, and gave pointers on how to drag the line a bit. After I hooked the fish, he told me how to land it, then he killed it quickly so it

wouldn't suffer and showed me how to scale, gut, and clean it. Then we walked back to the campsite, and I told my mother, "I caught a fish!" which was certainly an exaggeration and may in fact have been an actual injustice.

"Flying Squirrels in the Rafters"
Elizabeth Hand

You teach writing in New England. Anywhere else?
I'm on faculty at the Stonecoast MFA program here in Maine, but I also teach at various workshops across the country and have done so for about twenty-two years—Clarion and Clarion West, Odyssey, the Pike's Peak Writer's Conference, various other smaller workshops. I've also done workshops for elementary, high school, and college students—I especially love working with younger kids. A few years ago I did a series of poetry miniworkshops based on Arthur Rimbaud's life and work, with middle schoolers. It was a blast. This past summer I taught at Yale, which was fun but no different from any other writer's workshop, except for the setting, which was impressive.

When you teach writing, what do you try to unteach?
The habit of wanting to be a writer without first being a serious reader. I'm always taken aback by how many intelligent people set out to "be writers" (as opposed to simply writing) and have a very narrow repertoire of work they've actually read.

It's wonderful that so many people love Stephen King and Neil Gaiman—I do, too—but King and Gaiman are both well-read and widely read. That's one reason for their success. Watching movie and TV adaptations of books doesn't count.

I'm also continually surprised that many people just don't get how hard writing is to do. There are prodigies, as there are with any art, but for the rest of us there's a long, slow learning curve. Very few of us believe that we could sit down at the piano without having taken a course of study and bang out a challenging piano piece by Beethoven or Debussy or anyone else. But everyone thinks they can write a novel. That doesn't mean you need to have an undergraduate or graduate degree in writing—I don't—but you do need to put time in, learning your craft.

You studied theater in your misspent youth. Have you tried playwriting since? (Your colleague Jim Kelly has, and so have I, with spectacularly indifferent success.)

No, but in the last few years I've thought a lot about trying to write a play. I was in a very intense and competitive BFA program for theater, and after three years I realized that it was a lot harder to write even a mediocre play than I had imagined. I'd written four or five one-act plays for a children's/YA theater group when I was a teenager and seen them produced, which was a great experience. Transitioning from that to being a serious playwright was tough. I just didn't have the chops for it, and I didn't want to do something and fail miserably for the rest of my life. With fiction, I felt like I could fail miserably (and did), but eventually I might improve enough to succeed.

But I still love theater. There are a handful of performances I've seen in my life that changed me forever—a high school production of *Twelfth Night* which I saw when I was seventeen (the inspiration for my short novel *Illyria*); the Broadway preview of Tony Kushner's *Angels in America* in the early 1990s (which inspired me to write *Glimmering*).

One of things I most enjoy about living part of the year in London is having the opportunity to see amazing theater. Jez Butterworth's *Jerusalem* with Mark Rylance, which I saw in London a few years ago, is still inspiring me.

So yeah, I'd love to try to do that, but I need a good idea.

Plays are tough.

I think of you as a modern American Pre-Raphaelite. You seem to plant one foot in the past and to regard the present as provisional, like an experiment that is spinning a little out of control. That's not a question, but it begs comment.

I don't think of myself that way, maybe because I tend to think of Pre-Raphaelites as beautiful young women with long flowing auburn tresses and blank gazes. But it's actually a good suss, if you go back to the origins of the Pre-Raphaelite Brotherhood. They had a foot in two camps—the world of early Renaissance painting, and that of modern Victorian London in the mid to late nineteenth century. I love the PRB—my novel *Mortal Love* is set partly in that world—but much of their work is kind of musty in contemporary terms, and their attitudes toward women could be pretty exploitative. Yet at the time they were considered rebels. There's a moral here, though I'm not sure I want to know what it is.

Throughout my career (and my life), I've definitely felt that the world we live in is an experiment that's spinning out of control. I've been writing dystopian, post-apocalyptic, and apocalyptic fiction for almost thirty years, long before it became popular. My taste for reading and writing it has diminished radically as I've seen our own world surpass the darkest visions that I or anyone else could come up with.

Rock music seems to play a large role in your fiction. Ever been in a band?
No. I have no musical talent whatsoever, but I love music and musicians and performers in general. I'm the consummate fan. In another life, I would have been a groupie. I am a very good dancer, though.

Why Maine? Do you heat with wood?
I fell in love with Maine when my family vacationed here when I was a kid. We went camping, in those old Sears Roebuck canvas screen tents—five kids (I'm the oldest) and our parents—and then later we'd rent a house on a lake in the Long Lakes region. My father used to come up to Maine to hunt and fish when he was young, and his stories also informed my own experience. So for me, as for a lot of other people, Maine was always this magical place.

I visited it again as an adult in the early 1980s, when a college friend of mine got married there—she grew up in the area where I now live. A bunch of her friends came up for the wedding and I fell in love with Maine all over again, especially the Maine islands and the coast, which was not where my family vacationed. In 1988, when my then-partner and I were looking for a place to move to from DC, we flipped a coin and chose the Maine coast.

I've been here ever since. I knew nothing of backwoods living, so I had to learn, fast. A close friend of mine from those days, an artist, said that this was a good place to be poor, and for some years we were very, very poor. I came from a middle-class suburban background, with little experience of How The Other Half Lives, and it was a real adjustment and often very scary to be poor. But

I learned to get by, with the help of neighbors and friends and *The Tightwad Gazette*. It gave me a much better understanding of how poverty undermines lives in this country and an appreciation of how fortunate I was in my own upbringing. Americans don't like to factor luck into their life stories—everyone wants to believe she pulled herself up by her own bootstraps. Which a lot of people do, but I also took advantage of programs designed to help those with limited resources—WIC, HEAP, and so on. I don't have to anymore, and I'm grateful for that, but it enrages me to see politicians (like our current governor) attacking poor people and cutting the safety nets that helped me and so many others through tough times.

I do heat with wood—I learned about wood during our first winter at Tooley Cottage. I don't use wood at the cottage anymore, but we do use it at the house. In a typical winter we'll burn about four cords. I love heating with wood—we have a great stove with an isinglass window, so you can watch the flames. During the winter, which is about half the year, everyone lives around the woodstove.

Why Camden Town? Do you write there or just catch your breath?
My partner is a UK citizen and lives there, so for the last twenty-odd years I've spent a lot of time in Camden Town—not a "town" in the American sense but a district of London. I love it—it's very urban, gritty, totally counterpoint to where I live in Maine. It's very noisy—it's become a big tourist area, so there's lots of street life, lots of music, buskers, and drunks (many, *many* drunks) in addition to the normal vehicular traffic. I *do* work there, but for serious writing, I use the British Library or the Wellcome Library, both of which are about a twenty-minute walk.

But Camden Town is my London home. So yes, it's where I catch my breath and get some relief from stacking wood back in Maine.

In your novels there is almost always another hidden reality that intrudes on this one in alarming and often terrible or even beautiful ways. Is this a literary device or a deal you made with the Devil?
I could tell you, Terry, but then I'd have to sacrifice you on a stone slab beneath a full moon.

It's a literary device. But I've always wanted to believe in the existence of that other, hidden reality. In my writing I try to make it real and to depict it in as realistic a fashion as possible. I did have one uncanny experience when I was about thirteen, which I wrote about in "Near Zennor." Other than that, it's all wish fulfillment.

Cass Neary has been compared with Stieg Larsson's Liz Salander. What's the deal with these Scandinavian novelists? Does this have anything to do with global warming? Do you read mysteries? Why not?
I read some—I don't get to read enough for pleasure because of having to read grad student manuscripts and books for review. I've never read any of the Stieg Larsson books, or seen the movies—I tend to shy away from work to which my own books have been compared, not out of ego but so I can avoid being influenced. But I do love Nordic noir—I like reading about cold, miserable places. I'm going back to Sweden in a few weeks and will have the chance to meet some of the writers I admire. I'm excited about that!

And I do think the popularity of Nordic noir has something to do with global warming. So does the boom in adventure tourism in places like Iceland, Greenland, Antarctica, Alaska, Siberia, etc. With climate change, we're losing a large part of our world, in so many ways. Apart from the environmental and economic catastrophe, I think the loss of winter is going to be psychologically disruptive on a huge scale, at least for those of us in the Northern Hemisphere.

One sentence on each please: Amy Winehouse, Alison Bechdel, Paul Park.
Amy Winehouse sounds like she was teleported to our century from Swinging London circa 1966, one of my favorite eras; I love her, especially the song "Back to Black."

When I moved to Maine in 1988, some local alternative newspaper carried Bechdel's *Dykes to Watch Out For*, and reading that comic every week got me through some very tough years.

I've always believed that Paul Park and I are actually the same person split in two, like in that Platonic allegory of how the different genders came to be; he's a brilliant writer, and in person he makes me laugh harder than almost anyone else ever has.

You spend a lot of time dressing Cass Neary. Ever play with paper dolls? Ever consider licensing a Cass paper doll book?
Ha! I am *totally* going to come up with a Cass Neary paper doll book with my next publisher! That's brilliant.

    I was not a doll fan as a girl. I loved stuffed animals, the more obscure the better. I had a Steiff mole, fox, bat, and a toy skunk made of real fur. I'd make my own stuffed animals, too—a flying squirrel, a raccoon.

    I have very dim memories of a paper doll set, probably given to me when I was sick with chicken pox or measles and therefore desperate to be entertained. I did love doll houses—I loved rearranging the furniture. In another life, I'd be an interior designer. I also loved toy farms, where you could move around all the little farm animals. And dinosaurs.

    But back to paper dolls. I am a closet clothes horse—as in, I have some very nice designer clothes that rarely leave my closet. I've bought them on eBay and at vintage or consignment shops over the years but only get to wear them at conventions or public readings or the like. Cass gets to wear them sometimes, even though she's six inches taller than me. We do have the same shoe size, though, and I own many pairs of cowboy boots, some Tony Lamas, which I started buying when I was a teenager visiting my mother's family in Texas. I have ostrich boots, eelskin, lizard, and a really great pair of violet python boots. I hardly ever wear them—as Cass learned, Maine is a really bad place to wear cowboy boots, especially in the winter. The first time I was in Reykjavik I almost killed myself by wearing my Tony Lamas in bad weather.

    My real-life everyday wardrobe is Cass's and has been for the past forty years. Boatneck shirts, black jeans, black cashmere sweaters, Converse sneakers, boots. I don't wear heels and never have. Nearly everything I own is secondhand. A lot of it has seen better days. Cass would understand.

You and Paul Witcover did a comic together, right? Do you keep up with the "industry" today? Do you read graphic novels?
I have to admit that I don't even try to keep up anymore—there's just too much stuff, and too much great stuff, out there.

    That's not to say I don't read graphic novels and comics that come my way, but I don't seek them out as much as I used to. I wouldn't know where to start.

I recently did an essay on Hillary Chute's study *Disaster Drawn*, about war and trauma in graphic narratives. A brilliant book.

I'd love to work with Paul on another project—he's extraordinarily knowledgeable about comics, in addition to being a great writer. And he's a blast to work with. We made a good team.

Hard Light features an ancient device, a sort of primitive stone flip-comic. I'm assuming, perhaps naively, that you didn't make it up. Do you have one?
No, I didn't make it up—I wish I had! it's called a thaumatrope, and I remember seeing one when I was a kid. Basically you draw a picture on both sides of a big button or a round piece of cardboard—almost the same image, but with a slight change, the way you make a flipbook. You add a hole (or sometimes two), thread a piece of string through, then wind it up on the string. When the string unwinds, the thaumatrope spins. The images flicker, and your eye and brain register them as a single image that's moving, like a simple animation. It's a very basic example of the persistence of vision.

At the British Museum a few years ago, I saw an amazing exhibit of Ice Age art, stuff from all over Europe. And there was a little thaumatrope, a bone disc with a bison carved on each side and a hole drilled through the middle. On one side it's a young bison, a calf; on the other side it's an adult. So when you thread it and spin it, you see the bison go from young to old and back again, over and over.

An image of fecundity? Of death?

When it was found many years ago, scientists assumed it was a button. Then someone (probably some scientist's kid) added a string, spun it—and thus was (re)discovered the thaumatrope, Ice Age animation technology.

Only three or four of these have ever been found. In one, a man with a spear is menacing a cave bear; on the other side, he's flat on his ass and the cave bear is menacing *him*. It's like a prehistoric cartoon!

So thaumatropes are very real, if very rare.

I did make one for myself when I was working on *Hard Light*. Cardboard, of course, but it works. Inspired, I "made up" an ancient camera obscura for the novel. I'm still waiting for some anthropologist to dig up a real one somewhere.

You seem to me to be a regional novelist, in a way, but your region can be hard to locate. Where is Bohemia today?
Bohemia is a floating world, a moveable feast—it's anywhere you have creative people who form their own world and their own alliances, relatively free of the overlords of our consumer society. It may be tough to find, but it's there.

My Jeopardy *item. You provide the question after I provide the answer: They function as air bags for careless readers.*
Trigger warnings. Amazon reviews. Spoiler alerts.
  I know, that's three answers. That's why I'm not on *Jeopardy*.

Did you go to SF and fantasy conventions before you were a published pro? Who were the first people you met in the field?
I'd published one story when I went to my first SF con, which was Disclave, in 1988. At the time I was taking a writing workshop at the Writer's Center in Bethesda with Richard Grant, who became my partner for some years (and is my kids' father). Richard had introduced me to Steve Brown, the editor of the influential SF magazine *Science Fiction Eye*, which was where my first reviews and critical essays appeared. Both of them encouraged me to go to Disclave, so I did.
  It was a game changer for me. I met Mike Dirda there, who was an editor and critic at *The Washington Post Book World* (he went on to win the Pulitzer Prize a few years later), and he became a good friend. Mike asked if I'd like to do a book review, and of course I said yes. So that was the start of my career as a reviewer. You don't become rich from writing book reviews, but I've always loved it, and Mike gave me that break.
  A few months later, I went to my first Worldcon, again with Steve Brown and also with Paul Witcover, who's been one of my closest friends since 1981. I met a number of writers and editors there, some of whom became good friends. I also met my agent, who I've been with ever since.
  I always encourage aspiring writers to go to conventions. The infamous bank robber Willie Sutton was once asked by a judge, "Why do you keep robbing banks?" Willie replied, "Because that's where the money is." Cons are where they keep the writers and editors and agents and readers.

You once claimed I helped give you a start in doing novelizations and tie-ins. I apologize for that. Are you still doing that sort of thing?

That was one of the best things that ever happened to me! It gave me a chance to work another part of my writing brain, and it taught me how to work fast. I've always been very grateful for that.

I especially loved doing the Boba Fett juveniles for Scholastic—they were fun to write, and the Lucasfilm people were wonderful to work with. And I got the best fan mail ever ("You are my favorite writer in the whole world!") from little boys who had just read their first book.

As for doing another tie-in, I did stop doing novelizations a few years ago. But never say never, right? I'm a working writer, which means a lot of financial insecurity. I try not to turn down work, though I do want to focus on my own writing more than, say, any forthcoming Catwoman adaptations.

What did you think of that stupid movie about Thomas Wolfe and Maxwell Perkins, Genius?

I didn't see it, but I want to! I love bad movies about artists and writers. *Total Eclipse*, about Rimbaud and Verlaine, was silly, though David Thewlis had a great turn as Verlaine. I've seen it twice. *Fur*, with Nicole Kidman as Diane Arbus, was also pretty bad. Can't wait to see it again.

I think that John Waters should have right of first refusal on any biopic about a famous writer or artist.

You were into ecclesiastical terror long before Dan Brown. I'm thinking of the Benandanti in Waking the Moon. *Did you assemble that dark adversary from life or literature?*

From both. The Benandanti were a real group of people in medieval and early Renaissance Italy. I first came across them in *Ecstasies: Deciphering the Witches' Sabbath*, by the Italian historian Carlo Ginzburg, one of the best and most influential books I've ever read. I obviously embroidered on the real Benandanti for my own fell purposes in *Waking the Moon* and *Black Light*. Balthazar Warnick, my Benandante character, has made cameos in other books of mine.

Paul Park and John Crowley have also featured the Benandanti in their work, in very different ways. They're kind of an all-purpose secret ancient cult.

Do you have a drill for writing? You know: the where and the when, the cat, the coffee, the lucky pajamas, etc.
No. I mostly follow Mickey Spillane's advice: "Get your ass in a chair." I feel like I do my best writing at Tooley Cottage, which is my office, but I've written in hotel rooms, my parents' house, the British Library, and various other libraries. But not coffee shops or public places like that. I don't like writing in public, except in journals, or note-taking.

I don't have much of a special routine, though I do have a few songs I listen to, to psych myself up—"Valentine" by the Replacements, which I've used since first hearing it in 1987, and "Dice Behind Your Shades" by the Mats' frontman Paul Westerberg. And Neil Young's haunting "Pocahontas," which for me is Cass Neary's theme song. It gets at something so primal and rage-filled and true and sad about America, about loss and disenfranchisement. I know it's about our country's indigenous people, and Cass isn't Native American. But for whatever reason, that's the one song that immediately puts me in her head, and has since I started writing *Generation Loss* a dozen years ago.

What did you think of that great Swedish vampire movie, Let the Right One In*?*
I loved it. What an incredible story, what an incredible film, what a beautiful sad ending. The US remake wasn't terrible, just totally unnecessary.

It was terrible, but let's move on. Where do you write? Do you have a separate office? Is there a window over your desk? If you cleaned it, what would you see?
I'm very lucky in that I have a beautiful, tiny cottage that I use as an office. I bought it in 1990, when it was a derelict little fishing camp, a few weeks before my first child was born. We lived there, without running water or indoor plumbing, for eight years, before buying a "real" house a few miles away.

It was tight quarters, three hundred square feet when I bought it, four hundred square feet now. I raised two kids there (my son was born two years after we moved in), and for many years it was a work in progress.

I hired friends to do the renovation and new construction. A boatbuilder friend once told me that if I thought about Tooley Cottage as a house, it was a very small house, but if I thought of it as a boat, it would be a good-sized boat. That was helpful.

Now it's beautiful, though it's still tiny. I love it more than anything except for my family and friends. It's on a lake, with a large wetland, so there's lots of wildlife—moose, beavers, otters, foxes, bobcats, mink, deer, bald eagles, ospreys, blue herons, kingfishers, turtles, snakes, fishers, all kinds of migratory waterfowl and fish and amphibians. Once when the kids were little we saw a wolf—it was killed a few weeks later up in Ellsworth. Flying squirrels live in the rafters, which I know isn't good for the house, but still—flying squirrels!

It's also a mosquito and black fly preserve—it can be very buggy, because of the wetland. The window *is* kind of grubby, but it looks onto the water, which is only a stone's-throw away. It's a magical place, kind of a cross between Bag End and Merlyn's cottage in *The Sword in the Stone*.

But the truth is, when I'm working I hardly ever look out the window. I have to remind myself every few hours to stand up and go outside and look around. Sometimes I'm shocked to see where I am.

Do you read poetry for fun? What poets do you hate?
I do read poetry for fun, though I tend to return to the poets I've already read—Cavafy, Auden, Rimbaud, Bishop, Anne Carson, Anthony Hecht, Geoffrey Hill, Roethke, Eavan Boland, Yeats, Sappho . . .

I love poetry but I couldn't write it if my life depended on it. Maybe that's why.

Some of my teaching colleagues are poets, like T. Fleischmann and Brandon Som and Jeanne Marie Beaumont, and I love both reading their work and hearing them read it aloud. I like Billy Collins. He wrote a funny poem about a mouse discovering fire that I reread every year.

Of course there's a poet I hate—this awful Christian poet we were forced to read in parochial school. I won't tell you his name because I don't want to go to Hell.

You write beautifully. That can be an impediment for some authors. How have you managed to make (and keep) it an asset?
There's a definitely a danger in writing pretty, precious prose, and I've been guilty of it, especially early in my career. I'm probably still guilty of it, on occasion, though I hope not as much as I was twenty-odd years ago.

I like to try different things when I write. When I wrote *Generation Loss*, I did so with the intent of working in the noir mode, something I'd never done before. Very stripped down, terse, often dialogue-heavy prose. I hated writing that novel—there was a huge learning curve—and while I can't say I've mastered that voice, I think I've learned how to do it better.

With *Wylding Hall*, I wanted it to read like an oral history, so I created a series of fictional interviews with musicians, which was very constraining but also fun, maybe more like writing a play than a novel.

I still love to write lyrically, and in some ways that might be my more natural voice. But just because you can do something well doesn't mean you should do it all the damn time. Just because you know the right answer in class, you shouldn't always be the one to shout it out. Sometimes it's a good idea to keep your mouth shut. So sometimes I try to turn off the "lyrical" part of my brain and let a little breathing room into the narrative for another voice to speak.

Maine has one other famous writer, Sarah Orne Jewett. Have you read her work? Has Stephen King?
I read *The Country of the Pointed Firs* years ago and really enjoyed it. Her work holds up well. There's definitely something old-fashioned about it, but her depictions of Mainers and Maine are on the money. I know some folks who'd fit into one of her small towns even today.

I doubt that you get line edited severely. But I could be wrong. Am I?
No, you're right. I don't get a lot of line editing—I tend to edit my own work ruthlessly, and revise over and over and over again. I'd keep revising it once it hits the bookstores if I could.

What kind of car do you drive? I ask this of everyone.
A 2002 Subaru Outback with 241,000 miles on it. Part of it is held together with duct tape. I should send you a photo. It works really well. We also have a 2002 Volvo wagon that I inherited from my daughter when she moved to Maui a year ago. It has about 150,000 miles on it. It looks nicer than the Subaru, but the A/C doesn't work. In the olden days, you didn't need air conditioning in Maine, but with climate change you do.

I've never owned a new car. It just seems wrong.

What's that knocking noise from the attic?
Sarah Orne Jewett and Stephen King, duking it out.

"Who Does the Work in a Utopia?"
Cara Hoffman

Someone (it might have been you) once said that anarchism is about Responsibility, not Freedom. Really? Please explain.

Yes, really! Anarchism is about responsibility. But mostly because responsibility results in freedom. But I wonder if there is anything a person desires that isn't about responsibility. I live in Exarchia—a place that pushed the police out after the US-backed dictatorship fell. The Greek government expected Exarchia would destroy itself without cops there to control the population, but everyone in the neighborhood took responsibility for each other. Exarchia's autonomy is going strong after fifty years. The idea of anarchism being based in responsibility is an old one, though, not mine. It's based in part on Levinas's concept of spontaneous acts of responsibility for others, the idea is that if one is aware of an injustice, one is compelled to act. Or as the anarchist philosopher Simon Critchley writes, "The concept of anarchism, is not so much organized around freedom as around an infinite responsibility that arises around a situation of injustice." Anarchists and autonomists, who identify the authority of the state as a grave injustice, are compelled to take matters into our hands more universally. If the state reveals itself to be a system of extraction, not protection, then we are naturally responsible for caring for those around us, for ourselves, for our community, for the environment and all that. And this can take the form of helping provide food or housing, or delivering medicine to people; or for some it could take the form of sabotage, or burning a building or a car to dissuade gentrification of a neighborhood, or tactical engagement with an occupying police force that supports that gentrification. Petitioning those you think have authority is not how anyone gets freedom, and it never has been, it's just a waste of time. The idea of incremental progress toward freedom as governments and other criminals extort and exploit whole populations. Freedom is something you have to take. Freedom is something you help create. Ensuring that the people in your community are healthy, fed, clothed, housed, and not living in fear relieves stressors that enslave whole populations. That stuff takes moral and practical responsibility.

Who are you and where do you come from?
I'm a regular sort of person who comes from a place where there are woods and big empty factories and it rains all the time. Sometimes I think I have exaggerated how strange the town I grew up in is, then I visit and realize it's far weirder than I've described. Last year when I went to see family, I walked past a guy sitting on the porch of a molting Victorian house with no curtains in the windows and no furniture visible. He was wearing red rubber clown shoes and no shirt, holding a one-year-old baby. It is not uncommon to see people pushing a shopping cart filled with big bottles of distilled water down a completely abandoned street. At some hours of the day you can walk down a main road for miles and miles and miles without seeing a car or a person. People drive trucks affixed with large stickers of forest scenes on them. There is a maximum-security prison that looks like a castle with crenelated turrets and razor wire; a cemetery filled with the white unmarked tombstones of thousands of confederate dead; and, sunk beneath the river bank, the remains of a nineteenth-century amusement park. Clouds roil across the sky most of the year. On the odd times that the sky is clear, the moon is often visible during the day. Frogs sing all night in the spring. The accent of people in the town makes it sound like they learned to talk from sheep. The river is beautiful and freezes in winter and is named after the people who were massacred there. Everyone's house feels haunted. This may sound like a singular place to some, but there are dozens just like it throughout Appalachia and thousands more across the US, and I think that's what makes me a regular sort of person. I come from a place like that.

Do you read more SF or fantasy? Or neither?
Sci-fi. I love Philip K. Dick and have read all of his work including the bad novels and his *Exegesis*. I love the bad novels because they reveal the power of his ideas over his prose. And I love the *VALIS* trilogy. When I was a kid, I read a lot of Ray Bradbury and was a big fan of Harlan Ellison and of Rodger Zelazny's

The Chronicles of Amber books. My brother had a subscription to *Fantasy and Science Fiction* but he wouldn't let me touch the magazine because I might mess it up.

What's your current favorite movie?
I like reading books more than watching movies. But I do have three favorite movies: *Willy Wonka and the Chocolate Factory*, *Blade Runner*, and *Melancholia*.

How's your Greek?
It's abysmal. I told my friend I picked up his favorite raisin cookies at the bakery the other day and what I really said to him was that I got him his favorite altar boys. Every time I tell someone I am going to sleep, I accidentally say I am going to swim. But I understand things that are said to me or said around me a good deal of the time. This might be because it's an expressive culture.

You published several novels. What took you there? What novelists helped you get there?
I love the form of the novel very much, how completely transporting it is. It's an art form in which you can feel the infinite strands of chance. There are too many novelists whose work spoke to me, or taught me or whose prose made me swoon to list, but: Louis-Ferdinand Céline is at the top—I was devoted to his work in my twenties and early thirties; Marguerite Duras, who I think is the finest writer about freedom and autonomy and existentialist quandary; Tove Jansson, who wrote innately strange, beautiful work for children and adults; and David Wojnarowicz, though he didn't write novels. I feel the spirit of their work when I write—or that I share some of their experiences and worldviews and finding their work reinforced my own instincts and compulsions around narrative, form, and content.

One sentence on each, please: Four Loko, Bob Dylan, Queen's Gambit, *Billy Collins.*
If you like throwing up cough syrup you'll love Four Loko.
    Bob who?
    I preferred *The Man who Fell to Earth*, though Walter Tevis writes a good alcoholic; when I was a child, he shaped my conception of adulthood by depicting gin and bitters as the height of melancholic sophistication.

How bittersweet all these punctuations of flame and gesture.

What kind of car do you drive?
No car. I walk or take the train. The last car I had was fifteen years ago. It was a Nissan SX, which my kid and I referred to as the Nissan SUX.

How did you get started in writing? Anyone help?
A lot of people helped. My mother read to me every day. When I was in grade school, she was starting college and she read me *The Canterbury Tales* and *The Sun Also Rises* and *Portrait of an Artist*. When I was smaller than that, about three years old, she transcribed stories I would tell her and keep them in a folder and I was excited to be working on this short story collection. She wrote poetry and would read me her work as she was revising it. I think I also got some innate writing talent from my father. He was a chronic storyteller but he never wrote things down. A couple years before he died, he wrote one short story and it was perfect, stunning to read. It was in the early modernist style—restrained but filled with the clearest detail. It was just beautiful, atmospheric, the dialog was crisp and meaningful. It was handwritten all in one draft—a couple little cross-outs—but otherwise he got it perfect the first time around. I also talked a lot about writing with my brothers, and read them my work and they always had thoughts and ideas about it. I was lucky to have a family who took literature seriously and enjoyed talking and fighting about ideas. Everyone in my family treated me like I was already a writer when I was a child, and referred to me as a writer before I had achieved anything at all. That's the prehistory of who helped me get started, I guess.

Then there was Joe Schmidbauer, who hired me to work at a newspaper and taught me how to be a reporter. And the sci-fi writer Jon Frankel who read and gave notes on my early work and drafts of the novel that would become *Running*. And Goddard College—the antifascist school in Vermont where I worked with Rachel Pollack and Jan Clausen. And the journalist Annia Ciezadlo, who introduced me to her agent, Rebecca Friedman, who sold my first three novels. Rebecca changed the material circumstances of my life enormously, and she is a good friend. Writing is a solitary occupation, but no one does it all on their own.

What's your favorite magazine?
The Anarchist Review of Books. I read it cover to cover about twenty times before we go to print, and every time I say to myself, I can't believe how fucking good this magazine is.

Can you read or play music?
I can read music. I studied classical voice when I was young. I sang for many years in a choir in Manhattan, the St. George Choral Society, which was founded by Dvořák. I still sing and play classical and traditional folk music on soprano recorder, and I recently learned how to play guitar.

What kind of music do you listen to?
Arvo Pärt. The Velvet Underground. Punk. I listen mostly to David Bowie. I got the album *Ziggy Stardust* when I was nine years old and listened to it maybe every day until I was . . . until yesterday. And I will listen to it tomorrow. I am probably listening to *Ziggy Stardust* or *Station to Station* or *Low* right now while you're reading this. Or the band Powerwasher. Have you heard them? They are the best band to see live. I also like Asa Horvitz's work and his band VALES.

Are you a good cook? What's your secret skill?
No. My secret skill is to always be romantically involved with someone who can cook.

Do you have a drill in writing: regular time, spot, music, dope, and so forth?
I like things to be quiet in general and I love quiet even more when I'm writing. I like to write for long hours. When working on a book I usually write as soon as I wake up—take breaks to eat and write through evening until late at night. Ten or twelve hours of writing feels pretty good. But people need exercise and sunlight to live so I don't work like this anymore.

If you could (magically, fluently) read another language for six months, which would you choose?
Proto-Icelandic.

If you could live in any city you liked (other than Athens), what would it be?
New York, New York! (It's a hell of a town.)

What is Four Loko?
Four Loko is a highly caffeinated malt liquor that was taken off the market in the early aughts. You can probably still find some, but don't drink it unless you like speedballing. You also shouldn't drink a lot of it unless you live near a hospital. If both of those requirements are met, you should drink it.

Would you rather have a pony or a dog?
Pony. But a tiny one. What I would really like is a tiny deer. There is a deer called the southern pudu that's about as big as a cat. The tiniest deer in the world lives at the Queens Zoo and it is a southern pudu. One time I visited this deer in the dead of winter. No one was there, and it was small enough to steal or set free but it would not have been happy in my apartment or safe wandering the streets of the city, so the deer and I just looked at one another. It had a dappled coat like a fawn and a beautiful clear-eyed expression on its face.

Do you like Facebook?
No. Simon and Schuster wanted me to self-promote my books through social media and then suddenly I was on there, poisoning my brain with pictures of people's dinners and reading everyone's desperate attempts to connect or sell themselves. What a cesspit of anxieties. I liked the pictures of Chip Delany drinking coffee in his undershirt, but it wasn't worth staying on the site. Periodically there is a news story about how Facebook chat is the main way child pornography is disseminated throughout the world, or that a genocide was made possible by rapid unchecked disinformation promoted and spread by the platform, yet people still use it. I was happy to delete my account. If Facebook and Twitter were real places that could be set on fire, I would provide the matches.

You wrote two mainstream novels while you were traveling and with a kid. Was publication an ambition or a side effect?

Publication was an ambition. Always. I had written the bones of a novel when I was living in Greece in the late 1980s and early '90s, working in a hotel in the red-light district, and then back in the states I transcribed and finished it when my baby was sleeping. I had no document to prove I was educated because I had dropped out of school, and I was broke a lot of the time so I was trying to write my way out of poverty and be a good example for my son. I never had a steady job when he was young; or I should say unpaid writing was my steady job. I would only take work that allowed me time to write fiction and if the job got in the way of my writing, I quit. I worked at different newspapers, as a landscaper, a bartender, a prisoner advocate, a museum receptionist, I wrote PR briefly, worked for a farm sanctuary. And I wrote novels and stories when I got home, and on the weekends, and sometimes all night. My kid also had his music projects going on from an early age, so the two of us had a nice coexistence, writing and playing music in our own spaces in the apartment, then getting together in the kitchen to listen to one another's work and discuss it. When I was writing *So Much Pretty* this was harder because he started playing in a punk band and they practiced in the attic and were insanely loud.

In my midtwenties I got a New York Foundation for the Arts Grant that afforded me a little cushion to write a book of short stories that was published on an anarchist micropress, but for the most part my poor kid watched me fail at writing, a thing I loved, for sixteen years, and I yelled at him to be quiet so I could do it. I felt enormous pressure to get published in part so we could have money but also largely to show him it was possible to make a living as an artist and that the sacrifices we made were worth something.

This is absolutely a story about art and commerce and parental guilt. I was initially writing experimental, transgressive, existential stuff that I enjoyed—but the older my kid got, the shittier I felt about not making money. I knew if I wrote about this murder I had covered as a reporter, it would get published and I could make money because people love to read about dead women. And so I did it. I sold the book for a significant advance his junior year of high school, and it changed our lives completely. We put our stuff out on the curb and moved to New York City with just our books and clothes. Found a two-bedroom place in the East Village. And I gave him a percentage of the advance so he could have money in the bank.

I'm proud of *So Much Pretty* and that I was able to get all kinds of anarchist philosophy and Wittigesque feminism into a mainstream publication like slipping a pill in a dog's mouth by hiding it in peanut butter. And I'm proud that the book was about taking direct action, and I'm happy it's considered a classic and all that bullshit. But we all know that the reason that book succeeded wasn't because I worked so hard and we ate buttered noodles every night; it's because a corporation saw a way to make money with what I wrote. The reason I didn't make money before is because this country is a fucking brutal place where the rich fleece the poor. And I regret having bought into the bootstraps fantasy and the American fantasy of meritocracy. I regret it. I'm sure I would regret having done something like going to law school to support my kid much more. But becoming a successful writer by the standards of a capitalist oligarchy is not good example to set for a child.

What took you to Greece in the first place?
Ran out of money. Greece was warmer than northern Europe and so it was possible to sleep outside longer if I needed to. The second time I went to Greece it was for research.

Would you rather go to the Oscars or the Antiques Roadshow?
I would rather go to Economy Candy on Rivington Street and buy a bulk bag of Zagnut bars and eat them while I sit in Tompkins Square Park reading Cookie Mueller.

What poets do you read for fun?
Diane Seuss, John Donne, C. Russell Price, Cate Marvin.

Do you think writers have special responsibilities?
No. Special sensitivities maybe.

Who's your favorite sports hero?
Roberto Bolaño.
   When my partner's kid was little, he and I would play a game with baseball cards. We would show each other the cards with the player's name covered up

and try to guess who the player was. I would always tell him names of authors instead of ball players. We played this game enough that once when he went to Citi Field to get autographs he saw Bartolo Colón walking out of the dugout and called to him, "Roberto Bolaño! Roberto Bolaño!" And that is the sad tale of how I prevented a child that I love from getting the autograph of a baseball player he long admired.

Remember 9/11? Where were you?
I was working as a landscaper at a turf grass research facility in upstate New York. My job was mowing different types of experimental grasses that were used for golf courses. I rode a riding mower over acres and acres of land every day. That day it was beautiful and sunny and I was out in the fescue. When I came in to the pole barn for break, everyone was standing around the radio and my boss said the World Trade Center had been attacked and they didn't know how many people had died. And I realized that my brother was sure to get deployed to help kill more people, that my other brother was in the city at that moment dealing with whatever was going on there, and that I would have to pick up my kid from elementary school and talk to him about people dying.

You've written a couple of kids' books. How did that come about, and how has it worked out?
An editor at HarperCollins asked if I wanted to write a middle-grade book and I said yes. I had written a book for my kid when he was nine about a dog named Oswald Walker who drove an omelet truck, but my kid was the only one who read it. I never transcribed it or sent it out anywhere, so this editor must have had a sixth sense that I loved writing books for kids. I still read children's novels and am a big fan of Moomintroll and Paddington and *Harriet the Spy* and *The Mouse and His Child* and the worlds they inhabit. Writing children's novels has worked out great. It's incredibly fun. The first kids' book I wrote, *Bernard Pepperlin* is about a dormouse and his adventures in Manhattan fighting the Pork Pie Gang. You better watch out for the Pork Pie Gang. They're weasels from Ohio. They will kidnap you, play some awful music that stops time, try to gentrify your city—all of it! Take this as a warning: they are bad. Fortunately there's an underground organization of creatures you can join: rats, mice, frogs,

lizards whom people have flushed down toilets, bodega cats with missing ears, and they are going to *fuck the Pork Pie Gang right up*. And then I wrote another kid's book called *The Ballad of Tubs Marshfield*. Tubs is a musician and a frog who, with the help of an alligator witch, a bog lemming, and his cousin Lilah who was educated at the Sorbonne, commits a brave act of industrial sabotage.

It is very nice interacting with kid readers—they don't care about you at all, because they know that the characters are important and you are not. They love the characters and want to have long conversations about them and imagine things off the page. And they send you dioramas or pictures of weird looking cakes in the shape of an alligator witch or they pretend to be a bog lemming for a whole conversation. Adult readers always want to know about you as a person and it's boring. A kid knows it's all on the page. They already learned everything they needed to know about you when they read your book. Who gives a fuck about Roald Dahl when there's a tap-dancing centipede inside a giant peach floating through the sky carried by birds. Who cares about Tove Jansson when Moomintroll is fighting existential despair by building snow animals that come to life under a full moon? Adult readers ask personal questions and then tell you about themselves. Kids understand that it's the imagined world and all the characters in it that matter, not you and not them.

What do you wish I had asked that I didn't?
I bet you are wondering what my favorite amphibian is. It's an oak toad. They are incredibly beautiful. They like to go out in the rain and they have golden eyes.

"Correcting the Balance"
Nalo Hopkinson

Your work is often described, even by yourself, as "subverting the genre." Isn't that against the rules? Or at least rude?
Science fiction's supposed to be polite? Dang, maybe I'll take up poetry instead. To tell the truth, I kinda rue the day I ever let that quotation out into the world. I used it in a Canadian grant application fifteen years ago. In that context, when not a lot of science fiction and fantasy writers were getting grants from the arts councils because many of the jurors thought science fiction and fantasy were inherently immature, it worked. It allowed me to come out swinging and get the jury's attention. But as something said to science fiction people, it just sounds presumptuous. I don't remember how it got out of my confidential grant application and into the larger world. It was probably my own doing, and my own folly. Now the dang thing keeps coming back to haunt me. People quote it all over the place, and I can feel my face heating up with embarrassment. Science fiction and fantasy are already about subverting paradigms. It's something I love about them.

And yet, if I'm being honest, there is some truth to that piece of braggadociousness. No one can make me give up the writing I love that's by straight, white, Western male (and female) writers, but at a certain point, I began to long to see other cultures, other aesthetics, other histories, realities, and bodies represented in force as well. There was some. I wanted more. I wanted lots more. I wanted to write some of it. I think I am doing so.

Does the title of your debut novel, Brown Girl in the Ring, *come from the game, the song, or a wish to connect with Tolkien?*

Tolkien? Ah, I get it! One brown girl to rule them all! Well, no. The song comes from the game. ("There is a brown girl in the ring, tra-la-la-la-la / and she look like a sugar and a plum") it's an Anglo-Caribbean ring game, mostly played by girls. I used to play it as a little girl. All the girls hold hands to form a ring, and one girl is in the middle. When the other girls sing, "Show me your motion, tra-la-la-la-la," the girl in the centre does some kind of dance or athletic move that she figures will be difficult to copy. The rest try to copy it. She picks the one whose version she likes the best, and they switch places. And so on.

In my first novel, Ti-Jeanne the protagonist is surrounded by her life dilemmas and challenges, and things are getting worse. She's the brown girl in the ring, and she is young and untried. She herself doesn't know what she's capable of, but she needs to figure her skills out and employ them, quickly, before she loses everything she cares about. Tra-la-la-la-la.

Who is Derek Walcott and why is he important?
Derek is a St. Lucia–born poet, a playwright, a Nobel Prize winner, and a master wordsmith. These words are his, from his poem "The Schooner *Flight*":

> I'm just a red nigger who love the sea,
> I had a sound colonial education,
> I have Dutch, nigger, and English in me,
> and either I'm nobody, or I'm a nation . . .

Doesn't that last line just fucking give you chills, coming hard on the heels of what preceded it? Goddamn. *Much* respect. Derek started and for many years was the artistic director of the Trinidad Theatre Workshop. My father was one of the actors and playwrights in the company. He and Walcott eventually fell out and stopped speaking to each other. But in a way, that's beside the point. Walcott and my father are two of many talented Caribbean wordsmiths whose work I was absorbing as a child.

One of Walcott's early plays was a fantastical piece called "Ti-Jean and His Brothers." I believe it was modelled on a St. Lucian folk tale. Ti-Jean ("young John") is the youngest of three brothers who set out to beat the Devil, who appears in the play as that archetypical monster, the white plantation owner. The two elder brothers fail, and it's left to Ti-Jean to save the day. At some point during the writing of my first novel, I realised that since I was writing about three generations of women who were all facing the same central evils in their lives, there were parallels with the basic framework of "Ti-Jean and His Brothers," so I used the parallels to inform my plot. I wanted to make Walcott's influence evident, so I gave my three characters feminised versions of the brothers' names, and I embedded brief quotations from the play into my story. Walcott generously gave me his permission to do so.

Folktales are great for learning dynamic storytelling and how to structure the resonant echoes that give a plot forward motion. It wouldn't be the last time that I modelled a plot upon the shell of a preexisting folktale. I've discovered that it doesn't matter whether your readers recognise the folktale. It may not even matter whether the folktale is real, or one you invented. What matters is that it has structure, echoes, trajectory, and style.

Skin Folk won a World Fantasy Award, and there was talk of a movie. What's up with that?
The movie project isn't mine. The director who optioned it is the visionary M. Asli Dukan, of Mizan Media Productions. I believe the project is currently in the development stage, which means raising the money to make the film. That is the stage at which most film projects die stillborn, so if anyone who wants to see the final product is of a mind to support Asli with some hard cash, I know she'll appreciate it. Particularly when I speak at schools, people in the audience want to know whether there are going to be films of my books. Myself, I'm more jaundiced. I've seen what can happen when text-based science fiction gets zombified by Hollywood. Look at what happened to Gibson's "Johnny Mnemonic."

I know. I wrote the novelization of that unfortunate script.
My condolences! I've also seen what can happen when mainstream American film and television try to depict Black Caribbean people. You get the likes of Kendra the vampire slayer, Sebastian the crab from *The Little Mermaid*, and the eternal disgrace that is Jar Jar Binks. Seriously, would it be so hard to hire actors who can do accurate Caribbean accents? Though that wouldn't solve the depiction problem; mainstream American media seem to believe that Caribbean

people are little more than simpleminded, marijuana-steeped clowns who say "de" instead of "the." In any case, my work isn't going to make it to the big screen any time soon, given the types of characters that are in it. It'd be a lot of money for producers to invest in a project when they're not sure there's a big enough audience out there for it.

And because people are always quick to jump down my throat whenever I talk about institutionalised discrimination, let me acknowledge that there have been a few SF/fantasy films and television programs with Caribbean characters that weren't stereotyped. Actor Sullivan Walker as Yale in the short-lived series *Earth 2*, for example. Geoffrey Holder's voice as the narrator for the 2005 *Charlie and the Chocolate Factory*. There are probably one or two more, but not many at all.

Some people hear me talking like this and get pissed off at me. They don't tolerate critique of the things they love. They miss the fact that I may love those things, too. I just don't think love should be blind.

Anyway, we were talking film. When directors option my stories, I'm more confident if they are independent artists with some personal connection to some of my communities (science fiction, Black, Caribbean, Canadian, queer, women, and more). There are two other novels of mine in development: *Brown Girl in the Ring*, by Toronto's Sharon Lewis, and *The New Moon's Arms*, by Frances Anne Solomon of Toronto's Leda Serene productions. Both women, like M. Asli Dukan, have roots in the Caribbean.

You once identified the central question of utopia as "Who's going to do the dirty work?" (Ursula Le Guin would agree.) So how would you describe Midnight Robber's *planet Toussaint, where work is a sacrament (to some)?*
A sacrament? Did I do that? Not trying to dodge the question. Just that my memory is poor, and it's been a long, busy, often stressful few years since the time it was published. I'm trying to remember back to when I finished the novel, perhaps sometime in 1999. I suspect I hadn't yet come up with the notion that the big dilemma of science fiction is who's going to do the dirty work. I may have just begun asking myself that very question . . . ah.

I do remember this: the people of Toussaint have a maxim that backbreaking labour isn't fit for them as sentient beings. They've come from a legacy of slavery, of having been forced to do hard labour, and they're not about to forget it. But manual labour still needs to be done. So they mechanise it as much as possible. The machines that do that labour are unaware extensions of the self-aware planetary artificial intelligence that sustains their various support systems. So how you gonna keep your machine overseer down on the farm, once she's crossed the Turing threshold? They *programme* her not to mind doing all that work. They make her like her servitude. When you think of it, our brains are also wired to respond in certain ways to certain situations. But do we get to make that decision for other creatures? You could argue that we do so all the time, through domestication and by breeding other living things for specific traits. You could argue that that doesn't count, since other animals aren't self-aware. But anyone who's ever lived in close quarters with another animal for an extended period of time can present convincing evidence that many animals are indeed self-aware. You could argue that it's okay to mess with creatures who are less intelligent than we are. But as someone with a couple of cognitive variances and as someone Black and female, I have reason to be suspicious of intelligence tests. I'm not sure that we understand enough about cognition to be able to measure cognition effectively. For one thing, we're measuring it against human markers of intelligence. I wonder whether those are the only markers.

So, in *Midnight Robber*, there is a powerful human-manufactured sentience that we have programmed to love us and to want to take care of us. Was it wrong of us to do that to her? Ethically, it's a conundrum. That was deliberate on my part. The planet of Toussaint isn't exactly Utopia. I didn't solve the problem of who does the menial work. I just put it into the hands of a being that's been designed to accept those tasks. I may have had some of the human citizens voluntarily take on forms of manual labour as part of a practice of ethical mindfulness.

These are the people I meant, who see labor as a sacrament.
It's their way of acknowledging that work that looks after oneself and others isn't really beneath them. You know, something like the old proverb attributed to Buddhism: "Before Enlightenment, chop wood, carry water. After Enlightenment, chop wood, carry water."

I still haven't answered the question of who does the work in a utopia. I have an alternative history fantasy novel in progress in which I'm exploring the idea that everyone in a municipality is assigned menial tasks in a rotating schedule. But in practice, my characters have all kinds of ways of slipping out of their turn taking out the town's nightsoil or working on the building site of that new community centre. In the novel, it's a cooperative system, but not politically socialist. I'm trying to build something a bit different than our current political paradigms. I'm not quite happy with it yet as a world-building element.

My partner tells me I need to wrestle with systems of exchange in return for labour, money being the primary one that we use in this world. I need to look at effective alternatives to money. I'm daunted by that, but he's right.

You have a lot of uncollected short stories. Any plans for them?
Un*collected*, yes, but all but one of them have been published. I've actually collected them up into a manuscript, which I plan to submit to a publisher soon. Honestly, it's the formatting that's slowing me down, and the thought of writing intros to each story. Maybe I don't have to do that last bit.

You often speak of putting the "threads" of a story into a "weave." Not uncommon, yet from you it seems something more than metaphor. How did you get into fabric design?
On a lark, thanks to a company called Spoonflower which came along to take advantage of new technologies of printing with ink on fabric. Spoonflower's website democratises the process and makes it easy for someone with basic image editing skills to dabble in fabric design. They've built an online community of people interested in cool fabric. We range from hobbyists to professionals. We talk to one another, vote on one another's designs, and buy fabric to sew. It's like print-on-demand for fabric.

I sew as a hobby, have done since I was a teenager. When I hit the fashion-conscious teen years and my desire for new clothes outstripped my parents' income, they bought me a sewing machine. My mother taught me how to use it. It was an extraordinarily frustrating learning curve for someone with undiagnosed ADHD. Once, I glued the seams of a blouse because I was too impatient to stitch them. My mother was horrified. But I did learn how to sew, and how to get to a place of patience around it (plus some time-saving tricks that kept me from going supernova). Since then, I've always had a sewing machine. I have an ever-growing collection of clothing patterns, some dating back to the 1930s. I'm a big girl, almost always have been. There was a time when attractive clothing at reasonable prices just wasn't available for larger women. Being able to sew meant that I could make my own. It's easier now to find nonhideous off-the-rack clothing in my size, but when you make it yourself, the fit can be better, the clothing more unique.

Now that I can design my own fabric and have the designs printed, I can create and use iconography I don't find on store-bought fabric. Ever since I was a child, I've been hesitant to wear images of non-Black people on my body. Not because I hate white people or some rubbish like that but because I wanted to be able to love Black people and my own Blackness. Nowadays, you can find fabric with images of Black people on it that doesn't make you want to go postal, but good lord, does it ever tend toward the twee! I prefer images with a bit more bite, a bit more perversity, and a bit less saccharin.

I can make science fiction and fantasy imagery, too, that isn't all unicorns with flowing manes on a background of rainbow-coloured stars. I adapt a lot of historical imagery, and my own photographs as well, and sometimes I draw. I know nothing about design, and I haven't conjured up the patience to learn. I make fabric designs by trial and error. Some of them are hideous. Some of them are just okay, and some of them are successful. I'm always a bit surprised when someone who doesn't know me buys fabric from my online Spoonflower store: http://www.spoonflower.com/profiles/nalo_hopkinson.

I make stuff. I was a craftsperson and did a lot of my own cooking long before I took up writing. I have my mother to thank for showing me that it was possible to make things for pleasure, for sustenance, and to save money. Come the zombie apocalypse, I know I'll have some survival skills to offer.

You have edited several anthologies (including Mojo: Conjure Stories *and* So Long Been Dreaming*). Is this part of a plot to wedge more Black and female writers into the genre until they outnumber, overwhelm, and eventually drive out the white men? Or not?*
Good lord, you've sussed out my cunning plan for world domination! Excuse me for a second while I go work some obeah to keep you quiet. Please ignore the toad and the padlock lurking behind the curtain. Okay, I'm back. That toad's

never gonna croak again. So. How does trying to foster a more representative literary field translate to wanting to exclude white male writers? How would that be representative? I mean, I'm bad at math, but I'm not that damned bad at it.

Just now, once I was done burning a candle of a particular colour and padlocking a toad's lips shut, I glanced at the pile of books beside my desk. Among them are titles by Gene Wolfe, Steven Gould, Rudyard Kipling, China Miéville, Stieg Larsson, Hal Duncan, Charlie Stross, George R.R. Martin, Kim Stanley Robinson, and a certain Terry Bisson.

Whew. Frankly, you gave me quite a turn with the intimation that white male authors were in danger of extinction. If that were true, we'd have to immediately start the Society for the Protection of White Male Writers. We'd get a Board of Directors together, and we'd do a fundraising drive on Kickstarter, and make depositions to all the major publishing houses, and hand out T-shirts with our logo on them, and infiltrate government, media, the churches, and the multinationals. We'd become so ubiquitous that pretty soon, people would cease referring to us by our full name—TSFTPOWMW is so unwieldy, don't you think?—Instead, they'd just refer us as Society. Oh, wait . . .

I get it. You would have the status quo.
You said it, not me. Anyway, beside my bed are also books by Liz Hand, Ursula K. Le Guin, Samuel R. Delany, Madeleine E. Robins, Nisi Shawl, Ivan E. Coyote, Ayize Jama-Everett, Barbara Lalla, Olive Senior, and Rabindranath Maharaj. That list comprises some women, some Black folks, white folks, multiracial folks, South Asian, queer, Canadian, Jamaican, and Trinidadian writers. They are for the most part books I had to go a bit out of my way to find, which meant that I had to figure out where to look.

There are a lot of readers who pride themselves on not paying attention to the identities of their favourite writers. Some of them think this means that they're not prejudiced. I don't know anyone who isn't, myself included. But let's just say for argument's sake that those particular readers in fact are not prejudiced. How many books by writers of colour do you think you'll find on their bookshelves? I'd lay odds that if there are any at all, they will be far outnumbered by the books by white authors. Not necessarily because those readers are deliberately choosing mostly white/male authors. They don't have to. The status quo does it for them. So those readers' self-satisfied "I don't know" is really an "I don't care enough to look beyond my nose."

And that's cool. So many causes, so little time. But don't pretend that indifference and an unwillingness to make positive change constitute enlightenment. If you truly want to be a colourblind, unprejudiced reader, you can't do so from a place of being racism-blind, or you'll never have the diverse selection of authors you say you'd like. Why get pissed off at people who are fighting for the very thing you say you want?

Yet I don't think there's some conspiracy of evil racist editors. There doesn't have to be. The system has its own momentum. In order to be antiracist, you actually have to choose to do something different than the status quo. People who're trying to make positive change (editors and publishers included) have a hell of a battle. Fighting it requires a grasp of how the complex juggernaut of institutionalised marginalisation works, and what types of intervention will, by inches, bring that siege engine down. We're in a genre that is heavily invested in the romance of the individual villain and the lone hero who defeats that villain. We want to know who the bad guy is. Dammit, we want someone to blame! And there are people who say and do racist things, consciously in ignorance. You can try to change them, or to limit the harm they do. These are useful and necessary actions. But pulling the weed doesn't destroy the root system, and what do you do when you realise that we are all in some way part of that system? I don't know all the answers. I'm sure that some of what I say here is going to come back to haunt me with its ignorance or naiveté. Remember when Robert Silverberg published that essay about why the stories of James R. Tiptree, Jr. (pen name of Alice Sheldon) could only have been written by a man? I'm impressed by how graciously he later acknowledged that he'd been wrong. That's a grace to which I aspire. I have a feeling I'll need it. There are those who fear that if books get published according to some kind of identity-based quota system, literary excellence will suffer. What seems to be buried in the shallow grave of that concept is the assumption that there are no good writers in marginalised communities. That huge prejudice aside, there is some validity to the fear. If you want to vary your diet, you put a larger selection of foods into your mouth. You don't toss vitamins into the toilet. The latter would be attacking the problem from the wrong end.

So to speak. So what would be attacking the problem from the right end?
A few years ago, when I was about to put out the call for submissions to the anthology *Mojo: Conjure Stories*, I had two equal priorities that the received wisdom in this field says are antithetical: I wanted to choose stories based on the quality of the writing; and I wanted to end up with an anthology (about an African diasporic form of magic) that would actually contain a lot of stories by Black writers.

It took me some hard thinking to figure out the flaw in the logic that leads people to think that antiracist diversity and literary quality are mutually exclusive. This is what I came up with: there are many steps to editing an anthology, and they have different priorities. Efforts to broaden the representation have to happen at the beginning of the process, not at the stage where you're selecting for literary quality. If I wanted Black writers to send me their stories, I'd have to specifically invite them. And in an effort to right the systemic imbalance in numbers, I'd have to invite more of them than of anyone else. If I wanted the participation of non-Black writers (and I did), I'd need to invite the ones that I felt were creatively up to the task.

I knew that statistically speaking, if you invite people to something, one-fifth of them will attend. I knew that I had room for roughly twenty stories in the anthology. I multiplied that number by five and decided I would solicit stories from more than a hundred writers. "More than" because I knew I would reject some of the stories as unsuitable.

Then I made two lists of writers to invite who I thought could handle the material well: one of writers I knew to be Black, and one of writers I knew to be non-Black, or whose race I didn't know for sure; after all, some writers don't place a focus on their racial identities, and that is their right. I listed twice as many Black writers as those in the second group. In a way, you could say that I deliberately did the opposite of what would have happened in our current context of institutionalised racism if I hadn't thought about who I was inviting. Some might call that reverse racism. I think it was more in the way of revers*ing* racism (grammar's so important, don't you think?), if only for a small space of time in a temporarily and very conditionally autonomous zone.

I sent out the invitations, crossed my fingers, and waited nervously until the submission deadline. There was a chance it wouldn't work. The law of averages means that efforts to even out that kind of imbalance work in the aggregate, not necessarily in every single instance. I had to take that chance, and to also take the chance that if it didn't work out, I'd face disapproval from some of the Black readers in the field. Part of the job. At least I could say that I'd tried.

Once the stories were in, I read them and picked the ones I thought were strong, no matter who the writer was. Much of the time I wilfully disremembered the writer's name until I'd read their story; my natural forgetfulness comes in handy that way. I tried to read cover letters only after I'd read the attached stories. I didn't pay much attention to who was going to be in the anthology until I'd assembled the stories I wanted in the order I wanted. I believe that in fact I didn't assess it until I'd submitted the anthology to my editor and she'd accepted it. I'd have to recheck in order to verify this, but I think that about 50 percent of the contributors to *Mojo: Conjure Stories* are Black.

I'm glad it worked. It was probably my first lesson that demarginalisation has to start at the organisational/systemic level. Trying to do it person by person is starting too late in the process. Individuals are going to have a hard time making change if they're not receiving organisational support. You start as early on in the process as you can.

To certain white male writers I'd like to say, when those around you try to wrestle with issues of entitlement and marginalisation, please don't give us the tired trumpeting of "Censorship! No one can tell me what to write!" True, people *shouldn't* tell you what to write, but people will try to, for bad reasons and better ones. Your mother will try to tell you what to write or not write. Your husband will. Your editor, your government, your church, your readers, your nosy neighbour. Humans are an argumentative lot. Dealing with that as a writer comes with the territory.

Those books by my bedside? They include a book written by a white man about a white woman, one by a white man about South Asian people, one by a white woman about a Black woman, one by an American about a Londoner, one by a Black woman and a white woman about, oh, everybody; I could go on. Write whatever the blast you want, and if you live in an environment where doing so doesn't endanger your life or career, count yourself blessed.

When I hear a (usually white and usually male) writer trying to shut down a discussion about representation by bellowing that no one should tell him what to write, it sounds very much as though he's trying to change the topic, to make it all about him. To him I'd say, why not try to further the discussion, rather than trying to, um, censor it? What do you think needs to be done in order to make publishing more representative? Nothing, you say? The doors are already open but we just won't come in? Women, Black people (and purple polka-dotted meercats) actually "just don't write much science fiction"? Or their books are "only relevant to their communities" (which is often code for "those people are incapable of producing anything of real literary merit")?

Funny, how every one of those statements boils down to not being willing to change the status quo. You do realise that you're even drowning out the white voices amongst you that are trying to make some changes along with the rest of us? You do realise that a more representative literary field would be representative of *all* of us, yourself included?

Sure, there are people on both sides of that discussion who are full of crap. But as a smart white man once said, "Ninety percent of everything is crap." The crap doesn't invalidate the discussion.

Oy, I'm ranting again! This is what happens when you ask me to be an "outspoken author."

In Midnight Robber *the naming (and renaming) of things seems to be an important part of the story. (Granny Nanny instead of "electronic overlord" or some such.) What exactly are you "subverting" here?*
In my novel, Granny Nanny is a supercomputer that loves us. That's not new. She's like a planet-sized Tardis. The difference may be that the way in which I describe her is culturally specific. Granny Nanny is named after Nanny of the Maroons, a seventeenth-century African freedom fighter from Jamaica. She is one of our national heroes. In a West African diasporic linguistic context, Granny/Nana/Nanny don't necessarily designate a sweet, harmless old lady who bakes you cookies. It's a term of respect for a female elder, for a woman who has more years and more life experience than you do. Granny Nanny—the woman, not the AI—led an insurgency that fought off British soldiers and eventually gained freedom for a Maroon community in the hills of Jamaica. The soldiers were convinced that she could catch their bullets between her ass cheeks and

fart them back like a machine gun. She was an Afro-Jamaican woman guerrilla strategist on horseback, and I enjoyed invoking her memory in a science fiction novel. A lot of the time, all I'm trying to do is put some of my specific ethnocultural touchstones into science fiction and fantasy. When white writers do that, it's barely remarked upon. And sometimes it should be, because it's often wonderful.

Your literary background runs both wide and deep, from Russian lit to Shakespeare to classic SF to Caribbean folklore. How do the artist and the scholar get along in Nalo's head? Heart?
I'm not a scholar. That implies in-depth, perhaps guided study. I skim. I'm more along the lines of a knowledge geek who's been exposed to a lot of different cultures. They all get along well in both my head and my heart, but it often means that people don't pick up on all the references I'm making. I try to be aware of that when I'm writing. Sometimes I try to make sure that it doesn't matter if a reader doesn't get all the references. Sometimes I try to make it a bit of a game for the readers who don't know a particular reference, as well as a kind of in-joke for those who do.

Do you read comics—excuse me, graphic novels?
I do, whatever one calls them. My partner and I are verrrry slooooowly working on creating one. Some of my favourites are *Love and Rockets, Bayou, Finder, The Rabbi's Cat, The Invisibles, Dykes to Watch Out For, Fun Home,* and *Calvin and Hobbes.* The superhero comics from the Big Two mostly make me twitchy and cranky, though I'll usually go to the spin-off movies. The films make me equally twitchy and cranky, but there's my fannish pleasure in watching impossible science and impossibly beautiful people blow impossible shit up real good. And they give me lots of food for thought and ranting about everything from bad physics (when I can pick up on the incorrect science in a film, it's *really* fucking incorrect) to messed-up gender politics. Comics thrill me. They make me wish I were a comic artist.

You are often called a magical realist. Is that just a euphemism for fantasy, like speculative fiction for SF? Or does it actually get at something?

I haven't read tons of magical realism. I don't have as informed a feel for what magical realist writing does as I do for fantasy and SF. I sometimes feel that in magical realism (in literature, not in art), the supernatural elements are conceits that don't have to be followed through as rigorously as we demand from fantasy. It seems to me that in magical realism, the story as a whole takes precedence. The supernatural elements are only one of its parts. In fantasy, the fantastical elements are as central as plot and character. I think.

I love your description of geeks as people who "know too much about too many things that other people don't care about." What then are literary snobs?
I think the main difference is that all geeks aren't snobs, whereas all snobs are snobs.

Do you read V.S. Naipaul? Do you like Naipaul?
I read his earlier short story collection *Miguel Street* over and over when I was a kid. I really liked it. I think it still holds up fairly well, but I haven't read his newer work. He is, of course, notorious amongst his fellow Caribbean writers and everyone else for his outrageously racist and sexist statements. I don't like those. But I find him easy to ignore.

What kind of car do you drive? I ask every author this.
I don't have a car. You don't need one in Toronto. I believe the last time I owned a car was twenty-three years ago. I don't remember what kind it was. It was red. I hated it. I don't like cars. I don't like the expense, the maintenance, the danger of driving them, what they've done to the planet. Now that I spend part of the year in Southern California, I may have to get a car. This part of the world is built around the assumption of people having cars. It's difficult to get around without one and I have fibromyalgia. I get tired.

James Joyce never went back to Ireland. Do you see yourself growing old in Canada, or in the Caribbean? (Or growing old at all?)
I don't know where I'll grow old. Perhaps moving back and forth between a couple of places. The Caribbean is the home of my heart, but no one place has everything I'd want as a permanent home. Wherever it is, it'll probably be a big,

socially progressive city with lots of cultural, linguistic, ethnic and racial variety, lots of Black people, a mild climate, and a large body of water nearby. I haven't yet found a city that has all those things. I do plan on growing old, and I'm simultaneously terrified of it. I'm fifty-one years old, and the past few years as I entered what may be the latter half of my life were hellish. I experienced escalating illness, which led to destitution, homelessness, and near loss of my career as a writer. Things seem to be stabilizing now. I'm addressing the health concerns that can be addressed, I'm writing again, and I now have a professorship that is going a long way toward stabilizing my income. My primary (life) partner and I not only stayed together during those horrible years, but I think our relationship came out of it stronger. That in itself is a miracle, and unutterably precious. And yet I'm constantly aware that it's all temporary, that getting older will probably bring more and perhaps worse physical affliction to me and to my loved ones. Certainly, the longer I stay alive, it'll mean losing more and more of the people I love. I think of those afflictions and losses to come, and it makes me frantic with terror. I'm trying to remember that there will also be lots to gain in those years: new friends, new experiences, new competencies, new joys.

When you teach writing, what do you teach? What do you unteach?
Nowadays, I'm all about architecture and integrity. A story has to be given a deliberate shape that hopefully has some structural integrity and architectural wonder, and it has to be in dynamic movement along a trajectory. Is "dynamic movement" a tautology? I mean there should be pacing. I'm also all about allowing the reader to inhabit the body of a point-of-view character and experience the physicality of her or his world. I try to unteach the notion that a story is something told to a passive listener. I try to get my students out of the point-of-view character's head and more into that character's physical sensations. I try to model my love of words and meaning. I try to show them that editing is the fun part. It's the part where your word baby develops fingers and toes and eyes and starts looking back at you and reaching for things.

And being me, I'm now thinking about just how ableist a metaphor that is.

Did you initially see SF and fantasy as a gateway, or as a castle to be stormed? How has that perception changed?

That's a fascinating question. As neither. I think. You can breach gateways and storm castles, or enter gateways and inhabit castles. Maybe this is trite, but science fiction is a universe.

You totally work magic with titles: "Greedy Choke Puppy," "Ours Is the Prettiest," etc. At what point in the creative process does the title come to you?
Thank you! Often before the rest of the story. The title's sort of the distilled version of what the story wants to be. Before I quite know what the story is, the title whispers hints to me.

I like that. Now here's my Jeopardy *item. I provide the answer, and you provide the question. The answer is: Because they can.*
Why do cops routinely brutalise people? Why do bumblebees fly? Why do humans make art?

In the postscript to your ICFA speech, you took someone to task for separating Art and Labour. True, both are work. But isn't there an important difference or two?
Both are work, and both can be art. Hopefully, you're being paid for both. (And thanks for granting me that "u" in "Labour.")

Are you a Marxist?
No.

Three favorite movies?
Quilombo, by Carlos Diegues
　Pumzi, by Wanuri Kahiu
　　Lilies, by John Greyson

You seem to have stolen from Shakespeare (literature's master thief) in "Shift." What does a reader who hasn't read The Tempest *need to know?*
Let's see . . . in the play, Prospero is a rich white duke who's been exiled to a small island with his beautiful daughter Miranda. There he finds an ethereal fairy named Ariel who's been trapped inside a split tree by a white Algerian (African) witch named Sycorax. Sycorax had been exiled to the island earlier, while

pregnant with her son Caliban. Sycorax has died, leaving Ariel imprisoned and Caliban abandoned. Prospero frees Ariel and requires her servitude in return, but promises to release her eventually. Prospero takes Caliban in and teaches him to read, but when Caliban attempts to rape Miranda, Prospero makes him a slave (as in, no promise of release). Ariel gets all the flitting-about jobs and Caliban gets all the hard labour. Prospero repeatedly ridicules Caliban. Ariel helps Prospero and Miranda get off the island, and thus wins freedom. I think we're supposed to identify with Prospero and Miranda, but I was disturbed by Ariel's servitude and Caliban's slavery, and even though Prospero eventually pardons Caliban, I had trouble with the play's relentless mockery of Caliban as a "savage."

A few years ago I was visiting Kamau Brathwaite's literature class at NYU, and they were discussing Caliban. I had the insight that Ariel and Caliban could be seen as the house Negro and the field Negro, and I proceeded to mess with the story from there.

Someone once defined a language as a dialect with a navy. Would you agree?
I don't know if I agree, but it's hilarious! Whoever it was has a point.

Do you read poetry for fun? How about science? History?
Although my father was a poet and I know much of his work, I used to think that I didn't read a lot of poetry. But then I had occasion to check my bookshelves and discovered that I owned more poetry than I thought, and had read most of it.

I'd forgotten about children's poetry ("The more it snows, tiddly pom . . ."), not to mention Louise Bennett and Kamau Brathwaite, and Marge Piercy and Homer, and Lillian Allen and Dennis Scott, and, and, and . . .

There are poems I can recite by heart, and as a kid I read *The Odyssey*, *The Iliad*, and Dante's *Inferno* for pleasure, read them over and over, in fact. I don't think I could struggle through Homer nowadays, but I was more persistent as a child.

I do end up hearing a fair bit of poetry, as readings or spoken word or dub poetry performances, and as music. It's rare that I'll read a whole book of poetry from end to end as fun, but in sips and nibbles, I do read it. And I read science and history for fun as well as for research. Michio Kaku. *African Fractals. Death in the Queen City.* I also read critical theory for fun, and to find out what the hell it is that we writers are doing when we write. When it comes to fiction, I mostly read science fiction, fantasy, and comics, plus the occasional mystery or erotica/porn piece. But my nonfiction reading is more catholic.

Do you think the World Fantasy Award should be a bust of someone other than H.P. Lovecraft?
I have one of those. In appreciation for the merit of my work, the World Fantasy Award committee has given me a bust of a man who publicly reviled people of my primary racial background and who believed that we are by nature inferior to other humans. It is way creepy having racist old H.P. Lovecraft in my home looking at me.

I don't like that the bust is of him, but I love having the award. So I console myself in a number of ways: it was designed by Gahan Wilson, and how freaking cool is that? Lovecraft's own (part-Jewish) wife and his friends thought his racism was over the top. I gather his wife frequently called him to heel when he made anti-Semitic remarks; and I like imagining that Lovecraft is spinning in his grave as he's forced to view the world through the eyes of his statuettes placed in the homes and offices of the likes of Nnedimma Okorafor, Kinuko Y. Craft, S.P. Somtow, Haruki Murakami, Neil Gaiman, and me. I think the award should represent a fantastical creature, perhaps a different one every year. (I know that's probably too expensive, but since I'm fantasizing here . . .) A kitsune. A troll. A chupacabra. Anansi. A fat, happy mermaid with fish in her hair.

Do you outline plots, or just wing it? Ever write in longhand?
Nowadays, I have to write proposals for unwritten novels in order to sell them. I don't outline, at least not whole novels at a time. I tend to do it when I get stuck. I rarely write longhand. I type much more quickly. Plus I lose paper, whereas I rarely lose my computer or laptop.

Do you have trouble with copy editors or rely on them?
Both. Being copyedited is an occasion for taking a lot of calming breaths when I encounter wrongheaded or ignorant suggestions, but also for gasps of relief

when the copy editor catches something unfortunate in my text or makes a suggestion that lends a clumsy line grace. It also gives me an early insight into how my story is being understood, which means I still have time to make small adjustments. In my new young adult novel, *The Chaos*, I invented (I thought) the name of a pop star. The copy editor thought to Google the name, and discovered that it's the performance name of a porn star. Not an issue for me, except that she was not the character in my novel. I came up with another name.

You once described a first draft as clay. I like that. Can you describe your general procedure in writing fiction? Do you try to always sit in the same chair?
I don't. Sometimes I don't even have a desk at which to sit. I write and edit on my computer or laptop. I try to write in the early part of the day, since my mental energy peters out toward nighttime. I try to start with a solid meal before I take the ADHD meds which help my concentration. If I don't eat that first meal, the meds take away my appetite (but not my hunger), and by early afternoon my brain is so overclocked it's like bees buzzing in my head and I'm so ravenous I'm dizzy, but food tastes like ashes in my mouth. I usually need my surroundings to be relatively quiet. I generally can only go for short bursts, between fifteen minutes and an hour. I spend way more time trying to make myself sit and write than I do actually writing. It's pretty painful, but I give myself less grief now that I know it's how my brain is wired. The meds do help me to stop procrastinating and to focus. I've heard lots of people say that they fear that ADHD meds will ruin their creativity, but for me they are creativity aids. They help me to slow my thoughts down enough to register new ideas, and they give me enough concentration to write those ideas down.

I write scenes more or less in sequential order, but if I get stuck, I'll jump ahead to a scene that feels more tasty. If required, I'll backfill the rest in later. It's interesting how often I find I don't need to backfill.

Another thing I do when I get stuck is to step away from the laptop and go do something physical that I don't have to think about: wash dishes, go for a walk. My mind goes musing and I often come up with solutions that way. Or I'll try to describe the problem to someone. Sometimes the very act of doing so helps me solve the problem before I can finish articulating it to the other person, who's then left frustrated as I waft back to my computer in a creative trance. I use manuscript organizing software such as Scrivener. That allows me to see all the scenes at a glance, and to map out, shape, and move elements of the story around until they click into place. When I'm in Toronto, I'll often meet my friend, writer Emily Pohl-Weary, at a local library. She's the granddaughter of Judy Merrill and Fred Pohl, and a bitchin' writer in her own right. We'll take our laptops and each work on our own stuff for about three hours. We do goof off, but I get a fair bit of writing done in her company. I miss Emily.

Clute? Delany? Butler? Steampunk? Le Guin? Each in one sentence, please.
Clute's critical writing makes terrifyingly astute art. Delany: All hail the King.

Butler: I wish more people would talk about the ways in which she messes with normative sexualities, and I miss her very much and I don't care that that's really two sentences masquerading as one.

Steampunk: Cool gadgets, cool clothes, but whose hands assemble the materials?

Le Guin can make me cry with the simplest, seemingly inconsequential sentence.

You once said, "Fiction is NOT autobiography in a party dress." Okay. Then what is it?
It's what happens after you grind up a bunch of your personally received input, everything from life experience to that book about spices you read ten years ago, compost it within your imagination, and then in that mulch grow something new. I think that could even apply to autobiographical fiction.

You claim to have grown up in a culture without strict boundaries between literatures. Really? Not even between "high" and "low" art?
Yup. You can absolutely find that kind of snobbery in Afro-Caribbean culture, but it feels mostly toothless. The borders aren't as strictly policed. It's possible to have a literary conference in which both Nobel laureate Derek Walcott and dancehall singer-songwriter Lady Saw are headliners, plus bell hooks. In North America, there's no way that what I write would be considered in the same breath as, say, Michael Ondaatje's work. In the Caribbean, genre distinctions seem less important. Part of it might be that we don't have "alternative" culture in the way

that it manifests in Eurocentric cultures. As far as I know, there is no Caribbean equivalent of the hipster, or the science fiction fan, or the zinester. Perhaps that's because we're already marginalised from dominant Western culture, so we don't need or don't have the luxury of subdividing along minute genre fractures. There aren't enough publishers to have that kind of specialisation. The focus tends to be more on what each work is trying to achieve than on what genre it's in.

Your SF background seems heavily post–New Wave (1960s). Did you ever read the "Golden Age" all-guy crew like Heinlein, Clarke, Simak, Bradbury?
Absolutely, and still do. One of the proudest days of my life was when I got my mother to read Bradbury's *R Is for Rocket*. Her verdict? "But it's not about rockets and robots; it's about people!" I agreed.

You could easily (well, maybe not easily, but brilliantly) teach modern literature as well as writing. Given the choice, which would you prefer?
Thanks for the compliment. I couldn't, though. Geoff Ryman, now, he's brilliant at both.

In New York, I worked with some taxi mechanics from Guyana. Saturdays, they drank Teacher's and played cricket in the parking lot. What's the deal with cricket anyway?
Lord alone knows. My dad was a big cricket fan. Cricket to me is golf as a team sport, with better outfits, that goes on for what seems weeks. Just give me the Teacher's. Lots of it, if you're going to make me watch cricket. Yes, I am a bad West Indian.

"Encounter with a Gadget Guy"
James Patrick Kelly

You are often seen hiking in the New England mountains. What's the most awesome thing you've encountered there?
The view from Mount Willard looking south down Crawford Notch on a clear early autumn day.

I was a Boy Scout and so picked up the hiking habit early. I continue to be active outdoors year-round because the endorphin high is my drug of choice these days. I jog between fifteen and twenty miles a week and try to compete in at least one 5K or 10K road race a year. In the summer I wake up and swim half a mile first thing. In the winter I usually reach for my snowshoes or cross-country skis. All this exercise is actually a career move; I do my best story doctoring when I'm out of breath.

If you could have a drink with a dead SF writer (not a friend), who would it be?
I'm tempted to say Paul Linebarger, a.k.a. the great Cordwainer Smith, but instead I'm going to sidestep this one just a bit. Raymond Chandler famously had no use whatsoever for science fiction. In a letter near the end of his life he wrote a vicious parody of a scene from an imagined SF story, and ended the note with this question: "They pay brisk money for this crap?"

But many science fiction writers have been influenced by Chandler, and I am one of them. In fact, I've read and reread all the novels and stories, most of the letters, and several of the biographies. I've paid homage to Chandler more than once in my fiction and intend to do it again.

In addition to being a bit of a snob, Chandler was also an alcoholic, so I realize that drinks might be a chore. After all, I *am* an SF writer and have been sober now for some twelve years. But hey, I'd be willing to fall off the wagon for an evening if it meant connecting with the man who had Philip Marlowe say, "I needed a drink, I needed a lot of life insurance, I needed a vacation, I needed a home in the country. What I had was a coat, a hat, and a gun."

How Irish are you?
Other than my brazenly Hibernian name, not very. The ancestral Irish immigrant arrived on these shores before the Civil War. On my mother's side, however, I'm second-generation Hungarian. My grandparents were born there, and English was their second language.

But a kind of ersatz Irishness did impact my life. I attended the University of Notre Dame, of Fighting Irish football fame, in part because my dad followed their team. I think it was his oblique way of paying homage to our heritage. For the record, Notre Dame and I did not get along. Why did I choose an all-male school at the height of the sexual revolution? It's still a mystery to me! As soon as I realized my mistake, I loaded up on extra courses so I could graduate in three years. This was easier than it sounds; I was an English major.

Ever do hack work?
After escaping from Notre Dame, I started Real Life in the mail room of an architectural engineering company with offices throughout New England. As it turned out, what was most useful to this company was my ability to write comprehensible sentences. This skill, I discovered, was thin on the ground in AE firms. I began translating building proposals from engineering into English, and then writing press releases and promotional materials for the office I worked in, and then for the entire company. By the time I retired at the ripe old age of twenty-seven to write full time, I had the title of coordinator of public relations.

Early in my career I would have loved to write Star Trek novels, but I never found out what buttons to press to wrangle an invite.

You were at Clarion twice. Did you graduate or did they kick you out?
I flunked denouement. Thankfully, they let me make it up.

Back in the early days of Clarion, when it was still at Michigan State, attending more than once was rare but not unheard-of. But when I went the first time, it was drilled into us that the rule was *one and done*. For most students Clarion is an overwhelming experience. It certainly was for me. Not only did it vastly improve my command of the craft, but it validated my outrageous dream of becoming a writer. The magic of the workshop is that when smart people—your instructors and your fellow students—treat you like a writer, you convince yourself that they must be right!

And then the six weeks are over, and you return to your job and your real life. You have to work extra hard to catch up at work and on your relationships at home. Then the rejection slips land, and you doubt—what were you thinking?—and you find yourself deep in the dreaded post-Clarion depression. Happened to me, big time. I sold one silly story (that I have since struck from my bibliography) after Clarion and then there were months and months and deadening months of nothing. My career in public relations took off and consumed my fiction writing time. As I watched the dream fade, I wrote an impassioned letter to the late Glenn Wright, then Clarion director, begging him to break the rules and let me return to try to regain my momentum. That letter was probably the best writing I'd done since leaving East Lansing, and when Glenn passed it on to Damon Knight and Kate Wilhelm, they agreed.

They probably shouldn't have, although I doubt I would have had the same career, or maybe any career, if they had turned me down. One and done is a sound policy, although it is the case that several talented writers have attended the six-week Odyssey Writers' Workshop and then have gone to one of the Clarions. And Clarion grads have received degrees from the Stonecoast Creative Writing MFA program where I used to teach or gone from Stonecoast to Clarion. In any event, I did the workshop again. I realized later that one important outcome of going was that it killed my career at the architectural engineering company. They were willing to accommodate one six-week leave of absence, but a second one two years later was too much.

And the other outcome was that I finally passed denouement. As that second Clarion was coming to an end, I was pulling all-nighters to finish a story. I remember that it got critiqued on the second-to-last or maybe the last day. Damon and Kate, who founded Clarion and who always team taught the last two weeks, were writers in residence. The story was about an ambitious scientist who, against her better judgment, participated in an unspeakable experiment and in the process, all but wrecked her marriage. After much techno-mayhem, she alone was left of the research team; the experiment had succeeded at a horrific cost. In the denouement, she retreated in a daze to her office where she found a dozen roses from her estranged husband—a peace offering. In the version I workshopped, she decided impulsively to take the bouquet, go to him, and leave everything else behind. It was a bland conclusion to a There-Are-Some-Things-We-Are-Not-Meant-To-Know story. In her critique, Kate story-doctored my ending. She suggested that I have my hero toss all but a single flower out, stick that one in a bud vase, and sit down to write up the experiment, which would make her the new director of the lab. All it took was two sentences and one red rose to transform the piece into a chilling and powerful Scientist-Loses-Her-Soul story. This story—"Death Therapy"—was my second sale (which in my doctored bibliography becomes my first) and was reprinted by Terry Carr in his *The Best Science Fiction of the Year #8*.

And I've been story-doctoring in Kate Wilhelm's honor ever since.

One sentence on each please: Nisi Shawl, Colin Meloy, Star Trek, Dr. Johnson.
Nisi Shawl once washed my feet at a party, which deeply puzzled me; much later I realized that I should have been washing hers.

Colin Meloy is someone I had to look up because sometime in the early 2000s I stopped paying attention to rock music and filled the reclaimed cognitive space with jazz and audiobooks.

Star Trek is ultimately more of a force for good in SF, although very few fans realize why the transporter is murder.

I've been to Dr. Johnson's house, sat at his desk in his library, and thought about him but left no wiser than when I entered.

What is your favorite city? Why don't you live there?
New York, New York. I'm holding off on the move until my play is produced on Broadway.

My Jeopardy *answer: romantic comedy. You provide the question.*
What is the least understood genre?

You were on and once ran the New Hampshire Arts Council. How did that come about? What was it like?

My first involvement with the NH State Council on the Arts was when I applied to be on the Artists in the Schools roster. I was in the process of getting divorced and was casting around for a way to earn money to support my writing habit that didn't involve bagging groceries. I proposed to visit schools around the state to get kids to write and think about science fiction and the future. To do this I had to convince the council that I was an artist and I could teach. Back then in my experience writers and especially SF writers did not necessarily think of themselves as artists. Indeed, as I later learned, some arts councils in other states were turning SF writers down for roster spots for writing on the wrong side of the literary tracks. Not New Hampshire. I will admit that I learned to teach writing on the job. There were days when I waltzed in and was like Robin Williams in *Dead Poets Society* and others when I was like the saddest substitute teacher ever to lose control of a class. But I got better, and I liked the kids. I was actually getting more residency offers than I could accept when the professional staff approached me about serving on the council itself, which was composed of arts-friendly people from the business and nonprofit communities, arts donors and a couple of working artists, one of whom was leaving. I was honored and said yes, so the governor nominated me. The councilors are something like a board of directors; we met monthly to oversee the professional staff, set policy and approve grants—all for no pay. I loved it! Part of the job was to travel around the state listening to artists and arts organizations and finding ways to help them connect with audiences. I was twice nominated to four-year terms on the council and in my last two years I was elected chair, which meant that I traveled to a number of national conferences representing our little state. I might still be on the council, had I not joined the faculty of the Stonecoast MFA program. There just wasn't time enough for both.

What I learned as a councilor is that the arts are destined ever to struggle in our capitalist system. The vast majority of artists are among the working poor and many worthy arts organizations regularly face economic ruin. What government support there is never balances the books.

Arts organizations try to make an argument for better and more reliable support by talking about the arts economy and its collateral benefits. Towns with an active theater community are more likely to have upscale restaurants and posh housing stock. Streets with art galleries tend to draw the Rolex crowd. There's merit to this, I suppose, but for me the best argument for supporting the arts is that they represent the soul of our culture. Alas, our soul does not fit into a cell on a spreadsheet.

What drew you into writing plays? The money or the fame?
Both. And still waiting.

I started writing plays by accident. Back in the day I was on the Artists in Schools roster of the New Hampshire State Council on the Arts, which meant I traveled around the state talking about science fiction and fantasy and helping kids write stories. From 1989 to the early 2000s, I worked with K–12 kids in more than fifty NH schools and ate more bad lunches than I care to remember. Pizza washed down with a carton of chocolate milk! American chop suey and a mealy apple! As an unexpected bonus, I was invited to join an ambitious theater residency with the goal of getting the students to write, stage, and present a new play to the community. It was a magical experience. My fellow artists gave me gentle nudges when I strayed off course, and in part because of their expectations, and in part because of the kids' enthusiasm, we pulled it off. Word of what we accomplished traveled around the state and we did similar residencies around the state. After several, I tumbled to the notion that if seventh graders could write a creditable play with my help, I might be able to do it myself.

I started by adapting stories into one acts that got produced in local black box theaters. As you and I both know, it's kind of a thrill to sit in an audience that is enjoying your play. Some of my theater pals talked me into writing a couple of full-length historical plays. One was "I Have Not Yet Begun to Fight" about local NH hero John Paul Jones and featured an onstage battle between Jones's frigate *Bonhomme Richard* and the British *Serapis*. At one memorable performance, when the British captain called out at the climactic moment, "Sir, do you surrender?" the actor playing Jones blanked on his lines, replying simply, "No." Perhaps I should have taken that as an omen of how my theatrical career would go. But I did write another full-length play called *The Duel*, which had a nice four-week run in two of the biggest theaters in the state. It was about the encounter between Hamilton and Burr but with an alternative history twist. This was long before Lin-Manuel Miranda's *Hamilton*. At the end of the first act, both duelists miss. In the second act, New England has seceded from the Union, and the Civil War breaks out fifty years early, with Burr and Hamilton on opposite sides.

Since then I have limited myself to one acts and especially ten-minute plays, of which I've had maybe a dozen produced around the country.

You often teach writing. What's the hardest thing for people to learn? What's the easiest?
Endings are definitely the hardest and the most important. I'm no Isaac Asimov or Arthur C. Clarke, but I've always aspired to proclaim three laws of my very own. How about these? Jim's First Law: All great stories have great endings. Jim's Second Law: A story which reads great until its flawed ending is just an okay story. Jim's Third Law: A great ending will overshadow the flaws of a story which is otherwise just okay.

The easiest thing about writing is also the easiest to overlook. The only way to have a career as a writer is to send your stories out. Actually, this one isn't all that easy, because writers are good at finding reasons not to submit their work. Fear of rejection is the big one, but obsessive rewriting is almost as debilitating. As Valéry wrote, "A story is never completed, merely abandoned."

You do and sell Audible stories. How does that work?
I began reading aloud to my kids as a stay-at-home dad, classics like *Clifford the Big Red Dog* and *The Cat in the Hat*. When we graduated to the Oz series, I began to do voices. I remember casting the Wizard as a very broad W.C. Fields and the Scarecrow as Ernie from *Sesame Street*. As my career as a writer progressed, I was delighted to discover that fans at SF conventions would show up at readings to hear me pretend to be the characters in my stories. Readings are my favorite part of cons, and I'm grateful to write in a literary community which honors them as a hallmark of its culture.

I'm kind of a gadget guy and I used to record my readings on cassettes and copy them for friends. When recordable CDs came along, I would run off dozens, some of which I sold but most of which I gave away at cons as promotion.

But during the astonishing rise of the iPod and mp3s and podcasting and the downloadable audiobook, everything about recorded fiction changed. I was an early podcast adopter with my *Free Reads* podcast, which featured me reading my backlist of published stories. But one of the smartest career moves I ever made was to talk Jacob Weisman at Tachyon Publications into letting me record and podcast my standalone novella *Burn*, which he was about to publish. I posted a new chapter every week on *Free Reads*, and *Burn* got more than twenty thousand downloads in its first twelve months. I am convinced that it was the podcast rather than the print version that earned my novella its Hugo nomination and its Nebula win.

Meanwhile, *Free Reads* caught the attention of Steve Feldberg, who was keen to acquire SF for Audible.com. He approached me about transferring some of my *Free Reads* content to the Audible store and recording more of my stories. Lots more! Eventually I recorded and produced fifty-two short stories, novelettes and novellas for Audible, which were packaged into four collections or "seasons" under the titles of *James Patrick Kelly's StoryPod One, Two, Three,* and *Four*.

Alas, it was such a monumental task and the postproduction took so much of my time, that I gave up my regular podcasts, both *Free Reads* and *StoryPod*, in part out of exhaustion. These days I mostly let the pros publish my works on audio, although I still get behind the microphone from time to time.

What kind of car do you drive?
My current set of wheels is a 2014 Honda CR-V, but that is just quotidian transportation. My thrill rides have always had fewer than four wheels. In my twenties I itched for a motorcycle, but my wife at the time was adamantly opposed. Years passed—decades!—and in midlife I was musing about this forgotten two-wheel dream to my dear wife Pam Kelly when she shrugged and said she had no problems with motorcycles. I hadn't known this about her! Six months later, I swung my leg over my first bike, a Honda Rebel 250cc, which was fun but underpowered. Subsequently I moved up to Kawasaki Vulcan 400 and then to a Suzuki VStrom 600. A year ago, I decided that safety trumped buzz and made the jump to three wheels. My Can-Am Ryker 650cc is a trike with two wheels in the front and the drive wheel behind and a happy science fiction writer on the seat in between.

Do you ask Siri or use a map?
I have many thoughts about maps, all joyful. I never hesitate to ask Siri for directions and I always program long distance destinations into my car's GPS, if only to know when I'll arrive. On the other hand, I love to ride my motorcycle down back country roads until I am completely and gloriously lost. When I get home, I will then try to retrace my trip on Google maps. Google's satellite view, by the way, still feels like science fiction to me. I have spent happy hours peering at the Appalachian Mountain Club trail maps planning hikes for my wife and me to take. USGS topo maps fill me with delight. I have two historical maps hanging in my office and two more elsewhere in the house. I regard all of them as works of art. I'm totally a map guy.

You and Kessel did a number of anthologies for Tachyon. How did that come about? How come I never made it into any of them?
Wait a minute! Your story "The Cockroach Hat" was in our *Kafkaesque*, pal.

I may misremember, but our editing gig probably started when I wrote my column about slipstream in *Asimov's Science Fiction*. In any event, Jacob Weisman somehow got the notion that I knew something about slipstream and floated the idea of an anthology. My first reaction was that I hadn't read widely enough to pick the right stories, and so after consulting John Kessel, we came back to Jacob with the idea that we would be coeditors. I note here that I regularly talk to Doctor Kessel about matters of business and craft, since he is far wiser and taller than I am. Our idea, for this and most of the subsequent anthologies, was that we would not only choose the tables of contents but that we would discuss the commonalities of the stories. We had arguments to make about slipstream, Franz Kafka, cyberpunk and postcyberpunk, and the singularity, which we made in the introduction to each book. While some saw these books as attempts to establish a canon in various subgenres, we never did. We were just trying to provide context and start conversations around some wonderful stories and writers.

My personal favorite of these books was *The Secret History of Science Fiction*, in which we sought to demonstrate that, purely in terms of craft and conceptualization, there was no appreciable difference between genre SF and the mainstream crossover SF. Because John and I have shared this core belief since we first started typing professionally, it was cathartic to make our case.

We had a great run between 2006 and 2012 with these thesis anthologies. I'm not exactly certain why we stopped. Maybe it had something to do with Jacob passing on all the new ideas we pitched to him. Maybe it had something to do with the fact that editing was stealing time from our writing. Or maybe it was poetic justice for not including "Bears Discover Fire" either in *Feeling Very Strange* or *The Secret History*.

Three favorite SF movies? Three deplorables?
If I define "favorite" as films that influenced my thinking about our little corner of genre, I'd say *The Matrix* for its immersive VR, *Alien* for its workers' spaceship, and *Galaxy Quest* for being the best Star Trek film ever. Of course, this list represents a cruel betrayal of the fanboy who grew up consuming the stale cheese of Creature Features. He wouldn't have hesitated to cite *Forbidden Planet*, the first and best *King Kong*, and *The Day the Earth Stood Still*, since he watched them over and over and over again. Because I sat uncritically through so many bad SF movies at an impressionable age, I now have very little tolerance for the deplorables in recent release. I have no use for most of the recent Star Wars products. I sat through *Interstellar* only because I was with friends and I saw maybe half of *Ad Astra* on a plane last year.

My True or False Question: True or False?
There are more things in heaven and Earth, Horatio, than are dreamt of in your philosophy.

Did you read SF as a kid? What was the first story that lit you up?
I read all the SF in the children's section of my hometown library, especially the Two Toms (Tom Corbett and Tom Swift), often more than once. Then I asked the librarian's permission to cruise the adult stacks. (Fun fact: my pal Elizabeth Hand was probably just a few steps behind me. We grew up in the same town and have since compared notes about our many hours in that library.) So yeah, SF and I were not exclusive, but we dated heavily all through my teens. It's interesting, given my career as a short story writer, that I don't remember encountering any SF magazines until I got to college.

First story that lit me up? The truest answer here is *The Wizard of Oz*. Or rather all the Oz books, not only the L. Frank Baum novels but the sequels written by Ruth Plumly Thompson and John R. Neill. Is Oz SF? Well, I would argue that there is no robust definition of SF anymore, nor perhaps should there be. In the world I write in, SF now stands for speculative fiction and includes fantasy, horror, slipstream, weird fiction and on and on. But if I pretend that SF means stories about science or space or the future, then "A Planet Named Shayol" by Cordwainer Smith in *The Best of Sci-Fi 2*, edited by Judith Merril.

Our colleague Rachel Pollack once said, "Anyone who thinks guilt never helps anything has never been a writer." Was she onto something or just being a contrarian, as is often her wont?
As a survivor of an unrelenting Catholic education—kindergarten through college—I feel the shadow of guilt, earned and imagined, every day of my life. Not sure that it helps much, however.

Do you remember the Whole Earth Catalogue*?*
You realize that we date ourselves talking about such things, and SF is properly a young writers' genre, but of course I remember it. As I remember *The Mother Earth News*, *The Electric Kool-Aid Acid Test*, Firesign Theatre, *Zap Comix*, *Hair*, *Easy Rider*, and *Our Bodies, Ourselves*. How could I not? I was an eyewitness! I wrote "The First Law of Thermodynamics"!

"I Planned to Be an Astronomer"
John Kessel

Ever go back to Buffalo?
I haven't been back to Buffalo since my mother died in 2011, but I keep intending to do so. My brother, a flock of nieces. and my nephew live there, and I'd like to reacquaint myself with the place. It's always somewhere in my heart. The house my father started building when I was born, and that was in our family until I was in my sixties, still stands—owned by other people now.

I have a lot of memories of growing up a working-class child of Polish and Italian immigrants. It imprinted me with the ethnic mix of the first half of the twentieth century. Industrial capitalism and unions. The Catholic Church, which included 60 percent of the people of Buffalo in the 1950s, was ever present in my youth. The Great Depression, World War II, and the New Deal all happened before I was born but seemed to be ongoing realities in in my family. One reason I've written stories set in the early twentieth century is that I felt like I lived in it.

Your corner of the South is almost like New England, in that everywhere you turn there is a university. Has that worked for you?
I like the Research Triangle and have lived in Raleigh now for more than half my life. It draws people from all over the US and the world. I enjoyed teaching at NC State University, a major research institution, for forty years. Its closeness to UNC Chapel Hill and Duke, the vibrant cultural life, the good friends I have made make it a very good place to live.

I'll never be a southerner but I have learned a lot by living in the South. It's harder to ignore race as a factor in American life down here the way it was passed over so significantly where I grew up, and that has been good for me.

Plus, North Carolina is a beautiful state. The piedmont, the Blue Ridge mountains, the Outer Banks, the beaches down east.

Did you always plan to be an academic?
No. I planned to be an astronomer. I never considered that in order to be one I would probably have to be a college professor. The professor side of that, the teaching and academic life, was not something I spent time thinking about.

When I later, as an undergraduate, double majored in physics and English, I still didn't think in terms of being a professor. Even when I went to grad school in English at the University of Kansas, I didn't expect I would last long enough to get a PhD. I wanted to be an SF writer and, figuring that I would have a tough time making a living solely from that, was looking for whatever kind of job might support me while I wrote.

For three years, taking a break from doctoral studies, I was a copy editor and news editor for Commodity News Services and Unicom News, economic wire services jointly owned by Knight Ridder Newspapers and UPI. I was good at copyediting and enjoyed the work, though it was high-pressure. A wire service serving commodities investors, unlike a newspaper, is on a continual deadline. I learned a lot about how capitalism and markets work in the real world while I was there.

But gradually (it took me nine years from my BA to my doctorate) I thought maybe I could be an academic if I could get a job like Jim Gunn's[*]—one where I did not have to write scholarly literary criticism to justify my existence. When I finished the doctorate, I took a shot at applying to universities and was terribly lucky to get the job at NC State, where I started in 1982.

It turned out that I was well suited in some ways to being an academic, although in others I felt like a spy in the English department, someone who was not there for the same reason that others were. I was one of the last generation to be trained in the New Criticism in a literary history–based PhD program; I learned very little about the postmodern schools of criticism—structuralism, poststructuralism, deconstruction, Lacanian psychoanalytic criticism, semiotics,

---

[*] James E. Gunn (1923–2020), American science fiction writer, editor, scholar, teacher, anthologist. Gunn taught writing and literature at the University of Kansas for fifty years and founded the Center for the Study of Science Fiction.

new Marxism, reader-response theory—those schools of heavily theoretical criticism that were to dominate English studies for most of my career. In grad school I wrote a lot of papers and did a lot of close reading for courses I took, but my interests were always in fiction writing. I would not have finished a PhD if I had not been able to persuade the KU English Department to allow me to write a creative writing dissertation.

And I discovered that I could be a good teacher. I've genuinely enjoyed teaching both literature and writing, sharing my enthusiasms with young people, working with writers hoping to get better. Learning how to teach writing improved my own writing. Even though I can't take any credit, I do feel great satisfaction when one of my former students publishes a book.

What did Kansas and Gunn give you? What was he like? Did you get to know any of the other old-timers?

Through my years of grad study at KU I learned a lot about classic literature; I read tons of things from *Beowulf* to Chaucer to the Renaissance poets and Elizabethan playwrights, the history of the novel in England and the US, twentieth-century British and American lit, contemporary fiction. I was ignorant and soaked this stuff up like a sponge. I liked most of it but learned from even those works I didn't like. From the scholar Elizabeth Schultz I got my love of Herman Melville. Studying lit gave me models to aspire to.

Jim Gunn was a living example of the history of SF from the 1940s on, the last of the Mohicans in that way. He wrote science fiction and about science fiction. He knew everybody of the generation of writers who came of age in the 1950s and through him I met many of them: Brian Aldiss, Fred Pohl, Theodore Sturgeon, Gordon Dickson, John Brunner, Ben Bova, Samuel Delany, Harlan Ellison—all of them visited KU at one point or another while I was there. I was Gunn's grad assistant and therefore had to pick visiting writers up at the Kansas City airport and drive them back to Lawrence. I could ask them questions, talk about SF and writing it—though I was shy and did not want to annoy them. Some of them guest taught workshops and critiqued my stories.

Jim directed my master's thesis in fiction writing and was on my PhD committee when I wrote a creative writing dissertation. (I was one of three students who managed to get creative writing dissertations past the grad school in the early 1980s before they objected to such silliness and closed down the option.)

Jim read everything I wrote and commented on it. He was a tough reader. I was writing what was called New Wave SF at that time—my heroes were Ursula Le Guin, Thomas Disch, Gene Wolfe, Kate Wilhelm—and Jim was an old-school John W. Campbell/Horace Gold writer. He forced me to think about what I was doing, why I was doing it, how a story was constructed, and how it might be made better. "Stories aren't written," he said, "they're rewritten." I did not take to this immediately, though I came eventually to find revision the most rewarding part of the process.

He invited me into his home and was kind to me. Jim had a certain Midwestern reserve that was hard to get past. He believed in science fiction as a way to shape the future; for him SF was about ideas, and should have a positive effect on the world. I was more of a cynic and a skeptic. I always had a Kurt Vonnegut satirical side. But we both believed in reason and thought that SF was literature, not just disposable entertainment, and should be written to high standards. He was a good role model. I've tried to be as patient with my students as he was with me.

I visited eastern Kansas several times when I was obsessed with and writing about John Brown. Was Brown actually much of a presence there?
I don't remember Brown being a presence in the life of the people I lived among in Kansas and Missouri despite the fact that the things he cared about shaped so much of the place and are still live issues. But that John Steuart Curry mural in the Kansas State Capitol is astonishing.

John Brown lives! Smash white supremacy!

How did Sycamore Hill come about?
In 1980 and '81 I was living in Kansas City and Ed Bryant invited me to the Milford workshops that he ran in Colorado. Those were formative experiences for me. I had published only a handful of stories at that point. I'd admired Ed's work for years and at the workshop I met Connie Willis, Cynthia Felice, George R.R. Martin, Steve and Melanie Tem, and Dan Simmons, among others. For the first time I felt like I might belong to a community of writers.

When I moved to Raleigh I became friends with Mark Van Name and Gregory Frost, who were also early in their careers. Mark moved into a new house in the mid-1980s, and Greg casually observed that it was big enough to hold a workshop in, so in January 1985 Mark and I organized a five-day workshop along the Milford model. All the writers who came were men, most of them from North Carolina. It seemed to work well, so the next year we moved it to a house we rented on the campus of the Governor Morehead School in Raleigh, expanded it to a full week, and invited writers from all over the country, including Jim Kelly, Bruce Sterling, Orson Scott Card, Karen Joy Fowler, Susan Palwick, Rebecca Ore, and others. The thing turned into a yearly workshop.

This was in the midst of the regrettable Cyberpunk-Humanist business. I was interested in trying to get some of the most ambitious and outspoken writers of my generation together in the same room to see whether we might have a productive exchange of ideas, and support each other in our different ways of writing good SF. Most of the participants took to this idea, but some were not able to communicate across the natural divides that exist between writers. That was a learning experience.

Mark and I ran SycHill until the mid-1990s in Raleigh, then it went on hiatus for a few years, to be resurrected later at Bryn Mawr College in Philadelphia, run by Richard Butner and me with the help of Greg Frost, who had moved there. Later we moved to the Wildacres Retreat Center in the Blue Ridge Mountains of NC, where it still continues. In 2006 I handed it off to Richard, who has run it very successfully ever since. He's changed a number of elements, in my mind much for the better. I just got home yesterday from the 2023 Sycamore Hill.

Were you ever published in the Whole Earth Catalog? *I was.*
Nope. I used to read it back in my counterculture days.

If you could live in any city for a year (comfortably) which would it be?
There are a lot of cities I'd love to try that with. London, Berlin, Prague, Rome, Paris. San Francisco. Seattle.

One sentence or so on each, please: Guy Davenport, Kelly Reichardt, J.D. Crowe.

To my embarrassment, I have never read anything by Guy Davenport.

To my embarrassment, I have never seen a film by Kelly Reichardt.

To my embarrassment, I have never seen a performance by J.D. Crowe.

What poets do you read for improvement?
Among contemporaries I love the work of my colleagues Dorianne Laux and Joe Millar. Gerald Barrax, a wonderful poet, was my colleague at NC State for many years. I like Stephen Dunn. I like Hafez. Rilke. I love all sorts of classic poetry: Donne, Blake, Dickinson, Frost, Eliot, Williams. I come back to Yeats all the time.

I've tried writing a few poems myself but I can't say I have gone deeply into that place. Something always pulls me toward narrative. But nothing is more powerful than the distilled shock you get from poetry.

Funny how serious New Englanders (Small Beer Press) seems to have an affinity with your little knot of Southern writers (Rowe, Butner, et al.). Explain.
Throw in Andy Duncan (*An Agent of Utopia*). Kelly Link has North Carolina connections, so maybe that has something to do with it, but I rather doubt that.

Christopher (*Telling the Map*) and Richard (*The Adventurists*) and I (*The Baum Plan for Financial Independence*) are excellent writers of short fiction that fits into the offbeat sensibilities of Small Beer Press. Christopher's fiction has deep roots in the South, as does Andy's. I don't see as much of the South in Richard's. And as I said above, even though I've lived in the South for a long time and have set a few stories here, I don't consider myself a Southern writer.

I suppose that accidents of encounters with each other may have had something to do with it. If Small Beer likes the South, they like the weird South.

I found Pride and Prometheus *impressive and serious in spite of the silly title. Was the excellence of the Austen fabric scholarship or affection?*
On some days I think *Pride and Prometheus* is my best novel, or at least has my best protagonist, Mary Bennet. I am a big fan of Austen's fiction, but since I am an Americanist, I have never taught any of her work—though I've taught *Frankenstein*, the other inspiration for my novel, many times.

I'm not an Austen scholar, but I love her novels. She was so smart and funny, but also wickedly cynical. I read her books for the dark observations on British society that flow through them, but also for fun. I would say the book was powered by affection more than scholarship.

I was also drawn to fusing Shelley with Austen because they represent two major streams of literature in English. *Frankenstein* is a foundational text for science fiction, as Austen is for the modern novel of manners. Since I have spent much of my career trying to cross the sensibilities of these two forms of fiction, it was irresistible to me to try to draw these stories together. They don't naturally fit together; my novel starts in Austenland and gradually moves into the gothic as Mary Bennet falls out of the polite, privileged society, where she was born, into the madness and extremity of Shelley's novel.

Some Austen fans have complained that no woman of 1815 could have undergone the degradations I put my Mary Bennet through, but of course there were countless women in England at that time who suffered much worse. What those readers mean is that the people of the lower classes who lived those hard lives are invisible in Austen's novels. Such readers are complaining that my novel slips from one genre to another, and they don't want that. I don't give a happily-ever-after ending.

One of the unfortunate facts about the reception of *Pride and Prometheus* is that many readers, hearing the premise of a novel that crosses characters from *Pride and Prejudice* with the story of *Frankenstein*, think it must be a joke along the lines of the execrable *Pride and Prejudice and Zombies*. It is, as you say, a serious novel, with some attempts at Austenian humor, it's true.

One of the things I wanted to do in it was to present Mary Bennet as something more than the figure of fun that she is in Austen's novel. Flaubert said, "Madame Bovary c'est moi"; I say, "I am Mary Bennet."

One of SF's famous friendships is you and Jim Kelly. What's the story there?
I just spent a week rooming with him at Sycamore Hill. Somebody at the workshop asked if we had ever had a falling out. We scratched our heads and could not come up with anything. We may have had a disagreement here and there but nothing that has touched our friendship.

We met at the World SF Convention in Boston in 1980 when I noticed his name tag while I waited for an elevator and realized he was the author of a story I'd recently read and admired, "Death Therapy." He told me I was the first person who had ever recognized him as a writer. I liked his fiction from the start; he seemed to me to be smart and funny and full of invention, and he was writing things that I would have been proud to write myself.

We had similarities of background and temperament. Both raised Catholic but lapsed, both New Wave fans, both from New York State, graduated from college with English degrees the same year. I liked him as a person and as a writer. We exchanged manuscripts and offered comments to each other, talked writing and careers. We collaborated on some stories and then a novel. By the mid-1980s we had attended so many conventions together we got nicknamed the glimmer twins of humanist SF. Our careers have gone forward more or less in parallel, though we do not write as much alike as we did in 1985.

Even though we've never lived within seven hundred miles of each other, he is my dearest friend.

Your work has made it into film several times. How has that worked for you?
Only once: my story "A Clean Escape" was made into the first episode of the very short-lived anthology series *Masters of Science Fiction*. The script was by producer Sam Egan; it was directed by Mark Rydell and starred Judy Davis and Sam Waterston. Though it is expanded from my story, it does contain scenes that are right out of the story. I got to go up to Vancouver and see the episode filmed. It was cool to see my dialogue spoken by those actors.

I've had an option taken for a series titled *Clean* based on a couple of my stories. But no production yet.

You may have thought I had something else adapted because I had the pleasure of acting in a film: *The Delicate Art of the Rifle*, directed by Dante Harper, written by a former student of mine, Stephen Grant, and shot on the NCSU campus in 1994. It's inspired by the tower sniper, Charles Whitman, who killed sixteen people at the University of Texas in the mid-1960s. I play Dr. Max Boaz, a rather weird college professor.[†]

[†] Dante Harper, director, clip from *The Delicate Art of the Rifle*, YouTube video, February 27, 2021, 10 minutes, 44 seconds, https://www.youtube.com/watch?v=qucMpuFrFlA.

Did you teach writing or literature other than SF & fantasy?
Yes. I was hired to teach both American literature and creative writing, and for my first twenty years at NC State most of my teaching was in literature. Besides separate courses on SF and fantasy, I regularly taught the two-semester American literature survey and courses on major American writers. My students were mostly non-English majors taking them to fulfill a humanities requirement. I relished the opportunity to be the last English teacher most of them would ever have. I considered it my job to leave them with the idea that reading old books and poems might actually have some relevance to their own lives—and that it could be considered a peculiar sort of *fun*.

I suspect that most of your students at NC State were actual (born-and-raised) Southerners. What did you learn from them?
That the South is a more complicated place than I had imagined it was in my ignorance before I moved here. Plus, it's possible to like both Kansas City and North Carolina barbecue.

What are you reading these days?
Except for research reading for fiction—and I do a lot of that—since I've retired from teaching, I read haphazardly. Some old books, some new ones, some in genre and many without. I keep a list of books I've read. Among those from recent months are *Creatures of Will and Temper*, by Molly Tanzer; *Cora Crane: A Biography of Mrs. Stephen Crane*, by Lillian Gilkes; *The Strange*, by Nathan Ballingrud; *Crooked, but Never Common*, by Stewart Klawans; and *A Visit from the Goon Squad*, by Jennifer Egan.

What car do you drive? How come? I ask this of everyone.
I drive a 2018 Audi E-tron Sportback, a plug-in hybrid that I bought used about a year ago. It's the most fun-to-drive car I have ever owned. Before this I'd been driving underpowered Hondas since the 1970s.

I like it because it's environmentally friendly, relatively small, accelerates quickly when I need it to, and looks snazzy.

Ever write for comics?

When I started out in the late 1970s I scripted a comic strip, *Crosswhen*, a collaboration with my Kansas City friend Terry Lee, that appeared in the magazine *Galileo* from 1978 until the magazine's demise several years later. I can't speak for the quality of my scripts, but it was fun to write.

You have pretty explicit and progressive politics. Is the right right about anything?
That's a good question. The political right in the US today is appalling and my instincts are to say no, but when I look at it more objectively I can say that some of the things that the classic right professes to believe in, such as individual responsibility, should be incorporated into any mature political understanding. That doesn't contradict, in my mind, the necessity for government to curb capitalism, protect the environment, ensure social, racial, and economic justice, preserve democratic elections and institutions, and plan for a future that goes beyond the next quarterly earnings report. In the capitalist world we live in government is the only force large enough to counter the immense power of corporations and the wealthy.

Are you prepared for the Singularity?
The singularity is a fantasy, or at best a metaphor. So I guess if it happens, I will be unprepared.

Reflections of a Realist
Paul Krassner

Your first gig was with Mad *magazine, right? How did that come about?*
Actually, my first gig was when I was a kid working in a grocery store, separating cherries with green mold from the plain red ones. It was a kind of meditation. In my last year of college, I began working for *The Independent*, an anti-censorship paper, where I eventually became managing editor. The publisher, Lyle Stuart, was friends with Bill Gaines, the publisher of *Mad*, and when Gaines hired Stuart as his business manager, we moved our office downtown to what was unofficially known as "the *Mad* building."

I wasn't on the staff of *Mad*, but I wrote some scripts on a freelance basis. The premise of my first submission was "What if comic-strip characters answered those little ads in the back of magazines?" But the editor—Al Feldstein, who replaced Harvey Kurtzman—wouldn't include Good Old Charlie Brown responding to the "Do You Want Power?" ad, because he didn't think the *Peanuts* strip was well-known enough yet to parody. Nor would Popeye's flat-chested girlfriend, Olive Oyl, be permitted to send away for a pair of falsies.

Bill Gaines said, "My mother would object to that."

"Yeah," I said, "but she's not a typical subscriber."

"No, but she's a typical mother."

I sold a few other ideas to *Mad*, but when I suggested a satire on the pros and cons of unions, Feldstein wasn't interested in even seeing it because the subject was "too adult." Since *Mad*'s circulation had already gone over the million mark, Gaines intended to keep aiming the magazine at teenagers.

"I guess you don't wanna change horses in midstream," I said.

"Not when the horse has a rocket up its ass," Gaines replied.

At that time, there was no satirical magazine for grown-ups—like *Punch* in England or *Krokodil* in the Soviet Union or *Oz* in Australia—and so when I launched *The Realist* in 1958, I didn't have any competition. But I also had no role models for such a magazine. I just made it up as I went along.

Was the success of The Realist *a surprise?*
Yeah, absolutely. I thought it might reach a thousand circulation. And when it did, then I hoped it might reach three thousand. In two years, it did. Later, five thousand. Then ten thousand. Then twenty-five. Then fifty thousand. In 1967, the circulation peaked at a hundred thousand. And the pass-on readership was estimated at two million. But who really knows how many?

In any case, the readers had in common a sense of irreverence toward piety and pomposity. My credo was to communicate without compromise. I had no publisher or advertisers to answer to. The subscribers and newsstand buyers trusted me not to be afraid of offending them. And their urge to share fueled that Malthusian growth of *The Realist*. Word-of-mouth was the best kind of advertising and it was free.

Is there anything in your view that replaces The Realist *today?*
Well, because *The Realist* was personal, unique, originally published in the context of a blossoming counterculture, and undermined by the FBI's COINTELPRO (Counterintelligence Program), I say with all the false humility I can muster that *nothing* can replace *The Realist*. As for satirical publications, there's been *National Lampoon* and *Spy* magazine. And later, published in cyberspace, *The Onion*, *The Borowitz Report*, and *Ironic Times*. Incidentally, all issues of *The Realist* are now online at The Realist Archive Project. Meanwhile, irreverence has become an industry.

Ever meet Lord Buckley?
Nope. However, when I moved from New York to San Francisco in 1971 to coedit with Ken Kesey *The Last Supplement to the Whole Earth Catalog*, I also hosted my own radio program on ABC's FM station. My first appearance was on the morning of Easter Sunday, so I opened with Lord Buckley's classic jazzed-up performance of "The Nazz" (that's short for Nazarene).

Have you ever taught comedy? Like in college? Has anybody?
The closest I've come to that was in the '60s when I taught a course at the Free University in New York. It was titled Journalism and Satire: How to Tell the Difference. There are teachers of comedy now. Perhaps the best is Beth Lapides. I call her the mother of alternative comedy.

What do you think of WikiLeaks?
Well, let me put it this way: I trust WikiLeaks more than Wikipedia. I consider whistleblowers like Julian Assange, Chelsea Manning, and Edward Snowden to be heroic figures on an international level. In the '60s, we wore buttons that said "No Secrets" and we carried posters that proclaimed "Information Is Free."

Now, WikiLeaks has been transmutating those abstract ideas into worldwide public scrutiny of clandestine communications, ranging from embarrassing quotes to the revelation of international criminality. Here's an example: The Yemeni president covered up United States drone strikes against al-Qaeda in Yemen. He told General David Petraeus in a diplomatic cable, "We'll continue saying the bombs are ours, not yours"—sort of like vice-presidential candidate John Edwards's assistant claiming to be the father of a baby when actually it was Edwards himself who had impregnated his mistress.

It looks like pot is gradually getting legalized. Does this please you or dismay you?
It pleases my ass off. I mean, why would it dismay me? It dismays the DEA and the prison guards' union. It even dismays some growers, dealers, and medical marijuana dispensaries. In a truly free society, the distinction of whether marijuana is used for medical or recreational purposes would be as irrelevant an excuse for discrimination as whether the sexual orientation of gays and lesbians is innate or a matter of choice.

It dismays the Partnership for a Drug-Free America, which was originally founded and funded by the pharmaceutical industry, the alcohol industry, and the tobacco industry. Cigarettes are legal and kill 1,300 people every day—and that's just in this country—but marijuana is still mostly illegal, yet the worst that can happen is maybe you'll get a severe case of the blind munchies and eat a bunch of legal junk food.

What *does* dismay me, though, is that as long as any government can arbitrarily decide which drugs are legal and which are illegal, then anyone serving time for a nonviolent drug offense is a political prisoner. So, even though Colorado and Washington are the first two states to legalize recreational marijuana, I won't be satisfied until amnesty is declared, freeing all those stoners who are still living behind bars.

Incidentally, there was a questionnaire that was published in *High Times*, and one of the questions was, "Is it possible to smoke too much pot?" And a reader answered, "I don't understand the question."

Seems to me that American humor, at least since the 1950s, is primarily Jewish. I mean from Milton Berle to Sid Caesar to Lenny Bruce to, hell, Jon Stewart. Not to mention Paul Krassner. What's the deal with that?
First of all, I don't think of myself as Jewish. My parents were, but I consider all religions to be organized superstition. Ironically, anyone who thinks of Judaism as a race rather than a religion is accepting Nazi tenets. I don't believe that Jews were the chosen people or that humans were the chosen species. If that darned asteroid hadn't rendered all those dinosaurs extinct, would creationists be driving around only in cars fueled by batteries? But although I'm an atheist, I welcome diversity, as long as no theological dogma is allowed to become a law.

Anyway, sure, there was some truth to the stereotype of Jewish comedians, but that's changed. Steve Allen wasn't Jewish. George Carlin wasn't. Richard Pryor wasn't. Chris Rock isn't. Margaret Cho isn't. Conan O'Brien isn't. Louis C.K. was raised as a Catholic but is now an agnostic. Bill Maher is also an agnostic—his father was Catholic, and Bill was a teenager when he learned that his mother was Jewish. Stephen Colbert is a practicing Catholic, and he teaches Sunday School. As for me, I've had my foreskin sewn back on my penis.

Does that still hurt?
Only when I come.

You once described the Diggers as a cross between Mother Teresa and Tim Leary. Was that supposed to be a compliment?

I guess so. They served as social workers for the Haight-Ashbury community in San Francisco, and they took acid trips.

What do you think of hip-hop?
Besides passion and talent in show biz, I think of the hip-hop community as part of the ever-evolving counterculture. In the past several decades, we've gone from bohemians to Beats, from hippies to Yippies, from punk to hip-hop—it's essentially the same spirit continuing in different forms.

Ever been attacked by wild animals?
Only by cops swinging billy clubs and howling triumphantly.

Ever meet Woody Allen?
I interviewed him for *The Realist* in 1965. We concluded:

> **Q.** Are you concerned about the population explosion?
> **A.** No, I'm not. I mean, I recognize it as a problem which those who like that area can fool around with. I doubt if there's anything I can do about the population explosion, or about the atom bomb, besides vote when the time comes, and I contribute money to those organizations who spend their days in active pursuit of ends that I'm in agreement with. But that's all. And I'm not going to set fire to myself.
> **Q.** But do you agree with the motivation of the Buddhist monks who set fire to themselves in Vietnam?
> **A.** I don't think so. No, I think that they don't know what they're doing. I think they're nuts. That's *not* the answer. When all is said and done, it's not the answer. When you're home at night and you say to yourself, "Tomorrow morning I'll get up at eight o'clock and set fire to myself," there's something wrong. I wouldn't do it that way.
>   I can see dying for a principle, but not that way. At the very minimum, if you are going to die for something, you should at least take *one of them* with you. Go back to the Jews in Germany. If you have a loaded gun in your home, and the state comes to get you, you can at least get two or three of *them*.

I'm not opposed to violence as a course of action in many instances. Sometimes passive resistance is fine, but violence in its place is a good and necessary thing. But setting fire to yourself is not the answer. With my luck, I would be un-inflammable.

My Jeopardy *answer: "It seemed like a good idea at the time." You provide the question.*
Why did you stop beating your wife?

Watch any TV?
Less and less. Let's see . . . Bill Maher. *The Simpsons. Sixty Minutes. Louie.* Occasional movies or documentaries. If *Curb Your Enthusiasm* were still on, I'd watch. So, instead of Larry David, I watch *Seinfeld* reruns, despite the annoying laugh-track. I watch Rachel Maddow. I watch the real news and the fake news as they borrow clips from each other.

How come you have never hosted the Oscars?
Their invitation must've gotten lost by the Post Office.

Each in one sentence, please: Sarah Silverman, Sarah Palin, Thelonious Monk, Andy Warhol.
Sarah Silverman confessed her bedwetting trauma without the aid of a priest. When Sarah Palin was chosen as John McCain's running mate, and CBS interviewed her at home, a member of the crew told me that he saw the potential vice president remove from a shelf a book about seceding from the United States. I once interviewed Thelonious Monk for *Playboy*, and I was tempted to call him Felonious, but I figured that he'd already heard that too many times.

A few decades after Valerie Solanas shot Andy Warhol in 1968, his cohort, Paul Morrissey, said in an interview by Taylor Mead (who had played himself in Warhol's film, *Taylor Mead's Ass*, described in Wikipedia as a "sixty-minute opus that consisted entirely of Taylor Mead's ass, during which Mead first exhibits a variety of movement, then *appears* to shove a variety of objects up his ass") that "Solanas approached underground newspaper publisher Paul Krassner for money, saying, 'I want to shoot [Olympia Press publisher] Maurice Girodias,' and he gave her $50, enough for a .32 automatic pistol," which, of course, Paul Morrissey shoved up Taylor Mead's ass.

What's your favorite gadget?
You mean like my drone that delivers *The Washington Post* to Jeff Bezos? Or my invention of a combination dildo and anti-insomnia gadget called Dildoze? Actually, I like my answering machine, because I can screen all my calls. And as a result, telemarketers—whether they're humans or robots—automatically hang up. If a gadget doesn't have to have moving parts, then I say yay for my back-scratcher.

Was there anyone in the '60s counterculture you didn't meet? What would you say to them today?
Yeah, there were millions of 'em. At the risk of revealing my self-serving streak, I would recommend to them my own memoir, *Confessions of a Raving, Unconfined Nut: Misadventures in the Counterculture*, about which Pulitzer Prize winner Art Spiegelman wrote that "His true wacky, wackily true autobiography is the definitive book on the sixties." Oops, wait, you must mean *famous* countercultural icons. Well, I would've liked to meet Mario Savio. He gave that passionate speech in 1964, outdoors on the steps of Sproul Hall at the UC–Berkeley campus: "There's a time when the operation of the machine becomes so odious, makes you so sick at heart, that you can't take part! You can't even passively take part! And you've got to put your bodies upon the gears and upon the wheels . . . upon the levers, upon all the apparatus, and you've got to make it stop! And you've got to indicate to the people who run it, to the people who own it, that unless you're free, the machine will be prevented from working at all!"

Today I would say to him, "Thanks for inspiring the Free Speech Movement."

I would've also liked to meet Janis Joplin. Actually, I sort of did, but not really. We were both performing in a benefit at the Fillmore East. While I was onstage in the middle of an anecdote, she was walking toward the exit doors, and she was wearing anklets with these bells that rang all the way up the aisle. Later, hurrying out of the theater, she saw me in the lobby. "Hey, I'm sorry about my cowbells," she said, "but I hadda take a leak."

"Oh, that's okay, but ain't it better to *give* then to take?" She cackled and left the building. Today I would say to her, "Belated thanks for your empathy."

Have you ever been tempted to fake your death so you could read your New York Times *obit?*
That wouldn't be necessary, because NPR already has one in the can, and the radio journalist who did it sent me a CD, so I had the rare privilege of fact-checking my own obituary. And recently an AP correspondent was also assigned to prepare my obit. So now I can sign my books with this inscription: "This book will be worth more on eBay when I'm dead."

Three favorite movies?
Network. Sophie's Choice. The Night Porter. And a fourth: The Producers. Hmmm. There's a pattern there. Those last three were about Nazi Germany, and the first one was about creeping fascism in America.

Ever read science fiction?
Theodore Sturgeon: We became friends, and he wrote a column for *The Realist*. And when I was at *Hustler*, I appointed him as our book reviewer.

Harlan Ellison: We also became friends, and he wrote an introduction to my anthology, *Pot Stories for the Soul: An Updated Edition for a Stoned America*. "Basically, fuck dope," he began. "No offense, dude, but fuck dope."

Octavia Butler: My wife Nancy and I were seated at the same dinner table with her at a literary event, and discussing fiction, she offered a fine bit of advice on finding things to like about an evil character.

You were once the centerfold in Hustler *magazine. Any plans for a repeat?*
It's not on *my* to-do list. In 1978, after Larry Flynt had converted to Christianity, he hired me to mesh porn and religion. I suggested a scratch-'n'-sniff centerfold of the Virgin Mary. "That's a great idea," he said. "We'll have a portrait of the Virgin Mary, and when you scratch the spot, it'll smell like tomato juice." Anyway, I was completely naked except for wearing my old cowboy hat in the photo you're referring to. It accompanied an interview in *Hustler's* first born-again issue.

You once took LSD with Groucho Marx. So what?
You had to be there. But okay, I'll give you a snippet of the trip. Groucho told me about one of his favorite contestants on *You Bet Your Life:* "He was an elderly gentleman with white hair, but quite a chipper fellow. I asked him what he did to retain his sunny disposition. 'Well, I'll tell you, Groucho,' he says, 'every morning I get up and I *make a choice* to be happy that day.'" Then he went to urinate. When he came back, he said, "You know, everybody is waiting for *miracles* to happen. But the whole *human body* is a goddamn miracle."

Do you regard yourself as a journalist or a satirist?
Both, though I label myself as an investigative satirist. Currently, I'm working on my long-awaited—by me, anyway—first novel, about a contemporary Lenny Bruce- type performer.

Imbedded in your journalism career are two serious crusades: for abortion rights and against cigarettes. Any progress?
In 1962, when abortions were considered a crime, I never thought they would be legalized in my lifetime. After I had published an interview with Dr. Robert Spencer, without identifying him, I began to get calls from women who were pregnant but didn't want to be, and I became an underground abortion referral service, and in the process, morphing from a satirist to an activist. I was subpoenaed by district attorneys in two cities, but I refused to testify before their grand juries. Then came *Roe vs. Wade*, and I never thought that abortions would become a crime again in my lifetime, but now it seems like a possibility, one state at a time. States' rights aren't just for racists anymore.

As for cigarettes, in January 2014, the *Los Angeles Times* published my letter to the editor:

> Re "Smoking's global grip," Opinion, Jan. 21. Thomas J. Bollyky writes the following: "Step by step, the government cracked down on tobacco. Warning labels were added to cigarette packages (1965), cigarette advertising was banned on television and radio (1971), smoking on commercial airline flights was forbidden (1987), and tobacco products were put under Food and Drug Administration oversight (2009). U.S. criminal and civil

tobacco lawsuits exposed and punished tobacco companies for decades of obfuscation and malfeasance."

And yet that same government still uses taxpayer funds to subsidize the tobacco industry. American schizophrenia rules!

Hmmm. Did you know I was a tobacco farmer in Kentucky back in the '70s?
I do now.

Ever do Burning Man? I mean, you live in the fucking desert anyway.
Okay, please forgive me, but I've never been to Burning Man. Is that a countercultural sin? Do I have to say a hundred Hail Learys?

What kind of car do you drive? I ask this of everyone.
I never learned to drive. When I moved to San Francisco, I bought a used Volkswagen convertible for $500, stick shift of course, even though I didn't know how to drive. The hills in San Francisco scared me, and so friends would drive me from place to place in my own car, while I sat on the passenger side and took care of the glove compartment.

Remember Sing Out *magazine?*
Yes, I do. So what?

Are things getting better or worse? Or is that a fair question?
It's a fair question. I wish I had a fair answer, but one person's perception of "better" is another person's perception of "worse." I waver between hope and despair, between the Occupy Wall Street progressives and the Tea Party reactionaries. As Ellen Willis wrote in *Beginning to See the Light*, "My deepest impulses are optimistic, an attitude that seems to me as spiritually necessary and proper as it is intellectually suspect."

Backstage at a benefit concert, singer-songwriter Harry Chapin said, "If you don't act like there's hope, there *is* no hope." So then, hope is a placebo, and placebos work. But when an old friend told me that the official psychiatric *Diagnostic and Statistical Manual of Mental Disorders* had added "Optimism" to its listings, I'm embarrassed to admit that I believed him, if only for a moment.

On the other hand, I relish the irony that when I first met him, he was sixteen and attending my class Journalism and Satire: How to Tell the Difference. That's getting increasingly difficult these days.

"That's How You Clean a Squirrel"
Joe R. Lansdale

Where does East Texas end? (And don't say the Louisiana line.)
It doesn't stretch as far as Dallas, heading west, since that is what used to be called The Plains, though today The Concrete is more accurate. Simply put, if you go west and the trees disappear and the dirt gets black, you are not in East Texas anymore. Going north, it dies out before the Red River by some distance. Go southeast to Houston and you have gone too far. Houston is in the Coastal region, which though similar is still different.

East Texas has lots of shade, running water, and a meth problem.

Everyone (Hollywood included) agrees you have a gift for dialogue, but I think it goes deeper than that. There's a vein of indirection and understatement in all your prose that I identify as a southern thing. Just saying.
I think that's true, but East Texans can be very direct. It's said that we drawl, but if we do, we drawl fast. We speak faster than most southerners, and our culture is more southern than southwestern; and though those two overlap, we are more farmer types than rancher types.

I think one reason I do pretty well with dialogue is that we are storytellers here, or at least have been in the past, and that's a southern tradition. If the story has to do with somebody dead and their body tossed down into an old water well, or something dark in the woods, then all the better.

I always loved to listen to the older folks when I was growing up, how they talked. It impacted my writing by quite a bit. My parents were older when I was born, and they had gone through the Great Depression and therefore had a different viewpoint than the parents of many of the other kids I grew up with. My personal culture overlapped that of earlier periods, the Great Depression, and that of the 1950s and '60s; in our family I was probably the only counterculture kid, so I have that to draw on as well.

My father had a lot of great sayings from having been born in 1909 and having heard as he grew up sayings from the 1800s. His relatives, many of them, had fought in the Civil War. My grandmother on my mother's side was close to a hundred years old when she died. Came to Texas in a covered wagon. Saw Buffalo Bill's Wild West show when she was a child and was forever enraptured by it. My father had boxed and wrestled a little for money, riding the rails to fairs to fight. He couldn't read or write, though at the end of his life he got so he could read a little—newspapers, comics, simple paperbacks. But he could never actually be called literate.

My mother was a great reader when I was growing up and encouraged me to read. So did my dad. He knew how hard it had been for him not being able to read or write.

I often hear that story, of how southerners are all storytellers. Sometimes I think it's just one of their stories. But let's move on. Horror and humor seem closely linked in your work. Does one drive the other or are they just fellow travelers?
I think they are fellow travelers, though it can work the other way as well. A lot of the old frontier stories my dad told were both horrible and funny. People of his era could slap their knees and laugh over some pretty horrible stuff, but they were also kind and helpful people. I think they had to laugh at the horrors as a way of survival. It was rough-and-tumble humor, the sort of thing people today would be aghast at. Rightfully so, I guess, but when Dad told those stories they tickled the shit out of me.

Mark Twain said there's no humor in Heaven. Meaning, nearly everything we think is funny is based on the misfortune of others, as well as ourselves. Bad things can be funny, mostly in retrospect. As a character in my novel *The Thicket* said, "Everything in life is humorous, except your own death. But others will laugh."

You often mention Edgar Rice Burroughs as a "sentimental favorite" and an inspiration. Yet your writing hews much closer to noir and modernist realism. Who were your first actual models that you imitated, knowingly or not?

Burroughs inflamed my desire to write. He was the writer I originally imitated, and I think his headlong pace has stayed with me. I was already writing before I read Burroughs, mostly inspired by comics, *The Jungle Book*, *The Iliad*, and *The Odyssey*, Edith Hamilton's book of mythology. We also had the Bible and Shakespeare, and my mother gathered up books here and there, so I was always reading. But Burroughs set me on fire.

Later on my influences were legion. Lots of science fiction inspired me, writers like Philip José Farmer, Cyril Kornbluth, Fred Brown, Henry Kuttner, and a little later Ray Bradbury. And then Hemingway and Fitzgerald and Steinbeck, plus a little bit of Faulkner. Flannery O'Connor was major. I really didn't care for the Beats so much, but I learned a lot from reading Jack Kerouac, especially *On the Road*, which I liked. William S. Burroughs (the other Burroughs) put me to sleep, and I had to work too hard to get anything out of his cut-up style, which seemed more gimmick than story. I think at heart I'm a storyteller, and I want my style to accomplish that, which doesn't mean I can't be experimental.

I was also heavily influenced by Chandler, Hammett, James M. Cain, tons of noir writers, and many who wrote for Gold Medal. Those Gold Medal novels were mostly short and swift, and you could easily read one in a few hours. On weekends I used to devour two or three after morning martial arts practice, which is something I've also done for a long time. Over fifty years.

If you were to pick one book or story that "launched" you, what would it be?
For me it was a one-two-three punch. In 1986 *The Magic Wagon* come out, and it was reviewed well and treated like a literary novel, which gave me those creds (for whatever they are worth). *Dead in the West*, a pure pulp novel, came out the same year and started a sort of underground or small-press run that continues along with my mainstream publishing run to this day. "Tight Little Stitches in a Dead Man's Back," though it was not my first short story, got me a lot of attention and a nomination for the World Fantasy Award, which it didn't win (though I see places where it says it did). I've been nominated for World Fantasy many times, but no wins, so I'm correcting that confusion here. That story gave me my short story credentials. I also sold a nonfiction book that year that didn't come out until years later. Anyway, I made some money that year, and I started a three-pronged career in prose that's continued until this day.

I was introduced to your work by The Drive-In. *Is there a drive-in in Nacogdoches? Did you ever wonder what happened to all those little pot-metal speakers?*
I have wondered about those speakers. Once they switched to the radio, it was never the same again. I loved drive-ins. I don't know how much I would love them now, the heat and mosquitoes might not be too appealing these days. We had a drive-in in Nacogdoches, and we went often, but most of my Texas drive-in viewings were in Tyler, Kilgore, and Longview.

Back then they had movies made especially for drive-ins, things you couldn't see anywhere else. Most were terrible, but many were perfect for the young mind in search of horror, female nudity, and gratuitous violence. They also gave us a private place for sex, and talking about the sex we weren't getting. The popcorn wasn't too good. Always tasted like wet cardboard.

Your "Miracles" piece is pretty hard on religion. I get that. Were you raised as a Methodist or a Baptist?
Baptist. I actually am not against religion itself, but when people use it to justify bad behavior, or when they show how hypocritical they are, I always wonder if they've read the Bible they love to quote and shake. To justify some of the things many Christians justify, by quoting it selectively, irritates me. I don't believe there is a god, outside of the blind, uncaring power of nature. I don't mind Christians who try and live by the better attributes of their religion, but it seems to me, especially in the South, that most of what they get from the Bible is just the bad stuff. Reason for that is, it's mostly bad stuff.

The New Testament has its more positive side, but basically if you believe *Do unto others as you would have them do unto you* and know the Beatitudes, you can forget both books and, for that matter, Jesus. Thinking some guy who died over two thousand years ago is coming back is not much different from older religions that we now think of as mythology. So, yes, I can be rough on it.

Who taught you to drive? To write?
My dad and mom both taught me to drive, mostly my mom. My uncles a little. I taught myself to write from reading. I never had a course in creative writing, though I've taught a few, and am writer-in-residence at Stephen F. Austin State University. I don't think you can make someone a writer. You can assist them

and open a few doors, but it's always up to the person. Some people just have It. Others may know the alphabet, excellent grammar, and spell perfectly, but they seem to be trying to light a match underwater. It's just not there. I don't know why that is, but it's usually that way. Now and again someone, like Robert Johnson, who couldn't play the guitar worth a damn, will go off and come back a virtuoso, but that's rare.

Were you a fan of Bruce Campbell before Bubba-Ho-Tep? *Do you ever have any say in the casting of films from your work?*
I was a fan. My son Keith was a fanatic fan. He loves him some Bruce. He begged me to get Bruce for *Bubba*. I told him that wasn't my call, that was Don's call [producer, director Don Coscarelli]. Don called me one day and asked, "What do you think about Bruce Campbell?" and I laughed out loud.

Keith and I went on the set and met Bruce and Ossie Davis. We already knew Don and the other actors and people working on the film. Nice experience.

Bruce and I have been friends ever since. He's like the Elvis of B movies, but the thing is, the man can act. I've never thought he got his due. *Bubba*, in my view, is his finest performance, and Don's best film so far.

I was fortunate enough to meet Neal Barrett Jr. and even hung out with him (in Greenwich Village, of all places), but we never worked together. How'd you get so lucky?
Neal Barrett Jr. was a brilliant and neglected master. He wrote some survival stuff, but the best of his work, like *The Hereafter Gang*, is amazing. He and I were close friends for nearly forty years. I actually sought him out for advice when I was a young writer. He asked me, "Do you write regularly?" Yes. "Have you sold anything?" Yes. "Then why in hell are you asking me for advice? Keep doing it." Only writing advice I ever had (except a bit from Bill Nolan).

Neal was like family. I remember him being amazed that we didn't care for the beach. He and his wife Ruth loved it. He felt our children were being deprived. One day the mail came. Opened the envelope. It was full of beach sand and seashells. A note was included: "So your children will know."

Still have that sand. Miss Neal every day.

"Survival stuff." I like that. You are writer-in-residence at Stephen F. Austin University. Does this mean you never have to leave the house, except for Moon Pies?
I do leave the house to teach one long night a week, but I like it. I haven't taught lately, though. I've been traveling a lot, and I've gotten to the point where I can't stand to grade a paper. I may teach some more, but right now I'm investing that time in other projects.

Martial Arts Hall of Fame? Who do you have to whip to get in?
You have to have made a significant contribution. There are lower-level awards for Sparring Champion of the Year, Instructor of the Year, and so forth. The ones that count are the Lifetime awards, or System Creation awards. I have a little of all those from the International Martial Arts Hall of Fame, and the United States Hall of Fame. Also had one for using martial arts in my writing from the Texas Martial Arts Hall of Fame, but that hall has closed down. Too many cows in the hallway, I guess.

I love martial arts. These recognitions are nice, but it's the art itself I love, and for me, when you get right down to it, there is only one martial art—Martial Arts.

It says in your bio that you live in Texas with your wife, dog and two cats. Is that her real name or a nickname? Do the cats get along?
Ha. I am actually known as Dog to my wife and a few friends, and she is known as Bear. Our kids are of mixed animal genetics, I suppose. Little Dog and Red Panda, and we think the Red Panda, our daughter Kasey, might be some kind of raccoon. We have a fine family and pets. Our dog is a rescued pit bull, and our cat is old.

Love your Texas Observer *essays. How did you, a fiction writer, get involved in writing opinion pieces?*
My first sales were nonfiction, so articles weren't new to me. I've had quite a few published. I started writing for the *Texas Observer* because the editor called. He asked if I would cover a Poe exhibit at the Harry Ransom Center in Austin. I started the car, drove to Austin, saw the exhibit, and wrote a piece on Poe. They liked it, and so did I, so I began to do articles for them whenever I had the

chance. Then they changed editors. I did one for her, then she was gone, and then they changed editors again; I did one for him, and now they've changed editors again. So, we'll see. But so far I've written quite a few *Observer* pieces. I really enjoy doing it, especially the more nostalgic pieces.

You once said that you admire Hemingway's style but not his subject matter. What the hell does that mean?
I love the way he writes, but I couldn't care less about killing animals for trophies. He certainly wrote about more than that, but I didn't care for that aspect much. I don't see hunting as a sport. When I was growing up, it was part of how we ate. It wasn't the only thing we had going, but it was a nice supplement.

Hemingway influenced us all. I liked the fact that he had a kind of simple yet poetic style. I like his short stories the best: "The Killers," one of the finest stories in the English language; "The Battler," "Hills Like White Elephants," "The Short Happy Life of Francis Macomber," "The Snows of Kilimanjaro." I also like *The Sun Also Rises* and *A Farewell to Arms*, which is kind of a hardboiled Harlequin romance for men. *Islands in the Stream*, which many do not like, is my favorite.

Ever meet Molly Ivins? Or are there more than two liberals in Texas?
I did meet her. She was drunk at a signing at the Texas Book Festival, if I remember right. Neal Barrett Jr. was with me. I think she was hitting on Neal. She was witty and funny even in that short time.

You seem to show up on movie sets of your pictures more often than most writers. Is this because you are in disguise, or do they actually want you there?
I am given a lot of freedom and even say-so on all of the stuff of mine that has actually made it to film. I'm grateful. I think I'm so much a part of my stories that it's hard to separate me from the secondary creation of film. But I'm sure there may be others in the future who will not want me on the set. I've become involved in producing as of late, so I'm getting to spend time on the sets of other films not related to my work.

What kind of car do you drive? I ask this of everyone.

My wife and I have a Prius apiece.

Do you have a regular drill for writing? You know what I mean.
I get up, take the dog out (if my wife doesn't beat me to it), have coffee, read my e-mail and *New York Times* headlines, and start writing. My deal is three to five pages, and then if I want to quit, I can. If I want to continue, I can. I rarely miss that plan. I love to write, and I'm not one of those that loves "having written," like Dorothy Parker. I love doing it. I write five to seven days a week, about three hours a day most days. Once in a while I'll come back after lunch and work a little, but mostly it's just mornings. I show up and write, polish as I go, then give it a once-over when done. Day in, day out. For my birthday I write as a treat to myself, same for Christmas and other holidays. I used to not write when I traveled, but now I do, as I travel more. I wrote mornings before the *Hap and Leonard* TV show shoots, or in the evenings when it was done. I write. That's what I do. The short time period gives me workout time, which is getting harder as I age, and time to read and be with family, watch movies, play with the dog, the usual stuff we all do. Or should do.

Did you like Winter's Bone? *Know how to skin a squirrel?*
Winter's Bone. Loved book and the film, but they don't know from squirrels. You don't clean a goddamn squirrel by hacking it. You peel its suit off, from feet to head, and then you cut the head off, and then the paws, and then you gut from stomach down, not stomach up, so as not to drag squirrel shit back up into the body. That's how you clean a squirrel.

When I was young, I ate a lot of squirrels that we hunted. My dad told me once that if I started to enjoy seeing them fall, I needed to sit down and have a serious talk with myself. We ate for food, not sport.

What do Hap and Leonard never ever talk about?
They never talk about you. Or me either.

You weren't an English major, but you seem well read in the "mainstream" classics. What do you read these days for fun?

I read what interests me and always did. I love to read history as well as fiction. I tried to read all the classics, American and otherwise, to have some understanding of how literature developed. Some I loved, some I didn't. I read classics in the genres, science fiction, historical, coming of age, fantasy, mystery, crime, suspense, western, you name it. I read the foundations for movements, like the Beats, and so on.

So many writers I can read and in five minutes realize they don't have any history. You have to know what's gone before, know the rules in order to break them. I am sometimes embarrassed for the people teaching literature. You talk to many of them and realize they have only read the modern stuff, which is fine, but the other is important too. I read modern literature if it's something that appeals or seems impactful. Same with films, art, comics, and so on. One way to stay fresh is to constantly add fresh ingredients, otherwise your soup grows stale.

If you got tossed out of Texas, where would you live?
That's a toughie. I love Italy, but for long term, I'd need the USA. I like trees, but I don't like cold. Maybe Santa Fe, though I'd get tired of all that open space pretty damn quick. It would have to be someplace in the country. We live on ten acres of woods with a pond now, and we love it.

I do love Texas, though its warts are many and its sublime moments are few (except for us). We have peace and quiet and good people around, even if some of them love Jesus insanely and vote Republican.

Shit, you can't have everything.

I judge my neighbors on their character, actually, not on who they vote for or what mythology they serve. If they can rise above those things on a daily basis, and if I can rise above my own prejudices, then it's fine. Of course, they're wrong and I'm right.

Okra question: boiled or fried?
Pickled.

"A Lovely Art"
Ursula K. Le Guin

What have you got against Amazon?
Nothing, really, except profound moral disapproval of their aims and methods, and a simple loathing of corporate greed.

Even though you occupy a pretty high perch in American Letters, you have never hesitated to describe yourself as a science fiction and fantasy author. Are you just being nice, or is there a plot behind this?
I am nice.

Also, the only means I have to stop ignorant snobs from behaving towards genre fiction with snobbish ignorance is to not reinforce their ignorance and snobbery by lying and saying that when I write SF it isn't SF, but to tell them more or less patiently for forty or fifty years that they are wrong to exclude SF and fantasy from literature, and to prove my argument by writing well.

Your first Earthsea *novel (1968) features a school for wizards. Some critics claim that you used your SF powers improperly to travel thirty years into the future and swipe the idea from J.K. Rowling. Do you deny this?*
I plead the Fifth.

You once described yourself as a "fast and careless reader." I loved that! It reminded me of Dr. Johnson telling Boswell he rarely finished a book. Do you still regard this as an advantage?
Of course. It means I can get through shoddy books in no time, and can reread good books over and over . . .

One of the things I love about The Wild Girls *is its economy. You create a complex and strange world with a few swift strokes. William Gibson does this with art direction. How would you describe your technique?*
As improved by age and practice.

Should girls learn to sword fight?
I got in on my big brothers' fencing lessons when I was ten or twelve. It is a lovely art. I never planned to go out in the streets of Berkeley with my button foil looking for Bad Guys, however.

Your newest novel, Lavinia, *retells Virgil's* Aeneid *from a woman's point of view. Aeneas still plays the major role, though, and you seem rather fond of the dude. Do you like him better than Ulysses? Or Achilles?*
Ulysses is way too complicated to just like or dislike, but Achilles really turns me off. Sulky little egocentric squit. As if a lot of other guys on both sides didn't have to die young. I bet he went around with beard-stubble all over his face like all the sulky sullen half-baked heart-throb actors do.

Robert Louis Stevenson once said that our chronological age is like a scout, sent ahead of our "real" age which runs ten or fifteen years behind. What would you report back from your eightieth birthday?
I would like to be all cheer and bounce and lifewasneverbetter as old people—excuse me for bad language: older people—are expected to be. Unfortunately I find that at eighty I don't feel seventy let alone sixty-five. I feel eighty.

It isn't easy, but it's interesting.

You say you are not a "plotter." Do you start with an idea, or a character, or a situation? Or are they all the same thing?
Erm. Things come. People, landscapes, relationships among the people/landscapes. Situations begin to arise. I follow, watching and listening.

One criticism of the movie Avatar *was that there is no explanation for the convergent evolution. Is there one in your Ekumen books (I may have missed it)? Why not?*
Why not did you miss it? Why did you miss it not? Sir, I know not.

I provided a specious explanation of why everybody is more or less human: because everywhere local was settled by the Hainish. But that leaves out the indissoluble network of genetic relationship of *all* life on a planet. Such is the sleight of hand SF often has to play in order to get a story going. All we ask is the willing suspension of disbelief, which can and should return in full force when the novel is over.

You have generously mentored and promoted many emerging writers. Did anyone do the same for you?
I know everybody else remembers the early days of SFWA [Science Fiction Writers of America] as huge ego-competitions between X and Y and Z; but (maybe it was my practice at being a younger sister, or something?) I remember my early days in the SF world as being full of encouraging editors and fellow writers. Hey, what a neat bunch of people!

Seems to me it's easier to get published these days but harder to get noticed. How do you think you would fare starting out today?
If I hadn't connected with [literary agent] Virginia Kidd when I did, I might very well have had a much more constricted career and less visibility as a writer. Virginia was ready and able to sell anything I wrote—any length, any genre, to any editor.

I don't think it's easy to get published these days, though. Not published so as it matters. Put stuff up on the Net, sure. Then what?

Have you ever been attacked by lions?
Three separate dogs have bitten me, many separate cats have bitten me, and recently my ankles underwent a terrifying siege by a bantam rooster at whom I had to kick dirt until he backed off and stood there all puffed up and shouting bad language like a Republican on Fox TV.

Who needs lions?

Many authors (including myself) have imitated your shapeshifting dream-altered world in The Lathe of Heaven. *Was this idea original to you or did you swipe it from someone else?*

A lot of stuff in *Lathe* is (obviously) influenced by and homage to Phil Dick. But the idea of dreams that alter reality seems to me a worldwide commonplace of magical thinking. Am I wrong? Did I make it up? Doctor, am I all right?

What's an ansible? Is it like a Kindle? Where can I get one?
Anarres.

You didn't seem too enthusiastic about the TV series based on your Earthsea *novels. Why not?*
It wasn't a series, and it wasn't Earthsea, and can I go have a drink now?

You once described the downtime between novels as like waiting patiently at the edge of the woods for a deer to walk by. Are you a bow hunter?
Of the mind.

"Travel is bad for fiction but good for poetry." Huh?
Just reporting my own experience as a writer.

I share your modest enthusiasm for Austen's Mansfield Park. *I didn't like the movie, though. Do you like any of the recent Jane movies?*
Oh, as movies, sure. Not as Austen. There is no way I can dislike Alan whats-hisname with the voice like a cello.

What's your house like? Does your writing room have a view?
Nice, comfortable.
     My study looks straight out at a volcano which blew off its top two thousand feet thirty years ago. I got to watch.

Perhaps your most famous and influential novel is The Left Hand of Darkness. *What's it about?*
People tell me what my books are about.

One problem writers have with utopias is that nothing bad can happen. You don't seem to have this problem. Is this a function of literary technique or philosophy?

Both. Places where nothing bad happens and nobody behaves badly are improbable, and unpromising for narrative.

You mentioned as your favorite repeated readings Dickens, Tolstoy, Austen, et al. Are there any Americans you go back to? Any SF or fantasy?
Let me off this question. I read too much.

What kind of car do you drive? I ask this of everyone.
Ha ha. I don't.
    Charles is currently driving a Honda CR-V with about 120,000 miles on it. My favorite car we ever had was a red 1968 VW bus.

We all know better than to rate our contemporaries. But I would love to know your take on the late Walter M. Miller Jr., since he seemed to share your deep and radically humane conservatism.
He was a very, very good writer who I feel lucky to have read early on, so I could learn about the scope of SF from him.

The Ekumen and Earthsea series almost seem like bookends, one SF and one fantasy. Where would you put Lavinia *on the shelf between?*
My writing is all over the map; bookends won't work. Even shelves won't work. *Lavinia* is what it is.

Lavinia *shows a great love for Rome, or at least pre-Roman virtues. That seems contrarian for a staunch progressive. Or is it?*
I am not a progressive. I think the idea of progress an invidious and generally harmful mistake. I am interested in change, which is an entirely different matter.
    I like stiff, stuffy, earnest, serious, conscientious, responsible people, like Mr. Darcy and the Romans.

How's your Latin?
Mediocris.

Dragons are good in Earthsea. Or are they?

No. Nor bad. Other. Wild.

What have you got against Google?
Just its mistaken idea that it can ignore copyright and still do no harm.

In Always Coming Home *the future looks a lot like the past. What are the Kesh trying to tell us?*
What past does that future look like? I don't know anybody like the Kesh anywhere anywhen.

 The countryside, of course, is the Napa Valley before (or after) agribusiness ruined it, but gee, we have to take our paradises where we find them.

The Dispossessed *is about an anarchist utopia, at least in part. So is* Always Coming Home. *Would you describe yourself as an anarchist (politically)?*
Politically, no; I vote, I'm a Democrat. But I find pacificist anarchist thought fascinating, stimulating, endlessly fruitful.

In your acknowledgements to Lavinia, *you praise your editor, Mike Kandel. Is this the same Kandel who writes hilariously weird SF?*
He has translated Stanislaw Lem and others, marvelously. If he's written SF himself he's successfully hidden it from me. I wouldn't put it past him. Michael? What have I been missing?

*I'm working on the cover copy for this book right now [*The Wild Girls*]. Is it okay if I call your piece on modesty "the single greatest thing ever written on the subject"?*
I think "the single finest, most perceptive, most gut-wrenchingly incandescent fucking piece of prose ever not written by somebody called Jonathan something" might be more precise.

Ezra Pound described poetry as "news that stays news." How do you see it? What poets do you read most often these days?
Lately I've been getting news again from old Robinson Jeffers. It isn't cheery but it's reliable.

In The Lathe of Heaven, *the first SF novel to take on (or even mention) global warming, the only big cities in Oregon are John Day and French Glen. Where the hell is French Glen?*
Did I spell it that way? It's one word: Frenchglen. It's in Harney County, in farthest southeast Oregon; pop. about twenty-five.

Do you ever get bad reviews? Was one ever helpful?
Yes. No.

This is my Jeopardy *item. The category is Mainstream Fiction. The answer is "One would hope." You provide the question.*
Erm?

One more, please. The category is Sitting Presidents. The answer is "One would hope not."
I'm really pretty good at Ghosts and Hangman.

What's your favorite gadget?
My MacBook Pro.

What's your writing discipline? Has it changed as you've gotten older? More successful?
I never had any discipline, I just really wanted to write when I wanted to write. So I can't say that it has gotten any more successful.

What's your favorite city and don't say Portland because it isn't really a city at all.
All right then, snob. Frenchglen.

My favorite writer (next to you, of course), R.A. Lafferty, once said that no writer has anything to say before age forty. He also once said that no writer has anything to say after forty. Do you agree?
I would never disagree with R.A. Lafferty.

In your pictures you seem to be laughing a lot. What's so funny?
Cf. A.E. Housman: "Mithridates, he died old."

Will you sign my baseball? It's for my daughter.
If you will sign my fencing foil.

"Rooms Full of Old Books Are Immortal Enough for Me"

Jonathan Lethem

What was it like to get the MacArthur "genius" award? What did it do for you?
I was in Maine when I got that news. The fateful call. A peninsula neighbor also got one that year, a guy studying lobster fishing science, crustacean reproductive patterns under climate change and so forth. A big hero to the lobster-dependent community. The next day the local newspaper, the *Ellsworth American*, had an above-the-fold story, "Area Man Wins Genius Award." It wasn't me they meant. That was good perspective.

A joke that I'm stealing from Colson Whitehead: it's much like being Charly from "Flowers for Algernon." You peak for a year or two, and then you go back to being an ordinary person. It's a long time ago, and it's generous of you to recall I was briefly a genius—which, by the way, is a word the MacArthur people are always trying to deny but that attaches itself to their fellowships in a persistent folkloric way.

Another joke, which is my own, is that they don't send you special MacArthur money that comes in a special MacArthur wallet and which you can only spend on esoteric genius things. I paid off a couple of people's college loans, got my credit card out of the red, took a pleasure trip to New Zealand, and then lived on the residue for a few years instead of teaching. That's to say, it was rent, food, and health care. The direct results were *Chronic City* and the essay "The Ecstasy of Influence," two of the better things I ever managed, in my own opinion.

You seem to periodically but somewhat dependably come back to detective and science fiction. Is this a salute or homage to genre roots, or is something more devious or serious at work?

I'm relieved you notice. Sometimes I see people breaking me into two halves, as if after *The Fortress of Solitude* I became somebody other than myself. It feels sad to see this; it suggests that those making that division are utterly incurious about the books that followed, which include a surreal apocalypse with space travel, a gothic horror novel with ESP, a detective novel with ecological themes, and a postcollapse pastoral. Not to show ingratitude to your generous question, but I'd even quibble with "roots" and certainly with "salute or homage," as if I'm off to one side, tipping my cap to these things that in fact nourish and constitute me. The work is fed by many roots, almost all located in the voracious reading of my teenage years and early twenties. This list won't be exhaustive, and I've dropped these names before, but Delany, Kafka, Dick, Greene, Highsmith, Kavan, L. Carroll, Le Guin, Chandler, C. Stead, Willeford, Baldwin, Murdoch, Borges, Lem, Ballard, DeLillo. My books are the *branches*. From the inside, my writing feels like one continuous exploration, not a sequence of tactics. The differences are in publishing context and in the reception, not what I'm doing when I sit down. This all sounds immodest as can be, so I should add that I'm fully aware that it's a ridiculous privilege to be able to speak of having a "reception." Compared to most artists of any kind, I've been showered with attention. I'm absurdly lucky.

You inherited the chair at Pomona College once held by the late David Foster Wallace. Did you ever know or meet him?
By weird chance one of my childhood friends from Brooklyn went to Amherst and knew him, so during our respective college years I was told, "there's this guy in my dorm who's a writer too and he's really smart and you guys are interested in similar things and you should meet him." Then he became DFW and I became a bookstore clerk. Some kids I knew in college were also publishing books years before I could even place a short story in a magazine. Later on, he and I knew some people in common, so I always imagined we'd say hello at some point and I could tell him the Amherst story, but no.

What is Creative Writing at Pomona? Who takes it and why? What do you provide?
Pomona's an undergraduate college, so I'm not teaching MFA students, as so many novelists end up doing. Instead, we're in the realm of a liberal arts

education, with creative writing as a feature of the "humanities." I'm enclosed in a highly varied English department, and if you work with me a lot, the most that can produce is a college diploma as an English major. This takes a lot of pressure off, happily. We're not a professional finishing school for either authors or creative writing instructors; we're studying literature and daring to try to think about it and try to make some at the same time. That's to say, it's a good conversation that involves a lot of reading. I think of myself as a teacher of reading, really, apart from providing a few tips on where the quote marks usually go in a paragraph that includes dialogue, and why you probably shouldn't let your characters gaze into mirrors and describe themselves at length. I teach the kind of reading that encompasses reading your own drafts and the drafts of others, but also examples of published work ranging from canonical things to the work of young writers who might be just a few years or months out ahead of your own aspirations. It's fun.

Your nonfiction is often as personal as your fiction or even more. Does the apparatus of fiction (plot, POV, etc.) propel or constrain you?
That's interesting. I suspect you're right. I don't find anything constraining in fiction, so it may be that when I'm romping in that infinite playground, I forget to find "myself" directly interesting. There are so many other things to focus on. Anyway, "myself" will usually crop up uninvited, so I don't have to worry about it. By contrast, in my essays I trip up on notions of authority or subjectivity or positionality—the problem of who-the-hell-is-it-who-is-having-these-opinions? So I begin reflecting on my own person as a form of preliminary grounding, for the reader and myself. And then I wander into reminiscence and end up writing a confessional essay as much as opining on the matter at hand.

Do you write as a job or when the muse strikes you? Any particular routine?
I like everything better when I'm writing—myself, the sunrise, the sunset, food. I don't mean writing incessantly, just routinely. Usually two or three hours is the maximum, and sometimes it's a lot less. I like being regularly attached to a project that excites me and returning to it most days, if not every day, to make contact with my own thinking, to extend the notions a bit further, to refine some sentences I wrote the day or week before to make them clearer or funnier

or to produce more meaning than they managed the first time. It's been life-habit for so long that I think of it as more or less consonant with being alive—to be writing something. I can no longer imagine being without it, though of course I know I might be robbed of it, as one can contemplate being robbed of a sense or a limb.

The routine? Mornings are good. They don't have to be early. Just whenever you get up, after the coffee, get to the desk. It's morning right now.

Your essay on plagiarism, "The Ecstasy of Influence," was (to me) as rightly contrarian as T.S. Eliot's "Tradition and the Individual Talent." Did you pitch that to Harper's *or was it their idea?*
I sat in a restaurant and pitched it to an editor named Luke Mitchell, who has pulled out of me several of my best and most-committed essays over the years. Then came almost two years of work; it was the dissertation I thought I'd never have to write when I dropped out of college.

When you dropped out of college in your sophomore year, you hit the road. I did the same. Seems a sophomore thing. What did you know about Berkeley that drew you, or did you just end up there?
I threw myself at Berkeley, as if at a dartboard, when I needed to be distant from the East Coast. I think the Bay Area destination carried a faint residue of a Beat Generation script that had gotten into my head—a whiff of countercultural freedom, the Free Speech Movement, and the like. It was the copious used bookstores that kept me there for ten years—and the friends and lovers I met on the staffs of used bookstores.

Your Jeopardy *question: I provide the answer, you provide the question. Answer: Heaven without immortality.*
See above. I don't believe in immortality, but the used bookstores that are my heaven are going to outlive me, and that feels good. When the writer Richard Price was asked whether The Novel was dead, he said, "The Novel will be at your funeral." Rooms full of old books are immortal enough for me.

Is Plot for you a mentor, a taskmaster, or a companion?

I tell my students that I think plot is a chimera. There's often talk of it as if it can be identified, or intentionally produced, but I think plot is more a term of praise, one that pretends it is a quantifiable thing: "I loved the plot!" What you can identify, and design, happens not on some overall "plot" level, but locally, page by page. Things like implication, velocity, and causality and surprise. Occurrences tumbling out of other occurrences, and piling up with a pleasing sense of implication and possibility, and in unexpected ways, and at an agreeable rate. You can't really talk about plot the way you can point to the composition in a painting or the melody in a song. It's just what it feels like when that other good stuff accumulates.

Fairly early in your career, you showed up at some of the Famous Writer shows, Yaddo and suchlike. What put you on their radar? Was that a thrill?
I sought it all out, promiscuously, as guided by my reading, and by my teenage fascination with the lives of authors. I wanted to be a Yaddo guest, and a guest of honor at an SF convention, and to visit foreign cities where I would sit on panels where we needed interpreters to understand one another, and to see my books put into weird leatherbound volumes, and to publish in underground zines and the *New Yorker*. I wanted to guest-edit "Year's Best" anthologies and help revive lost authors and write introductions to G.K. Chesterton and Anna Kavan and Walter Tevis; I wanted to interview musicians for *Rolling Stone*; I wanted to blurb books and judge prizes and collaborate with other writers; I wanted to write a Marvel comic book; I wanted to do one of the most obscure things an author can do, I think: finish a book another writer had left unfinished when they died. I did that with Don Carpenter. I did *all* of those things, which made me silly with joy even when it was boring. But most of those things only have to happen once. The simpler acts of reading and writing are what I want to do all the time.

Do you still collect books? Vinyl records?
I never quit accumulating books, and some of the pursuits within that accumulation are specific enough to call "collecting." For instance, I'm trying to put together a run of the first hundred Ace Doubles—I currently have twenty-six of the hundred, including an "Ace-1," which I can't help bragging about. I love

books so much I am forced also to love cardboard boxes and barns and attics and storage spaces—I'm headed over to one of the storage spaces after I finish writing this morning, only I'm afraid I can't remember the combination of the lock. I started accumulating vinyl records again after a two-decade pause where I accumulated CDs and MP3s instead. But none of these things go away—I still listen to the CDs and MP3s and the vinyl.

The poem seems one of the few literary forms you have not tried, at least onstage. How come? What poets do you read for fun?
What are you, a mind reader? I was just wanting to tell you about my first-ever poetry collection, *Horse with No Cake: Selected Poems and Lyrics*, which is about to come out from Another Sun Press. Buy it on their website. It only took me forty years to accumulate enough of the things for a 120-page volume—and half of that is song lyrics, from my collaborations with musicians. Every single one of them was written in rueful appreciation of how difficult it is, what a remarkable form of disciplined attention, to center one's writing self in poetic work continuously, or even on a regular basis. It's beyond me. Instead, these things were mostly written to occasions, as gifts or asides, or in assumed voices. Still, I'm proud that the book exists. I won't live long enough to follow it up.

My favorite poets to read when, as a teenager, I briefly believed I might really be a poet, were the New York school and some of their relations: Kenneth Koch, John Ashbery, James Schuyler, Eileen Myles, Ron Padgett. I also read Surrealist and Dada poetry because I was into everything Surrealist, the collages and paintings and films and feuds. Then in the Bay Area I fell in with some poets: Steve Benson, Ron Silliman, Gloria Frym, Owen Hill, Tom Clark, others. I like the company of poets the way I like the company of painters, and I read my friends.

Does your car have a pet name? I hope not.
A story: The first car I owned entirely on my own—a New York kid, I was a late driver—was a Toyota Corolla gifted to me by an ex's pitying parents. All the silver paint was scuffed off to reveal a dull matte metal color. It was pretty run down. I got a vanity license plate reading SQUALOR. (My friend Angus MacDonald had a vanity plate that said RADIO ON, from the Modern Lovers song—the best vanity

plate I think I'll ever see.) I drove SQUALOR around Berkeley and Oakland for three or four years. Once the cartoonist Daniel Clowes invited me to his home, and when I drove up in SQUALOR he exclaimed, "That's your car? I love that car!" Later on, my sister drove SQUALOR, which turned out to be an indomitable car, and then she gave it away, and someone used it as the getaway car in the robbery of a Carl's Jr. True story.

John Crowley once told me that the secret subtext of his work is always: this is a book. Well, okay. So, what's the secret subtext of yours?
Isn't Crowley's the subtext of *every* book? I'm always so envious of other writer's answers to these aphoristic questions. Like for instance, "Why do you write?" to which Thomas Berger said, "Because it isn't there," and Bernard Malamud said, "I would be too moved to say," each of which seems too perfect to hope to match. Maybe the subtext of my books is "Wouldn't it be interesting to be someone else? How can I best approximate it?" Maybe that isn't even the subtext, just the text.

What's the deal with the jukebox on your website? Are you trying to hitch a ride on rock?
Is rock going somewhere? It looks to me like it just sits there. I'll keep an eye on it in case you're right.

Seriously, the sequence of collaborations with musicians has been one of the most unlikely pleasures of writing life.

Were you surprised when Dylan won the Nobel Prize? Are you still?
The morning after the announcement, before I heard any reaction, I happened to be listening to Claudia Rankine talk live on the *Brian Lehrer Show* on WNYC. She'd been booked, obviously, before the Dylan Nobel thing and just happened to be a poet on the radio the morning the news dropped. Lehrer asked her what she thought, and Rankine said, "His words are in all our mouths." Holding on to this simple acknowledgement of what seems an obvious truth—that he changed the language—was useful to me once all the debate started about what constitutes literature. I get that it bugs people because he could be seen as not needing the thing any more than he needed his Oscar, and there are writers on

whom the award would have shone a spotlight. Maybe there should be more prizes, or fewer. I don't know.

The Arrest is set on a little Maine peninsula occupied by out-of-the-way, oddball types. Is there actually such a place?
Yes and no—but you knew that would be my answer, right? I'm "there" now, enjoying the sight of some wild turkeys walking past the window facing my desk. Here at the start of summer I've been being an oddball with my oddball friends for the past week—swimming in the ocean, playing pétanque, eating fish that my friend Sergei caught, moving books in and out of storage spaces, and dreaming of opening a used bookstore so I can hang out there with whoever walks in. I'm grateful this place exists. Then again, *The Arrest* is fundamentally an allegorical space, a rubber reality, projected into existence by the fictional notions that occupy it. A cartoon, if the word doesn't seem too much a demurral from serious intent. Most of my books are serious cartoons, set in places that may share names with real ones, or not, but which are only obliquely depictions of those places, and serve mainly as a proscenium for my clowns and tragedians. So, no. Tinderwick, from *The Arrest*, isn't here, it's *here*—assuming you can see me right now, pointing my forefinger at my forehead.

I believe this is my baseline mode. It defines my short stories, and each of my first five novels (up to and including *Motherless Brooklyn*). The exceptions are three longer books about outerborough New York City. First *Fortress of Solitude*, where I began to do some social history work—tentatively. I was trained as a visual artist and was a failure as a student otherwise, so my capacity for study and research was a muscle that developed slowly. In *Dissident Gardens* I got a bit more deliberate about it. That's fiction as social history. And the book I'm writing now goes there again. But *The Arrest* makes no claim as an authoritative depiction of Maine or the towns on this peninsula. Its seriousness is as a conjuration.

Ever been down the Gowanus Canal in a canoe? I have.
I'm no fan of black mayonnaise, which is how the toxic chemical gunk at the bottom of the Gowanus has been described. Canoes tip. I might tackle it in a diving bell.

Were you in New York on 9/11?

I was. I wrote about it directly for a couple of magazines but couldn't get the feeling on the page to any real satisfaction. I shouldn't have included those pieces in *The Ecstasy of Influence* collection. I did better when I treated it askew, under other names, in *Chronic City*. I began writing that in 2006, at which point I was able to see the experience less in isolation, more as a crescendo of intricate historical nightmares—stuff extending on invisible strings beyond the moment itself.

Ever miss Brooklyn? (My wife asked me to ask you.)

Missing Brooklyn is so deep and basic to me that, when I'm there, I miss missing it.

"Working the Wet End"
Ken MacLeod

Did you steal the idea for talking squids in outer space from Margaret Atwood? Or from the squids themselves?
As far as I know the only SF writers who have talking squids in outer space are Steve Baxter and myself. I like telling people that I'm responsible for fifty percent of what Margaret Atwood insists she doesn't write.

The idea came out of a pub lunch with Iain Banks in 1980. We started wondering how much of the UFO mythos we could crowbar into a story that made some kind of sense. The Greys were easy: they're so humanoid they are (in our view at the time, anyway) unlikely to have evolved anywhere but Earth, and they're reptilian, so we figured they were probably derived from bipedal dinosaurs. Since there's no trace of humanoid dinosaurs in the fossil record, they must have been taken *off* Earth, which gets us an uplift scenario. That was where the squids came in: the only invertebrates that show potential for intelligence are the cephalopods, so squids were a good candidate for uplift too. And that gave us an explanation of the cigar-shaped motherships, which were so common in the early 1950s and are now so sadly rare: they have to be that size to make room for the aquaria for giant squids to live in. And they have flashing lights on the outside because cephalopods communicate by changing the colour patterns on their skin.

See? It all makes sense!

You are an actual working scientist. Is that what drew you to SF, or did it happen the other way?
I'm not an actual working scientist. Here's the real story: It was SF that drew me to science, or at any rate made me want to be a scientist. Because I was no

good at math, I chose the least mathematical science, biology, and specialised in zoology, and within that in vertebrate zoology. This was such a useless specialty that I was the only one in my class who took it.

In choosing my postgraduate work, I made the mistake of thinking I could at least make use of my high school applied mechanics, and chose a project on the response of bones to mechanical loading. After a year and a half of my slow and intermittent research progress, my supervisors said they couldn't justify my funding. But they kindly continued to supervise my research, which I struggled on with in my spare time for years, and eventually got an MPhil degree and my name on a published paper out of. By this time I had a job as a programmer, and my wife and two young children were in my graduation photo.

One of your characters (Elizabeth, in the Engines of Light *trilogy) asserts, "It is possible to learn from the past." You don't really believe that, do you?*
Of course I do. "History is the trade secret of science fiction"—that quote's attributed to me, but I think I got it from Asimov. History is also the trade secret of politics. Successful politicians left and right read lots of it and learn from it. Heck, just reading Macaulay's *History of England* is a political education, and not just for those who share Macaulay's politics: it's centrally about a revolution, after all.

In your work, intelligence is widespread in the universe, but it's mostly not biological. Huh? Aren't you a biologist?
Well, not quite, as I've explained; and in fact the widespread intelligences in the *Engines of Light* books *are* biological. They're dominant because they actively prevent nonbiological intelligence from coming into existence. That's the only way you could have such a scenario, because nonbiological intelligence is so obviously better adapted to space.

Think about it. Which is likely to happen faster: the evolution by natural selection of a species with superhuman intelligence, or the development of machines that can think faster than us? My bet would be on the machines. Even if you bring in genetic engineering, all that gets you is a given higher level of intelligence, which you can only improve by further genetic engineering. With artificial intelligence, you can in principle get improved performance just by increasing the clock speed or adding hardware, and beyond that you can upgrade the software or make it self-upgrading. That raises the prospect of runaway intelligence increase, which leaves biological mechanisms and reproduction in the dust.

This is of course Vernor Vinge's Singularity thesis, which—if human-equivalent AI is possible at all, and perhaps even if it's not—has an awful logic to it.

Flying saucers: do they come from Outer Space or Genre History?
Disc-shaped flying machines, and spindly humanoids with big bald heads, were imagined and illustrated in SF magazines in the 1930s, so in that sense they do come from genre history. The story that started the modern flying saucer craze, Kenneth Arnold's 1947 sighting, was of more or less wing-shaped flying objects, which he described as moving like saucers skipped across water. Somehow that got garbled to "flying saucers," perhaps because of the images from the pulps, and the hare was off and running. The whole mythos that has evolved since then is a mixture of misidentification, disinformation, urban legend, rumour, lies, hoaxes, honest mistakes, and so on, and it has interacted with SF all along. It would be interesting to trace these interactions and the mutual feedback between SF and UFO reports.

But having said that, the image of a silvery disc levitating above the landscape is immensely resonant, like the dreams we have of flying, and I suspect this is what gives the UFO mythos its power to fascinate.

Banks, Burns, Doctorow, Clarke, Stevenson (R.L. not Neal), Robson, Robinson: each in a sentence, please.
Iain Banks is my oldest friend, and one of the very few writers who can do both SF and literary fiction equally well, or indeed at all. Rabbie Burns is an eruption of freethinking, folk tradition, love, sex, and sheer poetry against a Kirk that tried to smother them all under a wet blanket of guilt. Cory Doctorow is a professional agitator who writes science fiction in his copious spare time (at least twenty minutes a day), and a dangerous man who should be watched. Arthur C. Clarke is unfashionable and underrated today but some of his work will be read hundreds of years from now, and he was second only to Asimov among the few public intellectuals SF has produced. Robert Louis Stevenson wrote (among many other things) adventure stories of great psychological subtlety

and insight. Justina Robson is a friend, so I can't be objective, but I find her a writer of astonishing range, power, and variety. Kim Stanley Robinson—well, there's the objectivity problem again—is one of the most serious SF writers, in the sense that he really means it: he isn't just playing with cool ideas but putting something on the line.

What is lablit? What does it mean to "work the wet end" of something?
Lablit is fiction about scientists—not necessarily or even usually science fiction, but fiction that has scientists as central characters and shows realistically what scientific work is like. I don't know where I got "work the wet end" from, but I meant practical lab or medical work as opposed to administration. I guess it could be applied to literature as well.

Publishing being the dry end?
You said that, not me.

Would you describe Night Sessions *as a police procedural or an ecclesiastical thriller?*
Both. It's a police procedural set in a possible future in which religion has been officially marginalised, and religious terrorism suddenly pops up from an unexpected quarter. But perhaps not so unexpected if you know your Scottish ecclesiastical history!

How come so many UK leftists are Trots?
Short answer: because Trotskyists in Britain moved fast on the CP's crisis in the 1950s, and moved with the times in the 1960s.

Long answer: in the 1960s in a lot of countries semimass currents arose to the left of the official Communist Parties. In some countries, including the United States and West Germany, most of the radicals who wanted to be revolutionaries became some kind of Maoists. In others, including the UK and France, much the same kind of people became Trotskyists. I think part of the explanation goes back to the 1950s, and especially the aftermath of 1956 and the Soviet intervention in Hungary.

The crisis of the Communist Party of Great Britain gave rise to a very serious opposition around a magazine called *The New Reasoner*, involving academics and people with real labour movement roots, which became what's now called the Old New Left. Some of these people were very open to Trotsky's arguments, and none of them were interested in adopting a new personality cult or clinging to the old one.

The funny thing is that in the United States the Trotskyists were much better organised than in Britain. For one thing, they were all in one party, the Socialist Workers Party (except for the Shachtmanites, who were busy becoming social democrats). In Britain they were all in one party too, but it was the Labour Party, and they were split into at least three mutually hostile groups. But the largest group was able to intervene in the crisis of the CP and rip off a couple of hundred serious people: intellectuals and trade unionists. Then they picked up more young people from the first wave of antinuclear activism—the Aldermaston marches and all that. They proceeded to lose or burn out the best of them, largely because their leader, Gerry Healy, was a thug as well as an ultraleft. The regime in Healy's group was far worse than anything anyone had experienced in the CPGB. Say what you like about Harry Pollitt (the CP's general secretary until 1956) he never thumped another communist, or threw anyone down the stairs. But other Trot groups were there to pick up people from the heap at the bottom of Healy's stairwell. What's worrying, actually, is how many went back up the stairs.

In the United States, the SWP fumbled the CPUSA's crisis, saw the CP left wing walk past them and into the increasingly ultra-left Progressive Labor, and followed up by failing to dive into the civil rights struggle. The mass movement they did dive into was the Vietnam antiwar movement, and even there they found themselves to the right of the young radicals who wanted to wave Vietcong flags. They came across as a very staid, conservative organization, rather like the CPUSA itself, and missed the 1960s. It took some doing at the time for a revolutionary organization to recruit almost no one out of SDS, but the SWP managed it.

Two of the British Trotskyist groups of the 1960s, the International Socialists and the International Marxist Group, were very much more open to the so-called counterculture. They didn't frown on kids with long hair who smoked dope. They waved their own Vietcong flags. They shifted farther and faster than the US SWP did on gay liberation, as it was then called. They had plenty of militant working-class struggles to pitch into, which the SWP didn't to the same extent (and it missed out on the ones it did have).

So Britain is infested with ex-Trots instead of with ex-Maoists, which is a small mercy.

What kind of car do you drive? I ask this of everyone.
A Mazda 2. I abandoned my Bentley when it ran out of peat.

Old-school tools like socket wrenches and WD40 show up in your Futures. Is this a shameless nod to the Steampunk crowd?
No. I don't know enough about Steampunk as a genre, and what I do know doesn't attract me much. If people want to dress up as Victorians, that's fine by me, but as a genre it seems backward-looking—indeed, that's its whole point. We can do better than that.

What is Semana Negra and why is it important?
Semana Negra in Gijón, Asturias, is an annual literary festival with a crowded and raucous funfair attached, complete with Ferris wheel. Its focus is on crime fiction, or "black novels" as they're called in Spain, with a periphery of attention to comics, westerns, horror, fantasy and science fiction. Hundreds of thousands go to the funfair, and thousands go to the book and film festival off in a corner of it.

Partly because crime writers in the Spanish state and in the wider Spanish-speaking world tend to be left-wing, the event has become part of the class struggle in the region. This July, my wife and I rode from Madrid to Gijón on *el Tren Negro*—the Black Train, which they hire every year to transport dozens of writers and journalists to the festival. We stopped in Mieres, a coal-mining town in the mountains of Asturias, where we were greeted by the mayor and a delegation of striking miners and taken on procession through the town for lunch. The train was delayed because striking miners in the adjacent province had blocked the track; it was a very bitter and militant strike. When we arrived at Gijón a brass band at the station played the "Internationale" as we climbed on the bus. You could get used to this sort of thing!

What is a Big Bad Book? Do you intend to write one someday?
Big and Bad are two separate ambitions. I intend to write at least one and hopefully more big books. One is a space opera that uses as many Golden Age tropes—telepathy, FTL, nearby aliens, sunken continents—as I can rationalise by setting it in the deep future of the universe. My mental working title for it is *Star Princesses of the Lost Galaxy*. The other is a long novel, *Dark Queen's Day*, an exercise in dark lord revisionism set after the next Ice Age. I've been tinkering with plans for that, off and on, for years.

The Bad Book idea comes out of a hankering to write a nonfiction bestseller that's not terribly rigorous intellectually—a high standard, but one I believe I could strive for, frankly. I'm thinking along the lines of a mashup of *Chariots of the Gods?* and *The Shock Doctrine*. This is in lieu of a pension plan, you understand, so I have abandoned all scruples and I'm wide open to suggestions.

You sometimes call yourself a Libertarian. Does that mean you take long drives with Ron Paul in his Oldsmobile?
Yeah, me and the Doc, we're like *that*—no. I respect his antiwar stand, but that's all. And I don't call myself a Libertarian, in the sense of a supporter of the Libertarian Party or anything like that. My usual handwave for my position is "hard-left libertarian" but in practice I just vote Labour.

Steve Jobs once told me that Glasgow was the Silicon Valley of the eighteenth century. What's it like today?
Postindustrial, reinventing itself as a tourist attraction, intellectual hub, and shopping centre, with a lot of poverty and long-term unemployment alongside some real development. Silicon Glen with Clearances.

Like many writers (like myself) you moved mothlike from the provinces to the capital. What was that like for you?
The capital, London, was stimulating but overwhelming. I brought to it a stupid provincial left-wing chauvinism about how much more radical the Scots were, and really underestimated how in outer West London I was living in an area with a socialist and trade union history and—in the 1970s—continuing strength that we can only look back on now with amazement. I met my wife

there, though funnily enough she grew up not far from me and knew lots of people I knew. Our children's early years were in Finsbury Park, which wasn't a bad place for kids to encounter the world.

Then way back in 1989 my wife and I got a hankering to move back to Scotland.

A bheil Gàidhlig agaibh?
No, sadly. My parents were both native speakers but they didn't speak Gaelic in the home, in a more or less conscious decision to have us grow up speaking English.

In a book like The Star Fraction *(or* Cosmonaut Keep*), are you planting a row of novels, or do they reseed themselves? How far ahead do you plan?*
With *The Star Fraction* I didn't even plan the book when I started it, let alone have sequels in mind. *Cosmonaut Keep*, however, was definitely planned from the beginning as the start of a series. I didn't plan for it to end up as a trilogy, but by the time I started *Engine City* I was losing my own suspension of disbelief, and decided to wrap it up as decisively and entertainingly as I could.

Are there any other serious writers in Edinburgh besides you and Rowling?
Some few. There's Iain Banks, Charlie Stross, Andrew J. Wilson and Hannu Rajaniemi just in SF, and Ian Rankin, Ron Binns, Regi Claire, Andrew Greig, Lesley Glaister, Brian McCabe, just to name some mainstream novelists and poets in my own circle of friends (and I've probably missed someone and will be dead embarrassed if he or she reads this and notices). Edinburgh's hooching with serious writers, and there are more coming up.

I love the title of your blog, The Early Days of a Better Nation. *What does it mean?*
It comes from Alasdair Gray's motto, "Work as if you lived in the early days of a better nation." It means what it says!

Favorite single malt? (This is for Stan Robinson)
Jura 16 Year Old is my current favourite, and Highland Park and Talisker are both very acceptable.

Who is Hans Moravec? Is he important and why?
Hans Moravec is a roboticist and AI guru who predicted in 2009: "By 2010 we will see mobile robots as big as people but with cognitive abilities similar in many respects to those of a lizard. The machines will be capable of carrying out simple chores, such as vacuuming, dusting, delivering packages and taking out the garbage" (https://www.scientificamerican.com/article/rise-of-the-robots).

To which I say: "What?" I mean, has this guy ever *seen* a lizard? But to me Moravec is important because he mapped out the path from robots to the Singularity and then to the Simulation Hypothesis, which is basically that the Singularity has already happened and we're living in a virtual reality created by our ancestors' creations. I plundered that whole line of argument for the Fall Revolution books and for *The Restoration Game*. I don't believe it for a second.

What is the most interesting difference between SF in the USA and in the UK? The least?
The most interesting difference is in the origins of each tradition's acquaintance with evolution, and how that has affected everything since. In Britain, we had H.G. Wells, who learned his evolutionary biology directly from Thomas Huxley. In the United States, I don't know who the equivalent of Wells was, but whoever it was seems to have picked evolution up from some social Darwinist like William Graham Sumner. This is like the difference between getting the gospel from Saint Paul and getting it from Norman Vincent Peale. To this day, British SF writers see evolution as a vast pitiless process that will eventually doom humanity, and US SF writers tend to see it as a chirpy homily to self-reliance. "Think of it as evolution in action."—Well, actually, they don't!

The least interesting difference, in my judgment, is spelling.

You recently took a position teaching writing. Is that a promotion?
I'm not exactly teaching writing—that's what the course tutors do. As writer in residence for the MA creative writing course at Edinburgh Napier University, my job is to advise the students about writing and just be there to talk to. I'm not even expected to read their work! I definitely see it as a promotion, and I love doing it.

In your works you seem not so much constructing as punching your way out of an already incredibly rich and detailed future. True or false?
False, I'm afraid. I have to construct my detailed futures quite painfully, though nothing like as painfully as I construct my plots and even storylines. World-building is easy; stories are hard.

What's next?
A novel provisionally titled *Descent*, which is at the moment in that very stage of painful construction that I've just mentioned. As usual I've planned it, made lots of notes, got excited, plunged into writing it, got about thirteen thousand words in and found I hadn't planned it enough. I always tell myself I won't do this again, and every time, I do.

What US writer would you most like to have a drink with, besides me?
Howard Waldrop.

I know that Dr. Johnson made it to the Hebrides, with the assistance of Boswell and a donkey. Did he get as far as Stornoway?
Was that Roswell or Boswell? I guess the donkey's a clue. I haven't read the book, but I have it somewhere and I intend to at least skim it.

Ever collaborate?
No. Except on the occasional interview.

Your books are often, and quite correctly, praised for their humor. Say something funny.
I have Ostalgia for the Free World.

"Put Your Twist in the Middle"
Nick Mamatas

You are a first-generation Greek American. Did your parents (or an old granny) speak Greek at home? Or was it already fading when you came along?
Greek is my father's native language, and my mother is a fluent Greek American who became more fluent after marrying my father. I also grew up around grandparents and great-grandparents and many aunts, uncles, cousins who all spoke Greek. My own Greek is pretty marginal, as my folks focused on my father mastering English when my sister and I were young.

I spent a lot of time when I was young in a little ethnic enclave on Long Island of not just Greek Americans but Ikarian Americans, from the small island of Ikaria; the dialect and accent are a bit weird. A rough analogue would be Quaker talk with a Cajun accent, though of course all the slang and idiomatic expressions are frozen in the 1950s–1960s as well.

I thought most Greeks were from Queens. But you grew up in Brooklyn and Long Island. Explain.
Port Jefferson used to be a working port, and a lot of Greeks are sailors, so boom. Once somebody built a church, the community was cemented. There was a big Greek community in Bay Ridge, Brooklyn, but I grew up in Bensonhurst when it was primarily Italian American. Think *Saturday Night Fever*.

A lot of your SF is satirical. I'm thinking of The People's Republic of Everything *and* The Nickronomicon. *Does that mean you think SF is funny?*
Not as funny as it should be! I was appalled to find out that Heinlein and the rest weren't necessarily being satirical or just running devastating thought experiments, but they really believed (or at least largely believed) the suggestions

their books seemed to make about human nature and how to properly reorder society. Science fiction is generally much better when you decide the authors mean the opposite of what they say.

I came to SF through the back door—*Hitchhiker's Guide*; Kit Reed, whose *Other Stories and the Attack of the Giant Baby* was the first book I ever bought with my own money as the cover looked very funny; *Omni* magazine (where I'd read Howard Waldrop stories, and Robert Silverberg's cute "Amanda and the Alien," plus all the cyberpunk I could eat); then Ellison, and so on.

Having said all that, nothing is worse than humorous science fiction and fantasy. Puns and pastiche—it's all pretty exhausting. Stories are funny when the characters crack a joke, not when they're named Sprazzlefork McAirlift or whatever.

What were you doing on 9/11?
I was woken up by a phone call from a friend who knew I was planning to go to the Borders bookstore in the basement of the World Trade Center that morning to pick up a copy of *In These Times*, in which I'd placed a short article about snitch lines kids could call to report their fellow students as potential school shooters (i.e., weirdos and nerds). She told me, "Don't go. A plane hit the towers." I thought to myself, *Wow, did the black bloc go crazy?*, and then the second plane hit. I then met a bunch of people at a twenty-four-hour diner (Greek, of course, and it was the only place that dared to stay open). We talked about martial law and what was happening and waited for word from my roommate, who worked in the Financial District. He lived only because he had spent the night playing Dungeons and Dragons at his friend's house on the Upper West Side. Then the phones started working again, so I called my mother. She reported seeing someone on the side of the road holding a sign reading "DROP THE BOMB TODAY! GO USA!" Then I started looking for the first antiwar protest or vigil I could join.

I'm one of a long string of adjuncts (Shawna McCarthy, Alice Turner) who taught Writing Science Fiction at the New School in New York. You went to school there, but we never ran into you. Explain.
Aha! I went to the New School for media studies, not creative writing, in the early 1990s. Though I always wanted to be a writer, I took a long side road into

film and video, and worked for the New School as a technical associate in charge of their video equipment while also picking up freelance work as a best boy and gaffer on film sets.

I soon realized that I'd never have a grandparent rich enough to bankroll a film of my own or old enough to drop dead and leave me that money. (I lost my last grandparent in 2019—Ikarian people are very long-lived; the island is one of those famous "blue zones.")

I didn't like getting up early to make the morning light. I knew a bit about the electrician business thanks to my father but didn't want to attempt to electrocute myself five times a day. So writing it was.

You've worked as an editor with Clarkesworld *among others, then Haikasoru, a Japanese publisher. How'd that come about? How's your Japanese?*
I don't speak a word of Japanese! I applied for the job at VIZ, which included Haikasoru and also editing Studio Ghibli–related art and picture books and other nonmanga titles, when my friend sent me a link to the application. I think VIZ was impressed that *Clarkesworld* had been nominated for a Hugo Award, and that I was not a manga/anime fanboy but rather someone well integrated into the science fiction field and scene. During the initial phone interview they asked if I liked manga and anime and I said, "Pfft, no!" It felt like a mistake even as the utterance left my mouth, but it was the right thing to say, as it turns out. I was hired to be an "English-language brain" for my Japanese managers, basically.

What drew you to SF, the science or the fiction?
Both. I don't write hard SF but I enjoy reading it. Haikasoru published more hard SF than was probably strictly healthy because I liked it so much. Engineering and the limits of physics are rife with dramatic potential. The problem is that economics is the flimsiest of social sciences and has the highest level of physics envy, thus all sorts of "hard SF" is nonsense that goes like this: "Entropy exists, therefore vote Ron Paul!"

I always ask interviewees what kind of car they drive. (It's in my contract.) But you claim not to drive at all. So what kind of skateboard do you ride?

No skateboard either. Nor a bicycle. My current ride is a pair of Doc Martens. Shoes, not boots. I usually walk four to six miles a day between commuting, errands, and such.

You taught writing in Berkeley. Fabulist Fiction. What can you teach about writing? What must you unteach?
Lots! Teaching is unteaching—you have to unteach television to teach prose. Most of it is basic: don't go backward, don't start with a character sitting alone and thinking about some interesting thing; start with the interesting thing. Your first thought about anything—character, dialogue—is probably something you heard or saw on TV as a child. Only your third or subsequent thoughts are truly yours. Don't type the word "Bang!" when a gun goes off. A premise is not a story. Put your twist in the middle, not the end. That sort of thing.

What do you mean when you say you write SF in a literary mode? I think I know exactly what you mean. Am I wrong?
I think about sentences and paragraphs a lot. I don't think of the elements of fiction—plot, character, setting, and so on—as a bunch of pistons in an engine that must all fire equally. More like a photograph with some parts in sharp focus and some less so, which is an attribute of all good photographs.

Dr. Johnson famously said that "only a fool writes for anything other than money." Or something like that. Anyway, were you ever one such?
Nope! Indeed, what brought me here is flipping through a copy of *Writer's Market* twenty-three years ago and seeing that literary journals paid in copies and horror and fantasy magazines paid in pennies.

One sentence on each, please: Kathy Acker, S.T. Joshi, Howard Waldrop.
Acker: a unique writer, which is extremely difficult to be in general and even harder when one writes one's influences so transparently (e.g., the plagiarisms). S.T. Joshi: a brilliant obsessive who unfortunately took a look at every school of literary criticism to emerge in the past seventy years and said, "No way, I'm in charge!" Howard Waldrop: the greatest short story writer (quickly Googles) alive. Whew! [Waldrop died in 2024. —Ed.]

Howard apparently lives for fishing. Do you fish?
I used to. My relatives fished a lot, but at a time when the Long Island Sound was being poisoned by all the toilets in Manhattan, so we were never very successful. I wrote an essay about it, "Unsound," which appeared in the anthology of fishing essays *Taut Lines*. I don't think I've fished in any way since 1994, when I was in Greece, in a motorboat on the way to see some relatives, and my uncle handed me a net. Didn't catch anything. We were going too fast, but we might have gotten lucky, so it was worth a shot.

Lovecraft seems to be an obsession of yours. Or is he an enthusiasm? What did you think when Lovecraft's image was abandoned by the World Fantasy Awards?
Definitely an enthusiasm rather than an obsession. I've met some pretty obsessed people and I'm not them.

I was in favor of the statuette being changed. I'd never thought it would be upsetting, but that's white privilege for you. It wasn't till Nnedi Okorafor raised an objection to the statue that I realized how awful getting one could be. If an award doesn't please its winners, then the award must change. I suggested that the Lovecraft bust be replaced by a statuette of a chimera, as fantasy can be a lot of things, and I recall that Jo Walton and some other big wheels thought it a good idea. In the end, the World Fantasy people went with a tree, and frankly it's ridiculous-looking and there is nothing *less* fantastical than a tree. But at least trees aren't racist.

According to the internet, you've published a volume of poetry. Cthulhu *something or other. How come I've never heard of it?*
Cthulhu Senryu came out of the signed limited edition of my first novel, the Kerouac/Lovecraft mashup *Move Under Ground*. I wrote an original senryu—a short topical poem form a bit like a haiku but with no need for a nature image and some need for humor or a comment on human nature—for each of the one hundred copies. Then they were collected into a little chapbook which was, at one, point, the number-two best-selling poetry collection on Amazon's Japanese website. You've never heard of it because it's humorous Lovecraftian verse. Why would anyone want to hear about that?

Do you read poetry for fun? I do. You should too.
I listen to it for fun. I particularly like it when people whisper poems on YouTube. "ASMR poetry" is probably my most frequent search string.

You claim to have taken the last typing class in your high school. Did it jump-start your career?
It did not. I actually did poorly in class, and when I got to college and found my way to the computer lab, where I spent hours a day on TinyMUDs, I learned to type with two fingers. Later, when I moved to the city and took a temp agency test, they'd never seen anyone do over one hundred words per minute with the hunt-and-peck method. But that only got me two days of office work.

What or who are Otherkin?
Otherkin are people who believe that their souls are those of mythological creatures: elves, dragons, and the like. Many of them seem to be either occultists or people with a dissociative identity disorder, but they all found one another and formed online communities. I interviewed several and wrote the first major article about them, for the *Village Voice*. I also started following several blogs written by Otherkin via Livejournal. When 9/11 hit, it was interesting to see how many people who on September 10 claimed to be nonhuman and sometimes non-Terran were suddenly proud Americans posting photos of crying eagles. Since then the phenomenon has gotten a bit sillier—otakukin are people who believe themselves to have the souls of this or that character from anime, for example.

My Jeopardy *question: I provide the answer, you the question. A: Voodoo dolls.*
Q: What is something that would probably be interesting to contemplate if it were possible to chip through four hundred years of racism and see it clearly, as through the eyes of a believer.

You have a serious profile in martial arts—Chen-style tai chi or some such. Does that mean you want your enemies to fear you?
I don't want any enemies, even though I guess I've created a few.
    Chen-style tai chi is a pretty good stand-up martial art that mixes wrestling (mostly joint locks, some throws) and dirty boxing if you train it right, but

almost nobody trains it right thanks to Mao suppressing martial arts during the Cultural Revolution. By sheer happenstance, I found a couple of people who have the real stuff, and I've used it against, for example, judo players in a tournament setting with some effectiveness. A fellow student of my teacher ended up spending seven months in a Milanese prison due to bad luck and used it several times in pretty harsh circumstances, so it works. It also cleared up my chronic bronchial infections and keeps me from stepping on my kid's Lego bricks.

You had a pretty good run in the term paper biz. Did you spend time studying the form or just wing it?
Well, I went to school myself, so I'd written a few. But no, I mostly wanged it. It helped that I was already a formalist and so was interested in and primed to see structures over content, and I could thus write about pretty much anything that didn't require original lab or field research.

You were already a working writer when you went for an MFA. How come?
Pure ignorance. I didn't come from a family that went to school so had no idea how school worked or how teaching worked. I got an MFA because I looked at ads for teaching faculty and they often said that applicants need to have published "a book." I had a few! So if I got an MFA, I could go teach at a university and have an easy life. I chose Western Connecticut State University because David Hartwell was on the board, so I figured it would be genre fiction friendly; because the program was low-residency, so no need to alter my life; and because the program insisted students write both creative work and practical work—so I'd just keep writing my usual fiction (creative) and articles/essays (practical) and get a degree for it. Well, once I got to my first residency, I read faculty member Kass Fleisher's memoir *Talking out of School*, which is about her own struggles with academe. One line that jumped out at me was something like, "Nobody tells you that you can only teach at schools one tier below the one where you got your degree." Well, as a then-new state-run low-res MFA program, WestConn was the lowest, and nobody told me how it worked till I got there either!

So I teach at WestConn occasionally.

Ever try comix? Any luck with movies?

Yup! I wrote a couple small comics, and a graphic novel for VIZ when I worked there for *All You Need Is Kill*, which is the novel on which the film *Edge of Tomorrow* is based. There was also a manga adaptation of the novel, which blew my Western attempt out of the water. Whoops! I was also the English-language adapter of Junji Ito's *Frankenstein* manga, which won an Eisner Award.

My short novel *Under My Roof* was optioned by a director of TV commercials, and I wrote the first and third drafts of the script. When we were pitching the book itself around in the old days, one of the Big Five publishers said to my agent, "Instead of a nuclear bomb, couldn't the kid have a girlfriend?" By the sixth draft of the film script, written by the director's wife, the kid had a girlfriend. By the seventh draft, that girlfriend was gone. They even shot several minutes of the film, so the option was realized and I got a payout. But no more footage was shot, and the director stopped answering my emails years ago.

So, sure, I'm luckier than 99 percent of all the daydreamers out there, and 95 percent of all the writers! No movie, though.

Most SF writers aspire to be a presenter at the Academy Awards someday. What are your chances?
Slim, but not none.

Around the turn of the century you wrote a number of articles for the Village Voice. *Do you ever get sentimental about New York?*
Yes, but only between visits. Giuliani and Bloomberg really ruined that town. Even the Bowery has been gentrified after three hundred years of resistance. I get sentimental about the 1990s, not about New York. Of course, now I live in the Bay Area, which is like a young adult novel dystopia. You're either a zillionaire with cosmic technological powers or a bad week away from being homeless.

You said it, Nick.

"Get the Music Right"
Michael Moorcock

Why Texas?
I was on the run. Looking for some fresh mythology.

You have played a central role in science fiction since the editorship of New Worlds magazine in the 1960s. How has that role changed from then to now?
I suppose I was more of a gadfly in those days where SF was concerned. I'd read almost none of the so-called Golden Age (1950s) SF. I bought a long run of *Astounding* when I became editor of *New Worlds* because I thought I ought to look at it, and found most of it dull and unreadable. This was also the experience of J. G. Ballard and others who had expected far more of American SF than it actually delivered (apart from a relatively small amount found mostly in *Galaxy*).

American 1960s "New Wave" was about improving the quality of SF, but we Brits were less interested in that than we were in using SF methodology to look at the contemporary world. SF magazines were the only ones that liked our ideas, but we had to provide rationalizations to those stories, more or less. Explication dulled down the vision.

Fritz Leiber, whom I greatly admired, told me that he and several of his contemporaries like Bloch and Kuttner had the same problem in their day. So you'd write, say, an absurdist story but you could only sell it if you added: "On Mars . . ." or "In the future . . ." and then stuck in a boring rationalization.

Anyway, we could only really publish in the SF magazines.

But we also felt contemporary fiction was anaemic and had lost the momentum modernism had given it. Most fiction we saw had no way it could usefully confront modern concerns—the H-bomb, computers, engineering and communications advances, space travel—not to mention changing social conventions and consequently language, politics, warfare, the altered psyche in the face of so much novelty of experience.

Almost all the literary fiction we read was actually retrospective (Durrell, Heller, Roth, or Bellow) or only pretending to tackle contemporary issues in a novel way (Selby, B.S. Johnson, the Beats, and others who saw themselves as the most interesting subject matter).

The reason we liked William Burroughs (*Naked Lunch*) was because his language focused on modern times and drew much of its vitality from modern idiom. We were inspired by him and Borges rather than influenced by them.

Many of our heroes (French existentialists, *nouvelle vague* movies) read SF and the *Galaxy* writers in particular (Bester, Dick, Sheckley, Pohl and Kornbluth, and, of course, Bradbury). In the 1950s there was far more acceptance of American SF in European intellectual circles than in the United States itself, where that retrospective tone spells "literature" to the *New Yorker* reader and in my view is the bane of American fiction, especially when linked to regionalism/provincialism.

Emerging from World War II into Austerity Britain, it was easy for us to see *1984* all around us. The three *New Worlds* writers generally linked in those days (and I was even then more writer than editor) were myself, Ballard, and Brian Aldiss. I'd come out of the London Blitz, Ballard from the Japanese civilian prison camps, and Aldiss from the war in Malaya, and we all had reason to welcome the A-bomb, perceiving it with far more ambiguity than most.

Post-1946 modernity was a bit on the grim side, but we felt that as writers we'd been given an amazing box of tools, an array of subjects never before available to literature, and we used those tools and subjects in ways that tended to celebrate postwar experience rather than denigrate it.

Our tastes in SF were often different. Brian liked *Astounding*, while I just couldn't read it. Ballard liked Bradbury. I preferred good pulp like Brackett and Bester. Richard Hamilton, the pop artist, thought all three of us were damaging the kind of stuff he liked. He'd used Robby the Robot at his first important exhibition at the Whitechapel Gallery.

I couldn't continue today to have the role I had then, because what we hoped would happen *has* happened. SF methods and subjects are now incorporated into modern fiction in order to deal with modern matters. Nostalgia is largely the preserve of fantasy and so-called Steampunk. (I suggested in a recent review that it really should be called Steam Opera since it has so many lords and ladies in it.)

Anyway: Then my role was to attack the old and celebrate the new. Now my role is to be careful not to discourage new writers. In my old age I carry a burden, if you like, of gravitas! This makes me a kinder critic.

An Elric film has been in the works (or not) for years. What's the current status? Any other Hollywood interest?
The Weitz brothers and Universal had Elric under option for some time, but I have no idea what's happening now. Michael Bassett, the English director who made *Solomon Kane*, is now interested. I've corresponded with him a bit, but to be honest, I don't much care about movies and tend to show little interest when I'm approached. I suspect Bassett would be a good choice, though.

You started out writing for comics, then dropped it until the mid-1990s (and Multiverse). *Do you still like the form? Why?*
I wrote a lot of commercial comics for Fleetway as a kid, but by the 1960s I'd had enough of what I regarded as a primitive medium. I had problems with the low-level racism/stereotyping prevalent at the time and found myself at odds with my bosses—refusing to write World War II comics, for instance. I wrote a bit of picture-journalism attacking what I saw as the trend of grown-ups to elevate juvenile forms, (especially in France) such as *Barbarella*.

Of course, I'd dusted off my old comic skills to write the Jerry Cornelius material for *International Times* in the late 1960s and early '70s, and I'd done a Hawkwind strip with Jim Cawthorn for *FRENDZ*, another underground newspaper. I did quite a lot with the underground in the 1960s and '70s.

Then along came Alan Moore, and I saw that it was possible to use comics in a fun, adult way in a commercial environment—as long as you had a good collaborator, as I did. By then I was friends with Alan, and you could say it was his example, as well as meeting a bunch of very bright kids at the San Diego Comic Convention, that made me want to get back into the medium.

So when I was asked to do a comic for DC I decided to try something ambitious, running three main stories at the same time and having them link up at the end.

That was *Michael Moorcock's Multiverse* in which I developed my ideas about a possible multiverse in which context determined identity, utilizing some Chaos Theory and Mandelbrotian notions of self-similarity.

I really like to carry fairly complex ideas in comics or, say, in the Doctor Who novel I'm just now finishing. Maybe to stop myself taking such notions too seriously. The clockwork multiverse.

Have you adapted other people's work for comics?
Well, only if you count Hal Foster. I "translated" the Spanish version of his Tarzan script back into English, mostly by guesswork, during my first publishing job on *Tarzan Adventures*. Oh, and I also did a two-part Tom Strong (Alan Moore's character).

You used to listen to the Grateful Dead while writing. Who do you listen to now, if anyone?
Grateful Dead. Messiaen. Mozart. Dylan. Mahler. John Prine. New Riders. John Fogerty. Ravel. Schoenberg. Ives. Chet Baker. Vaughan Williams. Elgar. Grateful Dead. Robert Johnson. Howlin' Wolf. Glenn Miller. Noël Coward. Beatles. Gus Elen. Grateful Dead. Next question.

That last one's not a group; it's an exit strategy.

In one of your novels (I forget which one), Charon, ferryman of the River Styx, explains and justifies himself by saying, "It's a steady job." Have you ever regretted not having a steady nine-to-fiver?
I started out doing nine-to-five jobs—messenger for a shipping company at fifteen, "junior consultant" (office boy) for a firm of management consultants, and editorial jobs (*Tarzan Adventures, Sexton Blake Library, Current Topics*). I've never regretted it. I'd hate to do it again.

Ever heard of writer's block? How do you deal with it? Or do you ever have to?

I've heard of it. Never really had it. My answer is to go into a different character, scene, etc. If you determine your scheme first, you usually know what's supposed to go where and when. Structure informs plot elements. Get the "music" right, too: what you hear in your mind. I tried to talk about some of this in *Death Is No Obstacle*, the interview I did with Colin Greenland in the 1990s.

Where the hell is the Multiverse? Are there entrances? What about exits?
It's everywhere. We're in it. No way in. No way out. No centre and near-infinite centres. Just points of entrance through the Second Ether. I first mentioned it in "The Sundered Worlds" in *SF Adventures*, 1962. Black Holes, but I didn't call them that. I don't like too much explication generally, but I've done quite a bit in my Doctor Who novel due out in October 2010.

Have you had run-ins with censorship? Or is SF too far under the literary radar? (I liked your comment about Bradbury's Fahrenheit 451*: "Why bother to burn books when you can make them disappear?")*
I've been censored in America more than anywhere else. First by Avon in *The Final Programme* (1967). The worst was by Random House in *Byzantium Endures* when they slashed a lot of the antisemitism from a book that is primarily about the Nazi Holocaust. NAL got nervous and made me change Reagan to Eagan in their version of *The Warlord of the Air*. Their lawyers got on it and did what lawyers do. Of course *Byzantium* isn't SF and I didn't regard the Cornelius stuff as SF, either.

Oh, and there's a version of *The Adventures of Una Persson and Catherine Cornelius* which was very thoroughly censored, along with another book whose title I forget, by the publisher. America has a free speech clause in her Constitution, unlike Britain, but Americans tend to self-censor in ways not generally found in France and England.

What do you do for fun (besides write)?
Due to my wounded foot, in recent years I've talked, eaten, and gone to movies (I live part of the time in Paris, where movies are worth going to).

Now that my foot's better, I'll add "walking" (though these days I'm more a *flâneur* than a fifteen-mile hiker). I used to enjoy mountain climbing a lot and "fell-driving," in which you take a big, preferably high-powered sedan up onto what are commonly considered hiking trails.

I am especially proud of being one of the only three people to drive England's Pennine Way in an on-road (2WD) vehicle. The other two were in the same car with me—Jon Trux and Bob Calvert. Hikers used to get outraged and curse us as we roared past.

Re your time with the band Hawkwind: You once spoke of what a pleasure it was to walk out on stage and see a whole crowd of people eagerly awaiting your appearance. Do you ever have that experience as a writer? Or is it the opposite?
I do love the stage. I'd have been a performer if I hadn't been a writer. I love reading and signing sessions too. I like people. A solo reading is harder work than playing in a band because in a band you have your mates to cover your fluffs.

But when I'm writing, I want the nearest thing to a monk's cell as possible. A friend once phoned when I was in the middle of a paragraph and I picked up the phone because I thought it might be Linda. "Bugger off!" I told him.

"That's no way to speak to a friend," he said.

"You can't be a friend," I said. "A friend wouldn't be phoning me while I'm working."

I hate people when I'm writing.

There is a subtheme of incest that runs through the JC (Jerry Cornelius) books. He is in love with his sister (before he kills her), and the deliciously strange Jherek Carnelian is in a romantic relationship with his mom. What gives?
Nothing much. I never had any siblings. Wish fulfilment? I probably just like the romantic/decadent flavour. Jerry also resurrects his sister, don't forget.

The critic Lorna Sage once said that I had too many "sleeping sisters" in my work (I think she was reviewing *Mother London*, which has a major female character asleep and dreaming through much of the book) and suggested that I preferred passive women.

A canard. All my women friends are far from passive. Hilary, my first wife, was by no means passive; neither is Linda, far from it; and my female friends like Angela Carter, Andrea Dworkin, and others, are/were all pretty aggressive/active.

The sleeping sister could be a holdover from the screamer-who-needs-rescuing convention of popular fiction.

Besides Elric and Corum, the Eternal Champions, and Cornelius, who seems to be a more high-tech version of the same, there is also Pyat, the cranky Russky of Byzantium. How does he fit into your pantheon—or does he?
Cornelius does what fantasy heroes can't do easily. I wanted him to confront contemporary stuff. He's far more knowing than standard fantasy heroes. I never regarded him as an SF character, let alone fantasy. The books were never published as fantasy or genre at all in England, but rather as straight "experimental" novels (I preferred to call them unconventional). I used Jerry to look at modern life.

Pyat was designed, or created if you will, for a very different purpose, though he originally appeared as a relatively minor character in the Cornelius quartet. I had felt compelled for some time to confront the Nazi Holocaust full-on (I have my share of survival guilt) and Pyat turned out to be the right guy for the job.

Pyat believes in systems. He sees society as a "correctable" machine. He is a modern man, if you like, in search of a soul. He represents the twentieth century's belief that society is a machine, which only needs the right engineering approach to make life perfect. In that sense his story riffs off "hard" SF of the kind you used to find in lots of pre-1940s visionary fiction. Wells grew increasingly to write this kind of utopian fantasy, and of course it is in Gernsback and all kinds of American stuff. Not only was society a machine that would respond to the right engineering—humankind itself was perfectible through the kind of genetic theories to be found in American and European thinking between the two world wars. Hitler based a lot of his "reasoning" on theories prevalent in the United States in particular, just as he based many of his racial laws on ideas first put into practice in America. Stalin had similar ideas and was also inspired by Hitler's methods. Mussolini, too, thought society and human individuals could be improved just as we improved planes, cars, and trains to go faster, be safer, not to mention more comfortable.

Hell, even Woody Guthrie sang about the power of electricity to improve our lives. The Grand Coulee Dam. Anarchists, too, subscribed to a slightly different and perhaps more humane vision of human society with the "right" systems in place.

It's against all this that Pyat is playing—as well as his terror, originally infecting him as a Jew in the Ukraine. (I've written more about the conception of Pyat in *The Daily Telegraph*, which can be found online at my website, Moorcock's Miscellany, in the Q&A section under published writing, or at the *Telegraph* site under Books: "A Million Betrayals.") Pyat was written from a sense of payback, of duty, a compulsion to use my talent to examine what was the single greatest crime of the twentieth century and see how it was allowed to come about.

Pyat claims to be many things that he isn't—an Aryan, an engineering genius, and so on. He's an unreliable narrator in a carefully reconstructed version of our own world. Cornelius is not unreliable in that sense (and neither are Elric and Co.) and readers are only invited to examine his actions from their own perspective of events.

It's an ongoing theme, if you like: I'm always asking if Romance is some specific kind of lie.

Your career spans the gap between the typewriter and the word processor. At what point did you make the switch? What was that like?
I was using a Selectric II for years. I still have it. I still have an Imperial 50/60 produced during World War II and a Smith Corona portable (should electricity fail). All my work from the age of nine was done on the Imperial.

Soon after I got to Texas in 1994, I was asked by ORIGIN, a game company, to write an original game that could also be a movie and a book. I wasn't sure of the scheme, but I liked the challenge.

At one point they asked me what kind of computer I was using. I told them I didn't have one. At this, an embarrassed silence fell across the room. At last the guy running the firm cleared his throat and asked, "Would you mind if we got you one?"

"You can get me one," I said, "but I can't say I'd use it."

So it duly arrived and within twenty-four hours, I'd taken to it like a duck to water. They were delighted. I wrote my first story on the computer within two days of getting it (a Cornelius short). They'd gotten me the top of the line, of course, and asked me what I thought of it. I said it was like a nondriver being given a Rolls-Royce and then being asked what he thought of it.

Mandelbrot supplied me with a map of my brain. Word supplied me with new applications.

What's your relationship to the very lively Austin music scene? Who do you hang out with in Texas? Writers? Rednecks? Ex-prezzes? Out-of-work musicians?
A few of my friends are musicians. Most of the people I know here I met through local politics and suchlike. Leftist activists in Texas really know the score. One of my best friends, Jewell Hodges, is ninety-two and has been involved in civil rights most of her life. She started life working in fields at the age of twelve, shoving cotton into sacks longer than she was tall.

Almost as soon as we got here, Linda was co-opted onto the local Family Crisis Centre board, and with another woman set about transforming it, with accommodation for threatened spouses and children, outreach, education, and so on; and I supported her in that, being an active pro-feminist.

We also got involved with the local food pantry, which Jewell was running when we got here. She asked me how we fed our hungry poor in the UK. I thought for a bit until I realized that we didn't actually have poverty in the UK of the kind she was battling in Texas.

Texas has no income tax and you feel obliged to involve yourself in activities which, as a European, you believe should be supported by taxes. So I self-tithe to balance that out. I know a few others who do.

Most of my musician friends in Austin start their gigs too late for an old man like me who has a long drive home afterwards! I did perform once or twice with pals in Austin.

I know a few writers—Howard Waldrop, for instance—whom I get on with. Though I have a few friends who are writers, I don't hang out with them much. It was the same in the UK and in France. I tend to be very loyal to my friends and maybe for that reason I don't have many close friends. But they're mostly from different walks of life. I enjoy company but am essentially a loner.

Do you ever go back and loot your works for ideas? Do you read your early stuff at all?

Very rarely. I almost never reread a book. I riff off the fundamental ideas underlying my books—multiverse, eternal champions, context defining characters, and so on. In the old days I'd write one draft in three days and have a friend read it for typos, possible inconsistencies, and I've never reread those. I've made a few revisions when readers point out plot errors or loopy inconsistencies, of course. A few of those early fantasies got to the bookstores without *anyone* having read them—me, editors, publicists.

I tend to have a good memory for books I've done, as if they were memories of my real life, though; so when it comes to sequels I seem to be able to take up a sequel pretty much where I left off. I have a terrible memory yet seem to remember books pretty easily.

Reading my own work is a fast cure for insomnia. Linda will confirm this. When I can't sleep, I go to get something by me and am dozing within a minute or two. This makes proofreading very hard.

If you were casting a Cornelius movie, who would play Jerry? Did you know he's from my hometown?
You're from Notting Hill? Not sure who—but Tilda Swinton is still my favourite choice. Someone did a Photoshop of her as Elric, which also worked very well. That's in the Image Gallery on my site, I think.

I was thinking about Johnny Depp.
Him too. But he's too busy playing pirate these days.

What kind of car do you drive? I ask this of everyone. Did you have a car in the Old Country?
We have an old Lexus SUV, which we bought new and cheap when my leg needed more room because of the wound, and that was about the only car that would take me.

I briefly owned a beautiful Citroën classic convertible with running boards and stuff. In the 1970s, I had a massive Nash (that's what I conquered the Pennine Way in), which in England was like driving a bus. I bought it because it could take a load of children and a load of band members.

But after our Fiat, we mostly had a Honda Civic in the UK. Linda made me stop driving when she discovered I didn't have a license. I'm useless at tests and exams. So although the driving instructor said all I needed were a couple of lessons and I'd sail through, I got worse and worse as we went along and gave it up as a lost cause.

Texas is littered with Lost Causes.

We mostly used public transport in London and we still use mostly public transport in France and the rest of Europe. I'm still an advocate for good public systems. One of my reasons for moving to Texas was because the then Democratic state governor wanted to bring a TGV to Texas and a light rail system for Austin.

I was *very* disappointed when Bush became governor.

You floated an interesting concept in Gloriana *when you said that modern art's relentless demand for novelty made bad artists worse, but good artists better. How does that work?*
I don't remember writing that! I can see how it might work, though. I think there are plenty of good journeyman painters and scriveners whose talents are wasted by attempted novelty. I was probably thinking of what happened on *New Worlds* when perfectly good run-of-the-mill writers tried to produce what they thought were New Wave stories and came up with crap, whereas good writers who were encouraged to expand (Disch, Aldiss, Ballard) produced superb stuff.

Do you regard the fact that SF is still a commercially viable literature a help or a hindrance?
It doesn't matter a lot. I liked it better before publishers didn't know what sold. There was a good patch that lasted into the 1980s even, when publishers were so uncertain about what the public liked that they were willing to give almost anything a go. By the 1990s, they'd worked out what sold and what didn't, and you saw a slowing down of interesting offbeat material and a tendency for categories and subcategories of generic stuff to become the norm.

I think it gets harder and harder to sell new stuff—stuff that breaks conventions—because now publishers and booksellers "know the market" and know what will sell (i.e., what *did* sell). So the chances of selling an offbeat novel masquerading in a commercial form get slimmer all the time.

I liked SF precisely for that potential for masquerade—avant-garde pretending to be space opera . . .

Ever get through The Faerie Queene? *Ulysses?*
Yes. *Gloriana* riffed off *The Faerie Queene*. *Ulysses* is best enjoyed when read aloud, as is Proust. But if you can read *Pamela* by Richardson or *One of Our Conquerors* by Meredith, you can probably read anything. It's books like *Dune* or *Lord of the Rings* that I find almost unreadable.

You are one of SF's most "literary" writers, and at the same time a militant populist in literature, opposed to high-canon thinking. How do you reconcile those roles?
By demonstration.

An innovative artist must create his own audience as he goes. Do you see yourself as an educator or an entertainer? ("Both" is a cheat.)
Both. I have been both most of my life. I've had magazines in which I could present arguments, publish examples. I used to say that the whole *New Worlds* thing was designed to create an audience for the kind of stuff that Ballard, myself, and others wanted to write.

I think we did that.

My entertainments always contain some sort of confrontational elements; my more confrontational stories have large elements of comedy in particular, and I'd say that was reasonably entertaining.

What do you think of McEwan? Austen? Wells?
McEwan, who is vaguely interesting for his subject matter, tends to dodge the issues like much middlebrow fiction and can be a bloody awful writer. As I can be.

Austen's a joy.

Wells is brilliant, often irritating. I have pretty much an entire collection of Wells, most of them firsts and in the original magazines from *The Time Machine* on. I have all of Austen in a nice edition. I have no McEwan, Amis (*fils* or *père*), and no Rushdie. I have all of Elizabeth Bowen, Angus Wilson, Colette, and plenty of Elizabeth Taylor, Rose Macaulay, and lots of Edwardian realists; all of Meredith, Eliot, Dickens; all of Stevenson, Conrad, lots of Ford

Maddox Ford, Jack London, Howells, Harte, Twain, California writers who could listen to the eloquence of the streets; a fair amount of Saul Bellow, and a bunch of contemporary writers. Today's English pantheon is pretty miserable in comparison.

You once said that your first approach to SF was a determination not to be marginalized. Was that the idea behind New Worlds? *Did it work?*
To a degree. I'm far less marginalized in the UK, I think, where a lot more of my nongeneric fiction has been published, won prizes and so forth. I get lengthy reviews for books that aren't presented as generic. I'm certainly not marginalized in that sense. My first hardcovers in England generally got good reviews.

Behold the Man and *The Final Programme* weren't reviewed as genre fiction. Only with the flood of fantasy paperbacks did people begin to get confused, I think. But *Gloriana* was extensively reviewed as nongeneric.

I tend to get treated according to the level of ambition people see in my books. I can be included, for instance, in a *Times* list of the fifty best writers since the end of World War II but still condescended to as some kind of literary barbarian by academics unfamiliar with my stuff. I'm comfortable with that. I think I make some critics and academics a bit uneasy.

If you look at a copy of *New Worlds* from 1967 on you'll see that a general audience is consistently addressed. I wouldn't let contributors address the "SF field." Reviewers reviewed Ballard and Borges together but had to address the general reader. We never spoke of that "field" in which I always imagined a bunch of sheep chewing and rechewing the same grass.

Many readers didn't know *New Worlds* had ever been a genre magazine. We were accepted almost from the start as a literary magazine. Ballard, Aldiss, Disch, and myself were frequently on radio and TV speaking for what the critics termed "the new SF." An anthology was prepared with this name. It attracted a wide readership amongst what you could call the English intelligentsia, particularly those who had liked, say, *Galaxy*, but needed something a bit posher in appearance to legitimize their enthusiasm.

We were fashionable in the 1960s the way the pop artists (some of whom were featured in *New Worlds*) and modern poets were fashionable. It was strange to come to the United States and find science fiction still marginalized, still condescended to. Snobbery seems much stronger in the United States, especially in New York.

But it's the same with rock and roll, I think. In the UK rock and SF were often linked—lots of musicians read SF, some writers performed in bands. I think we can see a major improvement even in America now, though. Writers like Michael Chabon have done much to force snobs to revalue—though I notice he's been attacked here for his enthusiasm for generic fiction.

I sometimes think America is now the *old* world as far as the arts and politics and social ideas are concerned.

Did you line edit at New Worlds?
Not really. There's a different approach in the UK and the United States, I think. American editing tends to come out of the newspaper tradition and seems excessive to me. If we had a problem I'd usually xerox the page or pages in question and underline queries to see what the author felt.

A curmudgeon (MM) once said that today's SF had gotten too sophisticated to take chances. Do you still make that charge?
Well, I always drew my inspiration from pulp and never much liked the movement to make SF "respectable" (which might seem odd, reading the above). I hated that as much as I hated the movement to make Black people whiter. My attitude was "like this or prove yourself a backward idiot."

So if we're talking about sophistication as respectability, I have to say it makes me miserable. The more invisible you are, the more chances you feel able to take. Rock 'n' roll, SF, and comics always show this, I think. Most artistic innovation comes through popular media or at least through obscure media. I chose SF and R&R precisely because there was no one looking over your shoulder when you did it—no critical magazines to study it.

Not when I started, anyway. There was just *Crawdaddy*.

You once suggested that anyone who wants to write fantasy should quit reading your stuff and read Mervyn Peake instead. Does that career plan still hold?
I didn't say Peake in particular, but yes, it still holds. If you want to write SF/fantasy, read everything but those genres. Peake is in many ways more in the

absurdist tradition I've always liked—Peacock, Jarry, Firbank, Vian, Peake. Even William Burroughs is an absurdist first, I think.

You're a musician as well as a writer. Do you still play? What? What was the state of popular music in England in the 1960s? Did modern jazz (Miles, Monk, Mingus) play a role in your postmodern liberation, or was it all rock?
It was all rock and modern composers like Messiaen. In the '60s it was still possible not to have to book tickets for Schoenberg, he was so unpopular. This changed during that decade.

I didn't much care for jazz after a brief craze for it in the '50s, when in Paris you could hear a dozen greats in bars up and down one tiny street. Now I appreciate it much more and like it better. My tastes have broadened. I used to think only string quartets were worth listening to.

SF has been swamped by fantasy. Are you partly to blame for that or do you consider your work a counterforce?
I write fantasy with more of an SF sensibility, I think. I write antifantasy. When Tolkien and I were really the only games in town, we both got our own nametag in bookstores, separate from the SF shelves. When Tolkienesque fantasy began to dominate I was knocked off the shelves by a bunch of Terries (nothing personal to you or Pratchett). That is, I sold when there wasn't a more escapist, comfortable brand.

Now I still sell pretty well, but it seems to be more to fantasy readers who don't much like Tolkien (or at least his clones).

The change in the United States came really when Donald Wollheim pirated the *Lord of the Rings* books and also found that *A Princess of Mars* wasn't in copyright. Larry Shaw at Lancer liked Jack Vance and me and was the first to publish my fantasy in the United States. I think my stuff probably is a counterforce at some level.

I don't think I'm to blame for Prof. T. My influences among modern writers were almost wholly American—Poul Anderson, Sprague de Camp, Fritz Leiber, C.L. Moore, Leigh Brackett, Robert E. Howard, Jack Vance.

Tolkien question here. The answer is "certainly." You provide the question.

Is Tolkien a sentimentalist who, like many writers (Sherriff, Deeping, et al.) emerging from World War I, needed to mystify and sentimentalize that conflict and/or their part in it? To make "sacrifice" noble. Are you sympathetic to but irritated by such attitudes which spilled over into the English middle-class sensibility so that they lasted (via BBC drama, for instance) long after the end of World War II?

Rowling question here. The answer is "perhaps." You provide the question.
Has Rowling discovered a strategy for continuing that especially English genre, the public-school story (Thomas Hughes, Talbot Baines Reed, Charles Hamilton, and many others), thus successfully continuing to spread certain English class attitudes well into the twenty-first century and across the world?

Do you wear a hat when you write? Do you have a regular work regimen? Coffee or tea?
I wear different hats. Currently I'm wearing a FLASH baseball cap for my Doctor Who novel. I prefer to work outside whenever possible and then I wear a wide-brimmed Panama.

Do you stay in touch with the old New Worlds *crowd (Sallis, Aldiss, Platt, Spinrad, Malzberg, et al.)? Why are they so grumpy?*
Are they? I'm scarcely in touch with anyone but Aldiss and Spinrad, and they seem actually less grumpy on most issues than they were in the 1960s. They were always fairly confrontational by nature, as I am.

I grumpily want to know why Malzberg pinched the title of my novel *Breakfast in the Ruins*. I'm not in touch with him at all or I'd ask him myself. Maybe they're grumpy because all their bloody mates are dying. That pisses me off too.

Why was the New Wave such a Guy Thing? Or was it?
Not for want of trying to publish women. We published as many women as we could encourage—Emshwiller, Arnason, Sargent, Zoline, Castell (Vivienne Young in art), and of course Hilary Bailey. Would you count Doris Lessing?

You have to publish by example, if possible, and I know we tried to publish women, but they were thin on the ground.

Judith Merril was strongly associated with the so-called New Wave. Much of the fiction I write and we published was decidedly pro-women in a way that a lot of guy fiction (the Beats, for instance) was not.

Precisely the reason I can't enjoy either Amis. There's always been a distinct smell of the saloon bar in much fiction. Could be why my "default" writer, the one I always turn to when I can't think of anyone else to read, is Elizabeth Bowen (especially *Death of the Heart*).

My close friend Andrea Dworkin loved SF and wrote some, and we sometimes discussed this. She thought there were a lot more women published now because women don't tend to submit work where they think it isn't wanted. Given that Joanna Russ, Ursula Le Guin, and others are associated with the so-called New Wave, I'm not sure that it was such a guy thing!

I always wanted something ambitious from Joanna.

Disch became somewhat bitter toward SF. In your Humble Opinion, was this critical or personal?

Tom was always a bit confused on this issue. He wanted literary respectability more than any other author I knew and used to say, "*The New Yorker* can smell the SF on me." (I just wrote a story touching on this, called "Stories" for an anthology called *Stories*.)

Once, when I got a full-page review in the *Times Literary Supplement* praising a book, Tom called me and said, "Congratulations. You've *won*!" I was baffled.

Tom was competitive, but he wanted his success to come from conventional institutions. He was far more a modern than a postmodern. He liked to think of himself as Henry James rather than Henry Kuttner. Yet he could be very generous and encouraging to new writers of SF.

He was always a snob, but never enough to hang out happily with other snobs. He was unhappy in New York, which is probably the snottiest town in the world, yet he hung on there wishing to be accepted—or accepted more.

That wasn't why he killed himself, though, I think. Essentially he killed himself because his partner Charles Naylor had died, leaving him terribly alone.

I was very fond of Charlie, but he was a worse snob than Tom in some ways, though much more "liberal" in some ways (anti-Jewish attitudes aside).

Unlike, say, Ballard who became increasingly radical into old age, Tom became increasingly reactionary until even the *Weekly Standard* (for which he wrote regularly) found some of his stuff went too far.

Is England or the United States more receptive to (or at least forgiving of) satire? The tradition seems to have remained healthier in the UK than in the US, though that said, there are some fine American satirists.

I don't know. Americans seem to place a higher value on *politesse* than the British. We're far more savage toward public figures. This is odd since free speech isn't in our Bill of Rights. I always have found it strange that Americans have to signal irony or humour in general by adding "joke" at the end of whatever they've said. Or by signalling quote marks. I've found I have to do it too sometimes or people take what I've said seriously. This spelling out of an ironic or sarcastic remark doesn't happen in England or France.

What do you read for fun?
Sexton Blake "story papers" (equivalent of dime novels) and others from between the wars. P.G. Wodehouse and a whole bunch of Edwardian comic/realist writers like Zangwill, Pett Ridge, Barry Paine, F. Anstey, Jerome K. Jerome. Scott, Q, Stevenson.

Do you read or write poetry?
Yes. Most of the poetry in my fiction, though, is parody (as in "Ernest Wheldrake," Swinburne's pseudonym under which he attacked his own work, as "Colvin" attacked mine). Otherwise I'm a crap poet.

You have written series novels, standalones, and short stories. What do you think is the distinction between short story writers and novelists?
Do you want me to be facetious? I suspect short story writers are temperamentally less patient than novelists.

Do you ever outline? Do you work from plot or character?

Not an outline as such, though I had to do one for the BBC when writing the Doctor Who novel they commissioned. I make extensive notes and then hardly ever refer to them. I tend to work from character, even with my fantasy novels. Writing Doctor Who was awkward in this respect since there's only so much you can do to work up his character.

Have you ever written a conventional screenplay? Do you like the form? (I do.)
I wrote one for *The Land That Time Forgot* and rewrote *The Final Programme*, and I've written a few that were never made. Usually I don't enjoy working with directors, though.

    I'm used to doing a story and then standing or falling by it, whereas I get frustrated when I finish a job and someone comes along to tell me it's not quite right ("It's wonderful, Michael. There are just a *few* changes we thought of . . .") My theory is that having to work this way didn't help Fitzgerald or Faulkner stay (or even get) on the wagon. I'd be a drunk in similar circumstances.

    The money's good, but there's a reason for that.

Your narratives are known for their velocity. Does this mean they are speedy to write as well?
I used to feel, as a journalist, that over three days on a book was uneconomical, so all my fantasies took three days to write. I'd support myself with journalism. *Behold the Man* took five days. *The Final Programme* took ten. The longest it took me to write a book before *Byzantium Endures* was six weeks (*Gloriana*). *Byzantium* took six months.

    These days it can take maybe a month for a first draft of a fantasy, with about two weeks for revision. Until *Byzantium* I rarely did more than one draft.

You describe yourself as an anarchist rather than a Marxist. What does this mean politically? Personally? Artistically?
It's a philosophical/moral position from which I can easily make quick decisions of pretty much every kind. My anarchism informs my pro-feminism, for instance.

    I happen to believe as a writer that words are action and that we have to be able to stand by our actions and accept any consequences of our actions.

Therefore if someone tells me they have been, for example, raped by someone claiming to have been encouraged by my work, I feel I have to examine that work to see if it can't be changed.

If someone tells me they hate or are dissatisfied by a book of mine, I tend to send them their money back.

I modified the Cornelius books as I went along because too many young men were poncing about thinking it was cool to pose around being "amoral." Like many writers attracted to SF, I'm intensely moralistic.

What has living in the United States brought to your work as an artist?
A little more understanding of a country which is often baffling to Europeans because they feel it should be a better version of Europe—certainly better than the Europe settlers left behind. That it is in several ways a worse version is a bit of a shock to us.

The anti-intellectual tradition and the overintellectualized tradition are both a bit depressing.

The tendency to live in enclaves concerns me. But the language of the South and Southwest gave me some good music for books like *Blood*.

Do you see anything stirring in contemporary SF outside the English language (United States and England)?
Not really. French SF and Indian SF are at last beginning to establish their own idioms, which is encouraging.

Some would say SF, like rock 'n' roll, has aged and is no longer the province of youth. Do you agree? Can this be reversed? Should it be?
It depends on what youth finds in it. I don't think you can bring the 1960s–'70s back. I know, however, that if I was sixteen in this world I wouldn't be looking to SF or contemporary pop music for inspiration.

My first novel, Wyrldmaker, *was a Moorcock (Corum) imitation. Do I owe you an apology, or him? Or do you owe me one?*
You owe me one (for that *y* in "Wyrld"). I loved your second novel, the one about the South. One of my absolute favourites.

Wow. Let's leave that in. How many projects do you generally have going at once? Is this a plan or lack of same?
Usually one novel or sequence of novels at a time, sometimes two or three (three at the moment). A short story or two. I'm usually writing a feature of some kind—a review, article or "diary" (I do a few a year for English newspapers, primarily *The Guardian* or the *Financial Times*. Maybe a comic, a memoir, an introduction, and so on. Usually at least one music project.

Does SF have a future? Or is it just reworking of old tropes? What writers do you see today as more forward-looking? Is there any new ground to break? This is a trick question.
That depends entirely on the individual whose imagination is sparked by a form. I know one intensely modernist intellectual writer, who used to be part of a well-known Oxford literary crew, who taught himself physics because he felt he should know about such stuff. Who then wrote an excellent and convincing time travel story, which appeared in *Asimov's*.

SF definitely has a canon, and your works are embedded in it. Is there anyone left out or overlooked that you would add?
I'm not sure. I have read very little SF since, say, 1964. If Harness isn't in the canon I think he should be.

Delete?
Oh, well. There's always some you feel are overrated. I've never understood the appeal of most "Golden Age" writers. In the end a good stylist will remain included, I'd guess—like Bradbury—while the clunkier writers will slowly disappear. Style tends to last, even when at first rejected (Hammett, Faulkner, Peake, Ballard) by the lit establishment.

Have you ever "taught" (academically) SF as literature?
I have never taught anything directly (oh—I taught my daughters to punch and to shoot!) but editing is a bit like teaching in that you try to find out precisely what the author's wanting to say and help them say it. But I don't believe I *can* teach, except by example.

I was asked to write a book on technique a few years ago and said I don't know any rules for writing. All I could do was tell someone how I'd solved a problem in the hope it would be of some use to them.

If you taught a survey course on SF that covered four novels and five short stories, what would they be?
Bring the Jubilee, maybe, *The Drowned World*, *A Canticle for Leibowitz*, *The Time Machine*. Short stories by Fritz Leiber, Bradbury, Wells, M.J. Harrison's, Forster...

Any regrets so far?
What about? This interview?
    I sometimes wish I hadn't written quite so many fantasy novels and spent a bit more time on stuff I took more seriously, like *Mother London*.
    I let obsession with work affect relationships too much, I think.
    The fantasy sequence I'm writing now is about the romantic lure of the exotic and how it can sometimes take your attention away from more important stuff, like politics and people.

"Punctuality, Basic Hygiene, Gun Safety"
Paul Park

You grew up in a college town. Defend.
These decisions about where to be born, where to grow up, one makes them almost arbitrarily, like the character details at the beginning of a story. But they are so hard to correct when things go wrong. I read an article recently by a man who had grown up in a Christian cult and then escaped into academia, only to discover many of the same structures: the abusive hierophants at the top, the un- or undercompensated labor at the bottom, the cruel assumption of superiority based on self-serving definitions of excellence, either spiritual or intellectual. My parents were priests in that cult, and it took me a long time to recognize the insidious ways in which privilege disguises itself as merit, or "merit," among upper-middle-class Americans. On the other hand, it's a lovely little town; I still live there.

Soldiers of Paradise was your first work. Or was it? Where did you try to place it? How did it end up with Hartwell?
I wrote a novel before *Soldiers of Paradise* about a murder in a monastery. I was living in New York in the 1970s, working in an advertising agency and hating it. So I quit to work in a squash club and write *Lamb's Blood*, which was never published. *S of P* came later, after two years in Asia. I was less green by that time and knew enough to get an agent, which took a year or so. Adele Leoni agreed to represent it with David in mind. He was with Arbor House then, and I remember the whole process taking about a week. The advance was not large.

Ever spend a winter on Block Island?

I did! Maybe in 1973? My parents had a house by the water, unheated except for a kerosene stove in one room. I ate a lot of Gorton's Codfish Cakes. I read Russian novels, and my dog and I walked all over the island, which was far more rural in those days. It would be easy to plot out a story that would make that winter a pivotal episode in my life, if you liked those sorts of stories.

You sometimes appear in your own stories. Is that by invitation?
I used to think it was a bad and politically retrograde idea to borrow anything from your own experience and put it in your work, except in the most glancing and indirect way. So calling characters "Paul Park" was my little joke. The name always seemed improbable to me, and artificial, since no one used it when I was a child. Once when I was working at Smith/Greenland I put it into a sample advertisement, and the client accepted everything but that detail. They told me, "No one could ever be named 'Paul Park,'" which seemed reassuring and right to me, and I took those words to heart. I had the art director substitute "Frank Masters," which the client liked and I did too, because it is a phrase that means something—I once had a student named Chace Lyons. Lately, of course, I've found characters more like myself haunting my stories, and I give them all sorts of made-up names.

When did you start fooling around with metafiction? What is metafiction, anyway?
A metafictional story is one that is aware of itself and knows that it is artificial. In most stories you are asked to imagine you are finding out about real people and their problems. So, for example, in this interview the reader might imagine an actual author answering actual questions in a way that suggests what he actually thinks. But what if that becomes increasingly unlikely? What if the response to a question about metafiction appears foolish or fraudulent, in a way that suggests either (a) that the interviewer is manipulating the answers and the author doesn't exist, or (b) that there is no author and no interviewer either, and the whole exchange is being manufactured by some unknown writer for a new purpose. Usually there is a metafictional break in the story, as, for example, here, where the reader understands they're being toyed with. In theory, the whole tone of the interview might change, as every subsequent answer is now suspect.

This way of thinking has always been interesting to me, as it turns out—recently I was cleaning up after a fire and came across some stories I'd written in school. Metafiction. I think it might be because I'm bad at conventional plotting, the straight line between A and B that "takes away all hope," as Grace Paley describes it.

Didn't you write a Dungeons & Dragons novel? How did that come about?
I was in Seattle teaching at Clarion West, and at a party I met one of the editors at Wizards of the Coast, who publish the Forgotten Realms books. My son had started to play the game with a posse of his friends, and I thought it would be fun to write a story for *Dragon* magazine, which I knew he read, and have it show up on his screen. Later, the same editor approached me for a novel, and I accepted under the condition that I could borrow the characters my son and his friends had invented for their game and base the novel under them. And one other condition: I could write it under a pen name, which would then appear in a metafictional novel called *All Those Vanished Engines*, about, among other things, a man named "Paul Park" who writes a Forgotten Realms novel under the same pseudonym and quotes from it inaccurately.

You seem more interested in ceremony than actual behavior. Are you aware of that? Does it worry you?
Is there such a thing as actual behavior, for conscious beings? How would that even work? Isn't everything a performance of itself? When I was living in the Congo, sometimes foreign guests would want to go to so-called tribal villages, where people who make a show of eating their traditional meals, wearing their traditional clothes, pursuing their traditional activities. So, melancholy and pathetic, and only tolerable if you remembered that everything is like that.

Do you ever workshop your own stuff?
No—that would be awful. And what would be the point?

You furnished the soundtrack for a museum installation. How did that come about?
I've done two museum shows, one at the Massachusetts Museum of Contemporary Art and one at CityPlace in West Palm Beach. In both cases I

provided the text for a mixed-media sound installation assembled by the artist Stephen Vitiello. Both turned into wonderful collaborations. They were his commissions, but he asked me to be part of the team, because when he accepted the assignment at MASS MoCA, he remembered from one of my author bios that I lived in the same town as the museum, and he asked them to hire me. They were like, "Who?"

Are you a Christian? What's with all the Jesus and Mary books?
I tried to be a Christian for a while, when I was in New York. I loved the smell of the old stone and polished wood. I loved the music. That sounds superficial, but I responded to those things in a way that still seems significant to me. I didn't love trying to convince myself I believed things I actually didn't. I got belief all tangled up with faith. Nobody really believes anything, it turns out. The books came later and are unrelated. At least I think they are.

Your father was a physicist, at Princeton for a while. Ever meet Einstein?
Yes, my father was at the Institute for Advanced Study in the early 1950s. He knew all those guys: Robert Oppenheimer, Richard Feynman. Not well, I think. Freeman Dyson was the only one who became a family friend. Once my father introduced my mother to Albert Einstein at a party. "I was expecting someone so much taller," she said. Later she suggested he might not have not found that funny.

One sentence on each, please: Carol Emshwiller, Mick Jagger, Ludwig Wittgenstein.
Carol Emshwiller is the only great writer whose smile can light up all of lower Manhattan. I regret pretending, when Mick Jagger checked into the racquet club where I was working, that I didn't recognize him and indeed had never heard of him, which was a pointless and pathetic lie. Despite quoting him once in a short story, I have never read a word of Ludwig Wittgenstein and never will.

Favorite whiskey?
Whisky, please: Laphroaig (Islay). For blended whisky (stirred, really): Ye Olde Earl (Edinburgh, London, Kathmandu).

You once brought me a bottle of Ye Olde Earl. Fortunately, it was tiny. You have taught writing at Clarion and several colleges. Ever have a real job?
No, I don't think so. I worked for the City Council in New York. I worked in advertising and in health clubs. I was a janitor. I worked in retail and sold Chinese antiques. I wrote catalog copy and artists' profiles. Now I'm a college professor. Real jobs are as chimerical as real Americans.

Do your students ever actually read SF? Do you have two or three things in particular you teach? Any things you have to unteach?
No. They used to have read Orson Scott Card but not anymore. I teach a number of different kinds of writing: Utopian Fiction, Imitations and Parodies, Science Fiction of the African Diaspora, Expository Writing for Art Historians, as well as Creative Writing. My college is generous that way, possibly because, to put it mildly, I lack formal credentials. I try to teach (a) punctuality, (b) basic hygiene, and (c) gun safety. I try to unteach Raymond Carver, show don't tell, and write what you know.

What was your first literature? Were you ever a reader of SF or fantasy?
I read myths and fairy tales, Arthurian legends, Tolkien, and Le Guin. I never read any comics or hard SF. I wish I had. It's too late now.

You were friends with James Sallis in New Orleans, and now with John Crowley in New England. So tell me, why is it that some major, even celebrated, writers, given the opportunity to jump ship from genre, don't?
I think it turns out to be hard. When I tried to strike away with the Jesus books, *The Gospel of Corax* and *Three Marys*, David Hartwell told me it was never going to work, that I'd never climb out of the box. He turned out to be right. The stain of genre doesn't necessarily affect the work, but it affects the perception and reception.

How come you haven't won any major awards? All your friends have.
It's true. Every single one of them. And not just participation trophies, either, but major, national awards. They put them up on the mantelpiece and dust or polish them. They survey them with quiet pride. Sometimes they stroke them

with anxious, feverish fingers, I hear. By contrast I am forever denied that experience. That glass case is closed to me. And yet . . .

Do you have a regular drill for writing? You know what I mean.
Nope. Not anymore. When I was living by myself, my routine was to piss and moan for a solid year until I had built up enough panic and distress, then pound out a book in a few months. That system turned out to be unconducive to domestic life and fatherhood. When the kids were young, I developed a more disciplined schedule and got up every morning at four so I could write before they woke up for school. Now they're gone, and I'm sorely in need of a new way.

You sort of slip and slide among genres. Do you use them as fences or chutes?
I never developed the hook of self-imitation, from which commercial success so largely depends. Do you think Jasper Johns *wanted* to paint all those flags and stars? This is especially true in genre, where one is rarely rewarded for change. I think it has helped me to never have made much money. If the Princess of Roumania books had been a great success, I could imagine sitting around thinking, "So, what about Bulgaria? Moldova? Transnistria?"

What's your position on the big bang? Evolution? Are you aware that they are just theories?
It's hard for me to believe in things I can't visualize—I mean actually believe in them and not just be comfortable saying so. The big bang theory sounds more like a religious moment than a scientific one, possibly because it seems so *fiat lux*. As for evolution, I don't dispute the facts of the case, just the theorizing that rise out of them, which seems to me reductive and depressing. In general, I have no interest in abstract thought.

Your wife is a theater professional. Ever write a play or a screenplay?
No, but I've thought about it. I'm not alone in this, I hear. *Three Marys* would make a good play.

When you were a kid, did everyone call you Pogo or just your mean sisters?

That particular cognomen, from the great Walt Kelly comic strip, started with my parents, who disliked the actual name they'd given me. Everybody called me that except in the most formal situations. And I don't think they were being mean . . . except, wait a second now. Wait just a gosh darn minute. "Dagnabbit," as Pogo might say.

The Gospel of Corax about the "lost years" of Jesus was based on what?
I was going on a hiking trip to the Garhwal Himal and had a few hours to kill while the Indian consulate processed my visa. So I walked over to St. Bartholomew's on 51st Street and Park Avenue, which is a beautiful neo-Byzantine pile. I sat in a side chapel, and the whole shape of the novel fell in my lap all at once: Jesus' trip to India. I had been primed for thinking about it for some years, ever since the time I'd spent in Rajasthan and Uttar Pradesh years before. I had gotten interested in theosophy because of all the references to it in Indian cities, roads named after Annie Besant or Madame Blavatsky. And it was commonplace in famous temples to hear people tell you Jesus of Nazareth had worshipped there. I was aware of the theosophist legend that Jesus had lived and studied, and even died, at Hemis Gompa in Ladakh—my great-grandmother had run a theosophical society in New Haven. There I was in St. Bartholomew's. Old stone, polished wood, half-heard music from the nave. It was as if the book was already in my hand.

You were part of the Mount Thoreau expedition in 2015. Are you an admirer of Thoreau or do you just follow Stan Robinson and Gary Snyder around?
The latter, sadly. I like to read people only after I climb the mountain named after them. It gives me a better sense of what they're like, what to expect. *Walden* had always seemed a bit hectoring to me. But I'd loved *The Maine Woods* and wrote about it for Laurie Glover's anthology. Step by measured step, until the man is way off the deep end.

What poets do you read for fun? Ever read mysteries? Why not?
I disapprove of mysteries. I'm not sure why. Disapproval is like that, for me. It comes from a place of stupidity. I imagine them as overdetermined and controlled, and I don't care to be told differently. Poets? I read a lot of poets. Right now today? Ocean Vuong and Celia Dropkin.

My Jeopardy question. I provide the answer, you provide the question. Answer: A boathouse on an undiscovered bay.
What is a fine and narrow cylinder of neglect?

You were one of the first to buy a Saturn, yet you rarely write about space travel. Explain.
Why write about it when you can live it? Those early models, I remember, when the company was still independent—downshifting into ninth gear on a summer night, at the old abandoned wooden ski ramp near my house, you could break out of the troposphere at an incline of sixty degrees, and she'd stop shuddering and shaking, and spilling all the coffee in your lap. Such bliss to hit that cold still quiet place. One tank of gas—Jesus. Past the Kuiper Belt, you could wrap up in a sleeping bag and coast. And in those early days they had refueling stations along the way.

If you could low-orbit any planet or satellite in the solar system for several hours, which would it be?
Haven't you been listening?

You were spotted at Everest Base Camp some years ago. What were you doing, collecting empties?
Yes, the place is a trash heap. I prefer the corpses higher up. The things people leave, they should take away. The things they take away, they should leave. Go figure.

So what's next?
I've been working on short fiction, mostly, for the past few years. And a novella called *Lost Colonies of the Ancient World*. It might be that I never finish it. Maybe it's important always to be working on something that defeats you. And I've been researching a new historical novel set in Roman Gaul. "Vercingetorix" is a name that holds, in my opinion, irresistible and universal appeal. I've been rolling it around my mouth since I was a child.

"But I'm Gonna Put a Cat on You"
Gary Phillips Interviewed by Denise Hamilton

How'd The Underbelly *come about?*
The Underbelly was initially written as an online serial a couple of years ago for the fourstory.org site because Nathan Walpow, a fellow mystery writer, asked me if I wanted to contribute to the site. Because Nathan had a background in fiction, he was also looking to add to the site, to augment the nonfiction with fiction, to broaden the site. Not just dry pieces about housing and homelessness. In fact nowadays the site runs stories about issues like housing, sustainable living and transportation, riffs on pop culture, to other fiction and even pieces on Cuba based on a trip the FourStory staff took to the island nation not too long ago. So, really, honestly, they're not dry pieces.

Anyway, Nathan knew I had a background as a community organizer and that my wife was an urban planner and ran a nonprofit. I drew on those experiences to write the novella. Essentially, the plot centers on a semihomeless Vietnam vet named Magrady who's now been sober for eight months. He was on and off booze and drugs for years and suffers from flashbacks. A disabled friend of his, a man in a wheelchair, who's not a vet, but lives on Skid Row, disappears, and Magrady has to find him. This sets the plot in motion.

The story takes place in Los Angeles, and that was the point of locating it in the sphere of FourStory, which is to say it takes place in a gentrifying downtown Los Angeles. And à la L.A. Live, this complex of venues recently built there that includes the Staples Center where the Lakers play and nightclubs, restaurants, and a large hotel, there's a mega development project in the book called the Emerald Shoals. This project like in real life has displaced working poor folks and impacted the homeless as the so-called urban pioneers move into converted lofts and the like. To reflect this one of the characters in the book is a community organizer named Janis Bonilla, who is a friend of Magrady's and also an organizer for a community empowerment organization.

Hopefully *Underbelly* walks the line between having substantive issues as context, helping to ground a story, and being on a soapbox with just having the story as an excuse for a polemic.

Is it bad literature to write polemic stories?
If I want a polemic I'll read nonfiction. As storytellers, it's our job not to be the opiate of the masses but if you're going to tell a story, it should have characters that resonate with the reader and have a plot and structure and is just not an excuse to go on forever.

Take for example John D. MacDonald, a mystery writer who created the Travis McGee character and series. It seems to me he got consumed at the end of his writing career with his own conservative politics, and there would be long passages in his books having his characters ranting on about environmentalists, treehuggers, and lefties, but the job of the writer or storyteller is to tell a story. Obviously you want to have these realities in your work but you have to be clever about weaving that stuff in your story.

I think people's points of view certainly come into play, so that's fine, but I'm also interested in having characters having different points of view. It makes for better drama, right? Characters always want something, and invariably these interests collide.

Another example is a book of mine called *Freedom's Fight*. The novel is about African American soldiers and civilians during World War II. In the book we see the racism and conflicts the all-Black units encounter with white soldiers. Because of Jim Crow policies, Black troops weren't sent into combat until end of 1943, beginning of 1944. The story also unfolds through the eyes of a Black woman reporter, Alma Yates, for the *Pittsburgh Courier*, the largest Black weekly newspaper at the time.

Via her, the reader gets glimpses of what's happening in the States. The *Courier* was part of something called the Double V Campaign, victory at home and victory overseas. During that time there were arguments among civil rights organization and on the left about the role of the Black soldier. Why should they fight and die for freedom abroad if they didn't have freedom here at home, versus the pressure for African Americans to show white America they were good, loyal citizens.

Freedom's Fight came about as my way to tell a slice of this bigger story. I think I'm accurate in stating there are less than a handful of novels about Black soldiers during this period—though certainly there are several informative non-fiction books such as *The Invisible Soldier* by Mary Penick Molley, *Lasting Valor* by Medal of Honor winner Vern Baker and Ken Olsen, and *Brothers in Arms* about the 761st tank battalion by Kareem Abdul-Jabbar and Anthony Walton.

But if you watched the TV miniseries *Brothers in Arms* or now the recent *Pacific* on cable, you wouldn't have any idea that there were all-Black units who fought in those theaters of conflict, but there were. My late dad Dikes was in combat at Guadalcanal, his brother, Norman, was at D-Day Plus One, and the youngest brother, Sammy, served in India. My mother, Leonelle, had a brother named Oscar Hutton Jr., who was shot down and killed over Memmingen, Germany, as a Tuskegee fighter pilot.

Given all that, I tried not to make *Freedom's Fight* preachy, but, hopefully, entertaining historical fiction with a sociopolitical grounding, and even some hardboiled elements—there is a murder mystery subplot, dimensional characters and action on the battlefield.

Speaking of which, when did noir get a grip on you?
I stumbled into it at as a kid, I played sports as a kid in school, but because my mom was a librarian, I was literally forced to read. When I came home from grade school I'd have to read *Pinocchio* and *Grimms' Fairy Tales* for an hour before I could go out and play. I initially rebelled against this, but damned if I didn't come to like reading. And there's some pretty rugged stuff in those Grimm stories, including cannibalism and murder.

I still remember at 61st Street Elementary, they taught us the Dewey Decimal System, and I went to the school library and plucked off the shelf *20,000 Leagues Under the Sea* by Jules Verne. I was eight or nine and hadn't even seen the Disney movie of the book, so I don't know how I knew about it, but somehow I knew who Verne was.

How does that get us to noir? I started to develop a love of reading. Somewhere in this I was reading a lot of pulp stories because Bantam was reprinting Doc Savage and the Shadow. At this time I'm starting to watch mystery and detective stories on TV and I heard about Dashiell Hammett so I picked up some Hammett and read some of his short stories. It would be a while before I read his Sam Spade novel the *Maltese Falcon*. But Hammett got me hooked, I liked the way he wrote, I liked his patter, and I liked that he wrote these tough and, in many ways, unsentimental stories, and from there I branched into Ross Macdonald, though that was a little later.

Then in 1970 when I'm still in high school, playing at the Temple Theater in my neighborhood in South Central was this movie called *Cotton Comes to Harlem*. I didn't know then about Chester Himes—the movie is based on his book of the same title—but the film looked cool what with two Black actors dressing 1970s slick in the lead roles as Harlem cops. The stars were comedian Godfrey Cambridge as Gravedigger Jones and Raymond St. Jacques as Coffin Ed Johnson, with Redd Foxx in a supporting role as, yes, a junk man—this before his fame as Fred Sanford on the TV show *Sanford and Son*. Foxx I knew from his ribald party records—and I'm talking vinyl LPs, long play, here—my dad would play for his friends when they came over for beers. Naturally I was sent off to bed but always managed to hear some of Foxx's dirty jokes through my slightly cracked door.

This early 1970s is the beginning of the blaxploitation cycle of movies Hollywood ground out, a lot of them with mystery and crime plots. Seeing *Cotton* gets me to Himes. At some point I began reading his work, a blend of oddball characters, crazy plots, and rumination on race relations in America. What always struck me about noir and hard boiled stories is one I enjoyed them because they were crime stories, walks on the wild side. And two, they always looked at what exists in the shadows, the flip side of human personalities. Plus they're great morality tales.

But sometimes the bad guy wins. What kind of morality is that?
Maybe that's the hard truth, the real truth that life teaches us. When there are ambiguous endings or the bad guy wins. Thus the metaphor for capitalism, I suppose. The character in the novel out to take down the bank or knock over the racetrack is the stripped-down robber baron with no pretense at anything else than being a gangster capitalist. Could be noir is a trap of the proletariat.

Your character thinks he or she can change their station in life if only they can get away with this crime . . . but they're sucked down. Though this can happen to well-off characters. Hell, sometimes the working class gets the upper hand in noir. But only sometimes.

Recently too I saw read this mention of a nonfiction book entitled *American Homicide* by a historian named Randolph Roth. Roth posits that high homicide rates "are not determined by proximate causes such as poverty, drugs, unemployment, alcohol, race, or ethnicity, but by factors . . . like the feelings that people have toward their government and the opportunities they have to earn respect without resorting to violence." Roth also stated that looking at FBI stats from the first six months in 2009 taken from the urban areas Obama carried in his election for the presidency, saw the steepest drop in the homicide rate since the mid-1990s.

Of course you also have a rise in neofascist racist groups, and I include the teabaggers in this mix, as a result of Obama's presidency, so there's that. But it does suggest there can be further interesting takes on noir if you track Roth's theories.

How'd you cross the bridge from reader to writer?
In my twenties, because I was involved in community activist work, anti-apartheid and police abuse organizing and the like, and because I had a bent for art in those days, but that was only because I wanted to draw and write comic books. This meant I'd wind up being on the committees to write and design the flyers for a march or a demonstration. Fact for a while in the mid- to late 1980s, I was the co-owner of a print shop in South Central we'd started from the funds my comrade the late Michael Zinzun had put up. He was one of the founders of the Coalition Against Police Abuse, CAPA, and had won a suit after being beaten by the Pasadena Police Department and losing an eye. Our shop, a union shop, I might add, was called 42nd Street Litho and we'd print pamphlets, newsletters, and flyers. I was always involved with writing some of those given the various organizations I was involved in as well. But like Raymond Chandler, I didn't start till I was in my thirties writing fiction. By then I figured out what I wanted to do was write a book.

Specifically I'd been fired from a union organizing job in 1989. I'd been working for the American Federation of State, County and Municipal Employees, AFSCME, and this particular local, Council 10, represented the groundskeepers and some of the library personnel at UCLA, the university here in Los Angeles. Having time on my hands and talking it over with my wife Gilda, I decided to take this extension class being taught at the university about writing your mystery novel. The class was taught by Bob Crais, who then was coming out of TV as a script writer on shows like *Hill Street Blues* and *Cagney & Lacey*, and had turned to writing mystery novels.

In Bob's class we deconstructed the first Spenser novel by Robert Parker, the *Godwulf Manuscript*, about this illuminated artifact being stolen. We then had to come up with an outline and the first fifty pages of our own novels. It's there that I came up with my private eye character Ivan Monk and the people in his world. The class was over in, I think, ten weeks, but I went on and finished that first book. I didn't get it published but was happy to have just written it.

I guess I always knew I'd write a mystery novel because that's what I'd been reading, all kinds of people from the established pantheon—Chandler, Hammett, and Macdonald—even Dorothy L. Sayers and her Lord Peter Wimsey stories, to Black writers like Donald Goines and Iceberg Slim, Robert Beck. Iceberg, from whom rapper-actor Ice-T derived his stage moniker, had been a pimp and consorted with all types of low life individuals back east. He retired from the "Life," and came west. He drew on those harsh experiences to craft his street level fiction for paperback originals for the white-owned Holloway House here in L.A.

Goines, a former Air Force military policeman (he enlisted underage, using a fake birth certificate), rooty-poot pimp, petty thief, heroin addict, truck driver and hustler, among his other pursuits, wrote sixteen paperback originals for Holloway House, starting with *Dopefiend*, published in late 1971. His writing routine was grind out pages in the morning and go score dope in the afternoon. His last two books would be released posthumously in 1975. One was *Kenyatta's Last Hit*, a series he wrote about this politicized gangster, and attributed to him, *Inner City Hoodlum*.

But as Eddie Allen relates in his biography about Goines, *Low Road*, *Inner City Hoodlum*'s parentage was not Goines's solely, but also that of a writer named

Carleton Hollander. Allen states Hollander had to heavily edit and finish the uncompleted manuscript that Goines had left behind. I also know from my friend Emory Holmes, who was an editor two different times at Holloway House, that Goines's use of heroin often impaired his page outage. You see, Mr. Goines exited this world in as violent a fashion as any depicted in his books. He and Shirley Sailor, who lived together and had two children, were shot to death in their apartment at 232 Cortland in Detroit, their bodies found on the morning of October 22, 1974. Fortunately, the murderers hadn't harmed the children. Like some Ross Macdonald mystery embedded in the past but reverberating to the present day, the killers remain unidentified.

So in those days you'd find Goines's books and Iceberg Slim's in my neighborhood in South Central at the Thrifty's, the CVS drug store of its day. You wouldn't find them at the B Dalton and the Pickwick bookstores. Now you can find their stuff at the chains. These two cats, for good and ill, are considered the godfathers of what's called ghetto lit now.

Circling back to the *Godwulf Manuscript*, and apropos of the kind of stories Goines and Beck wrote, what I remember in that book is Spenser beds a mother and subsequently her grown daughter in the course of the story, because he was that kind of stud. Maybe that was the lesson we were supposed to learn about PI characters.

Well, after writing my first book, I knew I had to write another book. After the LA riots or the civil unrest, depending on your political point of view, in 1992, at that time I was working at a nonprofit, the Liberty Hill Foundation. Then and still today, they grant money to community organizing. So I knew a lot of the players in LA, the mainstream local power brokers as well as grassroots people and some of the ones involved in the gang truce. Knowing this range of folks, I thought I could then write a mystery novel set after the riots—a mystery set amid a changing racial and political landscape. It was titled *Violent Spring*, with my PI Ivan Monk delving into the death of a Korean merchant in South Central. The book eventually got published, despite some publishers telling me in their rejection letters to drop the sociopolitical aspects of the novel. The book even got optioned for HBO and I did the Hollywood shuffle. Hilarious.

But now I was hooked. I'd written one book, I had to write the next one. 'Cause you're only as good as the last book . . . your last trick. Which gets us to today, twelve or so novels later and some short stories, anthologies, and scripts I've banged out. The deal is to keep repeating the trick, which is especially arduous given the state of publishing today. Or maybe it's easier, because you don't have to worry about a publisher buying your next book. Anyway, maybe it's a good thing you won't need to publish your book in the traditional way. It's gotten harder and harder to sell a book given it's all about the P & L—the profit and loss on your last book.

Is that because of e-publishing and the Kindle?
Yeah, because with the Kindle, iPad, and what have you, and just to bite the hand that feeds, why do we need publishers, if there's no real book, no physical copy? So what is the publisher's role if they're not "publishing" a hard copy of the book? We now have some cases of young writers like my boy Seth Harwood, who wrote *Jack Wakes Up* and *Young Junius*, who have gone this route. Initially they publish an e-book, even doing podcasts of reading the chapters. They then work the social media, Facebooking and twittering and who knows what else, building up an audience. So they can quantify a readership based on downloads and hits, and counterintuitively, the same people who got the book for free or cheap electronically, a good number of those folks, went out and bought their books when these works came out as real books. I mean, a book you can feel and smell, man.

It seems to me then that there is still an attachment by some people to the book as an artifact. They want a hard copy sitting on their shelf. Will this be the case with the new generation?
I don't think so. I hope so, but young people growing up in a paperless society won't need or want the hard copy of the book. For them a book isn't an artifact. Conversely, there are still books that catch fire. There seems to be young people, among other people, who will go out and buy those books.

What I'm curious about is what is the demographic breakdown of those who are buying hard copy books vs e-books. I would bet it's heavily young people.
My wife Gilda recently read a book on her iPhone, *The Devil in the White City* by Erik Larson. And because she was engaged in the story, she didn't care that

she was reading it on this little device, though she showed it to me on the iPhone and the text was pretty readable. The fact remains we still need and want stories. There will always be a need and a hunger for stories. That's just how our brains are hardwired. I guess something about order in the chaos that's life. And we're storytellers, whatever form that takes. Someone still has to come up with the plot, the characters and situations. But it seems to be the case now that when the publisher takes on your book, they expect you to quantify and deliver your audience.

I try not to think too hard about the future of publishing. If I did that, I'd never write another book. I just keep telling my stories and being optimistic that it will still find an audience.
I agree.

What's your muse?
Deadlines. Seriously, I'm reluctant to say that I have a muse because to me, as a commercial writer, a genre writer, I write better if I have a deadline. The pressure. If I had any muse, it would be the ghosts of my mom the librarian and my dad the mechanic who always encouraged me, particularly about writing. Especially my dad, Dikes, because he didn't have much of an education. He had to drop out of school in the sixth grade. I grew up hearing his stories. He was born in 1912, so was a teenager and grown man during the Great Depression. He dug ditches making highways for the Works Progress Administration, was a lookout as a kid for a bootlegger in his hometown of Seguin, Texas, was an iceman delivering blocks of ice to cold water flats in Chicago, delivered bodies to the mortuary, chopped cotton for a quarter for a day's work, and so on.

Eventually his older brother Norman came out to LA and got a job and had Pop come out too. I grew up hearing his stories, of being a young man on Central Avenue, the jazz clubs and night spots then as given the segregation of LA, Blacks were on the east side of the city and Central Avenue became the Stem, it was called, of Black life. Hotels, doctors, dentists, newspapers like the *Eagle* and the *Sentinel*, they were there on or around Central Avenue. He got drafted, going to the war . . . I grew up hearing those stories, and those are the tales that stuck with me then and even today.

Los Angeles itself is certainly an inspiration and a continuing character for me. I think LA can be plumbed for a lot of ideas. As thin as the *L.A. Times* is now, there's always something you read in the paper, see on the news, hear somewhere that invariably sparks an idea in me. I carry that around with me and make little notes. At some point it worries your brain enough that you have to write the story.

I'm also fascinated with the retelling of tales often told. How many versions of timeless iconic characters like Frankenstein, Sherlock Holmes, and Robin Hood are there? Yet there always seems to be room for more—allowing for different angles and perspectives on the characters. Or take the late comedian, the monologist Lord Buckley, Richard Buckley. This big, six-foot-six onetime lumberjack white guy from the sticks in upper California, who reinvents himself as a bebop hipster with a baritone voice, a pith helmet, and Salvador Dalí–type moustache doing an aristocratic English accent knocking it back with Black slang.

"But I'm gonna put a cat on you who was the coolest, grooviest, sweetest, wailin'est strongest cat that ever stomped on this sweet, swingin' sphere. And they called this here cat, the Nazz."

This is part of Buckley's version of the life of Jesus of Nazareth. Cool and crazy. See, it's all in the telling.

Someone, I forget who, said, you will write when it hurts more not to write. Agree?
(Nods) Plus writing is such good therapy. I don't know what I'd do if I couldn't write.

And LA is such a rich cauldron to draw from: various classes, races, cultures, undocumented immigration . . .
Absolutely.

They're not going to stop coming. Until we help stabilize Mexico's economy, stop selling them guns and genetically modified corn. No border can stop it. We are all part of a continuum.
That's right. Our job is to go out and get those stories and tell them.

What's noir then?
Looking at this book you have here on your table about William Mulholland, who engineered the bringing of water, or some would argue helped steal that water, to make what has become the modern metropolis of Los Angeles, drives home the concept of LA as the seat or crucible of noir. Even though the word 'noir' is bandied about a lot these days, to me the term refers to a doomed character or characters consumed or at least driven by lust, greed, gluttony, revenge . . . one of those baser instincts of us humans.

Invariably this bent mental state gets the character all caught up; when they should turn left they turn right, when they should keep walking, they turn the knob on that battered door and their fate can only spiral down into the velvet whirlpool. Noir means doomed characters in search of a doomed destiny, but they don't know this and they can't help themselves. They're self-deluded but they're making themselves self-deluded by lust or greed. Usually it's one of the seven deadly sins but there are only two or three of those that really trip people up. Ha.

They can't see up for down, wrong for right, because they want something. It's usually not a big thing. It's a reasonable thing. They want money but they don't want a lot of money. A couple hundred thousand, let's say. Or you desire your neighbor's wife 'cause she looks so damn good in that summer dress.

So noir is personal?
It's your own undoing that you, if not willingly, at least subconsciously, participate in and bring about. When you should make a left turn, you make a right. When you should lock that door, you open it. Because you're driven, obsessed. Often it's a situation you've put yourself in. Noir will kill ya.

> Denise Hamilton writes crime fiction set in contemporary, multicultural Los Angeles. Her novels have been short-listed for every major mystery award. She is also the editor of the Edgar Award–winning short story anthology *Los Angeles Noir* (that Phillips has a story in) and subsequent anthologies *Speculative Los Angeles* and *Los Angeles Noir 2: The Classics*. Visit her at www.denisehamilton.com.

"Living off the Grid"
Marge Piercy

Cape Cod? Isn't that a weird, or at least rather sandy, place for a writer to live?
Not at all. There is a long history of writers, painters, and radicals living on the Outer Cape. I don't understand what sandy has to do with it. We grow just about all our own vegetables, our own fruit, many perennials, a garden of organically grown roses, all in the soil you seem to scorn. It's a fecund place.

When I moved here, at a time when in part due to COINTELPRO, the movement in NYC was destroying itself. This was a very cheap place to live. I've written about that in an essay . . . "Gentrification and Its Discontents." My house was built for $25,000 by a bunch of stoned hippies. When I moved here, there were many people living off the grid. Several Communists had spent their underground years during the McCarthy era on the Outer Cape. It's still viewed as the wild and woolly boondocks by people who live in the more suburban parts of the mid-Cape and upper Cape.

The last decade or so, we've been inundated by wealthy summer people between July 4 and Labor Day, and now many suburban types with money have retired here; but there are still remnants of how we lived then. There's still a barter economy that's important to us, and a lot of writers and artists still live and work here—fewer in Provincetown than there used to be, as it's turned way too expensive—but just as many in Wellfleet.

The Outer Cape is very liberal politically, and most residents are ecologically oriented. There's a tradition of acceptance of all kinds of lifestyles and orientations. Gays and lesbians were comfortable here for probably a century before that was true on the mainland. Black sea captains operated out of the Cape while slavery was still legal.

You have not only consistently published poetry but gained a wide circle of readers who are not poets themselves. That puts you in rare company. What do you think of Edna St. Vincent Millay? E.E. Cummings? Gary Snyder?

I admire Gary Snyder and his ecological commitment very much. Edna St. Vincent Millay was outspoken and feisty. I admire E.E. Cummings's musicality, less for his visual-only poems, not at all for his occasional anti-Semitism.

What does the current state of Detroit mean to you?

That the money and whites fled. That those who made their money out of the labor of hard workers did not give a damn what happened to them. That great music and writing and all kinds of art can still come from a place that is dear to me. That it is possible for Detroit to survive with new ideas but it will be difficult. Growing up in Detroit prepared me to be a lefty and a feminist.

I wasn't white when I grew up. Jews and Blacks were always lumped together in racist and anti-Semitic propaganda handed out by the Silver Shirts on street corners and pumped over the radio by Father Coughlin. The neighborhoods with housing bans (most of Detroit) made no distinction between us.

Even though you are a bona fide New York Times *bestseller, you describe yourself (in your memoir* Sleeping with Cats, *I think) as a midlist writer. Is that humility or pride?*

I never made the kind of money bestsellers do, and because I am a midlist writer, I can no longer get my fiction published in New York. My poetry does well enough to still get published by Knopf. I'm too old, too left, and too feminist to be a true bestseller author or to be interesting to the young Ivy League trust fund people who are most of the New York editors today. One of the reasons we started and ran Leapfrog Press for ten years, until we could no longer afford to continue, was to publish other serious midlist writers who could no longer find editors in New York houses—of which there are fewer and fewer. Those that remain are like other corporations that produce face creams and detergents. There's little pretense they're doing more than watching the bottom line. The demise of midlist writers is self-fulfilling. The few New York publishers left put all their effort into a few titles. The rest of the list has to do their own publicity, if they can, and hope that the occasional reviews that still exist help. Then when you come along with your next book, all they look at is how many copies the last one sold.

Dystopias are easy. You are one of the few writers who tackle serious utopias. What are the rewards of that endeavor?
Science fiction, speculative fiction, whatever you want to call it, is one of the ways to explore social issues in fiction. You can explore what it's going to be like if current trends continue. You can change a variable and see what that does.

Dystopias are not as easy as you seem to think. In *Woman on the Edge of Time* and *He, She and It*, I tackle both types. I think *He, She and It* is more relevant today because what I describe in it is happening and happening rapidly. But the reason for writing utopias is to provide a positive image of what can be worked toward, instead of fighting for more of the same, more McDonalds, bigger McMansions, more powerful SUVs, yet more media, cheaper plastic surgery, deadlier and more automated weapon systems. Utopias offer the writer's imaginative portrait of how things might be if we make it so.

What's a worming?
It's a group criticism/self-criticism session familiar to anyone who has read *Fanshen* or anybody who was active in New Left groups toward the later 1960s.

In the utopian vision of Woman on the Edge of Time, *there are no cities, or at least no Big Cities. What happened to the girl who wanted to eat New York?*
I lived in NYC twice, the last time for seven years. What I saw was not delightful: the increasing ownership of the city by the ruling class, the poor and finally also the middle class being pushed out, terrifying police work (believe me, the Red Squad were no philanthropists), real estate prices from hell. Pollution. Being right next to an aging nuclear power plant—but so are we here on the Cape, with no way to evacuate when the local Fukushima clone blows.

I lived in many cities for the first half of my life—Detroit, Chicago, Paris, Boston, San Francisco, Brooklyn, and Manhattan. My lungs were weakened by years of smoking and breathing pollution. I was gassed several times in antiwar demonstrations. By the time I moved to Cape Cod, my lungs were seriously damaged and I was sick. My lungs cleared here.

You have a distinct poetic style combining (for me) the easy lope of Whitman with the taut line of Dickinson. Can you say something about contemporary poets who have influenced you?

You named the poets who influenced me just when I was beginning to write poetry at fifteen. Influence is a matter of adolescence and early adulthood. I'd say the other major influences in late adolescence were Muriel Rukeyser and William Butler Yeats. Muriel was very important to me, as a writer who wrote honestly, passionately, and well about being a woman, as a writer with politics, as a writer whose work was written to be said aloud.

After going through college and learning that proper poetry had to be composed of sestinas written about works viewed in the Uffizi in Florence on a Guggenheim, I dared to go back to writing in my own voice and about my own life after hearing Ginsberg read. Although I tried numerous times for Guggenheims—for instance to do research for *Gone to Soldiers* and for *He, She and It*—I have received extremely few grants or any free money in my life. I've worked since I was twelve, and what money I have I've made from working for it.

Was your great-grandfather really a pirate?

Great-great-grandfather. I have no idea. My mother told me that about my father's father's father's father, but my mother loved drama and was leery of the Piercys. I know little about my father's family other than that the men went to sea a lot. I saw a memorial to a Piercy captain in the cathedral in Kent.

I know far more about my mother's family and my grandfather on that side, who was a radical and was murdered by the Pinkertons for unionizing the bakery workers in Cleveland. I know about my great-grandfather who was a rabbi in a *stetl* in Lithuania and finally married my grandmother and grandfather when he was fleeing the Czar's police after an unsuccessful revolutionary attempt. I was very close to my maternal grandmother, whom I've written about in my memoir *Sleeping with Cats*. She gave me my religious education, gave me a strong sense of female-based Judaism, told me tales from the *stetl* and from her own difficult and hazardous life. Magic realism? She was a master of tales infused with that.

You got started as a writer pretty early. Or would you call it late?
When I was fifteen, we moved from a small asbestos shack where I slept first in my parents' bedroom and then in a room that was for storage and a passageway, to a much larger house where I had a room of my own upstairs, away from my parents although across the hall from boarders. The bathroom I could use was downstairs and my room was tiny and unheated, but I loved it and began to write seriously in an attempt to deal with contradictions in my life and assorted traumas. A girlfriend I was close to died of a heroin overdose that year, my sweet cat was poisoned by my next-door boyfriend because our little house was sold to an African American family—the neighborhood was predominantly Black but segregated by blocks. I had gone to school with Blacks and played with them since I was little, so it was hard for me to understand our neighbors' fury. Of course their kids went to a parochial school that was all white.

After my beloved and loving grandmother died, I revolted against Orthodoxy starting with my anger at the rabbi at her funeral. Nothing in my life or around me was the way it was supposed to be according to TV, according to school, according to the propaganda everywhere about America. I had been in a sort of proto-gang where I felt accepted—until we moved. I had been sexually active early but stopped when we moved, as the girls in this new neighborhood were "good girls." I felt like a different animal than those around me. I had already developed some left politics, called myself a socialist. I did not fit in anyplace I could see. I started writing both fiction and poetry. I wrote much better poetry than fiction for a long time. But it all started in a desperate attempt to understand myself and my life and Detroit around me.

You went to Cuba back in the 1960s. What was that like? Do you think of yourself as a socialist today?
I was invited by the Cuban government to spend the summer in Cuba in 1968. It was a very vital time. The blockade had not stifled the economy that much and the arts were free and percolating. I was one of the founders of the North American Congress on Latin America—NACLA—one of the only New Left groups still active today. I subscribe to their newsletter, one of the best sources of information on what's really going on south of the border. I had friendly relations with the Cuban delegation to the UN. That was why I was invited.

I spent the first month trying to explain the New Left to party people and seeing all the official sights. Then I was turned loose. I traveled around Cuba freely, met amazing dancers, painters, filmmakers, poets, all kinds of men and women who'd fought in the revolution, and peasants in the countryside. I argued with party members about sex roles and freedom for sexual orientations, but loved a lot of what I saw and experienced. Cuba is very beautiful and there are lots of pristine wild places still, amazing bird, reptile, crustacean, mammal life. I like Cuban food.

In New York, life was edgy. I received death threats with some regularity from right-wing groups. I'd been beaten in demonstrations. I had been under surveillance in New York—mail cover, at one point a live tap on my apartment, and strange guys in the basement of the apartment house. The men who worked in that building were from the Dominican Republic; they resented the American invasion there and were sympathetic to me and my politics. Plus, I spoke Spanish fluently then and used it every day with them and in the neighborhood. They always warned me about surveillance. If I ever doubted, Ira found proof years later, after I had moved to Cape Cod.‡

I had a huge old-fashioned desk I used till I got my first PC in 1982. The desk was not a good place to work on a computer, so Woody built a new desk for me. The old desk had to be broken up to be burned. As Woody was prying it apart, he found an electronic bug on the bottom of one of the drawers. A tiny mike and wires leading away.

Yes, I'm a socialist-anarchist-feminist.

Is Vida based on anyone real?
I knew a lot of the people in the Weather Underground and kept in touch with them. Three of them are still close friends. The character Vida was not based on any particular individual or individuals. I don't work that way. I did not agree with about half of their politics at that time, but I am loyal to friends. And I was proud of how so many of them ran rings around the FBI. *Vida*'s still one of the most accurate portrayals of life underground, what led to it, and how the people survived.

---

‡   Her partner Ira Wood, a.k.a. Woody.

You teach a lot, and you and Ira Wood have written a how-to book on writing. Yet in a poem you say that all one can learn is someone else's mannerisms. So which is it?
I don't actually teach a lot. I give a lot of readings, some speeches and three or four workshops a year. I've taught in college on three occasions, two of them for just a quarter or a semester. I did my best, but I was out of my element in academia.

Woody and I both teach craft workshops. You can teach craft. Beyond that, it's pretty much bullshit. If you take four writing workshops, you'll hear four opinions, four definitions of excellent, four sets of instructions and recommendations for writing. The worst workshops are given by people who only write books about how to write but pretty much can't do it themselves. The best way, we always say, to learn to write memoirs is to read memoirs and learn from those that don't work for you as well as from those who do. Look at how they did things. Separate out the craft elements. If you want to write detective stories, read them. If you want to write historical novels, read them.

You seem to share Rexroth's old-fashioned idea that the poet has a public and political, as well a personal artistic, responsibility. How would you describe that responsibility today?
The idea that poetry should be devoid of politics is a modern heresy designed to diminish any slight power we might have, to render us irrelevant. It is a notion that poets before about 1940 would have found really weird. Shakespeare's plays are rife with politics; same with Milton, Dryden, Pope, Wordsworth, Shelley, Byron, and that's only a few British poets. All the Irish poets had political ideas. Go back to the Romans. Find one without politics!

Poets and novelists and memoirists and essayists are all citizens like your plumber or neighborhood cop or clergy. If you don't take an interest, politics may come down on your head, may take away your livelihood, pollute your air, give you cancer from the food you eat, teach your children garbage and false history, make you pay for wars you don't believe in and actually hate.

Do you have a different strategy for writing poetry and fiction? A different schedule? A different desk in front of a different window?

Ideas for novels can't be mistaken for ideas for poems and vice versa. I do both usually all the time but seldom on the same day. I can write prose for a lot longer duration than I can poetry, which is much more intense and concentrated.

You once compared talent to phlogiston. Was that a compliment?
Phlogiston is the substance that the scientists and philosophers of an earlier time used to explain fire. So it stands for any invented thingie that people label the cause of a phenomenon they don't understand.

I read Dance the Eagle to Sleep *when there actually were rebels fighting underground in the USA. If you were writing it today would the protagonists still be teens?*
No, they'd probably be sixty-five-year-old women.

Like me, you were drawn to SDS even though a bit too old. Out of school. Was that a problem?
I joined SDS after searching around to find a group opposing the war in Vietnam that I could agree with. I was a premature antiwar activist, from about 1962 on, before we had officially entered the war. I had a friend who spent time in Vietnam and wrote letters about what was really going on. I had trouble finding anybody else who cared for some time.

I went to one of the big rallies in Washington in 1965 and joined SDS then. I organized off campus in Brooklyn from 1965 on. I worked for *Viet Report* and tried various ways of relating. Then we started NACLA and I was fully involved there. I did power structure analysis and created and ran a database on power structure, the CIA, interlocking directorates among the ruling class, etc. I was recruited into the regional office of SDS because I was one of the few people around who had any experience organizing off campus. I had done some in civil rights and local politics. I was a precinct captain in Chicago during the Kennedy election.

Nobody thought I was much older. I've always looked younger than I am, still do. I was in an open relationship and had many relationships in the Movement. Bob Gottlieb and I started Movement for a Democratic Society to do off-campus organizing after Progressive Labor launched a coup and took over the regional office of SDS. We had teachers, social workers, city planner groups, affinity groups like the Motherfuckers (primarily a motorcycle gang), street theater, buying co-op, child care, and so on.

What kind of car do you drive? I ask this of everyone.
When I drive at all, it's an old stick shift Volvo. Mostly Woody does the driving, in a truck with four-wheel drive, a Toyota. Most year-rounders here on the Cape drive trucks.

Do you read poetry for fun? Who?
Martín Espada, Dorianne Laux, Joy Harjo, Laura Kasischke, Wisława Szymborska, Tony Hoagland, Philip Levine, Adrienne Rich, Rita Dove, Lucille Clifton, Yehuda Amichai, Paul Celan, Kevin Young, Leslea Newman, Nelly Sachs, Maxine Kumin, Audre Lorde.

One might say all novels are historical. But City of Darkness, City of Light *and* Gone to Soldiers *definitely are. Can you say something about how research informs your work? What about other novelists (thinking in particular of James Jones and Hilary Mantel)?*
Generally I've done a lot of research on the period before I begin work. I work on characters then for some time before I write. After first draft, I know what I need to research and generally do a lot of it all the way through to final draft. The research for *Gone to Soldiers* was seven times longer than the novel. For *Sex Wars* (my most recent novel), my research came to 1,900 pages.

What interests me in history is how those periods influenced the present. In *Sex Wars*, one of the alarming aspects is that in the period after the Civil War they were dealing with the same problems and issues we are dealing with today: the rights of women and minorities, immigration, abortion, contraception, income inequality, prison reform, election manipulation.

Bernard Cornwell does excellent research for his novels.

If you had to abandon fiction or poetry, which would it be?
No contest: poetry would win. You can write poetry in a jail cell. If you have no paper, you can memorize your poems. You can say a poem in front of a firing squad. Poetry is highly portable. Novels are not. These days I'm inclining more

toward short stories than novels. As I get older, I like shorter forms better than longer ones. But poetry will always win out. I also make more money these days from my poetry—readings and advances—than from fiction or other prose.

"Radical, Sacred, Hopefully Magical"
Rachel Pollack

Does Tarot work?
Yes. Not only that, it will do the work you hire it to do. It has a long résumé.

Your career with Tarot seems quite successful. Do your followers know you are also a fiction writer? Is there leakage between the two realms?
Not that much, which I find both strange and frustrating. Strange, because you'd think that people who say that my Tarot books are vital to their lives would be very interested to read my stories (since Tarot is somewhat specialized, I would not necessarily expect that of my fiction audience). But that does not seem to be the case. And frustrating, both because who doesn't want a wider audience, and I think people's views on Tarot might open up somewhat to read my fiction. I am the same person, after all. I don't turn a switch in my brain to write one, then the other.

The Shining Tribe Tarot artwork—yours? Are the cards different? How much alteration and invention is acceptable?
Yes. I had planned to sketch them out, then hire an artist to do the final pictures. But I had trouble finding someone who was willing to stay close to my visions of what they should be. Then the great artist Niki de Saint Phalle, who had invited me to consult with her on her Tarot sculpture garden in Italy, told me I needed to do them myself. So I became more serious about the drawing. The influences are to a large extent tribal and prehistoric art from around the world, but they're also connected thematically to the more well-known versions of the cards. Not everyone sees that, however, which has caused some people to think they cannot "work" with the deck. Something

I find very satisfying is that the strongest response to the pictures has come from artists.

What's a Traveler? What do you think of the movie The Fisher King?
The Travelers are meant to be the reality behind all the traditions of sorcerers, magicians, witches, shamans, root doctors, alchemists, and so on, from the earliest humans to the present day. They are always set apart, keeping their existence hidden from ordinary society, yet also completely up to date, having their own dark web, called Jinn-net, and using "spirit drones" to deliver supplies for their magical workings. I've had a great time writing these stories. Each one adds to the lore, building on the ones before it.

I love *The Fisher King*—seen it three times. Mostly it's the brilliant construction and the powerful performances, but I also found it thrilling because I studied King Arthur in college and know the original story of the Fisher King and the Wasteland. The title of my Jack Shade collection, *The Fissure King*, actually came from a writer friend named Nancy Norbeck. We were discussing a *Doctor Who* episode with an alien called the Fisher King, and Nancy said that the first time she heard a character say it she took it as "Fissure." I realized that the expression, as both a title and a character, was perfect for an original novella that would tie together the four previously published stories. I asked if I could use it, and Nancy was kind enough to agree.

What or who got you into Tarot? Or were you raised in that religion?
As I'm sure you know, Tarot is not a religion. It began as a card game in the Renaissance, then in the late eighteenth century it began to be seen as both a repository for ancient doctrines and a device for fortune-telling. Growing up, I never heard of it, and even after college I only knew of it as a sort of plot device in T.S. Eliot's great poem "The Wasteland," which is based on the Fisher King, among other things. Then, in the early spring of 1970, I was teaching at a state college in upstate New York, and another teacher said she would read my Tarot cards if I gave her a ride home. As soon as I saw them I knew they were something I had to have. They were pretty obscure back then, and it took some searching but I finally found a deck.

That time, 1970–71, was a great watershed for me. I discovered the Tarot (or the Tarot discovered me), I came out as a transwoman and a lesbian, and I sold my first story, to Michael Moorcock's *New Worlds*.

What are the two parts of Why?
Origins and purpose.

Why does the Sun exist? Because pieces of dead stars coalesced to form a next-generation star that reached a critical mass and came to life.

Why does the Sun exist? To create just the right conditions for organic, self-aware life to come into existence on the third planet, and with life, eventually, consciousness.

Who was Lou Stathis?
My second editor on the comic *Doom Patrol*. Lou was tough. I learned a lot from him, but he also was a champion of my work. Sadly, he died, way too young, of a rare brain condition inherited from his father (who'd also died of it), and the editor who took over had a different vision of what kind of work he wanted to see.

You have been acclaimed as "One of the Most Important Women in Geek History." Gosh. Does this come with benefits?
Ah, if only. The fact is, though, there is a great benefit, and that is hearing from the people whose lives my work has touched. I also get invited to teach (usually Tarot) in places like Australia and China, and that's pretty terrific.

Tell us about Doom Patrol. *How did that come about?*
I greatly admired the work being done on it in the late '80s (the comic began in the '60s), by a writer-artist team named Grant Morrison and Richard Case. At a party I met the editor, Tom Peyer, and after gushing about it confessed it was (then) the only monthly comic I really wished I might someday have a chance to write. Tom told me that Grant was ending his run, and if I wanted to send him a sample script he'd consider it. So I did, and it became my first issue. In the months leading up to the change-over I wrote a series of dumb letters in the voice of a gee-whiz fangirl. The first said something like "Gee, Mr. Peyer, *Doom*

Patrol is just the coolest thing ever! Grant Morrison is, like, totally a complete genius! If he gets sick or dies or something, can I write it?" I sent the first to Tom without telling him, and he liked it so much he told me to send one every month until the time came to make the announcement. In the next to last one I threatened him with some kind of mob action (his head in the toilet bowl, I think I said) unless he let me write it. Then in the last I apologized, adding, "The thing is, I already told my mom I was doing it, and she told all her friends." So Tom, as the editor, announced, "Well, there it is, she told her mom, so what can we do? Rachel Pollack is the new writer on *Doom Patrol*." And amazingly, there are people to this day who believe that's how I got the job.

A historian of comix (there are many) once said that your character Coagula "perfectly explained to Robotman how gender identity works." What did she tell him?
First of all, a nitpick—"comix" refers to the "underground" work by 1960s–70s cartoonists, such as R. Crumb. The work published by the big companies has always been called "comics." Coagula, whose actual name was Kate Godwin (we almost never used the secret hero name—the characters in *Doom Patrol* didn't have secret identities) doesn't so much explain gender identity to Cliff (Robotman) as identity itself. Though Cliff is a human brain in a metal robot body, he's been falling for Kate, and then someone tells him she's trans. He freaks out and confronts her, saying, "You used to be a man!" Kate says, "No, Cliff, I was never a man." Then he says, "But you had a penis, right? And you cut it off!" Kate then says, "And what about you, Cliff? Do you have a penis? Are you a man?" She then goes on to say we are who we are because we know who we are.

What were her superpowers?
She had alchemical powers based on the old slogan "Solve et Coagula." A gesture with her left hand could make something dissolve, then the right could cause it to coagulate. But really, her main superpower was belief in herself.

If, as some believe, science fiction is a bastard child of literature, then comics are . . .
The bastard child of movies? Or maybe it's the other way around. Not sure.

What kind of car do you drive? I ask this of everyone.

A red Nissan Versa named Katrina, for the mysterious "High T" in the story "The Beatrix Gates."

Did you enter the SF/fantasy field as a fan or as a writer? Were you made to feel welcome?
Oddly enough, I did not know fandom existed until I became a pro writer. I wish I had, I'm sure my high school and college years would have been a lot more exciting. And I was definitely welcomed.

Is there a lot of paperwork involved in gender change? Licenses, deeds, IDs?
Not as much now as there used to be! Or maybe it's just a lot easier.

What poets do you read for fun?
Questions like this always throw me because it changes—and because I read more prose. I've liked Joy Harjo a lot—Muscogee (Creek) poet who writes in English. And I was, am, very influenced by a movement called Ethnopoetics, radical modern translations of ancient poetry and shamanic/magical texts. there's an experimental poet/fiction writer named Selah Saterstrom I enjoy. Her work is influenced by magic and divination. I read "The Wasteland" every April ("the cruelest month") and short passages from *Finnegans Wake* every February 2, which is James Joyce's birthday. Technically, the *Wake* is a novel, but its language is more musical than any poetry.

What pulled you into writing, story or words?
Tough one. I would have to say story, but the way it's told is so vital.

Is "Burning Beard" from the Bible, or does it only pretend to be?
Well, it's what Jews call midrash, a kind of expansion of something in the Bible, in this case the life story of Joseph, from Genesis. But it's a pretty radical form of midrash!

I think of you as a "stand-aside" writer. I expect a certain formality in your prose, which elevates everything. Even the humor.

I like that. Thanks. The only thing I'd add is that I think I do that even more with strong emotions, particularly in parts of "The Beatrix Gates."

Ever hit a bad patch in either career?
When *Godmother Night* won the World Fantasy Award it was already out of print, and its American editor, who was a champion of my work, told me that the publisher had told him there was "no way" they'd publish another fantasy by me.

You write in longhand first with a fountain pen. Any other drills, charms, or tricks as a writer?
Just pushing myself to write a certain number of words a day. I sometimes like to say, "Anyone who thinks guilt never helps anything has never been a writer."

What were you doing in 1968?
Marching, shouting, chanting. Actually, I was in grad school for a year, which was awful. I also cast my first presidential vote. I couldn't bring myself to vote for Hubert Humphrey, so voted for the radical Black comic Dick Gregory. Later I found out that Gregory, for all his terrific politics on many issues, was an anti-Semite. That was a lesson I never forgot.

Your first publication was with a pen name. How come and what was it?
Not really a pen name, just my birth name. I sold my first story before I came out and changed my name. And as I say in the essay "Trans Central Station," you can find it easily enough, but I'm not going to give it, out of respect for all those trans people who must fight so hard for people to acknowledge their "real" name, the name they give themselves.

Shamanism, Tarot, Judaism, Paganism, Witchery—are all these present in your everyday quotidian life or are you just saving a seat for them?
You forgot Goddess worship! They're all there, but in my own mix. A friend once told me of a form that asked your "faith," and I thought, if I had to answer that, I might put down "Heresy."

You had an encounter with cancer. Anything to say about that? Turning point, hinge, bump in the road?
It was an amazing experience, largely due to the great outpouring of love and support from so many people literally all over the world. I had cancer twice, actually, with the second time requiring a very radical treatment known as "stem cell replacement therapy," requiring three weeks in the hospital. But it's two years now, and it seems to have worked.

I know you have a suspicion that certain science fiction writers were secretly trans. Care to comment? Why not?
I like that "Why not?" it's respect, really, for people's privacy, in this case mostly the families, since two of them are dead.

And I get this from their writings, not any knowledge of their private lives.

My Jeopardy *answer: Young Adult. You provide the question.*
"What is the most dismissed subgenre in writing today?" The finest book about slavery ever written by a white person is a YA book, *The Astonishing Life of Octavian Nothing, Traitor to the Nation*, by M.T. Anderson. And one of the greatest fantasy works of modern literature, *His Dark Materials* by Philip Pullman, is not even YA; it's a children's book.

Violets were once big business in Rhinebeck. Also, Rufus Wainwright was born there. Is there a connection?
Didn't know about the violets, but Rufus Wainwright's mother, Kate McGarrigle, wrote one of my favorite songs, "Talk to Me of Mendocino."

One sentence on each please: Guy Davenport, Marion Zimmer Bradley, Ray Lafferty.
Pass on the first two. For the third, R.A. Lafferty is one of the great neglected writers of SF, somewhat like Cordwainer Smith. My partner and I used to refer to him as Great-Souled Lafferty. (That's two sentences, but I figure I had credit from the other two writers.)

Ever been torn apart by wild dogs?
Keep thinking I should say yes, but nothing comes to mind.

Rejected by (or disappointed in?) mainstream feminism, you discovered the "Goddess movement." How did that come about, and what the hell is it anyway?
I'm not going to get into the hostility to trans women that arose in the radical feminist world, but the Goddess movement was the rediscovery of the powerful female deities, temples, and stories before the rise of the so-called Great Religions.

Thank you for not telling us about your cats.
Anytime.

How would you describe your politics today?
Radical, sacred, hopefully magical.

Were you ever a Nice Jewish Boy?
I've always been Jewish, even when I thought I wasn't, and I'm pretty sure I've never been a boy, even when I thought I was. As for nice, I've always tried to be, but I've also always tried to be tough.

"A Real Joy to Be Had"
Kim Stanley Robinson

David Hartwell once said that the Golden Age of Science Fiction is twelve. Was that true for you? What was your first literature?
I didn't know science fiction existed until I was eighteen; then I fell in pretty deeply. The first book I remember reading was *Huckleberry Finn*, and I still have that copy of the book with me, it has a gorgeous cover depicting Huck and Jim pulling a caught fish onto the raft, in vibrant colors. For years I pretended to be Huck Finn. My parents subscribed to the Scholastic book of the month club, and I read those when they came in the mail pretty much the day of arrival. I read everything that caught my eye at the library when I was a child, then as a teenager did the same, but became a fan of locked-room detective mysteries, chiefly John Dickson Carr but also Ellery Queen, and all the rest of that crowd from the 1930s. Then just as I was leaving for college I ran into the science fiction section at the library, all the books with their rocket-ship-and-radiation signs on the spine, and that was very exciting. In college I majored in history and literature, and on the side majored in science fiction, absorbing the New Wave pretty much as it happened.

Did your parents read to you as a kid? Did anyone? Do you read to your kids?
Yes, my mom read to my brother and me at bedtime, and then I read on by myself with a flashlight. I read at bedtime to my older son throughout his childhood and youth at home (my wife read to the younger son), and we made our way through all of Joan Aiken, the entire Patrick O'Brian sequence, many kids' books I remembered from my childhood and found in used bookstores, and many more. Now that my son is off to college I miss that very much, and have tried to horn in on the younger son, but no luck. It's sad to be done, and I have

to say, along with everything else, it certainly helped me with my public readings of my own work. My mouth just got stronger and more versatile.

Do you touch type? Do you write on a computer? I hear you and Karen Fowler like to write in cafés. What's that about?
Yes, I touch type, and I can go really fast, although not accurately. I write by hand in a notebook, and then on a laptop for fiction. I'm trying to work outdoors now, in the shade of my front courtyard, it's very nice. Being outdoors helps a lot.

I wrote in cafés for many years, and I liked that too. I liked seeing the faces, which often became characters' faces, and I liked hearing the voices around me, I think it helped with dialogue and made my writing even more a matter of channeling a community. Karen Fowler joined me in this at several cafés downtown, all of which died, we hope not from our presence, although we may have killed three. It was good to meet with someone going through the same issues, it was a kind of solidarity and also a bit of policing, in that there was someone to meet at a certain time, who would then be watching in a way. It was a great addition to a friendship. But now Karen has moved, and on my own I'm finding I like my courtyard better than any of the cafés left in town. I thought I was getting tired of writing, before, but now I realize I was only tired of spending so much time indoors sitting around. When it's outdoors it feels completely different.

Were you ever tempted to keep a journal? Did you give in?
Tempted maybe, but I never gave in. Except in this way: long ago I started filling out a Sierra Club weekly calendar, which has only a narrow space for every day, with a week per page—you know the type. So every day could only be given a few sentences at most, basically a bare description of what that day held, very minimal. I now have twenty-three years of those filled out, and my wife and I have a game where I keep the ones from ten and twenty years before on the bed table under the new one, and I tell her what we were doing ten years ago and twenty years ago on that day. It is a way of placing us in time and our own lives that is very interesting, and we get some good laughs and often some groans. Twenty years ago we were young, without children, living in Europe, dashing all

over in trains and planes, seeing romantic cities like Venice and Edinburgh; in the present, going to work and buying groceries, the entry for every day almost identical. But oh well. It's also a very interesting test of the memory, because sometimes we won't remember events or even people, but other times a single sentence will bring back a very full memory of an event; and that memory, there in the brain waiting, would never, never have come back to us if we hadn't had the spur of the sentence in the journal. So, as memories may need to be remembered to hold fast as structures in the brain, this is a good thing in itself. We've become convinced that an evolutionary accident has left us in the curious state of having brains that can remember huge, huge amounts of incident, but we have no good recall mechanisms in us to go back and get them, so they sit there as knots or configurations of synapses, doing nothing but waiting. Very strange.

As for journals, I love the journals of Henry David Thoreau and Virginia Woolf, and often feel they are the whole story as far as literature goes. They are novels written as first-person hyperrealist accounts of a single consciousness, say. And we don't have any other novels that come even close to doing what they do as far as getting inside the head of another human being—except possibly for Proust's novel. So they are considerable works of literature in that sense and I often wonder if a journal would be the best way to go if you were intent to do this particular thing, which it seems to me most literature does indeed want to do. But neither Woolf nor Thoreau had kids. There's a time problem here, and also it takes a certain mentality to keep at it year after year, which is what is required. Also, with both of them, when really bad things happened, their journals went silent, usually for months and sometimes for years. So there seems to be some kind of problem there with what the journal can actually face up to, as a form. Maybe.

I know that you write and publish poetry. Have you published outside the SF field? Have you published fiction outside the field?
No, all my poetry is stuck inside my stories and books. It helps me to think of my poems as being by someone else. And all my fiction has been published in SF magazines or books, although sometimes brought out as "general fiction," by my publisher, but booksellers know which section to put it in after it's off the front tables.

Are there special "chops" for writing SF? Are there ways in which SF is less demanding?
I don't know, I guess there are some techniques particular to SF, maybe the ways in which the future background is conveyed, or something like that. I can't imagine it's less demanding than any other kind of fiction, it feels about as demanding as I can handle, anyway. My near-future and my far-future stories feel about the same in terms of writing, although I will say that when I came back from years on Mars to write about Antarctica, it was a huge relief to have other people making up the culture for me, rather than trying to do it all myself. In that sense I think SF is a bit harder. But it's all hard, and none of it is "realism," so I think distinctions here are very fuzzy.

What part of the process of writing fiction do you like best? Least? Is there a process to writing fiction?
I like the writing. These days I write only novels, and I like most the last three to six months of writing a novel, when I bear down and really go at it like a maniac. There is a real joy to be had in submitting to a task like a madman. It feels like things are coming together, and the process is one of identifying problems and then solving them on the spot, and then moving on. So there is a problem-solving aspect to it that reminds me of hiking cross country in Sierra, where every step is a decision, like every word coming up in a sentence. You get into a flow and then it's problem, solution, problem, solution, and that goes on at a smooth good pace for a long time, and at the end you're somewhere else. Often when in this flow state I will have a couple of hours pass and it feels like only about fifteen minutes have passed, and that I take it is the blessed state, the Zen state, prayer, what have you. Writing as hiking a prayer.

The part I like least . . . Well, first draft when faced with a hard idea can be tough. It makes you feel stupid. But I have learned to ignore that and grind on, and so it's not so bad once you get in the habit. I don't much like dealing with editorial comments, but truthfully, my editors now are so good that that part is not so unpleasant either, because it's helping the book and that always feels good. I like readings. I don't like the wasted time associated with business travel, but this is not a very bad thing either. I guess I mostly like all of it. I don't like people telling me what fiction is or is not, in the sense of what I can or cannot do (see below).

Do you research and then write, or do the two overlap?
I usually research as I am writing, on a need to know basis. If I did my research first, I would never get started writing. I call this the Coleridge problem, because he listed all the things he would need to learn before he could write his epic poem, and he never wrote his epic poem. And I find the research is so much more effective when it is specifically to support a particular scene or chapter. So in the *Mars* books, *The Years of Rice and Salt*, and the climate books, I researched as I wrote and it worked very well to suggest to me what the scenes needed or, better, how they could be extended or made even more interesting. It's a good stimulus to fiction, researching on the fly.

Where did the idea of The Years of Rice and Salt *come from? That's got to be one of the great undiscovered high-concept ideas of SF. Mostly we recycle old ones (apocalypse, first contact, and so on). Was that a "eureka" moment, or did it just leak in from somewhere?*
Thanks, I like that idea myself. It came to me in the late 1970s, and it was indeed a kind of *aha* moment, in that I was thinking about alternative histories, wanting ideas, and thought of the one for "The Lucky Strike" too, and looking over the alternative histories I decided what was needed was the most major change you could think of, that did not simply change the game so much that it wiped away everything. Because you want comparison. So that Harry Harrison's novel in which dinosaurs evolve to high intelligence instead of mammals, is an alternative history in a way, but not—useless as such, because the comparisons are invalidated because the difference there is too huge to be able to play the game. So I was thinking, well what would be the biggest change that would still work in terms of comparison to our history, and it seemed to me that Europe's conquering the world was so big that if it hadn't happened—and then it hit me, and I said *Wow* and ran to write it down quick before I forgot it and ended up wandering around moaning saying I had a good idea but I can't remember it now, it won't come back—which has sometimes happened to me.

So, once I had the idea, I knew I couldn't write it, that what it implied was beyond what I was capable of expressing. I wondered if I would ever be capable of such a thing. I have a couple of good ideas I've never written because I can't think how to yet, but after the *Mars* novels I figured I had worked out the method, and I was feeling bold. I'm glad I wrote it when I did. I don't know if I have the brain cells for it now. Although that's partly that book's fault, because I blew out some fuses writing that one that were never replaced.

Antarctica—you were there. Was that scary or just fun?
It was fun. I was having fun every waking moment, and I seldom slept. It was so beautiful, and alien; like being on another planet.

I did have one scary twenty minutes, when we were in a Kiwi helicopter, pilot about twenty-eight, a real vet, and copilot about twenty-four, and we were trying to fly around Ross Island's north end to get from Cape Crozier back to McMurdo, rather than taking the straight route around the south end; and we were flying toward a cloud bank and the copilot, flying, said to the pilot, "You don't want me to fly into that do you?" and there was a silence of about ten seconds before the pilot said no, and we turned around. But then we had about twenty minutes flying back toward Cape Crozier, where it wasn't clear that the winds would allow us to land. Under us was black water with orca pods visible (very cool before) and the steep snowy side of Ross Island. And there are a fair number of crashed helicopters still half-buried in snow all over Ross Island and the dry valleys, so we knew what could happen. In the end the copilot stuck the landing straight into the wind at Cape Crozier and we retired to the penguin scientists' hut there and hung out for twenty-four hours until the winds died down.

Other than that, it was heaven. I would love to go back.

You're pretty good at landscape. What's that about? Is it a fictional skill or something else entirely? You're also pretty good at erotic scenes.
Thanks. I like landscapes and think they are worth some sentences to describe. Also, I've seen some landscapes and paid attention when in them, so that I feel I can bring something new to the page when I write them, something I saw myself rather than read in a book. There are a fair number of writers who write down only things they have learned in books and in their personal relationships. They think that being nifty or tasteful with the word combinations is enough to make it good writing, but I'm not so sure. I think new perceptions out of the world are better. So this is something I can bring.

As for erotic scenes, I decided long ago that I wasn't going to put violence in my stories just to jazz up the plots, like Hollywood and TV—that that was fake too. It was all out of books and TV and movies, and the writers didn't know what they were talking about, and if I tried I wouldn't either. It's guesswork, it's lazy, it's a cheat. So, but fiction these days and maybe always is pretty reliant on sex and violence, and so without violence, that left sex. Everyone's an expert there, so the test for writing about it is finding ways to make it sexy. That's not easy, but it is fun to try.

Someone once described your Mars *books as an infodump tunneled by narrative moles. I think it was a compliment. What do you think?*
No, not a compliment. I reject the word "infodump" categorically—that's a smartass word out of the cyberpunks' workshop culture, them thinking that they knew how fiction works, as if it were a tinker toy they could disassemble and label superciliously, as if they knew what they were doing. Not true in any way. I reject "expository lump" also, which is another way of saying it. All these are attacks on the idea that fiction can have any kind of writing included in it. It's an attempt to say "fiction can only be stage business" which is a stupid position I abhor and find all too common in responses on amazon.com and the like. All these people who think they know what fiction is, where do they come from? I've been writing it for thirty years and I don't know what it is, but what I do know is that the novel in particular is a very big and flexible form, and I say, or sing: Don't fence me in!

I say, what's interesting is whatever you can make interesting. And the world is interesting beyond our silly stage business. So "exposition" creeps in. What is it anyway? It's just another kind of narrative. One thing I believe: it's all narrative. Once you get out of the phone book anyway, it's all narrative.

And in science fiction, you need some science sometimes; and science is expository; and so science fiction without exposition is like science fiction without science, and we have a lot of that, but it's not good. So the word "infodump" is like a red flag to me, it's a Thought Police command saying, "Dumb it down, quit talking about the world, people don't have attention spans, blah blah blah blah." No. I say, go read *Moby-Dick*, Dostoevsky, Garcia Marquez, Jameson, Bakhtin, Joyce, Sterne—learn a little bit about what fiction can do and come back to me when you're done. That would be never and I could go about my work in peace.

But I thought you liked infodumps.
I do! But let's call them something different and also think of them differently. Think about all writing as narrative, because it is (outside the phone book and other such places). Scientific abstracts, *TV Guide* summaries, all writing has information that traverses time in the telling and in reality too, so *it's all* narrative. So, okay, some of these omnipresent stories are about us, and some of these stories are about the rest of the world. And what I think the people who speak of "expository lumps" or the smartasses who reduced that to "infodumps" are saying is, you can only talk about us. The proper study of mankind is man (Pope) etc. Well, that's just silly. Why be so narcissistic? There are many, many stories that are extremely interesting that don't happen to be about us. That's what science is saying, often, and that's what I'm saying in my science fiction. So, my *Mars* novels are a narrative, the story never stops for even a sentence, even in the list of tools that goes on for two pages, it's just that sometimes it's the story of the rocks and the tools and the weather, and sometimes it's the story of the people there in interaction with all that. I know it reads a bit differently and freaks some people out, but I can see others like it as well. Even some of the people freaked out read on, irritated and mystified.

What do you think of the current state of Earth's Mars enterprise?
Well, the robot landers are sending back some fantastic photos. And the orbiting satellites. A balloon floating at low altitude and taking good photos and moving images would be mind-boggling too. As for human landings, those would be exciting, but they seem a long way off. I don't know if we are going to see them in our lifetimes. But I don't think there's any hurry there. I'm not in the group who say we have to go there fast to save our civilization. I don't believe it's true. We need a healthy Earth and a sustainable civilization, and the Mars project will come. So it may be some time.

How come you only drive Fords?

Ha, well, my dad worked for Ford Aerospace and so he got to buy Fords at dealer cost or lower, and his family too, so this was something he could do for us. I've driven a Cortina, an Escort station wagon, and a Focus station wagon. Those have been good cars, and my wife has driven two Tauruses—we won't talk about those. I want my next car to be a little electric station wagon that I can sleep in the back and fit in my bikes and bales of hay. If Ford makes one, fine. If not, I may be off somewhere else.

You're a big supporter of Clarion, the science fiction "boot-camp" workshop. Why?
I'm a big Clarion supporter because I tried to express my thanks to a dead person. Maybe not the best idea.

Clarion gave me a six-week party and a group of good friends, a cohort, a block party in the small town that is science fiction. It gave me tangible evidence that I was serious about becoming a writer, and taught me a lot of craft points, some of which I agreed with, others not. It gave me some time with six fine writers and people (Delany, Wolfe, Zelazny, Haldeman, Knight, and Wilhelm) whom I've read with intense interest and pleasure ever since.

What do you think of the current MFA-in-writing boom? Do you think working in a commercial field (like SF) sharpens or dilutes a writer's vision?
I think getting an MFA in creative writing is a bad idea. If you want a graduate degree to help get a job, then the PhD is stronger and gives you more options. With an MFA you need also publishing credits to get a job, so it is not sufficient in itself, as a PhD is, and it only gives you a chance at teaching writing anyway, not all literature. So it's weak in that sense. If you are going for that MFA in order to learn more about writing, I'd say any other graduate degree will give you more raw material for your writing, while you can teach yourself writing on your own. You will be anyway.

I don't know what working in a commercial field does to a writer's vision. A lot of the effect must be unconscious. Ultimately you seem to be saying, does the desire for readers change what you write? Surely it must. But isn't the desire for readers pretty basic to writing? So, maybe it sharpens your vision, in those terms.

Have you ever thought of yourself as part of a "school" in SF? Did it last? Was it fun?
Oh, I hate all literary schools, not just the ones in SF but everywhere. In science fiction they are particularly small and stupid: marketing ploys, herding instincts, white guys wishing they were back in high school and were the tough guys smoking cigarettes out in the parking lot. That's a deeply stupid thing to wish for—gee, I wish I was back in high school. Sorry, but no.

I was called "literary science fiction" for a while, that's the kiss of death in terms of sales, then I was a victim of certain cyberpunks' need to have somebody to mug to show they were punks, that was fine, but a "school" was invented to "oppose" them in a rumble like the Sharks and the Jets, so then I was a "humanist," that was dumb; then I wrote the *Mars* books and I was suddenly "hard SF," but hard SF is only hard in its attitude toward the poor, in other words right wing, so that didn't seem to fit very well, even though I talked about technology. Now people have given up. Sometimes I am called "utopian SF," but that cannot be a school, as there is only you and me and Ursula in it—a study group more than a school. Well, I just don't believe in them. I believe in science fiction, which is a kind of small town in literature, not highly regarded by big city people, but I like it, and I like the big city too. The whole point is to be as idiosyncratic as possible, the town madman. Although in our town that's a tough label to earn.

Were you ever close to any of the "old-timers" in SF? Which ones? What did you get from them?
Not really close, but I loved the several interactions I had with Jack Williamson, one of the kindest, smartest people in writing, modest but incisive. He published science fiction from 1928 to 2008—isn't that eighty years? I'm having trouble believing my math. Anyway, he was great.

I've met Asimov and Bradbury, and talked with Clarke on the phone, and they are all generous friendly people. I guess I get from them the sense that the community is a real community, that the people in it function like neighbors in a small town, helpful to the young people.

Your first big series was the Orange County *or* Wild Shore *trilogy. Did you feel you owed that to your birthplace or was it because Orange County, CA, somehow concentrates all the tendencies good and bad in modern America?*

That trilogy is called *Three Californias*, as the handsome Tor trade paperbacks say. I guess it was a little of both. I wanted to ground some of my science fiction in my actual home town, and I also felt like I was the beneficiary of a lucky coincidence, in that my home town seemed to me to represent some kind of end case for America, some kind of future already here for the rest of the country to witness and hopefully avoid following. I'm not sure that was a true perception, but it had to do with the westward movement in American history. When people reached the Pacific, there was nowhere else to go, so the leading edge of malcontents and dreamers was stuck there and had to make something of it. LA is the big exemplar of how that can go wrong, San Francisco of how it can go right, and Orange County is like the purest expression of LA. And in my time it was so beautiful, then it was so destroyed, and it was so drugged out. It seemed a good spot to talk about America, so I used it. It still feels like a lucky thing, and I think it was fundamental to me becoming a science fiction writer in the first place. When I ran into science fiction at age eighteen, I said, *Oh, I recognize this. This is home. This is Orange County.*

My favorite of that series is Pacific Edge, *the utopia. What's yours? Are there any particular problems in writing a utopia?*
My favorite is *The Gold Coast*, for personal reasons, but I think *Pacific Edge* is more important to us now. Anyone can do a dystopia these days just by making a collage of newspaper headlines, but utopias are hard, and important, because we need to imagine what it might be like if we did things well enough to say to our kids, "We did our best; this is about as good as it was when it was handed to us. Take care of it and do it better." Some kind of narrative vision of what we're trying for as a civilization. It's a slim tradition since More invented the word, but a very interesting one, and at certain points important: the Bellamy clubs after Edward Bellamy's *Looking Back from the Year 2000* had a big impact on the progressive movement in American politics, and H.G. Wells's stubborn persistence in writing utopias over about fifty years (not his big sellers) conveyed the vision that got turned into the postwar order of social security and some kind of government-by-meritocracy. So utopias have had effects in the real world. More recently I think *Ecotopia* by Callenbach had a big impact on how the hippie generation tried to live in the years after, building families and communities.

There are a lot of problems in writing utopias, but they can be opportunities. The usual objections, that they must be boring, are often political attacks, or ignorant repeating of a line, or another way of saying "No expository lumps please; it has to be about me." The political attacks are interesting to parse. "Utopia would be boring because there would be no conflicts. History would stop. There would be no great art, no drama, no magnificence." This is always said by white people with a full belly. My feeling is that if they were hungry and sick and living in a cardboard shack they would be more willing to give utopia a try. And if we did achieve a just and sustainable world civilization, I'm confident there would still be enough drama, as I tried to show in *Pacific Edge*. There would still be love lost, and there would still be death. That would be enough. The horribleness of unnecessary tragedy may be lessened, and the people who like that kind of thing would have to deal with a reduction in their supply of drama.

So, the writing of utopia comes down to figuring out ways of talking about just these issues in an interesting way; how tenuous it would be, how fragile, how much a tightrope walk and a work in progress. That along with the usual science fiction problem of handling exposition. It could be done, and I wish it were being done more often.

Your two early "standalones" anticipated some later themes: superlongevity and terraforming in Icehenge. *And in* Memory of Whiteness *the exploration of ten-dimensional space. What keeps you coming back to these themes?*
I like the superlongevity theme because I'd like to live five hundred years, and also from time to time when I think back on my past, it feels like I've lived five hundred years, so it works as both wish and metaphor. And the whole thrust of medicine leads toward that wish, I think. So it's good science fiction. Same with terraforming Mars, which is very achievable, and even the idea of terraforming other places is interesting to contemplate. It's also a good metaphor for what we now have to do here on Earth, for the rest of human time.

As for ten-dimensional space, physicists keep coming back to it, ever since Kaluza and Klein in the twenties, and I keep thinking, *What the heck can it mean*? It seems to stand in for all the deep weirdness of modern physics and what they are saying about this world we live in, but apparently don't see very well. Also, if you have foolishly taken on a time travel story, it's the only way to make it look like it makes sense.

Are you sorry Pluto is no longer a planet?
No, not at all. I think it's a good lesson in words.

These books came out at about the same time as the Three Californias. *Were they written earlier or in between?*
I somewhat wrote them all at once or overlapping through those years. It went something like, *Icehenge* part 3, *Memory of Whiteness* early drafts, *Icehenge* part 1, *Wild Shore, Icehenge* part 2, and *Memory of Whiteness* final drafts. *The Gold Coast* and *Pacific Edge* came later.

You once said that a writer had to perch on a three-legged stool. I think you meant that you had three readerships: the SF community, the science community, and the more "literary" types. Does that still work for you?
Yes, I think that might describe the three parts of my adult audience, although I think college students and high school students form a group as big as any of these three. Also, leftists, environmentalists, and wilderness people. I like all these readerships very much and indeed am deeply grateful to them, as providing me my career and my sense of myself as a writer. I'm not a writer without them. So, thinking of the SF community as my home town, I guess I think of the "literary" community as another small town, with pretensions, while scientists are the real big city. But they tend to act like a big city, in that they don't know each other and usually don't read fiction. Word of mouth doesn't work as well there as in the other communities. Younger readers use word of mouth and also listen to their teachers, a bit, so they are crucial. Getting word to people who would enjoy my books if they were to give them a try—this is the big problem, and ultimately it comes down to word of mouth. So again I depend on my readership. It's a real dependency!

You are firmly ensconced in a genre (SF). Many writers regard that as a trap, and others as an opportunity. How do you see it? Is working in a field with a developed, opinionated and rambunctious "fandom" a blessing or a curse?

It's the hometown. It's a floor and a ceiling, in some respects. I love the genre and the community, but want readers who don't usually think of themselves as SF readers to give me a try, as they have in the past for Bradbury, Asimov, Frank Herbert, Ursula Le Guin, and so on.

These days there seems to be a lot of permeability. Chabon's *The Yiddish Policemen's Union* was a great SF novel, an alternative history, but that's SF too, and it was widely read and enjoyed by people. Maybe Philip K. Dick's takeover of the movies helped break down part of the barriers.

Anyway there is no reason to pretend it's a ghetto and we are oppressed artists that the world won't give a break. In the 1950s that was true and drove many writers mad. Now to hold that position (which some do) would be only a confession that you'd rather be a big fish in a little pond than swim in the big ocean. I like the ocean, but I love SF too. And really, to have a literary community as a kind of feedback amp on stage, loudly talking back to you and ready to talk at any moment—any writer is lucky to have that. The solitude and alienation of many writers from their audiences strikes me as sad. It's solitary enough as it is, in the daily work.

You wrote your PhD thesis on PK Dick. Did you ever meet him? He seems to be on the verge of replacing Asimov as the most familiar SF name. How do you think he would fit into today's market?

I met PKD once in a hallway at Cal State Fullerton in 1973, where we both had come to see a lecture by Harlan Ellison. PKD rose to his feet during the Q and A after the reading to thank Ellison publicly for raising the level of respect for SF in the general culture. PKD really felt the put-downs of the literary culture back in the 1950s. Afterward in the hall I said to him how much I had enjoyed his novel *Galactic Pot-Healer*. He looked at me like I was insane. He may or may not have said thank you, or anything. But I'm glad I did it.

I guess he is "the SF writer" in American culture now. I think it's fitting. We live in a PKD reality in a lot of ways, crazier than Asimov's vision. So many of PKD's visions now look prescient and like perfect metaphors for life now. He had a big gift that way.

Many of his novels were written in two weeks on speed, and it shows. In today's market (especially if all his movies had been made) he would have been able to afford to slow down. He was skillful. If he had to start in today's market, he would do okay. If he were still alive and had his real start, he would be huge. And his books would be very interesting no matter what. He was a good novelist.

Tom Disch once said that all SF is really fantasy. Was that just Disch or is there a grain of truth in it?
I think it's a little of both. Imagining the future; that has to be fantasy, by some definitions. But some of these fantasies of the future can conform to what we think is physically possible, and that would be science fiction, by my lights. A fictional future, meaning there is a historical connection explained or implied between that future and our now, with whatever's in that future sounding physically possible. This would rule out faster-than-light travel and time travel, which are in science fiction all the time, so maybe that's what Disch meant. But you can dispense with those and have a "real" SF I think.

Disch got very angry at the SF community, as his home town that had somehow rejected him despite his great work. Too bad. It's not the whole of his story, by any means, but part of it. I like many of his books and stories, but distrust anything he said about SF. He was too angry.

SF writers are always complaining about the state of publishing. What do you think would be the proper role of SF in a proper publishing world? Would there be genres or categories at all?
I don't know! That's a real alternative history. If there were no genres or categories, people might be more open to trying new things. That would be good. I'd love to try it. But it's not the world we have. Going forward from now, I guess I think every science fiction section in every bookstore should have a sign saying "SCIENCE FICTION—YOU LIVE HERE, WHY NOT READ ABOUT IT?" or "SCIENCE FICTION, THE MOST REAL PART OF THIS STORE." Something to remind people of reality, which is that we are all stuck in a big SF novel now, and there's no escape. Might as well accept it and dive in.

You are a minimalist in your long-distance Sierra treks: superlight pack, no tent floor, no poles even, no stove, just a pellet and stones. Does any of this apply to your writing? I know you cover a lot of ground.

No, in my writing I am more of a maximalist. I'll try anything, include anything; I don't think I have a method that works for everything, as the literary minimalists seemed to think.

I hike ultralight in the Sierras because I can be just as comfortable in camp, while suffering less on trail when I've got my house on my back. It's a version of the technological sublime. My mountain experiences are philosophically complicated, but they feel like bliss to me, like devotion or prayer in a religion, so I do it and enjoy it, and at home like to think about it too. But I will spare you my ultralight ultracool gear list and technique.

If you were to take up a trade, what would it be? If you could play music, what would you play? Do you listen to music when you work?
I like working with stone and would love to be an artsy drywall mason, like Andy Goldsworthy or the more local and practical drywall stone artists in New England. I'd be good, I think. It's like novel writing, the pattern work, and I like stones.

I play the trumpet and would love to play like Louis Armstrong or Clifford Brown, but good luck with that! Every trumpet player says that, but it can't be done.

I do listen to music when I work, mostly music without lyrics in English, and lots of different kinds. I pick the music to fit the mood I want for the scene I'm writing. I don't really hear it while working, but I'm sure it has an effect.

Who are your favorite poets? Who do you read for fun?
I like Gary Snyder and W.S. Merwin among living poets, also many more American poets, especially Stevens, William Bronk, Rexroth, and the whole twentieth-century American tradition, also the English romantics, and the Elizabethans. I like poetry. I read it for fun, usually one poem last thing before sleeping after I've read a half hour or so in a novel. I'm always reading a novel, I love novels, and I try to read widely, try new writers. Nonfiction I read for work or at meals.

Your recent Global Warming *trilogy (*40 Signs of Rain, 50 Degrees Below, 60 Days and Counting*) was about global warming, which leads to a deep freeze! What do you think of Obama's "green" agenda? Is it headed in the right directions?*

Climate change will mostly be warming, but that will add such energy to the world system that the turbulence will lead to areas of greater cold in winter, as well as more severe storms, and so on. So I followed a scenario that describes the "abrupt climate change" that the scientists have found in the historical record, that results when the Gulf Stream is shut down at its north end by too much fresh water flooding the far north Atlantic. That could happen with Greenland melting, though now they think it is lower probability than when I wrote (oh well).

I like Obama's green agenda and hope his whole team and everyone jumps on board and pushes it as hard as possible.

One thing happening is that the Republican Party in the USA has decided to fight the idea of climate change. Polls and studies show the shift over the first decade of this century, in terms of the leadership turning against it and the rank-and-file following, which is like the Catholic Church denying the Earth went around the sun in Galileo's time—a big mistake they are going to crawl away from later and pretend never happened. And here the damage could be worse, because we need to act now.

What's been set up and is playing out now is a Huge World-Historical Battle between science and capitalism. Science is insisting more emphatically every day that this is a real and present danger. Capitalism is saying it isn't, because if it were true it would mean more government control of economies, more social justice (as a climate stabilization technique) and so on. These are the two big players in our civilization, so I say, be aware, watch the heavyweights go at it, and back science every chance you get. I speak to all fellow leftists around the world: science is now a leftism, and thank God, but capitalism is very strong. So it's a dangerous moment. People who like their history dramatic and non-utopian should be pleased.

Have you done any audiobooks? What about film or TV?
I haven't read for my audiobooks, but several of my books are available as audiobooks. No film or TV, though the AMC channel is in the early stages of developing *Red Mars* as a TV series. That would be nice, but it's a long way from happening right now.

Where does A Short, Sharp Shock *fit into your canon? Is it fantasy?*
I think of it as my version of fantasy, what I think fantasy ought to be: strange, new imagery, a possible science fiction explanation (science fantasy is that sub-genre of science fiction set so far in the future that it looks like fantasy, done well by Vance and Wolfe). My vision of fantasy does not seem to have been picked up on, but what can you do?

    I wrote it when our first kid was born and I was not sleeping much or writing much. I decided I would write no matter what, and it might be best to try a dream narrative. It was right before *Red Mars*, and I knew I would be spending years on a very rational, historical project, so I thought it might be good to discharge some craziness in the system before I embarked on that. I very much enjoyed working on *A Short, Sharp Shock* and I appreciate my publisher Bantam keeping it in print.

You wrote a wonderful book about Everest, Escape from Kathmandu. *Was any of that based on personal experience? Was your prediction about Mallory and Irvine based on secret info or just luck?*
Yes, a lot of it was based on the trek my wife and I took in Nepal in 1985. We ran into Jimmy Carter, laughed hard every day, enjoyed our Sherpa handlers, who took care of us like pets, and loved the country and the mountains. I'd like to go back and write a book called *Return to Kathmandu*, using George and Freds again. There have been so many changes in the twenty-three years since, but I bet much is the same too. I got some calls right, about the revolutionary forces, and also about the Mallory find on the north side of Everest. That was just luck, but I could see how it would be possible.

How would you describe your politics? What was your relationship to the antiwar movement and the political currents of the '60s? Were you an activist? Are you today?
I call myself an American leftist and try to point to all the left activities in American history as a tradition of resistance, activism and successes. Indeed today I read in the paper about the election of a leftist president in El Salvador, and the chant was "The left united will never be defeated." Very nice thought, especially since the divisions in and among the leftisms have been such a problem.

Those are so often what Freud called "the narcissism of small differences" and that is an important concept everyone should study.

I was at UCSD during the anti-war movement, or I should say, after 1970. In the 1960s I was in Orange County in high school and it might as well have been 1953, except for the news of distant places. At UCSD things were more up-to-date, and I transitioned into antiwar sentiments as part of my group cohort feeling, and my draft number (89). I saw Marcuse and Angela Davis speak at a rally at the gym and gathered on campus a couple times, but I was a follower. By the time I had ideas of my own, the war was over.

I am only an activist today in the local politics of my town, Davis, California, where I am trying to fight a real estate development proposed by the university. It's pretty draining and uphill work. I think of my writing as an activism, and we give financial support to a lot of activist causes.

You were a student of the famed postmodernist Fredric Jameson. How has he influenced your work?
Famous Marxist Fredric Jameson, you mean. What he managed was to rearrange everyone's definition of postmodernism from a fashion or a style, to a period in the history of capital and the world. So that was quite an accomplishment. And his persistence over the years has given a kind of lens for leftists and everyone else to understand modern history in Marxist terms. So, that has been a major influence on everyone, I think, even if for most people it is indirect.

For me it was direct. Fred is very educational in person, a great teacher, and after our time together at UCSD I kept reading him, and by reading all his work gave myself a good ground for understanding world history and our moment today. That's a great thing for a novelist to have. I've stayed in touch too and he is a good person to know, perpetually interesting.

I understand that you live in a utopian community. How does that work? Is it pre- or postmodern?
A little of both, I guess. The model is an English village, really, about eighty acres, a lot of it owned in common, so there is a "commons" and no fences except around little courtyards. There are a lot of vegetable gardens, and the landscaping is edible, meaning lots of fruits, grapes, and nuts.

It's really just a tweaking of suburban design, but a really good one. Energy mattered to the designers and we burn about 40 percent the energy of an ordinary suburban neighborhood of the same size. That's still a lot, but it's an improvement. If every suburb since this one was built (1980 or so) would have followed its lead, we would have much less craziness in America; because the standard suburb is bad for sanity. But that didn't happen, so for the thousand people who live here it's a kind of pocket utopia. Not the solution, but a nice place to live right now, and it could suggest aspects of a long-term solution. It's been a real blessing to live here.

You gave one of the Google talks. Was that cool or what? What did you tell them?
It was a lot of fun. The Google people were great, and their free cafeteria is out of this world. They put the talk online so you can find it on YouTube. It was my first PowerPoint talk ever, so that was a bit clunky, but fun. It was configured as a talk to the Googlers, telling Google what it could do to fight climate change and enact utopia. I'm not sure the folks at Google.org (their charitable/activist foundation) were listening, but it was worth a try, and basically a way to frame my usual talk about what we all should do. Mostly I say, go outdoors and sit and talk to a friend: this is our primate utopia and very easy on the planet.

Your latest work, yet to be published, is about Galileo. Or about the relationship between science and politics. Or is it ambition and religion? Or work and age?
A bit of all those things, but mostly I was thinking science and history—what science is, how it has affected history, how it could in the future, and also about Galileo's actual work, which is ever so interesting. He was a great character.

What's your favorite city?
San Francisco is my favorite city, but I also like New York, London, Edinburgh, Paris, Venice, Sydney, Vancouver, and Kathmandu.

You broke into print the "usual" (old) way for SF writers—through short stories. Do you plan to go back to short fiction? What do you think of today's dwindling story "market"?

I don't rule out going back to short fiction, but I like novels better and that's what I'm focused on; that may never stop. I think it's too bad about the dwindling market and wonder if reading habits are changing with the internet. In a way shorter fiction should possibly benefit by the quickness of web life, but I don't know. I'm enough outside it not to be thinking about it too much.

SF used to have an agenda—the future, and in particular, space travel. Does it have an agenda today?
I don't know! I think it has to have the agenda of the future. But when the future doesn't include space travel as the obvious next step, it gets a lot more complicated. Things on Earth don't look so science fictional. And yet the whole world in a sense is in a science fiction novel that we write together. So it's all very confusing. My response is to say, "Just keep writing, one novel at a time, and hope for the best."

Do you think there is life on other planets? Intelligence? Do you think we will even "make contact?"
I do think there is life on other planets, and also intelligence, but what kind of intelligence I think is very mysterious. Making contact will be a serious problem, maybe too much a problem to ever really happen, partly because of the size of the universe (bigger than we think) and also the potentially inexplicable nature of alien intelligence, so that we won't be able to communicate with it (the *Solaris* problem, after Lem's great novel).

How come there is no space travel in Years of Rice and Salt? *Do you think space travel is a Eurocentric enterprise?*
No, I think any technological civilization would think about space travel, because of the moon, and the simplicity of rockets, and so on. I didn't have it in *Years of Rice and Salt* partly by accidental omission, partly because that book only takes history about seventy years past us; and I think without Percival Lowell, we might not have gotten to the moon yet, and might not for another century or so. That was a freak event, with a genealogy that runs from Lowell's fantasia to the novels of Lasswitz/Bogdanov/Wells to the German Rocket Society to von Braun to WWII to NASA. Without all those elements, including Lowell's

hallucinations about Mars, we might still not have gotten to the moon. So, in my alternative history, I thought it was okay to leave it out. It would have only gotten a sentence or two anyway if I had thought of it.

"Load On the Miracles and Keep a Straight Face"
Rudy Rucker

Your new book, Nested Scrolls, *is an autobiography. Does that mean you've run out of ideas?*
I feel like I always have new ideas, but certainly some of them are beginning to look a little familiar. I get SF ideas by extrapolating, from speculating, and from imagining surreal juxtapositions.

In 2008, I had a cerebral hemorrhage—a vein burst in my brain and I nearly died. Coming out of that, I decided that I'd better write my autobio while I still had time.

One of my goals in writing *Nested Scrolls* was to get an idea of the story arc of my life—as if I were looking back on a novel. My conclusions? I searched for ultimate reality, and I found contentment in creativity. I tried to scale the heights of science, and I found my calling in mathematics and in science fiction. I was a loner, I found love, I became a family man. When I was a kid, I felt like an ugly duckling, and over the years I grew into grace—thanks in large measure to my dear wife, Sylvia.

Aren't novels a rather messy exercise for a mathematician? Do you have the whole thing in RAM when you start, or do you make it up as you go along?
In some ways mathematics resembles novel-writing. In math you start with some oddball axioms and see what theorems you can deduce from them. You have very little control over the course that your reasoning takes. In novel-writing, you start with an outré scenario and see what kind of plot emerges from the situation. Here again, the details of your work tends to come as something of a surprise.

In science fiction, it's useful to be able to think logically, which is something that comes naturally for a mathematician.

But of course SF novels are more than logical exercises, and that's why I love writing them. I like the possibility of expressing myself at various levels—sometimes it isn't until later that I realize something I've written has to do with some deep obsession of mine.

Frek and the Elixir has been described as a YA (young adult) novel. Is this because it has a kid as a protagonist, or because only kids can understand it?

Tor didn't actually market this book as YA, although that might have been a good idea. When YA books catch on, they can sell very well. But in *Frek*, I wasn't fully focused on teenage problems, as is usually the case in YA books. Although the thirteen-year-old Frek has some abandonment issues with his father, he's also dealing with the social issue of many species becoming extinct.

In order to give *Frek and the Elixir* a classy feel, I modeled the book on the "monomyth" template described in Joseph Campbell's classic *The Hero with a Thousand Faces*. Campbell's archetypal myth includes seventeen stages. By combining two pairs of stages, I ended up with fifteen chapters for *Frek*.

I'd like to revisit the world of *Frek* and write a sequel. I liked those characters, especially the flying cuttlefish called Professor Bumby. I had him as a professor in my abstract algebra course in grad school.

Your webzine Flurb *reads like a who's who of outside-the-box SF writers. Who would you most like to get an unsolicited manuscript from, living or dead?*

I've had a lot of fun editing *Flurb*, and as a personal matter, it's convenient to have a magazine which will always publish my stories. I sleep with the editor's wife, as I like to say.

I started with asking my old cyberpunk friends to contribute, but over time I'm getting more over-the-transom material from younger writers. Regarding your question, I'd be happy to get manuscripts from Robert Sheckley, Philip K. Dick, Thomas Pynchon, or Jack Kerouac. It's not so well known that the Beats were very interested in writing SF, and they talked about it a lot. They viewed SF as an indigenous American art form, along the lines of rock 'n' roll or jazz.

If you look at it in a certain way, William Burroughs's novel *Naked Lunch* is an SF novel. But there's a certain goody-goody nerd element among SF people that tends not to want to acknowledge that.

What is Time? Seriously.
Kurt Gödel, the smartest man I ever met, claimed that the passage of time is an illusion, a kind of grain built into the fabric of our reality. To the extent that we can sense Eternity, it's present in the immediate Now moment. Another point to make is that, insofar as time is real, it's like a fluid we swim around in. As John Updike puts it, "Time is our element, not a mistaken invader."

Okay, I'm regurgitating quotes there. A simpler answer: time is breath. Does that answer your question?

No. You seem to have a knack for running into famous characters: Anselm Hollo, Martin Gardner, Gödel, Wolfram? If you were forming a band, which would play lead guitar? Would Turing be in the band?
I'd probably like to be lead singer, like I was in my short-lived punk band, the Dead Pigs, in 1982. In this case I'd choose Johnny Ramone as lead guitarist. If I had a better voice, I'd want to work with Frank Zappa, but in reality I don't think Frank would let me sing. Maybe I could play kazoo. And of course I'd be happy singing with Keith Richards or Muddy Waters.

Being in a band was one of the more enjoyable things I've done. Much of my career has consisted of mathematics, computer hacking, and writing. These are solitary activities, so it was fun for me to be in a band and do something in group. Come to think of it, that's another reason I like editing my webzine *Flurb*.

I don't think Alan Turing was all that interested in music, but I'd enjoy having him as a friend. He was interested in writing science fiction, as a matter of fact, and he also had an interest in heavy philosophical trips. I'm currently writing a novel with the working title *The Turing Chronicles*, which centers on a love affair between Turing and William Burroughs.

I feel like I'm getting to know Turing and Burroughs via the process of writing about them and maintaining internal emulations of them. I've often done this in the past—I call it "twinking" someone. I twinked the mathematician

Georg Cantor in my novel *White Light*, Edgar Allan Poe in *The Hollow Earth*, and the painter Peter Bruegel in my historical novel about his life, *As Above, So Below*. Bruegel was the best. He's a wonderful man.

Do you ever write longhand? Do you own a pencil?
In my back pocket I almost always carry a blank sheet of printing paper folded in four. I write ideas down on the paper, and when I get home, I type the notes into my computer. Generally I've got a notes document going for whatever book I'm working on. I do write longhand on my pocket notes paper. Sometimes I can't read the writing later on. I used to take copy-books on trips with me and write longer passages in them, but now I almost always travel with a laptop.

Does anyone ever "own" a pencil? They're just things you rummage for, briefly use, and immediately lose. But now and then, if I have a pencil, I might use it to draw something on my pocket square of paper. More commonly I use a Pilot P-700 pen, preferably Extra Fine. I've been using these for going on fifteen years now, and I worry about them going out of production. Every now and then I buy a big stash of them, like fifty or a hundred.

You sometimes collaborate on short stories, with Paul DiFilippo, Marc Laidlaw, John Shirley, Bruce Sterling, Eileen Gunn, even myself. Is this laziness or ambition?
As I already mentioned, writing is a somewhat lonely activity, so I enjoy collaborating on stories. There's no reason not to. The thing about short stories is that they're really hard to sell, at least for me. There's only a very small number of story markets, and often I end up having to publish a story in *Flurb*. And even if I do sell a story, it pays very little, and it can take several years before the story appears. It's not a satisfying market at all, so I might as well have some fun in the writing process by collaborating.

When you write together, it's something like a musical collaboration, a spontaneous give and take. I find that, in order to blend the prose, I tend to imitate the other author's style. Like the way that actors in Woody Allen movies usually seem to talk like Woody.

If you could spend twenty-four hours in any city on the planet, with money in your pocket, which would it be?

First of all, I'm not going for just twenty-four hours. Why travel so far and turn right around? That's idiocy. I'm staying for at least four days and maybe a week.

As for destinations, I'm a huge fan of New York City. I love the noise—you hear it as soon as you get out of the airport, a filigree of sirens overlaid onto a mighty roar. The museums are great, and I know a fair number of cozy, inexpensive restaurants filled with hipsters and city slickers. I'd catch some ballet, and maybe a rock band. Just walking the streets in NYC is a great entertainment as well. And as long as you're paying, Terry, maybe I'll stay at the refurbished Gramercy Park Hotel.

I'd love to spend a week in Koror, a funky town in the archipelago of Palau. I'd go diving, riding a Sam's Tours boat out to the Blue Corner, which is perhaps the greatest dive spot in the world. I'd probably stay at the Palau Royal Resort, and I'd snorkel at the hotel beach, admiring the richly patterned mantles of the giant clams.

A lot of scenes in my SF novels are drawn from my dive experiences. SCUBA is really the closest thing we have to floating in outer space and to visiting alien worlds. Well, NYC is fairly alien as well. Life in the hive.

Your film career was cut short after The Manual of Evasion. *What went wrong?*
Well, you're talking about the acting part of my film career. *The Manual of Evasion* movie was also called *LX94*, as it was made in Lisbon in 1994. Terence McKenna and Robert Anton Wilson starred with me, and some excerpts are online, although the complete movie is hard to find. The director of that movie, Edgar Pêra, is a really good guy. I went to visit him in Lisbon again in the summer of 2011.

What I'd really like is for one of my novels to be made into a film. We came close with *Software*. It was under option to Phoenix Pictures for a decade and they paid for about ten screenplays, none by me. *Master of Space and Time* was another near miss. Michel Gondry wanted to direct, Jim Carrey and Jack Black were going to star, and Daniel Clowes wrote a script. A dream team.

But the producers didn't want to lay out the money. It still seems like the big-money people find my work a little too gnarly. Maybe I'm ahead of my time. That could change at some point. But it's not a prospect I obsess on. I joke that they can't make any of my novels into movies until they've made every single one of Philip K. Dick's novels and short stories into a film. And that's going to take a while.

You are (in my mind, at least) a "hard SF" writer in that the machinery of your work is always math and physics. What do you have against wizards?
I don't like it in a fantastic story when there are a large number of unexplained loose ends. In the context of TV series, I think of *The X-Files* or *Lost*, where the scriptwriters are continually piling on new complications, and none of the earlier mysteries are being solved, and the narrator just gives you these big-eyed woo-woo significant looks.

It isn't really that hard to devote a little effort and figure out a logical framework for the story you want to tell. For a professional SF writer, it might take a day. But for some reason, TV and movie people are literally unable to do this—and they're unwilling to hire an SF writer as a consultant. They'll spend a hundred million on the effects, but they won't give some poor SF vet a hundred K so the story makes sense. I don't understand it.

Back to books, my feeling is that you can be just as logical in a fantasy story as in a science-fiction story. But there seems to be a convention in fantasy that you're not expected to cash the checks that you write. You do any old thing, and then move on to something else and you never circle back. I guess I care more about logic than most people do. Must have something to do with the PhD in mathematics.

My most recent novel, *Jim and the Flims*, is to some extent a fantasy story—a large part of it is set in the afterworld, and my characters are battling with otherworldly beings who are basically demons. But I found it natural to think of some pseudoscientific explanations for the goings-on, and working the logic into the story made me feel more comfortable.

What drew you into math, chaos or order? What drew you into literature?
From the start I liked math's tidiness and power—the numbers and the geometric diagrams. As for literature, I always loved reading and traveling to other worlds. I read science fiction as a boy, and Beat literature in high school. I came to appreciate the radical, countercultural aspects of literature as well.

I wanted to major in English in college, but my father nagged me that I should major in something hard that I couldn't learn on my own. He made the point that I could read novels without taking classes about them. So I decided to major in physics. But then I didn't take the right courses freshman year, and only the math option was open for me. I was okay with that because I found math easy. If you understand what's going on in math, you don't have to memorize very much. Most of what you need to know follows logically from a few basic principles. And I like that math has a lot of gnarl—chaotic patterns that emerge from seeming order.

When I finished college in 1967, I had the option of going to fight in Vietnam or going to grad school, and I picked grad school. I'd been a very poor student in college, and I only had a C average. So I had some trouble getting into a PhD program. As it happened, I married my wife Sylvia the week after graduation, and Rutgers University was eager to have her enter their graduate French program. The French chairman put in a word with the math chairman, and they let me in. I ended up getting my doctorate at Rutgers, a PhD in mathematical logic. And by the time I was done, my average was more like an A than a C. I'd finally found some course material that interested me.

I wrote my first novel, *Spacetime Donuts*, around 1976. I was amped up from having seen the Rolling Stones play live in Buffalo, New York. Ultimately, writing was to be my real career, and teaching my day job.

As it happened, I switched from teaching math to teaching computer science when my family and I moved to San Jose, California, in 1986. This was a good move for me. It meant I got to ride a twenty-year wave of computer science, from PCs up through the Web. I never took a single course in computer science, but eventually I taught most of them. I enjoyed the hands-on, experimental nature of the subject, and some of it permanently changed the way I think.

Are you prepared for the Singularity?
I have complicated thoughts about the so-called Singularity. First of all, I think it will be quite a long time, maybe a hundred years, before we get close to human-level artificial intelligence. I have this opinion from having taught AI as

part of my job at San Jose State. The AI field's existing techniques are a handful of cheap parlor tricks.

Second of all, I don't think we'll ever see standalone devices that are vastly more intelligent than people. What we'll see will be intelligence amplification (IA) tools, so that people can create at a higher level. But it'll still be the people doing the creating.

Third, I don't think we'll see injectable nanotech elixirs that can restore a person to a state of youth. I feel that a hysterical fear of death on the part of guys like Ray Kurzweil has clouded the discussions of the Singularity. I think it's lame and juvenile to worry so much about dying. Didn't Ray take his acid in the Sixties like he was supposed to?

Fourth, I think we'll soon be able to create interactive emulations of individual people that I call lifeboxes. The secret for lifeboxes is to use really large databases rather than extreme AI. If you're a writer and a blogger, you're well on the way to having created your lifebox. Singulatarians are, however, obsessed with a much stronger version of the lifebox, that is, with the notion of creating an artificially alive android-like replica of yourself and thereby achieving a kind of immortality. It's not all that well known that I was one of the very first people to present this "uploading" idea in a science fiction novel, that is, in *Software* in 1982.

I have a strong feeling that the conventional notions of a Singularity don't go nearly far enough. A couple of years ago, I got impatient with the prevalent style of hype about the Singularity and, wanting to move past it, I wrote a novel called *Postsingular*. Charles Stross's *Accelerando* helped me see how to write this book. You load on the miracles and keep a straight face.

Postsingular and its sequel *Hylozoic* are based on the idea that gnarly, naturally occurring processes can serve as programmable computations. So you might be gaining information from an air current, or a candle flame, or the rocking branch of a tree, or an eddy in a stream. You might in fact program one of these processes to be an emulation of yourself.

As I was eager to get the ideas of *Postsingular* into circulation, I followed Cory Doctorow's example and released an edition of my book for free online under a Creative Commons license. The release didn't seem to hurt the hardback and paperback sales. But now that e-book sales are finally ramping up, I don't think I'll do CC releases anymore.

For a dude from Kentucky (I'm another), you exhibit a shocking lack of provincialism in your life and work. How come? Has this been a hindrance?
It's a bit of an American tradition to have a rube from the sticks become a cultured cosmopolitan. Harold Ross, the founder of the *New Yorker*, was from Colorado. William Gibson grew up in Wytheville, Virginia.

One reason I learned about more than Louisville was that my mother was from Berlin, and I have a lot of relatives in Germany. We went there several times when I was a boy, and I spent most of the eighth grade in a Black Forest boarding school.

Certainly I was still somewhat provincial when I arrived at Swarthmore College in 1963. But after college I married Sylvia, a Hungarian woman whose family lived in Switzerland, and we ended up visiting them in Europe nearly every year thereafter. And in the US, we were of course attending graduate school, working at universities, and culture-vulturing any and all available events.

Speaking of Kentucky, Terry, I always enjoy seeing you at SF events, as you have the feel of a distant cousin from down home. A fellow Kentucky ham, both of us well cured.

I don't get your transrealism thing. Hasn't the novel always been made out of the stuff of the author's life? Is there any other way? Or do you think SF is different?
It's not really the case that every novel is made of the author's life. People very often settle for writing about stock situations, or about scenarios they've encountered in other books or in movies, or about arbitrary things they've completely made up. What impressed me about the Beats when I started reading them in high school was that they were writing about their actual lives—and in a confessional, self-revelatory kind of way.

My notion of transrealism is that, if you're writing SF, and also writing about your life, you can enhance or mutate your experiences in interesting ways. I see the familiar power chords of SF—time travel, antigravity, alternate worlds, telepathy, etc.—as standing for certain kinds of archetypal emotions or experiences. Time travel is memory, flight is enlightenment, alternate worlds symbolize the great variety of individual world-views, and telepathy stands for the ability to communicate fully. If you're using the power chords, but also writing about your life, you end up with something richer than realism and more engaging than sheer fabulation.

Genre fiction like SF is even more at risk of having flat, two-dimensional characters than is normal literary fiction. Perhaps some SF authors imagine that their ideas and situations are so fascinating that they don't need realistic characters. Sticking to a transreal approach is a fairly easy way to ensure that your novel will be lively.

What's the difference between the infinite and the absolute? Do they coexist?
In the branch of mathematics called set theory, infinity is a fairly garden-variety kind of number, and there are lots of different infinities. One is known as alef-null, the size of the set of all natural numbers. Another is called the continuum, and it's the size of the set of all points on a line. My early novel *White Light* is about a young mathematician interested in figuring out the exact relationship between alef-null and the continuum.

The absolute, on the other hand, is more of a philosophical notion. It's the ultimate, inconceivable, largest possible infinity. God, for instance, would be an absolute, and not a mere infinity.

In mathematics, the class of all possible sets is an absolute. There's a semi-theological axiom of set theory known as the reflection principle. It says that whenever we think we've conceived of the class of all sets, we're thinking of some smaller set. That is, any property enjoyed by the absolute is reflected in the properties of some lower-level infinite set. And any notion you have of God also applies to something smaller. Does that answer your question?

No. What's on your iPhone? What's not on your iPhone?
I have about thirteen gigabytes of music. First I ripped my CDs, then a bunch of CDs from the library, and then I started ripping my old vinyl records, which is an interesting but time-consuming process. What kinds of music? Punk rock, Frank Zappa, blues, reggae.

What's not on my iPhone? No books yet—I'm still holding back from reading digital editions, although just in the last year I've finally started seeing some actual e-book sales on my royalty statements.

Bruce Sterling got me to attend an Augmented Reality (AR) conference in San Jose last year. An example of AR is when you hold up your iPhone and see the world with things overlaid onto it. I got this cool *AR Invaders* app, in which

I see UFOs flying around my living room or in the sky over my deck, and I can shoot them. A perfect tool for any SF writer.

Do you think math models the universe? Or the human brain?
Math is the abstract science of form, and seems to be ideally suited for modeling anything at all. It's a universal construction kit. This said, I sometimes feel like the whole idea of science, logic, and math is a little off-the-beam for modeling the universe and the brain. From the inside, life feels like emotion, sounds, colors, and memories, arranged in a mushy and not-particularly-mathematical way.

Our professional organization, Science Fiction Writers of America, is currently lobbying Congress to repeal the Scaling Law. Good idea or not?
Terry, you're a card, and sometimes I'm not sure what you're talking about, or if you know either. I'll assume that with the "Scaling Law" you're referring to the empirical fact that society's rewards for creativity are distributed according to an inverse power law—in which an author's financial reward is inversely proportional to his or her popularity.

Rather than lying along a smoothly sloping line, a Scaling Law payment schedule has the form of a violently down-swooping curve, akin to the graph of $1/x$. It's as if society wants to encourage very many books that are precisely of the kind that it likes the most, and to discourage those works that vary in the slightest from the current ideal. The swooping, hyperbolic Scaling Law curve loads money on the best-selling authors, while portioning out much smaller amounts to the scribes out on the long tail. Disgruntled writers sometimes fantasize about a utopian marketplace in which the Scaling Law distribution would be forcibly replaced by a linear distribution. But this wouldn't work, as I discuss in my nonfiction book *The Lifebox, the Seashell, and the Soul*. Scaling laws are a much a part of nature as are gravitational laws, or the laws of probability. Coming to understand this has greatly helped my serenity—seriously. Sometime math can actually make you happier.

One lesson I can draw from the Scaling Law is that it's okay if my best efforts fail to knock the ball out of the park. There's simply no predicting what's going to catch on, or how big it's going to be. Trying harder isn't going to change anything. Relax, do my work, and don't expect too much. Almost nobody wins, and the winners are effectively chosen at random. Along these lines, the science fiction writer Marc Laidlaw and I once dreamed of starting a literary movement to be called Freestyle. Our proposed motto: Write like yourself, only more so.

A flipside of the Scaling Law is that maintaining even a modest level of success is hard. The gnarly computations of society keep things boiling at every level. As a corollary, note that there's no chance of making things easier for yourself by sending your outputs to lower-paying magazines. They're still likely to reject you, but they'll be ruder and more incompetent about it. Ah me, the writer's life.

You and author Michael Dorris were teenage pals. Did you share any interest in literature, or was it all girls and cars?
I seem to remember that Dorris and I were preoccupied with finding erotic fiction to read, combing the louche bookshops of downtown Louisville. Otherwise our tastes weren't very similar. I recall that he liked James Michener's *Hawaii* and I liked Jean-Paul Sartre's *Nausea*. And in the backs of our minds, both of us dreamed of somehow becoming writers. But we didn't talk about it much. I wish very much that he were still alive. Even though he's dead, he's still my friend.

Your novels (and stories, like the ones in this volume) are known for their irreverent and wildly humorous social satire. Why do you hate America?
In the fourth grade I was remanded to a private boys school where I felt bullied and picked upon. And after my college years I had to deal with a government that wanted to draft me and send me to die in a pointless war in Vietnam. I never fit in well. As I described in my novel *The Secret of Life*, I've always felt like a visiting alien.

Your German grandmother introduced you to the work of Pieter Bruegel the Elder at an early age. You later wrote a serious (and wonderful) novel based on his life, As Above, So Below. *Was writing historical fiction a stretch for you?*
In some ways, writing historical fiction is akin to writing fantasy or SF. In each case, you're imagining a complete world that exists in parallel to the world we live in. I considered bringing SF elements into my Bruegel novel, but I

decided I didn't want to drag the master into the gutter. His life and times were strange enough on their own.

Something I like about Bruegel's paintings is that sometimes they seem to illustrate a moral or a folktale, but nobody's ever been able to figure out exactly what the tale is. The Flemish godfather makes you an offer you can't understand. And it's especially the things you can't understand that seem worth knowing.

I remember being very sad when I finished writing *As Above, So Below*. I felt I'd grown very close to Bruegel during my years of work on the book. He'd become like a close friend, or an alter ego. When the book appeared, I was actually living in Bruegel's hometown of Brussels on a grant. His house still stands, and I walked by it in the rain. I felt like Bruegel's ghost was right there with me. He liked my book.

Bruce Sterling once compared the cyberpunk movement (you, Gibson, Cadigan, Shirley, and of course Bruce) to the Beats. Was that accurate? Which were you? And don't say Kerouac; he had no sense of humor.
I was William Burroughs—the oldest of the group, rather professorial, and perhaps the gnarliest. In my *Seek!* collection, I have an essay, "Cyberpunk Lives!" that draws this comparison. One of the things I write about in that essay was the time in 1981 when I met Allen Ginsberg in Boulder, Colorado. I asked Allen for his blessing, and he slammed his hand down on the top of my head like the cap of an electric chair, crying out, "Bless you!" It was great. I met Burroughs then, too, but I didn't get very close to him. I managed to give him a copy of novel *White Light*. Bill said, "Far out."

My Jeopardy *topic: SF Today. The answer is, "Because girls just want to have fun." You provide the question.*
Why is supernatural romance so popular?

Do you like guns?
Guns aren't for me. If I kept a gun in my house, I probably would have shot someone by now, possibly myself.

How did you learn to paint? Did it involve unlearning something as well?

In 1999, my wife and I took an oil-painting class in night school at the local museum. I took to it right away.

My level of manual control is low enough that I tend to surprise myself with what I end up painting. Sometimes these surprises show me things that are a good fit for the novel or story that I'm currently working on—you might say that I'm channeling information from another part of my brain. But it's fine if I don't use the images in my fiction. The main thing is that I'm feeding my soul and getting into the moment and, if I'm lucky, turning off my inner monologue. Given that painting doesn't involve words at all, it's even more meditative than writing. I love the luscious colors.

Painting has taught me a few practical things about writing. When I'm doing a painting, for instance, it's not unusual to completely paint over some screwed-up patch and do that part over. I think this has made me feel more relaxed about revising my fiction. And I've also noticed that the details that I haven't yet visualized are the ones that give me the most trouble. But the only way to proceed is to put it down wrong, and then keep changing it until it works.

If there's anything I needed to unlearn, it was the belief that I needed to paint human figures with complete accuracy. Approximations are fine, and I can brush away at a given figure until it looks reasonably okay. We have cameras for accuracy.

"Your soul isn't in fact immortal on its own, but is, rather, a pattern of information that God stores in His memory so that He can resurrect you." Explain.
In the Passion scene in the Gospel according to Luke, the Good Thief says, "Lord, remember me when you come into your kingdom." And Jesus seems to agree with that, and says, "Verily I say unto you, today you will be with me in paradise."

I once had an interesting discussion of this passage with my old science-writer mentor, Martin Gardner. Some religious sects have taken the exchange between Jesus and the Good Thief to mean that your soul isn't in fact immortal on its own, but is, rather, a pattern of information that God stores in memory so as to resurrect you. Sometimes the word "soul sleep" is associated with this notion.

Keeping it simple, to me the Thief/Jesus exchange suggests that the soul can in fact be represented as software, that is, as a pattern of information that God (or a sufficiently large computer memory) can store.

Of course, realistically speaking, when it comes to immortality, we're grasping at straws. These days I'm more inclined to think that it's going to be a matter of lights-out and that's all she wrote. That used to bother me, but now it seems okay. I think when you're younger you're concerned about living long enough to do things you feel you need to do. But I've been lucky, and by now I've pretty much checked off everything on my list. Not that I wouldn't mind another twenty years.

Your work describes a universe in which anything can happen and often does. Is this a literary device or wishful thinking?
One reason I write is so I can travel out of my ordinary world. I like running with any crazy idea that pops into my head, fleshing it out and giving it substance. I really do feel that there are some as yet unsuspected levels of reality, and SF can help us find our way there.

There's a kind of transreal aspect too. When I write a novel, I am to some extent leaving this world and going into another one—the world of the novel. So it's natural that in my novel, the main character leaves his or her world and goes off into some other dimension or alternate reality. Because that's exactly what I'm doing by writing the book.

"Gear. Food. Rocks."
Carter Scholz

On the cover of this book [Gypsy] you appear to be heading out into the Universe on foot. Are those clip-art stars or an actual destination? Won't you need more than two poles and a daypack to get there?

The star field is the sky surrounding Alpha Centauri as seen from Earth. You can read *Gypsy* to learn just how much more you'd need to get there, but the ultralight principles are shared. That pack holds everything I need for seven days out.

What drew you into (or toward) science fiction? What was your first sale?

My family was profoundly unliterary. I remember a short shelf of Reader's Digest Condensed Books, my father's engineering texts, my mother's Gregg shorthand manuals, and that was it. So in adolescence I read my way, with the indelible joy of escape, through our public library's science fiction shelves. Afterward, I found further indelibility: Eliot, Beckett, Kafka, Faulkner, Joyce, Pound. I was drawn to the core modernist works, not so much to the Updike and Cheever domestic realism that was dominant at the time, despite my living in the landscape it described. What it said wasn't true to my experience in 1960s suburban New Jersey. Science fiction seemed the nearest extant thing to modernism, and to my experience.

My first sale was an accident. I attended the 1973 Clarion SF Workshop, and my characteristic, class-traitor response to that was to write a long, non-SF "mainstream" story about the last NASA Apollo mission titled "The Eve of the Last Apollo." Kate Wilhelm, one of my instructors at Clarion, had asked me to send her a story for a forthcoming workshop anthology, so I sent this, with a cover letter apologizing for its inappropriateness. She passed it, literally, across the kitchen table to her husband, Damon Knight, and he said, so he told me,

"It's mine!" He published it in his legendary hardcover anthology *Orbit*, even though it wasn't SF by any definition but his. All us young'uns who knew them then owe Damon and Kate: they spent a lot of publishing capital helping us unknowns.

You have been published both in and out of the science fiction category. Was this by design or chance? Do you consider genre a help or a hindrance to the serious writer?
I think a serious writer largely ignores category and genre when at work. Category is what your publisher calls you, and where you get shelved in the bookstore. Genre is more complicated; that involves the whole history of your reading, your affinities, and so it implicates category as well. But yourself and your idea of literature is always bigger than that.

I submitted my novel *Radiance* to Bryan Cholfin, then an editor at Tor, a science fiction publisher, because he'd been kind enough to buy a couple of stories from me for his magazine *Crank*. Bryan literally walked across the hall from Tor to PicadorUSA, both owned by St. Martins, subsidiaries of Macmillan, then owned by Bertelsmann—I don't know the current Borg masters. Bryan did me a noble, spirited service by his walk, and he'll always be my friend for that, though it did neither of us any negotiable good. Genre depends a great deal on your point of view.

I wrote an essay many years ago that claimed Beckett's *The Lost Ones* as SF, and Gaddis's *JR*, also most of Calvino and Pynchon and Borges (whose first publication in North America, I note with genre satisfaction, was in the pages of *Fantasy and Science Fiction*, then edited by Anthony Boucher). I don't mean to appropriate them into our category, but to proclaim that this mode of "imaginative" storytelling, rather than the strictly "realistic," has been with us far longer and is more fundamental.

Gypsy is what we in SF call a "starship novel." You didn't invent the form. Do you recall when you first encountered it?
As a teenager in that public library. Probably "Far Centaurus" by A.E. van Vogt. In van Vogt's story, the first starship is so long in its traveling that a newer faster-than-light ship is invented and overtakes it and has a colony up and running before the slow ship arrives.

I've never seen an SF story take full stock of how hard, maybe impossible, interstellar travel is going to be. *Gypsy* is my attempt to do it "with the net up," as the "hard SF" writers say. Even in the most rigorous hard SF, you always reach the hand-wave moment where the net drops to permit some bit of story development. I wanted to play it straight and let the story come out of the constraints of the physics. Even the made-up parts, such as the ship's fusion engine, aren't my invention. I drew all the extrapolated technologies from published research papers and hewed to their limits. I'm not a physicist, but I grew up and was educated during the Cold War, when math and science education were priorities, so I understood enough to be able to run gravity simulators on my computer to model the Alpha C system, spreadsheets to model various flight times, and so on. All the mechanics of the journey—all the moving parts, the times and trajectories—are as accurate as I could make them, physically and astronomically.

So I've come full circle. My first published story was a mainstream story about a returned astronaut in the 1970s alienated by his experience from domestic "realism." This story is truly hard SF, the first I've ever written, with physically realistic constraints on what can happen.

You have also written for music magazines. Did you like the Beach Boys? Do you now?
I wrote for music technology magazines, such as *Keyboard* (thanks, Dominic Milano), which is not the same thing at all. The question should be, "Did you like MIDI?" Who are the Beach Boys?

You also play jazz piano, are an accomplished if amateur astronomer, and make pretty good wine. What's your best guess of a thread that unites these talents?
Attention deficit disorder?

What's a gamelan? Do they get good mileage?
Gamelan is the orchestra and the music of Indonesia, which is a made-up state comprising many cultures, each with its own distinct music. I first heard Balinese gamelan on a Nonesuch Explorer album, those glories of the 1970s, but I ended up playing for many years the very different Javanese form under the tutelage of

Pak Cokro, Midiyanto, Jody Diamond, and Ben Brinner. Considering the average distance my teachers covered from Yogyakarta and Surakarta to Berkeley and back over all those years, I'd say the mileage is considerable. Pak Cokro's own mileage is even better: he has a recording on *Voyager*, currently twenty billion kilometers out and counting.

Ever miss New York? What brought you to the Bay Area? What keeps you here?
Sure I miss it, but the New York I grew up in has forever passed for me. My last visit was in 2010, when my younger stepdaughter looked at colleges. It seemed like aliens had taken over midtown. As a kid I used to ride the elevator up to the observation deck of the Empire State Building fairly often—a couple of times per year. I think it cost a quarter. When Amalie and I went up, as I'd promised her, the tab was somewhere north of a hundred bucks for us both. The Whitney and the MOMA are now displaced, and my beloved Hayden Planetarium has been replaced by something created by consultants. My Soho, in the late 1970s, centered on Sam Rivers's and Rashied Ali's jazz lofts, and that locale and scene is so gone it's not even lamentable.

I had friends in Berkeley, and I came for a visit in late 1977. I decided to stay on January 1, 1978. It was a gorgeous day, seventy degrees, and I was driving with a friend on Highway 1 in Sonoma County. We stopped to eat some lunch overlooking the ocean up on a two-hundred-foot cliff. My mind was already blown. Then a pod of whales breached below us. I knew I was staying.

What keeps me here is the sheer physical beauty of the place. We're so blessed that the California Coastal Commission (thank you, Jerry Brown), the East Bay Regional Park District, and the East Bay Municipal Utilities District have secured so much open space in and around our urban sprawl. Above all, the Sierra Nevada keeps me here.

What do you and Kim Stanley Robinson talk about when you're tramping about in the Sierras?
Weather. Wildlife. Gear. Food. Rocks. Route. Proust.

What was the origin of your novel about the Livermore Labs, Radiance? *Have you ever worked in high tech?*

For a time I did a little technical writing and coding for some very low-tech outfits, but my primary sources are credited in the acknowledgments: Andrew Lichterman and Daniel Marcus. Andy ran lawsuits against the Lab, and Dan worked there, so I had access to fairly intimate knowledge of the place from two very different perspectives. But the origin was simply living in the Bay Area. You couldn't not be aware of the Lab, especially during the SDI period, which *Radiance* covers. I consider it primarily about the California landscape, physical and psychic.

You seem equally adventurous in music and literature. At least in SF and jazz. Do you find the balance between pattern and innovation, expectation and surprise, similar in both or different?
Very similar. SF and jazz, these days, are generally not all that adventurous. They're mostly (not entirely) in archival mode, reliving and remixing past glories. And what glories. Both SF and jazz had a great run in New York City in the 1950s. The number of SF magazines and the number of jazz clubs, combined with the affordability then of life in the city, enabled a good number of really fine artists to make a living without a day job, to play every night or publish every month, enough to make a real scene.

The scenes crossed others as well, such as the avant-garde. Horace Gold, the editor of *Galaxy* magazine, hosted John Cage and Morton Feldman in poker games at his home in Peter Cooper Village, where I grew up. Orrin Keepnews—the Riverside Records producer who did so much for the careers of Bill Evans, Thelonious Monk, and so many others—started out as a book editor at Simon and Schuster and worked on several early SF hardcover titles. Culture is a wild seed, so who knows, but I see some of the 1960s born in this cross-fertilization.

This year, 2015, is the fiftieth anniversary of the AACM (Association for the Advancement of Creative Musicians), born in Chicago. Check them out.

You and Jonathan Lethem authored a book together. What was that process?
When Jonathan lived in Oakland, he and I had often had lunch together. One day he showed me a notebook entry that in its entirety read "KAFKA/CAPRA." He said, "I think there's a story there." I went home and thought about it and wrote a thousand words about an émigré Kafka in 1930s Hollywood. We passed

it back and forth. In the course of this collaboration, we found that we'd each previously written a story involving Kafka. If we'd each write one more, he suggested, we'd have a slender book. Jonathan's energy turned this frail beginning into a real book, first from Subterranean Press (thank you, Bill Schafer), then from Norton (thank you, Aimee Bianca).

One of James Baldwin's favorite novels was The Princess Casamassima. *Did you know that?*
No.

Jeopardy answer (you provide the question): The Rapture of the New.
What is this morning?

You write as well as play music. How does musical composition differ from literary? Procedurally, I mean.
When you play, that is, improvise, which is composing in real time, you don't get the liberty of afterthoughts and fixing mistakes. But procedurally I think both kinds of composition start with improvisation, on some theme that's maybe a little vague at first, which gains more definition and direction the more you work on it. As a "composer" of music, you're doing this out of real time, which can be a benefit or a disadvantage. As a writer of prose, you're way better off hiding from real time.

What kind of car do you drive? I ask this of everyone.
A 1995 Honda Civic CX. It was stolen a few years ago. I learned from the internet that it was, at that time, the most stolen automobile in the USA—that year and model. It's easy to break into. The internet says you can open it with a tennis ball: make a slit in the ball, hold it against the door lock, squeeze it just right, and the air pressure holds back the tumblers. Nice going, Honda. Still, a great car. I got mine back and hope to keep driving it till I'm too old to care. Its appearance already shows that.

Do you listen to music when you write?
Never. Too distracting.

What are you reading this week? Next week?
This week, the scurrilous verse of John Wilmot, earl of Rochester. Next week, I wish I knew. (That's the title of a song by Harry Warren.)

Why do drivers take so long to get moving when the light changes?
Idiocracy.

Each in one sentence, please: James Salter, Don Pullen, Cecelia Holland, Antoni Gaudí.
Outsiders all; all underappreciated, except for Gaudí. I'm going to cheat with semicolons.

Salter wrote like some kind of tortured but undisgraced angel; he hid his Jewishness, and his angelic writing was always in some fear or disdain of its god Hemingway, but his integrity was his own.

Also his disappointment.
My first piano heroes are Monk and Evans, but Pullen could play anything—jazz, gospel, Afro-Brazilian, and, most powerfully, free.

Cecelia Holland can write about any period as if she'd lived her whole life in it, coming away with a fine understanding of how individual wills and a cultural moment create very particular moral complexities; if she'd written only three or four such novels that would be impressive, but she's written thirty or forty, which inspires awe.

I haven't ever stood within Gaudí's architecture, but the photos I've seen are stunning and remind me of standing within Simon Rodia's Watts Towers, and of the work of the German painter Hundertwasser, both I believe inspired by him, and both underappreciated.

Favorite Shakespeare play?
Tamburlaine Part 3. But it was actually written by Francis Bacon.

You are a charter member of a legendary San Francisco writers' workshop that almost never meets. Is that a problem or a strategy?

We consider it both. We're meeting "soon." That's the title of an underappreciated Gershwin tune.

"The Fly in the Sugar Bowl"
Nisi Shawl

What's the deal with you and dolls?
Dolls are how we learn to be people. We pretend we're human with dolls so as to get the hang of it. I'm still paying attention, still being educated.

What (or who) drew (or pushed) you into science fiction?
I can't remember a time when I *wasn't* into science fiction or some form of fiction operating outside consensus reality. Early influences include Rod Serling's *Twilight Zone* series, Ruthven Todd's Space Cat books, *The Wonderful Flight to the Mushroom Planet* by Eleanor Cameron, *Mary Poppins* (and all the sequels), *Tatsinda* by Elizabeth Enright, *A Wrinkle in Time* by Madeleine L'Engle, and everything Edward Eager ever wrote. When I was in sixth grade, I persuaded the librarians at the downtown Kalamazoo branch to let me read books shelved in the adult SF section and discovered Ray Bradbury, Theodore Sturgeon, et al., and it was all over.

What period in history interests you most?
Currently I'm most interested in two periods: the late Victorian/Edwardian era and the late 1950s and early 1960s. *Everfair* was set in the first period, but even before I began work on it, I was drawn to that time as one of enormous change and consequential choices. Regarding the second period, I've written two-thirds of a novella, *The Day and Night Books of Mardou Fox*, set in the 1960s, which is also the background for my forthcoming middle-grade fantasy, *Speculation*. And I set a flash story there too. It's called "More than Nothing," and it's part of Tor.com's *Nevertheless, She Persisted* anthology.

I suppose part of my fascination with that time stems from my personal connection—I was born in 1955 and have memories of my life from nursery school onward. Also, though, it was an amazingly optimistic time for Black people. We were making progress in terms of our civil rights, our culture was strong and beautiful, particularly our music—the Blue Note jazz scene, Motown—just a magical historical moment.

What tech device do you find most helpful? Least?
Most useful has got to be my smartphone. I don't have to cart around a laptop to read my email, access documents, watch movies, accomplish lots of laptop-centric tasks. Least useful tech device? That's a harder pick. If it's not useful, I'm not using it, and I tend not to think about things I don't use. I suppose dishwashers qualify. I eschew online calendars also. Which is most unuseful? Hard to judge.

What poets do you read for fun or pleasure?
Umm, none? If poetry is thrust upon me—if I come across it in a mixed-format book or someone dedicates a piece to me—I may read and enjoy it. Generally, though, I find it too intense, even though I've been known to write it. Reading a poem is like drinking a tumblerful of lemon juice.

The exception is song lyrics. Those I can handle.

Does science model the universe or the human mind?
Oh, science can't help but model the human mind, because it's born of the human mind. It's probably the closest we'll get to modeling the universe as well, though.

My Jeopardy *item (I provide the answer, you provide the question): Writing while white.*
What's the default setting for authors in this place and time?

One sentence on each, please: Jordan Peele, Paul Robeson, Alison Bechdel.
Sure would like to meet Jordan Peele and hang with him for a day. Paul Robeson has all my love and respect. (Did you know I named a character in my cyberpunk

story "Deep End" after him?) Does Alison Bechdel know Samuel R. Delany—and if not, does she want to?

What car do you drive? I ask this of everyone.
I drive a 2018 Honda Fit. I bought it when my mom was still alive because at the time I drove a standard (stick shift) 1996 Honda Accord, and she couldn't operate the clutch. She had a partially paralyzed left leg, so I bought my first automatic with her physical abilities in mind. I had once borrowed a friend's Fit—an earlier model—and I was impressed with its carrying capacity and ease of parking. The friend reported it as being nicely reliable too. My Fit's not a real smooth ride, and there's a wide window stanchion that impinges on my view when I look out the left side, but otherwise I like it. It's painted a shiny, metallic blue and bombed with crow shit. I named it Melina, after the Greek singer/actress/activist Melina Mercouri.

How did you research Everfair? *Was it hard to do or hard to quit?*
Researching *Everfair* was hard in that there wasn't much to go on when it came to certain areas of knowledge. Particularly scarce was information on the indigenous people of the Upper Congo in the 1890s—people who were decimated and, in some cases, completely wiped out. But the research was fun and also deeply rewarding. I created several characters I wouldn't have thought of, basing them on surprise facts.

And some of my research was deeply physical too. In addition to reading books and articles, I ate relevant foods, listened to relevant music, and collected and pored over photos, maps, and floor plans.

My method is research-as-you-go, which is why I can't use the sorts of retreats that cut you off from the internet, the starting point of many of my inquiries. Questions come up as I write, and the answers I find shape the story's subsequent lines, paragraphs, pages . . . That thing where you put in a note telling yourself to add a description later? I don't do that. For me, that doesn't work. I need it all to be there. One detail leads to another.

What's with the sequel?

I'm not sure what you're asking. It exists. Or rather, it will; there will be a sequel. My working title is *Kinning*. I gave an outline to Tor and I signed a contract and there's a deadline. The sequel concerns infectious empathy, community, hierarchy, and a struggle for succession. I'm going to try to limit myself to only four viewpoint characters: Tink, Bee-Lung, Princess Mwadi, and Prince Ilunga. But Rima, Rosemary, and Laurie will be prominently featured too.

What's the origin of Writing the Other? Is it a book or a class? What if you're writing a book about someone who isn't a writer?

Writing the Other: A Practical Approach is a book based on a class based on an essay based on something I overheard a friend say twenty-seven years ago. The book was published in 2005, and there've been many classes derived from and associated with it since then. We hope to do an update soon.

Were you ever part of fandom?

Sure. I would say I was part of fandom when I attended my very first convention. Confusion, it was called, and the guest of honor was C.J. Cherryh, whom I idolized. I dressed up as her, in fact: streaked silver through my afro and donned a flight suit like one of her characters. I also attended a World Fantasy Convention in Chicago and got fed cookies by Gene Wolfe.

We're talking the 1980s and '90s. At that time I was an exception; hardly anyone of African descent went to cons besides me. For years and years I was what Nalo Hopkinson calls "the fly in the sugar bowl." I used to go up to every Black person I saw at any given convention, introduce myself, shake their hand. Because I could. Because there would be maybe two or three of us among a thousand plus white attendees. Couple of East Asians if the scene was ultradiverse.

Since Race Fail, which gave rise to Con or Bust, that has changed. At a recent WisCon there were over a hundred nonwhite attendees out of around eight hundred total. No way I could introduce myself to every single one.

Yet fandom still has profound issues when it comes to racial equity. I have still felt unwelcome and frozen out at conventions. The behavior I have problems with isn't necessarily explicitly racist. It doesn't have to be, though, if I've become sensitized to that sort of thing by fending off multiple microaggressions every day.

You mention "Race Fail, which gave rise to Con or Bust." Huh?
Con or Bust, a nonprofit giving travel grants to fans of color attending science fiction conventions, grew out of its founders' dissatisfaction with the resources available to POC wishing to make their participation in fandom more visible. Race Fail, remember, was about white fans doubting the existence of nonwhite fans. By helping nonwhite fans attend cons (which are crucial in the construction of SFFH's community), Con or Bust literally changed the face of that community.

What is the filter in Filter House*?*
It's a biological means of feeding oneself. See, there are these very small sea creatures called appendicularians, and they create "filter houses" out of mucus to trap food particles and funnel them into their bellayz. A filter house is like a very tiny, three-dimensional, underwater spider web. As an appendicularian grows in size, it creates larger and larger filter houses for a better fit. The discards become a large part of the constant fall of organic matter sinking down through the ocean and providing sustenance to deep layers where light isn't so readily available. (This foodfall is also known as "marine snow.")

I guess I was thinking of the book as collecting stories the way a real-life filter house collects food. And then it detaches and drifts into the depths of your mind? Something like that.

Were you ever published in the Whole Earth Catalog? *I was.*
You got me there. My most outstanding hippy cred is taking a shit with Wavy Gravy.

Your move to Seattle is celebrated (on your website) as: "This mermaid has returned to the sea." Huh? Aren't you from Michigan?
I lived on the Atlantic when I spent eight months in Scotland. For me, those waters are haunted. My godmother, Luisah Teish, attributes this to ancestral memory. Thousands of African captives jumped or were thrown into the Atlantic Ocean. Tossed overboard alive when deemed unprofitable as merchandise. Escaping to their deaths from stinking hellholds. The waters of the Pacific missed out on absorbing those horrors, so it's to them I turn for my salt and tides. Which, apparently, I need.

Ecologically speaking, there are many similarities between the Seattle area and my home state of Michigan. Flora, fauna, at times even climate. And we're far north here, bordering on Canada. I like that. I'm used to it. Feels like I can leave the country by walking in the right direction.

There's more to it than that, of course. I attended two writing programs here back when I was still based in the Midwest. I did divination before deciding to move and was told in resoundingly definite terms that this was the place. But the previous two paragraphs are true enough for jazz.

Did you know Octavia Butler? What do people today get wrong about her?
I did indeed know Octavia and got to hang out with her a bunch while we both lived in Seattle. We went to restaurants, shops, and plays together, among other expeditions. We talked on the phone. I had her over for dinner, and she reciprocated.

The thing I find most annoying and ignorant these days is when lesbians claim her as one of their own. Listen, unless she was deeply, deeply closeted, Octavia was a heterosexual. I'm queer—currently preferring they/them pronouns and identifying also as bisexual. Octavia was no homophobe, but in all our many conversations she never so much as hinted to me that women attracted her. People grow, and sexuality can change and develop. At the time of her death, however, and as far as she was concerned for her entire life prior, she was not a lesbian. Period.

As you approach our present in your "Crash Course in the History of Black Science Fiction," you celebrate "the emergence of self- and small press publishing as a black SF force to be reckoned with." Really? Isn't this just making the best of a bad thing?
Ninety percent of being Black is about making the best of a bad thing. Case in point: chitterlings.

Self- and small press publishing, though, are definitely on the rise. Their moment has come. They're far more nimble than traditional publishing houses and thus able to more quickly capitalize on niches and trends just rising to prominence. Case in point: PM Press.

Who is Carl Brandon?

Carl Brandon was a hoax. Terry Carr and Pete Graham perpetrated him on fandom in the 1940s and '50s as a means of rendering the community less blindingly white. When we founded the Carl Brandon Society (CBS) in 1999, Ian K. Hageman suggested it as a suitable namesake. You can learn more in Carr's essay, which Jeanne Gomoll reprinted in the fundraising book titled *Carl Brandon* she put together for the CBS.

Ever go to Burning Man?
No, but I've done dog sitting for people who went. Does that count? In the 1970s and '80s I attended the annual Rainbow Family Gatherings, which I categorize as Burning Man precursors.

You're a critic as well as a writer. What's your take on cyberpunk? High fantasy? Mundanity?
I have written cyberpunk and enjoyed reading it—though mostly what I like challenges any even temporary status quo associated with the genre. I mean, back in 1992, people were already convening a symposium about its overness, which made me rather sad, as I hadn't yet gotten a crack at smacking it down. It was dying without my hand on the murder weapon.

My cyberpunk stories are basically the six published so far in my Making Amends series: "Deep End," "In Colors Everywhere," "Like the Deadly Hands," "The Best Friend We Never Had," "Living Proof," and "The Mighty Phin." I plan two more: "Over a Long Time Ago" and another still sans title. I suppose "Walk like a Man," included in this book [*Talk like a Man*], qualifies as well.

I haven't answered your question, though, have I? Eileen Gunn's "Computer Friendly" is the kind of cyberpunk I admire and want more of. That help?

"High fantasy" gives me the heebie-jeebies as a term. What's it higher than? What's it high on? I do love some literature that has been classified as high fantasy—most notably Lord Dunsany's novel *The King of Elfland's Daughter*. *Lilith*, by George MacDonald, fits in there as well, right? It's a favorite of mine too. Lyrical prose is one of the things I appreciate about so-called high fantasy. Its focus on the upper classes is one of the things I do not appreciate about it.

Your third named category, Mundanity, I'm going to assume refers to the movement founded by Geoff Ryman, in which traditional SF tropes such as faster-than-light travel are bypassed in favor of futuristic elements actually extrapolated from current scientific knowledge. I think it's a noble concept, and it has produced some beautiful, laudable work, such as Ryman's *V.A.O.* Tragedy's more believable against a rigorously constructed background.

Where does Afrofuturism fit into all this? Or does it?
Afrofuturism is not a subgenre of SFFH, like the things you asked me about. It's a means of encompassing many different genres and subgenres. It's an aesthetic movement rather than a set of guidelines for ways to construct or read a story. Authors Milton Davis and Balogun Ojetade have named certain parallel subgenres in light of their contributors' Afrofuturist bent: steamfunk, sword-and-soul, etc. I call *Everfair* AfroRetroFuturist, stitching together the "retrofuturist" name steampunks give themselves with Afrofuturism. No need to choose one over the other.

Ever done a graphic novel (comic book)?
No, I haven't. I'd like to, though. My friend, artist Steve Lieber, thought I should do a script for my Louisa May Alcott send-up, "The Tawny Bitch." Comic books are such a different art form! I figured out a lot about the differences just drafting an outline to work from.
Everfair would be a cool comic, wouldn't it?

Do you follow (or attend) Superhero movies? Online games? What do you do for fun?
Answer questions like these.

What question were you hoping I would ask that I didn't?
I'm not sure how this could have been framed as a question, but I was hoping to talk a bit about how, as a teen, my friends would have deemed me rabidly apolitical. My first true love destroyed draft records with fake blood attacks and organized a months-long sit-in at the Post Office. His best buddy fought cops in the streets of Chicago at the 1968 Democratic Convention with nothing but a wet bandana between him and clouds of tear gas. By contrast, my most radical act as an adolescent was probably playing a wooden flute in a bank lobby. Even though some of my earliest memories include walking picket lines with my

parents, for a long while those sorts of actions simply were not my jam. Poetry, magic, those were my preferred modes of revolution.

Nowadays, of course, I'm up for all of them. To paraphrase Marlon Brando's character in *The Wild One*: How am I rebelling against the patriarchy? "How many ways ya got?"

"Pro Is for Professional"
John Shirley

You're tough to pigeonhole, John. You are celebrated as a postmodernist in McCaffrey's Storming the Reality Studio, but you are generally published as a genre writer. Is there a contradiction? Or is this a postmodernist disguise?
I never felt like a postmodernist in the philosophical sense, but I can appreciate its forward-looking sensibility and its relativism. I believe in having a moral and ethical compass, but I'm down on dogmatism.

I'm a genre writer partly because I make my *living* as a writer, and that's where the market was for a guy like me when I started. Also, science fiction seemed to me to be in line with the surrealism I admired in art. The genre has its appeal—it provides a kind of literary computer program, where you can model alternative societies and various social futures, and see what might work and what might break down, and what the unintended consequences of trends might be. And it seemed to be a place for outsiders to find a role—and it was. Look, they even took Terry Bisson in! And, for example, Alice Sheldon . . .

William Gibson felt like an outsider too. He once said in an interview (paraphrasing here) that if a weird cat like Shirley can find a niche there, so can I. So some genres are places for outsiders to find a home. And where else can you get paid to create bizarre imagery?

But I'm an outsider within genre writing too. I am. And of course I like to pretend to transcend genre, to be sui generis . . .

How did you get started as a writer? Was there a breakthrough moment or book that made it real?
I published in the alternative press at first, around 1970, so that helped. But really it was the Clarion writers' workshop. I was accepted to that and had a small

windfall that made it possible to pay for it. I was bottled up at Clarion with the likes of Ursula Le Guin, Harlan Ellison, Frank Herbert, Avram Davidson, Terry Carr, Robert Silverberg. I was there with Gus Hasford, who went on to write *The Short-Timers* [the novel that was the basis for the film *Full Metal Jacket*], and Vonda McIntyre, Lisa Tuttle, Art Cover—a group of talent-charged people.

I was barely civilized at the time. Ellison jeered at the reek of my dorm room. I took acid there one day. But still—I got a great deal out of the basic Clarion experience. Especially criticism—the criticism I received was golden. My first pro publication was in a Clarion anthology.

Carr and Silverberg went on to accept stories by me for their anthologies. Damon Knight's Milford West workshops in Eugene were a great help. He and Kate Wilhelm taught us—Joe Haldeman and Gene Wolfe were students, with me, back then! They taught me to read my own writing as a reader would and that helped mature my prose, which was necessary because it was often, well, *premature*, as it were.

I think of cyberpunk as SF plus noir (or vice versa). How would you describe it? After all, you were there.
Your description is not far from mine. And I always quote Gibson: "The street has its own uses for things." People on the street, or the poor, the underclasses, can appropriate technology and use it against the power structure; use it to challenge the status quo. Look what happened in the Arab Spring. Look what Anonymous does, or WikiLeaks. It's not all good. But it's all cyberpunk.

"Dystopian" seems a rather gentle euphemism for the worlds you create. Have you ever written a utopian novel or story?
I sometimes take things in a metaphysical direction—I prefer that term to "spiritual." I'm influenced by Aldous Huxley, who did that so well in *Time Must Have a Stop*, and *The Perennial Philosophy*. In those metaphysical explorations we find doorways "out" of the worst of the human dilemma; or a transcendence of it—a right relationship to our condition. Right congruence.

Usually even my darkest novels, like *Everything Is Broken* or *Demons*, have a resolution where things are at least improved; where there's hope, a direction to go in. But getting there can be hell.

The Other End is a novel of alternative apocalypse, where I make up the Judgment Day I'd like to see. It's a Judgment Day without an angry God, but there's still . . . something. And that's a kind of utopian vision, I guess.

The idea of city personified animates your classic City Come A-Walkin'. *Fritz Leiber had a different take on the same theme (and same city) in* Our Lady of Darkness. *Was the old German an influence?*
I don't think I read *Our Lady of Darkness*, but another Germanic fellow (he was Swiss) was an influence: Carl Jung. *City Come A-Walkin'* is a bit influenced by Jung's ideas of the collective unconscious, but mostly influenced by my stays in San Francisco at an impressionable time, and by the music and lyrical content of Patti Smith. I simply perceived cities that way—each had its own mind. City as a kind of organism. *City Come A-Walkin'* was also influenced by my involvement in progressive, edgy, prepunk rock 'n' roll. I was trying to capture that feel, that energy, that pulse.

I have always tried to fuse things, to bring contrasting art forms into some kind of creative unity. It seems contradictory to fuse storytelling with surrealism (hence someone had to make up the term "magic realism")—real surrealism shouldn't be rational enough to have the internal logic of a story. But I have tried, anyway, and succeeded at times, or so I am told. J.G. Ballard of course did it in novels like *The Crystal World*. He has always been an inspiration.

I often think of SF and Fantasy as this jumble shop of ideas to be examined, reused, appropriated, and returned—a commons, if you will. Your thoughts on the copyright/commons debate? Should music be free? What about literature?
I'm a person who makes a living from intellectual property. I have an album—mostly songs, not readings—that came out in January 2013, from Black October Records. So I don't leap headlong into Creative Commons for books and music.

Having said that, I do think it's possible to worry too much about, say, free music downloading. *South Park* made fun of Metallica: the poor Metallica musician had to buy a *slightly smaller* private jet because of music piracy! Well, I don't have a private jet but I don't like it when *The Crow* (I was co-scripter for the movie) is pirated, as I get money from DVD sales.

And yet my son has almost convinced me that there's room for it all. For example, a lot of artists put free stuff up on YouTube to publicize their work. If you offer a song free, people will buy your album. I have some of my short stories free at my blog in hopes of encouraging people to buy books.

Tell us about your work with Blue Öyster Cult. Was this a natural fit?
I wrote lyrics for them—eighteen songs. BOC is "the thinking person's hard rock band." Their music is intricate, their lyrics vary between deliberately ironic and chilling. They often used horror and science fiction imagery, stuff that had the resonance of Lovecraft or Bradbury. They had a vision of a dark underlying reality behind the accepted human world, and I identified with that point of view. You find something like that in the shadowy organizations behind a futuristic neofascism in *A Song Called Youth*, my cyberpunk trilogy—even though I tend to disdain conspiracy theories. And in fact my first novel is called *Transmaniacon*, which is the name of a Blue Öyster Cult song. In my rather jejune way I dedicated it to them and to Patti Smith (who also wrote lyrics for the Blue Öyster Cult—as did Michael Moorcock). The band was aware of me because of the book, and many years later I got the invitation to write lyrics for them. And jumped at it.

The Crow has a dark history. What was your share in all that?
I found the comic, which was obscure, took it to a producer who optioned it (attaching me as screenwriter). It's not an accident the comic was movie-like, since James O'Barr, the creator of *The Crow*, was into Japanese samurai films. I wrote the first four drafts of the script but didn't get along with one of the producers.

I wanted to have a ruthless corporate scumbag be the main bad guy in *The Crow*, but the producer I had the run-in with came from a family that owned a big corporation. He insisted on changing it, I argued with him, and soon I was out. They brought David Schow in for a rewrite, and he did fine. So Schow and I share the credit.

Obviously the real shadow on *The Crow* was the death of its star, Brandon Lee, during filming. Just an accident, something stuck in the barrel of a prop gun, and a powerful blank shell . . . but it could have been avoided. The movie was mostly done when he died, and they paid a settlement, then finished the film in post, and it was a hit. All in all it was a good movie, seething with stylistic originality, because despite the tragic accident, it had the right director, Alex Proyas.

Any movie projects in the works? There were rumors about Demons . . .
My novel *Demons* has been optioned a few times. The Weinstein brothers optioned and reoptioned it, and they had a director attached, and a script. But then the recession hit, and the Weinsteins almost went broke. They had to ditch most of their film projects and refinance, so the film was dropped.

But there's interest, still. *Demons* is a nightmarish novel, with spiritual overtones, having to do with demons invading Earth the way hostile extraterrestrials do in other tales. And it's an allegory about how far industry is willing to go in sacrificing innocent people for the sake of profits . . .

Your nonfiction book on Gurdjieff shows not only an understanding but a sort of affinity. How did this project come about?
It was the product of fifteen some-odd years of intense reading in spirituality and philosophy. People like Alan Watts and Aldous Huxley and William James and Meister Eckhart and Lao Tzu and Ramakrishna and Emerson and Thoreau. Zen writers like Shunryu Suzuki. Sufism, Christian mysticism, certain forms of Gnosticism—even old C.S. Lewis. In philosophy, Plato (the *Timaeus* dialogue), Spinoza . . .

Then I read an interview with Jacob Needleman about Gurdjieff's ideas on the human condition. And I felt, yeah, that's right! Needleman's book *Time and the Soul* had a great influence on my thinking. So I became a student of Needleman and, through him, of Gurdjieff. Essentially, Gurdjieff says that we're all psychological machines; that we're asleep when we think we're awake. But even though we are unconscious, there are moments of freedom and liberation. And it's possible to develop something inwardly that can be freer yet, and more conscious.

Me, I wanted practical results. I didn't want to jabber about spirituality. I wanted to be free. I wanted to be in command of myself—I'd been such a bull in a china shop, in my life! Most of all I wanted to be more conscious. How could I get there, practically speaking? The Gurdjieff Foundation provided specific methods. To my astonishment, the methods really helped. I am not conscious, but I can see the signposts to a fuller consciousness.

So when Penguin gave me the chance to do a serious book on the subject, an intro to Gurdjieff's life and ideas, I jumped at it.

But while I'm influenced by Gurdjieff, and use his methods, I'm influenced by Zazen methodology too, and by the teachings of Krishnamurti. Yet it's not a vague mishmash. I am focused on a specific methodology, one you find in all the greatest metaphysical traditions, when you get to their inner, esoteric circle.

You have strong connections in cyberpunk, in underground comics, and in rock music. How did this come about? Does it all still fit together?
It overlaps more than fits together. Frank Zappa influenced underground comics; underground comics—for example, the work of Paul Mavrides and Jay Kinney and [Victor] Moscoso and Spain Rodriguez—influenced me, and so did Zappa and so did Captain Beefheart and so did King Crimson . . . and so did composers like Stravinsky and Varèse, for that matter. And Penderecki.

Groups as diverse as Blue Öyster Cult, the Rolling Stones, the Sisters of Mercy, Hawkwind, the Velvet Underground, artists like Jimi Hendrix, Patti Smith, Iggy Pop, John Lydon . . . they were all voracious readers. Most of them had read the better science fiction. Patti Smith was especially influenced by Baudelaire and Verlaine, as I was. And people in that scene had an appreciation for filmmakers like Fellini, like Kubrick, like Roeg . . .

Somehow it all made up a counterculture to the counterculture. We were outside the counterculture per se; we were our own underground counterculture, and it all overlapped.

Which do you like better, writing for TV or for comics (leaving aside the money)?
I've only written for comics once: a five-issue miniseries for IDW titled *The Crow: Death and Rebirth*, which is a sort of reboot of *The Crow* set in Japan (and in Japanese Buddhist hell). It was a good experience in some ways, frustrating in others, but I got my story told. It's out in a graphic novel now.

So I haven't had that much experience with comics. But it wasn't as committee-oriented, in terms of the writing, as television. You're always filtered through producers and executives, "suits," in TV and movies. Few people get to be *auteurs*. I'm still waiting for my first really satisfying film or TV writing experience. I had a bit more artistic freedom writing the comic.

Do you have a daily routine as writer? A certain bow tie, an heirloom chair, a time or word-count quota? (People like to know these things.)
So you know about the bow tie and the chair? Well, it's true: I tie a bow on a chair, and then the chair tells me what to write.

Beyond that, I try not to get up too late in the day, I try not to spend too much time online, and I usually end up writing from about noon till three. I take a break, then write till dinner. If I'm writing a work-for-hire piece I assign myself a certain number of pages per day. If I'm writing out of my own wellspring of inspiration, which naturally I prefer, I try to write at least five pages. Sometimes it will be more. Thank God for revision. I often start the writing day by revising what I wrote the previous day to get into the swing of the narrative.

That's fiction. Nonfiction, of course, I write nude, on my roof (in all weathers), wearing a balloon-animal hat.

What are you reading right now for fun?
Are we allowed to read for fun? I usually read biographies or historical fiction, at this time in my life. Now reading *1356* by Bernard Cornwell. I'm also a big fan of Patrick O'Brian and tend to reread him. I like reading something that edifies me and entertains me at the same time. Guilt free!

Did you learn anything useful from your stint in the Coast Guard?
Sure. I learned that I had a hell of a lot to learn. I learned that I was a clumsy, fairly absurd, loutish young snot. I learned respect for men who risk their lives to rescue people, too. It was all a bit like Kipling's *Captains Courageous*, but I didn't pull it off as well as his snotty boy did.

There is a persistent theme in your work: the battle between the young and the old. The good guys being usually the young. Has this changed over the years?
Not entirely. Over the years, I've accrued more understanding of elders, and of some traditions. But of course lots of traditions are vile and need to be dumped.

Racism is traditional, customary in some places—a thing being customary doesn't make it good.

You will of course find more older people in my novels now that I've grown up. But when reediting earlier books I find I still connect with most of the writing. My *A Song Called Youth* (I think of it as one novel, and it is—in the Prime Books omnibus) was titled that because I knew, even back then, that youth has its own point of view. And it's all relative.

A reader described Everything Is Broken, *your anti-libertarian thriller, as* Atlas Shrugged *turned on its head (a contortionist metaphor worthy of Cirque du Soleil!). What inspired that work?*

Ugh, I hate to be compared to Ayn Rand at all. If it's on its head, it's because my thinking is the opposite of Ayn Rand's. What inspired the book was a reaction against Randian thinking, against Libertarianism, against the Tea Party. *Everything Is Broken* is a crime novel/disaster novel fusion that, underlyingly, is also an allegory about the value of community and the need to fight back against the Ayn Rands out there.

How would you describe your politics?

While I can see some virtue in some selfishness, and I believe in independent thinking and constantly critiquing government, I think we still have a profound need for a well-organized, democratic, centralized government. I have a streak of socialist in me, but I believe in a free market modified by regulation; capitalism modified by, for example, socialized medicine, social safety nets. It's not a choice between government and anarchy. It's about allowing some space for the anarchic in a structured society.

I'd like to see Elizabeth Warren run for president. We need a woman president next time. Hopefully, if it's not Warren, our woman president will be a progressive Independent, or a Democrat.

What was your intro to left politics?

I think seeing the photos of the My Lai massacre, when I was a boy, influenced me to ask: What the *hell* is going on? Those grim, grisly color photos of murdered women and children radicalized me. Years later my radicalization was moderated by experiences on the street, back when I was a drug user. I came to appreciate a properly run police force.

Looking at history, I see some social progress—like the end of legal slavery and the beginning of empowering women. The rise of unions helped establish the middle class. Some of that's been undone, but the fight goes on. I appreciate the Occupy movement. It didn't have a clear message but no one else was doing anything that honest. Some of those people will in time develop a more effective political movement, and I'll welcome it.

What do you find most frustrating about the left? Is the right right about anything?
I find knee-jerk political correctness frustrating; I find the left's self-righteousness and lack of pragmatism frustrating. And the sheer cynicism of many who *were* on the left and now just shrug and sneer—that, too, I find frustrating.

I think we need conservatives. It's a kind of thesis, antithesis, synthesis thing, and we need them to push back against us, within reason. But you know, even conservatives get "progressive" after a while. Few of them would consider taking the vote from women. They digested that much social evolution. They have digested some degree of environmentalism—and now in the age of global warming they're getting a real schooling.

And conservatives are correct that unions can be exploitative, and too expensive for a community if they become greedy. Only, that shouldn't mean getting *rid* of unions—it should mean *modifying* unions, a bit. It doesn't justify the kind of union-busting on a state level we're seeing now, in places like Michigan.

What do you mean by "reverse terraforming"?
Turning the habitable world into an uninhabitable world through world war or environmental irresponsibility. Like global warming.

Do you think writers have a particular social responsibility? What is it, then?
I only know that I personally have a sense of social responsibility—yet as a writer I also feel another kind of responsibility: to entertain. It's a balance. Dickens was powerfully entertaining—but he sure made his point, and a sharp, penetrating point it was. There were actual social reforms prodded into being by his novels. Steinbeck, Upton Sinclair—more than once, novelists have prompted reforms.

Yes, I know, we've gotten stuck with Fox News now, and the *Citizens United* decision, the Koch brothers. We're in danger of falling into a corporatist dictatorship. But we're not there yet, and books like *Brave New World* and *1984* and *Fahrenheit 451* have helped. So did books like *Catch-22*. Solzhenitsyn schooled us about the excesses of USSR-style communism. *Uncle Tom's Cabin* helped end slavery. Novels can be our social conscience.

Have you ever collaborated with anybody besides E.A. Poe? How did it work out?
The Poe collaboration was just finishing an unfinished story by him, in an anthology called *Poe's Lighthouse*. I hope he approves of my collaborative efforts but I haven't heard from him. Yet.

I've also collaborated on stories with Rudy Rucker, William Gibson, Marc Laidlaw, and Bruce Sterling. That's good shit, man.

Ever been attacked by wild monkeys?
Oh, you laugh. We'll likely all be attacked by them, and other tropical creatures, as global warming chases them north! The worst will be the diseases, though. Say hello to tsetse flies, Montana.

You wrote of drones (in A Song Called Youth, *if I remember correctly) long before they flew into the consciousness of the public. Do you ever worry that the CIA is mining your books for ideas?*
I was recently told by someone that he gave the early version of those novels (I've since revised and updated them) to people high in the US military in the early 1990s. However, I refuse to apologize to al-Qaeda.

The military has confessed to mining ideas from *Star Trek* and Arthur Clarke and Larry Niven. In *A Song Called Youth* the drones are basically a tool of the oppressors. The heroes of the novels are the resistance to a corporatist neofascist theocracy—and drones represent danger. And some of that's coming true.

But I think drones can be used legitimately. Sometimes. Better get used to them. Police forces are buying them up.

What kind of car do you drive? I ask this of everyone.
A Toyota Echo on its last legs, if it had legs. I want to get a Chevy Volt next.

There's a legend that you introduced William Gibson to SF. True?
The legend has it backward. I introduced science fiction to Gibson. He was already a reader of SF (and a great deal more). He had already published one piece in an obscure SF zine called *UnEarth*. I showed his unpublished stories to the editors of *Omni*, and to Terry Carr. Carr later bought his novel *Neuromancer*.

But what really "introduced" Gibson was his excellence as a writer. When I read his stories I was immediately impressed by his wit and the beginning of what was to be a kind of literary mastery.

Do you prefer writing short stories or novels? Does one ever morph into the other?
I have shamelessly woven short stories into novels for years and have developed novellas, like *Demons*, into novels. You bet. I'm a pro, that's one thing pros do. No, "pro" there is not short for prostitute; it's short for professional.

R.A. Lafferty? Ayn Rand? Rudy Rucker? Hunter Thompson? Each in one sentence, please.
Lafferty had an incomparable originality in his way of looking at the world, which showed me that good science fiction didn't have to be science-based. Ayn Rand ended her life on welfare. Rudy Rucker is a lead guitarist of ideas. Hunter Thompson was a huge talent who perhaps influences some writers too much.

Do you listen to music when you write?
I typically do, as it seems to soak up distractions, for me at least, and it creates atmosphere and even conveys energy—but it has to be music of a certain order. The lyrics can't be out in front or on top; I can't be listening to Dylan while writing or I'll start writing Dylanesquely. Instrumental music works if it has the right feel—if it feels like the "soundtrack" of what I'm writing. I can also listen to certain bands where the lyrics don't intrude. Mostly they don't intrude because they're embedded in a wall of sound. Like Motörhead, for example, or the Stooges' *Fun House* album. Rammstein is ideal because it's high energy, the right mood, and the lyrics aren't distracting because they're mostly in German so they're just sounds to me.

What city is best for writers today? Tomorrow? If it were 2056, what city would you want to live in?

New York City is always best for novelists. That's where most of the publishers are, hello. I lived there for years and loved New York. I'd live there again in a hot second. I live in the next best place now—the San Francisco area, which is pretty agreeable to writers and artists. Lots of smart, stimulating people here. Stories on every corner.

If you're writing films, you don't *have* to be in LA, but it can help. So it's about the people you interface with. But for some people the best place to write might be deep in a redwood forest.

In 2056 I want to be under the dome that's protecting Seattle, maybe, or Toronto. Cooler, safer. The Black Winds will be blocked off by the dome. Defensible . . .

When they do the John Shirley biopic, who do you want to play yourself? (And don't say Johnny Depp; he doesn't have your looks.)

William Hurt could play me as I am now. Me as a young person, I don't know—some actor yet to be discovered who can play "out-of-control youth" and embody paradox. Good and bad, kind and selfish, hardworking and slothful. As a youth I was all those things at once.

I know you and your wife Micky take film seriously. What filmmakers do you watch? What bands or musicians? What writers?

These days I'm pretty eclectic about film. I like Peter Jackson's stuff and I enjoyed the *John Carter* movie and *Skyfall*. But I also like, say, Terrence Malick and David Fincher. I like certain Korean filmmakers, Bong Joon-ho or Park Chan-wook. I like the Swedish filmmaker Tomas Alfredson. I think some really creative stuff is being done in science fiction films these days, like *Chronicle* and *Looper*.

Did cyberpunk die . . . or do a butterfly?

It was eaten alive, co-opted. Today it shows up in film and television, it's in comics, it's even in some so-called military SF. But that's justice. We cyberpunks devoured and digested Philip Dick, Alfred Bester, Cordwainer Smith, Ellison, Delany, John Brunner . . .

My Jeopardy *item: The answer is Fox News. You provide the question.*
What news channel should someone with a conscience and deep pockets buy? Please!

You seem to keep a line open to Hollywood. Ever tempted to live in LA?
I have lived in Los Angeles and would again if I had the right project there, something I needed to be on site for. I'd love to be a hands-on producer on a show of my creation, so I could choose what really matter: the writers, the directors, the actors. In that order of importance.

If you are ever elected US president, what will be your first executive order?
Not sure, probably something environmental. I will pick the one that will most annoy the Tea Party types.

"A Source of Immense Richness"
Vandana Singh

Did you fall into SF or climb into it?
I fell into it, from a planet called the Third World.

Who are you?
I am an amalgam of recycled star cores and hydrogen, formed so that the universe could talk to itself. Just like you and that rock over there. In addition, I am a nonlinear combination of various apparent contradictions: earthling and alien, animal and tree, mammal and earthworm, to name a few.

What kind of car do you drive? (I am required to ask this of everyone.)
I've almost forgotten I have a car. Isn't that wonderful? I haven't driven it much during the pandemic. My steed is an aging Toyota.

Do you have a favorite city in the US? In India?
Not really. I have favorite places in cities, but cities as we currently conceptualize them are not my thing. There's a spacetime location in Delhi where/when I lived as a teen, with fruit trees and wild birds, clean air and blue skies, but it no longer exists. There are a couple of cafés in Boston I like. And the Japanese Garden in Portland, Oregon.

Several of your stories feature food. Are you a good cook?
No, but I'm good at eating good food. I am a middling sort of cook with a limited repertoire, but I love good food across cuisines. I miss proper Indian cooking. I frequently wish someone would cook for me.

You grew up in a literary family. How did that come about?
A long family tradition that valued learning. I grew up in a vast family of grandparents, aunts, uncles, cousins, parents, and siblings, and because there were no cell phones then and hardly anyone we knew had a TV, we read voraciously. We were not rich, but almost all the adults had college degrees. We didn't have much, but my parents had steel trunks filled with books on every subject under the sun, so I taught myself elementary German, memorized Greek myths, learned anatomical drawing, read writers well above my age level, and learned to immerse myself in the magic of story by the time I entered my teens. I also listened to accounts from elders on subjects as varied as ancient Indian poetry, the Ramayana, the relationships between languages, folktales, the wretchedness of the caste system, and the fight for independence from British rule. So it was a rich intellectual atmosphere for a child to grow up in.

What do you like most about New England? Least?
I like that no matter which way you throw a tennis ball, you're going to hit a university. The place is thick with them! What I don't like is the winter when it's being wimpy and not a real winter. We've been having too many of those lately. Rain in January!

What current controversies in physics do you find most interesting or intriguing?
The nature of dark matter and dark energy; why the universe's expansion is accelerating. Whether there are other universes than ours. What life as we don't know it—on other worlds and maybe our world—might be like. The nature of quantum information. The nature of time. Whether a unified theory exists or if the laws of the universe are more like a tapestry that shifts and shimmers as you examine it. The possibility of formulating theories with concepts and mathematics that don't exist yet.

"The universe is much more like a hippie's pipe dream than it is like an accountant's ledger." Explain, please.
Ah, that's my ad for my modern physics course. After a hefty dose of Newtonian physics, in which we have a well-behaved, predictable universe, in which you can calculate the trajectory of a ball or the orbit of a planet with pretty good

accuracy—after all this good behavior, we find ourselves in a strange place where the flow of time is affected by speed and gravity, particles may wink into or out of existence, light can be wavelike or particle-like, and you, the observer, become part of the experiment—well, that beats any drug-induced hallucination I've ever heard about, and it has no unpleasant side effects.

What writers have influenced you?
This is a very long list, so I'll just name a few. I grew up on the short stories of the great Hindi writer Premchand. From him I learned that a writer's empathic imagination can extend beyond their social stratum and gender. Because poetry and music are part of the air I breathed in Delhi (that was before the pollution) I also absorbed into my consciousness the ancient Sanskrit poets Kalidasa and Jayadeva, and medieval poets of my city, like Ghalib. Through them I discovered the power of metaphor. They reinforced that we lived with other species, that in their world clouds could be messengers, and that human love, despite being absurd, could stand for metaphysical union. There were the great epics, like the *Ramayana* and its multiple versions, from which I learned about the rhythm of story, and that the arc of plot could turn on one act by an unimportant character.

More recently and from this part of the world, I have been inspired and encouraged by Ursula K. Le Guin, who showed me that science fiction could be my country too, allowing me to take my first giddy steps into this strange land. I learned from Octavia Butler that hell is only a small spacetime interval away, always. And from all of them and more people than I can name in this small space, I learned to love this thing we call imaginative literature as (almost) the only hope we have.

You lived in Austin. To teach or study? Did you connect with the Austin music scene?
I lived in Austin as a young, married woman with a child, as part of a ten-year period of exile from academia, which I sorely missed. What I loved about the almost three years I spent in Austin was the time I got to spend with my small daughter, counting primroses in the park or playing with our dog, and learning how to see the world anew through a child's eyes. There were other not-so-nice things in the suburb of Austin where we lived, including some rather blatant

racism, but I did get to be part of the music culture there—specifically the Indian music scene. There was a rather large population of people from India, and classical Indian music concerts used to be held regularly. We saw many great artists perform. I have a little training—only about three years—in North Indian classical vocal music, and I grew up in a musical family, so that meant a lot.

What music do you listen to most?
Depending on my mood, it could be North Indian classical, Bollywood oldies, reggae, classic rock, R&B, Western classical, jazz, or folk music from around the world.

Do you keep hours, habits, routines, or rituals as a writer?
Well, I have a very busy day job as a professor at a small university, so I don't get to write much during the semester. The only semiregular habit I have is to write about two or three times a week, even if it is only a paragraph, to keep the creative juices flowing. When summer comes I do this more regularly, and often the random little snippets become seeds for a story. I wish I could say I have mysterious rituals, like dancing to drumbeats by the light of the moon while waving a scimitar, but alas that would not be true.

What science writers do you read with pleasure?
I don't get to read much popular science, but I do read *Scientific American* and *New Scientist* as well as specific journal articles for research or curiosity.

Do you like American films? What about Bollywood? Are movies part of growing up in India?
I would like to be more literate in film. I haven't seen very many films, apart from a few classics. Bollywood is certainly an important part of growing up in India, but I was too much of a bookworm to care much about movies when I was growing up. And we didn't have a TV until my teens, which was too late for me to get habituated to the screen. But I have seen many, if not most of the Hindi classics, and I know a number of the songs. During my last winter break I started to explore Kurosawa. I do admire good movies—the medium

is so different from writing, and therefore the aesthetics and imperatives are different too.

Ever spend time in the Himalayas?
Yes, from childhood visits to hill stations, to a life-changing trip in the summer between the end of high school and the beginning of college, and my most recent visit in 2019. The life-changing visit at the age of seventeen was with a group of Delhi students to visit the Chipko movement, a now-famous eco-feminist movement of Himalayan villagers for forest rights and environment. Although this trip was decades ago, I remember details with vivid clarity. It was one of those paradigm-shifting things that shake you loose from all previously held assumptions about the world. So while I fell in love with the Himalayas during my childhood, it was that visit as a teen that cemented a permanent relationship marked by a constant ache of longing when I am away. In 2019 I got to see a part of the range I had never visited before, in the Eastern Himalayas, and felt as though I belonged there as much as the bamboo and pine growing on the mountain slopes. Other people might be haunted by ghosts; I'm haunted by an entire mountain range.

In terms of reading and writing, what are the most interesting differences between Hindi and English?
Well, they are both Indo-European languages, so there are, first of all, similarities, for example in the roots of many words. Against this backdrop of deep-past common origin are some intriguing differences. In Hindi the verbs tend to be at the end of a sentence, and the script is far more precise than that of English. We have more letters as a result. There are sounds in Hindi that don't exist in English. Also, while multiple literary styles abound in Hindi as well as English, it is easier to be emotional in Hindi than in English, to express passion without sounding purplish, although purplitude may also be embraced with abandon, as in the most unabashed Bollywood movies. As is true with comparing most languages, there are concepts that exist in Hindi that can't be translated into English. It is my mother tongue, so I find in it an indescribable sweetness. Certain phrases evoke childhood memories, aromas, tastes of favorite foods, voices of people long gone.

Why are there so many different languages in India? Is that a feature or a bug?
It's definitely a feature. There are many cultural groups in India that have different histories, including linguistic histories. And apart from the officially recognized languages, of which there are over twenty, there are thousands of dialects. It's often hard to talk across these, which is why the colonial language, English, has such a hold still. There are plenty of quarrels across languages, but for me it is a source of immense richness to have so many languages and therefore so many different ways to see the world. Although I only know Hindi really well, I can sing in Bengali, and I used to be able to speak fairly good Tamil.

A sentence on each, please: Lee Smolin, Vandana Shiva, Molly Gloss.
Lee Smolin: you can trust him not to string you along. Vandana Shiva: I haven't followed her work lately, but a certain phrase of hers resonates: monoculture of the mind. Molly Gloss: Her writing is full of silences that speak—spare, passionate in the most understated way, evocative, and unforgettable.

Which of your children do you like best?
I only have one, so that's easy! She's my heart's joy.

Do you read poetry for pleasure? Who?
I grew up in a poetic culture, so it's as natural to me as breathing. Among Indian poets, I've already mentioned a few above, but there are also Sahir Ludhianvi, Dushyant Kumar, and Jacinta Kerketta. Among poets from other parts of the world, I love Neruda, Rumi, Hafez, Byron, Wordsworth, Keats, Angelou, Hikmat, Harjo, and so many others. I don't have any kind of deep knowledge of their works, but poetry is part of my basic four food groups.

My Jeopardy *item. I provide the answer: Keynes and Feynman. You provide the question.*
An economist and a physicist walk into a bar and discover that they are not at all keen on each other, although the beer is fine. Who are they?

How's your novel going?

It isn't! I don't have time to write anything that long, so my head is filled with larvae of novels, some in chrysalid sleep, others growing fat and impatient, and still others moribund.

"No Regrets, No Retreat, No Surrender"
Norman Spinrad

You were a key member of SF's legendary New Wave in the Sixties. Did you just stumble into that, or was it a destination?
I was there in Los Angeles when Harlan Ellison cooked up the idea of the *Dangerous Visions* anthology, and after we talked about it and what it might include, my "Carcinoma Angels" was the first story bought for the book. Published in '67, it marked the birth of the "American New Wave." But I knew nothing of the British New Wave, led by Michael Moorcock and *New Worlds* magazine (named by Judith Merril), and I don't think Harlan really did either.

When *Bug Jack Barron* was rejected by Doubleday (which had had it under contract) and was bouncing around New York without finding a publisher, I took the manuscript to the Milford SF Conference, a sort of pro workshop in the wilds of Pennsylvania. There I met Mike for the first time and learned about the British New Wave, which was something rather different and more stylistically complex than our version. Mike got enthusiastic about *Bug Jack Barron* and decided to serialize it in *New Worlds*.

That's when all hell broke loose.

I believe it was actually denounced in the British Parliament. How come?
They were pissed because the magazine was financed partly by the British Arts Council, and it was publishing this deliberately impolite novel about uncomfortable stuff like racism, sex, celebrity, and immortality, not to mention politics.

Soon after the brouhaha over *Bug Jack Barron*, I decided to move to London (the "Swinging London" of the time) to be where the action was.

Those must have been heady days for a young writer from the Bronx.

It was wild enough. And I wasn't the only American writer on the scene. Tom Disch was there, and John Sladek. And William Burroughs, too. I spent some time with him at a conference in Harrogate, way up in Yorkshire. On the way back to London, we had to change trains, and Burroughs bought a bunch of those sleazy British tabloids, which he loved. I remember him cackling at the lurid lead story, which was the Manson murders.

Life imitating fiction?
That appealed to Burroughs. A few months later, I was in Los Angeles writing for the *Los Angeles Free Press*, and Manson family members and wannabes were hanging all over us because the paper had said some nice things about Charlie. And even after we found out how guilty he was, we had to keep making nice because we didn't want his minions to dislike or discorporate us. But that's another long story.

And a particularly American one.
Yes, but the Brits had their own tough customers. At the Harrogate event a Communist minor guru interrupted a panel discussion to denounce the "elitism" of the conference and demand that the seating be altered into a more "egalitarian" (roundtable) configuration. But when I looked down, I saw that all the chairs were nailed to the floor. When I pointed this out, I was told that it didn't matter. Chaos ensued at the conference. John Calder, the honcho, and Nigel Calder, running the panel, were stymied. Shouts and threats were traded. On and on it went. I knew that the seats were immovable. I realized that the idea was just to create such a scene and disrupt the event. So I stood up and pointed out that the chairs were nailed to the floor.

"You, sir, are a fascist and a bastard!" the commissar roared at me. Then he turned on his heels, led his posse out, and the panel continued. The next day the story was in most of the British papers and I had my fifteen minutes of fame, albeit as a fascist and a bastard. In that order. My name was even misspelled "Norman Spinard."

I guess it could have been worse.

Things can always get worse. One *New Worlds* fringie in those days was Sonny Mehta, a lowly genre paperback editor then, who would fuck up my career at Knopf many decades later when he had become the most powerful publishing executive in New York. "Please don't let on that you knew me when," as Bob Dylan has put it.

But that too is another out-of-sequence, long story.

Was it easier to get published in those days, or harder? Or should I say, to make a living in SF?

It was easier to get short stories published—there were more magazines. About the same as today for genre novels, but the money was less. I mean, there was a kind of half-assed auction for *The Iron Dream*, and the winner was $3,000. I remember Larry Niven was over the moon when Ballantine raised the advance for his next novel from $1,500 to $1,750! And Niven was a Doheny heir.

You have certainly stuck it out. Would you be drawn to the field as it is today?

Early on, Harlan Ellison gave me some good advice. "You're a writer," he said, "and some of what you write is going to be SF, but write all sorts of things, whatever you can—science fiction, mainstream fiction, journalism, scripts, whatever may present itself." So for most of my career, I haven't relied totally on SF to make a living. I've written TV scripts (*Star Trek*, as everyone knows), feature films, all sorts of journalism. I wrote a monthly column for *Knight* magazine, a *Playboy* knock-off, which covered my rent. I was a regular weekly film critic and political columnist for the *Los Angeles Free Press*, which paid very little, but more or less covered the rest of my monthly nut at the time. More recently, I've written the prose in art show catalogs. Still write regular literary criticism. Just finished a stage play adaptation of *Greenhouse Summer*, first such thing I've ever tried.

I guess Harlan knows whereof he speaks, although I doubt he could match you in eclecticity. Is that a word?

I guess now it is. That's something I also learned from my dad's stories about finding work in the Great Depression. If there was a job of any kind open, he'd go for it. He'd tell 'em, Yeah, sure, I know how to do that. If he'd been offered a gig as a brain surgeon he'd probably have bought *Brain Surgery for Dummies* and given it a try if he could bullshit them into hiring him.

I've also written a number of so-called mainstream novels that were published as such—*Passing Through the Flame*, *The Mind Game*, *Pictures at 11*. And two historical novels, *The Druid King* and *Mexica*. Songs, too, which haven't earned me much money. All sorts of things except rubber checks. Never bounced a check, and "eclecticity" is probably a big reason why.

But what about SF itself? Would you be drawn to the field as it is today, if you were just starting out?

The "field" as it is today—I assume by that you mean the SF publishing situation. Which sucks, literarily and economically too. SF probably wouldn't attract me as strongly as it did in the 1960s. Besides, these days, if I was writing the same kind of fiction and had never been pigeonholed as an "SF writer," I'd have a much better chance of getting my work published as general fiction. In France, that's how my more recent novels are being published.

But in an alternate universe where I was starting all over again, I'd still be writing more speculative fiction than anything else. I'd have written and would continue to write the same things that I've written, am writing, and will continue to write. Literarily, politically, no regrets. No retreat, baby, no surrender.

Speaking of France, you've lived in Paris longer than in New York, your original briar patch. How did that come about? How does a kid from the Bronx become not only a Parisian but a player in the arts and literary scene there?

Way back in the 1970s in Los Angeles, I got a call from Peter Fitting, an academic interested in SF, who told me that Richard Pinhas, a French musician who had named his band Heldon after the fictitious country in *The Iron Dream*, and his wife Agnetta were coming through LA and wanted to meet me.

I said okay, but not without some trepidation on the part of myself and Dona, since fans of *The Iron Dream* might turn out to be neo-Nazis. They didn't. Instead they became close friends for decades.

After Dona and I moved back to New York, and eventually broke up for several decades, I was Guest of Honor at a major SF conference in Metz.

I discovered that I had a literary and political reputation in France thanks to the French publication of *Bug Jack Barron*. So I did radio and TV in my primitive French, made more friends, and started going to France for weeks at a time.

During one of those trips, my musician friend Richard—who just about *invented* electronic rock and ambient computer music before he or any other musicians even had computers—asked me to write a simple lyric and record two cuts as a singer on his forthcoming album *East/West*.

I told him I was no singer. He told me not to worry, I would sing through a vocoder. So in France, I became a cyborged singer, which much later became the inspiration for *Little Heroes*.

Much later, I visited Paris on vacation with my then wife, novelist N. Lee Wood. She had never been to France, and we both fell in love with Paris. I had long fantasized about living there but was reluctant to move there alone. But now was the time to do it.

This was early-to-mid Glasnost days, and I was inspired to get a contract to write *Russian Spring*, which despite the title is largely set in Paris, and I spent a year there writing it. By the time the novel was finished (after a trip to Moscow, which despite the title, we had to do in the Russian winter) the Berlin Wall was coming down, and we were culturally connected and decided to stay.

Lee and I eventually divorced, and I decided to stay in France where I was a literary lion, half-assed not-quite rock star, occasional political commentator, sometime screenwriter, and eventually even involved in the gallery and museum art scene, writing exhibition catalog copy. Invited to literary and SF events all over Europe.

Like Utopiales, in Nantes. It was a treat for me to get to rub shoulders with European SF legends like you and Brian Aldiss and Christopher Priest.
And bend elbows as well. The French tradition of the open literary bar helps.

Eventually I reconnected with Dona Sadock, who lived with me in Paris for two years or so after 9/11 (which we experienced pretty damn close in New York City) until real estate and monetary complications forced our exile to New York, where we now live together as I write this.

But we still spend three or four months a year in France. Wouldn't you?

To quote Dylan again, "Honey, do you have to ask?"

In your famous Woody Allen interview (in which he ends up interviewing you!), you said you felt more "culturally connected" in France. Is that because they have the crazy idea that SF is actually Literature?

Partly, I suppose, it's because my writings are considered literature, not SF in general. But it goes deeper than that. In France, literature, art, and film are more culturally central than in the US. Every little village wants to do some event that puts it on the cultural map, and is willing to spend money to do it. The French Ministry of Culture, combined with the Foreign Ministry, has sent me to Mexico and New Caledonia, in effect as a cultural emissary of France, not the USA. The French Consulate in New Orleans was a great help to me and my video biographer Ben Abrass in doing research for my novel *Police State*.

I wrote a commissioned article for *Le Monde* about all this, called "The French Exception." When there were commercial negotiations between the US and the French, Hollywood kept insisting that France's subsidy of its film industry violated "free trade" rules. The French in effect told them to get stuffed. Because film is an art, a part of the national cultural patrimony, and any civilized country of course must regard that as more important than mere commerce.

And France still sticks to that position.

The US doesn't even have a Ministry of Culture. It has "endowments" of the arts and of the humanities (NEA, NEH).

And neither is a cabinet position. All that makes a difference. As I think I more or less said in the Woody Allen dialog, when you're a writer in France and you walk into a bank, you're at least an artist if not a celebrity. When you're a writer who walks into a bank in the US, you're an unemployed bum.

Speaking of unemployed bums, you have been president of SFWA (Science Fiction and Fantasy Writers of America) twice, and also president of World SF. And you were a Guest of Honor at Worldcon in 2013. Does all this mean that you have a political as well as literary agenda? Are there changes you want to see made in the way writers are treated (or treat themselves)?

Well, being Guest of Honor at a Worldcon, or for that matter at any SF convention, and being on panels and such, I don't regard as having a political agenda.

That sort of thing is literary on the one hand, and PR or promotional on another—and of philosophical, scientific, personal interest on yet another, if we can allow three hands.

In SF three hands are allowed.
But being president of anything is, of course, ipso facto a political role, and therefore to one degree or another, successful or not, involves championing some sort of "political agenda"—though not necessarily what the French call "politique politicienne," meaning more or less party politics or pursuit of a political career. My agenda was mostly about making writers' associations more professional.

But while I'm being French about it, I do admit to being *engagé* as a writer. That's hard to define in English; it sort of means the opposite of "apolitical," meaning that I, or at least my characters, often do have their political agendas, which I may or may not agree with, and the stories can and do sometimes turn on specific political conflicts—the outcomes of which can and usually do reflect my own political stance on the matters at issue.

However, I try not to be didactic when writing fiction. When I want to address political matters, I do so directly, as in "The Abnormal New Normal" in this very book [*Raising Hell*]. And I think doing that keeps me from turning my fiction into political screeds.

Finally, like any other writer, I am also a citizen of something; and as a citizen, I've been politically engaged since I was maybe as young as six or seven. My family was politically engaged to the point where mornings were spent in an intricate dance of getting done in the bathroom, eating breakfast, and passing around the morning newspaper, then talking about it over breakfast, schedules permitting, so that the kids and the adults could start the day up-to-date on the news.

From a Democrat or Republican perspective?
Labor, all the way. I was told early on that ladies and gentlemen do not cross picket lines unless they have a damn good exceptional reason. And when at the age of no more than seven, when I asked Jimmy Hauser, a virtual uncle and committed Communist, for something that would give me an overall picture, he handed me H.G. Wells's *Outline of History*.

One more question. As a New Yorker, born and raised, how do you like the city these days?

Not so much. I don't like being in New York, first because it feels isolated from the wider and more diverse worlds of Europe. I don't like being in New York because it's the capital of the US publishing industry, which has pretty much blackballed me for nearly a decade, resulting in four novels published or being published in France, but none in the USA. And after fifteen years in France, I have many more friends there than remain in New York. New York is also monstrously expensive to live in.

As the song goes, "If you can make it there, you can make it anywhere." But doesn't that mean that it's easier to make it anywhere else?

Afterword: For Terry
Nalo Hopkinson

THE FIRST TIME I spoke with Terry, it was via email. I was a newly published writer. I knew who Terry was and enjoyed his work (*Bears Discover Fire*!). I had stumbled upon an online bootleg, unattributed, of his lovely comic short story "They're Made out of Meat." I found his email address and informed him of the copyright violation. And he responded! It was a short and sweet email. He thanked me for letting him know and told me it's a story of his that is frequently reproduced without his permission. He had stopped following up every time.

I was awed and perplexed by his low-key generosity to the thieves. I don't know, were I in his place, that I would feel the same. Writing is hard work! Writers deserve to be credited.

I finally met Terry in person, I believe at the massive science fiction gathering Utopiales in 2001, in Nantes, France. Terry came up to me, introduced himself, and gave me the gift of *Nova Africa*, a French-language translation of his novel *Fire on the Mountain*. Then, quick as he'd shown up, he bustled away again. At the time, I think *Fire on the Mountain* was only available in the French version. My spoken and written French are passable, but reading complex literature in French is an uphill battle. I tried, but I couldn't do it. But I see now that PM Press published it in English. I know what my next novel purchase will be.

Fire on the Mountain is an alternate history. The review of the book on the Big Pulp website says that it "travels 100 years of alternate history to examine a world in which the Civil War is known as the Independence War, and the American south has become the distinct nation of Nova Africa. Bisson's narrative slides between 1859, following the nascent abolitionist movement and the seeds of rebellion, and 1959, where we see the results of that rebellion, a socialist nation filled with scientific advances and wonders."

In subsequent years, Terry had me as a guest at one of his literary salons. He also invited me to be featured in his Outspoken Authors series, at a time when my life was so fraught that I could barely write anything at all, and certainly not to deadline. He waited patiently, encouraged gently, and then coaxed me through his editorial process. The resulting chapbook in that series is one of which I am very proud.

In addition to his fine writing and supportive, wry presence (damn, I miss his sense of humour), Terry's outspoken leftist politics—not an easy position to take in the United States—were among the reasons I admired him. In his interview by TB Calhoun, he rejects the distinction between writing as art and as political project. And he lived his beliefs. For several years he contributed as a writer and editor to the newspaper of the John Brown Anti-Klan Committee. He did jail time for refusing to rat out members of John Brown to a grand jury. In the 1980s, he and his wife Judy ran a mail-order service that sent revolutionary books to prisoners. He was friends with political prisoner Mumia Abu-Jamal and wrote a biography of him. He also worked repairing cars and as a tractor mechanic. His advice to aspiring writers was to learn a trade. His aforementioned humorous short story "Bears Discover Fire," revolutionary in its own quiet way, mentions in passing the value of being able to mount and fix one's own car tyres. He appreciated the problem-solving work of the trades he practised. Problem-solving also happens to be essential to writing speculative fiction.

It often seems to me that the central problem of speculative fiction is one of labour: in other words, who does the dirty work? Who collects the garbage, digs the ditches, cleans up our messes? In our world, those jobs are usually poor-paying and systemically get relegated to or forced upon disadvantaged communities; working-class people, people of colour, women, prisoners. Speculative fiction tries to imagine solutions. Futuristic machines. Magic. Robots. In fact, the word "robot," coined in 1921 by the writer Karel Čapek and his brother Josef, comes from the root of the Czech verb meaning "to work." Problem is, as those labour-saving devices become complex enough to make the kinds of discerning decisions that humans do, they might in effect become self-aware intelligences on a par with humans and therefore deserving of the same rights and considerations. So now who does the dirty work? The goalpost keeps moving.

One alternative to creating and programming machine slaves is to change our systems for getting the back-breaking work done; to change our ideas of who should do it, how they are looked upon in society and how they should be compensated. Say what you will about the various types of leftist ideologies, they pay at least lip service to the notions of shared labour and of respecting hard labour. Science fiction, as well as being a fun genre full of adventures and advanced technology and aliens and new worlds, has always been political, in that it has always wrestled with the big questions such as human rights, class, equity, and community structures. When I consider what directions radical science fiction and fantasy—yes, fantasy can be radical—might take as we move forward into the future, I think imagining systemic change will continue to be a key direction. Terry did this in his time with works such as *Fire on the Mountain*. He was one of the people who made room for people like me to participate in this literature at all. I disagree quite strongly with his negative view of hip-hop, but I suspect we could have had a fulsome, reasoned, and respectful discussion on the topic. I miss Terry. Not that we were close friends. It was my good fortune to stumble into him from time to time and to sometimes have the opportunity to work with him. But as with the late Octavia Butler, I miss knowing he was there, you know?

Elegy
Rudy Rucker

I MET TERRY IN 1984. We felt an immediate rapport. We're beatnik science fiction writers from Kentucky. We grew up wanting to be Beat authors, and to some extent we did that.

I'm from Louisville, Terry from Owensboro, which is the third-largest city in Kentucky, as Terry would testily remind me, annoyed that I was unsure. Louisville was, after all, the big city.

Terry retained his Kentucky accent. His rasp and drawl gave our chats a pleasant, down-home tang. I always felt safe and comfortable with him. He was like a brother.

Re growing up in the provinces, Terry has a wonderful, telling passage in his marvelous autobiographical novel, *Any Day Now*. His character has walked out past the end of a street in his small town. "He kept his eyes on the ground until he was far out in the field. Then he looked up. There was the Universe. It was all stars. He lit a Kent and watched the smoke drift up into the Universe. Nobody in Owensboro even knew it was there."

Terry is perhaps better known for his stories than for his novels. He once made in interesting comparison: "Writing a story is like fixing a car. You work on it for a couple of weeks and you're done. Writing a novel is like being a farmer. You're out in the field for years."

My favorite of Terry's SF novels is *Pirates of the Universe*. A work of genius, with the furthest-out SF I've ever seen. And it has a *transreal* quality, that is to say, it's SF is grounded in the details of the author's life; the hero is from somewhere like Kentucky

I started seeing more of Terry after 2002, when he moved to the Oakland hills with his partner Judy Jensen, who is, among other things, an extreme quilter. At some point my Sylvia got into the craft, and that made another thing the four of us had in common.

We relished our get-togethers. Most years Terry would organize an Oscar-watching party, as befitted his self-anointed status as the world's greatest film critic. His daughter Welcome wondered why she was the only one who was annoyed by Terry's self-confidence. I told her, "That's because he's your *father*." And a very good father he was.

Terry was a man of letters. He edited dozens of short books in the PM Press Outspoken Authors series, each including an incisive interview by him. And he was the convivial emcee of the monthly SF in SF readings organized by Rina and Jacob Weisman.

Terry was at all times knowledgeable, worldly, witty, good-humored, and radical. His wide-ranging autobiographical novel *Any Day Now* reflects his and Judy's life in a commune. And his revelatory alternate-history novel *Fire on the Mountain* is about a world where a slave revolt in the American South leads to a successful revolution and secession.

SF writing can be a collaborative affair, and I had the pleasure of writing two fun stories with Terry. One is "Where the Lost Things Are," about two old men and their wives. It's inspired by the following phenomenon: when you drop a pill on a tiled bathroom floor, the pill instantly disappears forever. But if you go over to where the lost things are, you'll find huge mounds of pills, wallets, spectacles, and so on.

As another joint effort, I published Terry's *Billy's Book* under the aegis of my very small press Transreal Books. In today's benighted marketplace nobody else would print it—although later another edition appeared.

The Billy stories are parodies of children's stories, the kind of thing some urbane wag might have published in the 1950s *New Yorker*. They're deep, simple, caustic, and punctuated by Terry's stylistic trick of fastening on some phrase and repeating it multiple times in his narrative. Like riffs or beats.

Good times.

I visited Terry and Judy a couple of weeks before he died. Though ailing, he was his same wise and congenial self. He was toying with a tool chest of wrenches, rearranging them.

His last words to me?

"See you on the other side."
The man was a hero.

Elegy
Peter Coyote

THE OWENSBORO BOY

1960 September afternoon. His shaggy white-blonde hair,
eager saunter across the dazzling grass,
whistling John Coltrane's "Blue Train." Species-signal
seeking its own kind. I named the tune, fell in step
and we rolled for the Student Union and the first
of sixty-four years of coffee, poetry, and good talk.

sixty-four years, five months later, his matted hair, gummy eyes,
his wrists so thin his hands dangle like platters
as I help him sit up, pulling against the suction cup of his sheets,
kiss his forehead. "I've always loved you Terry."
His best effort—"I know." Barely this side of the light
and slipping. Mine fading with him.

Terry there the night we took peyote.
"My hands are dizzy," he said and we left this world together.
Under the stars I said, "I'm some kinda little wolf,"
turned away, dog-trotted until dawn
through the fields, clear eyes, panting, not yet knowing
I had discovered who I was and was not.

Our friendship survived his taking my girl.
His leaving school months into our sophomore year.

Chesty jocks, offended by his shaggy hair,
jumped and sheared him—(my shame I didn't think
to cut my own.) The mutts had no clue—the prizes,
the respect he'd win from famous men and women

while they tread-milled at safe jobs, combovers and mid-life
questions. Terry could snap one tooth from a comb,
sluice you through the gap to worlds where bears discover fire.
Those beefy shits could never corral his high flights and wild mind,
his trade of "The Mason-Dumbass Line" for Frank O'Hara,
at the Five Spot, Ginsberg at the White Horse, Birdland, Miles.

Before heading East, he helped me fix and tune the two old cars
we'd hustled to carry "The Grinnell Fourteen" to Washington.
A three day fast on the White House sidewalk—
responding to the Cuban Missile crisis, the theft of our carefree youth
supporting Kennedy's Peace Race while John Birchers
shadowed us, gnawing fried chicken, throwing the bones.

The president, in Arizona, saw us above the fold in *The New York Times*,
invited us in to talk. Terry there when Marcus Raskin, Chief of staff to
McGeorge Bundy, blooded executioner of Vietnam, burst into our rooms,
euphoric to tender the president's invitation. Inspired us with vision
and significance of what we'd done, as his son Jamie does today
dispelling the rancid air of Congress.

Pre-internet letters to dozens of schools, eliciting students to replace us
and they did. Terry driving the second car back to Iowa
when Ohio Troopers snagged us bringing an invite
from billionaire Cyrus Eaton, for a celebratory breakfast,
tour of grounds and stables.
We brought along the scruffy hitchhiker who stuffed his pockets
with fluffy breakfast rolls

Terry left to claim New York.
An empty space in the Student Union booth.
Years before we met again—a Colorado dirt road,
Running Deer and me changing a flat, boiling coffee over a small fire.
First one out of the loaded hippie van that stopped to help,
Bisson—like me now, a long-haired communard

Hugs and elation. Never out of touch again despite
his later anger when I worked for California Governor Brown,
sponsoring poets, painters, musicians in prisons and schools.
My pride was Soft Fascism to Terry, his steel already tempered
by three months contempt for refusing to snitch out Puerto Rican revolutionaries
plotting to blow off the head of the Statue of Liberty.

He'd joined the Weatherman in gale-force winds.
Moved West again from Brooklyn
where we repaired our motorcycles in Oakland,
greasy-black fingers staining hand-rolled smokes, Terry
spitting snoose into a chipped green cup. We'd wives and children
now, divorces and ragged losses—his three and six kids,

my two and two, until he'd docked in Judy Jensen's stable harbor,
flinty Kentucky quilter who kept him safely moored,
the twenty years and books he wrote, the children she bore.
She weeps softly today, unabashed before me in her rocker.
Their talk—*The cancer's winning, Judy, I'm quitting
all this shit*—tears squeezed out of her by the papery ruin

of her lover sleeping in the bed beside our chairs,
his mouth agape, still as a beached fish,
the electric blanket barely raised by his breath. We sit
quietly. Death has no ears, for tongues stopped with loss.
We are old friends and can be silent with one another.
Guest arrive, she is calm and gracious. The sky

cracks open outside. My inspiration and model,
the one who never missed the joke,
the one who never lied, the one who never abandoned
or cheated the life of an artist, is dying.
Even the heavens are weeping.
Safely home, I stab my pen onto this sheet of paper.

     For Terry Bisson

About the Authors

Eleanor Arnason is the author of six novels and more than fifty works of shorter fiction. Her novel *Ring of Swords*, acclaimed by the *New York Review of Science Fiction* as one of the best SF novels of the 1990s, won a Minnesota Book Award. Her novel *A Woman of the Iron People* won the Tiptree and Mythopoeic Society Awards. Other works have been short-listed for both the Nebula and the Hugo. She has been called "the acknowledged heir to the feminist legacy of Joanna Russ and Ursula Le Guin," and Andrea Hairston has called her "a treasure." Ms. Arnason lives in the Twin Cities Metro Area.

Terry Bisson was an author, editor, political activist, and friend to many. He was a Hugo and Nebula award-winning writer of seven novels, numerous short works of fiction, and over a dozen children's books. He was the author of *On a Move: The Story of Mumia Abu Jamal* and was the series editor of PM's Outspoken Authors pocketbooks. PM Press published his books *TVA Baby*, *Fire on the Mountain*, and *The Left Left Behind*. He also wrote the long-running "This Month in History" series for *Locus*. His progressive politics landed him in jail for refusing to give testimony to a grand jury investigating the radical underground. He operated Jacobin Books, a mail-order book service that sent books to prisoners, from 1985 to 1990. He was as much an activist's activist as he was a literary powerhouse. More about him and his work can be found at terrybisson.com.

Michael Blumlein was the author of *The Movement of Mountains*, *X,Y*, *The Healer*, *Ageless*, *Longer*, the novella *The Roberts*, and the story collections *The Brains of Rats* and *What the Doctor Ordered*. He was nominated twice for the World Fantasy Award and twice for the Bram Stoker Award, received the

ReaderCon Award, and was short-listed for the Tiptree Award. He wrote for the stage and for film. His novel *X, Y* was made into a feature-length film. His stories have been widely anthologized and taught in a variety of settings, from high school through college and medical and law schools. In addition to writing, Dr. Blumlein was a practicing MD and a faculty member at the University of California in San Francisco. Much of his career has been spent caring for the underserved. After a long battle with lung cancer, Michael passed away on October 24, 2019. Tributes, a memorial, and more on his work can be found at michaelblumlein.com.

John Crowley is the winner of three World Fantasy Awards—including one for Lifetime Achievement and one for his novel *Little, Big*—as well as two Mythopoeic Awards. In 1992 he received the literature award from the American Academy of Arts and Letters. He is the author of thirteen novels, his first *The Deep* in 1975, and his most recent *Flint and Mirror* in 2022. He taught creative writing at Yale University from 1993 until his retirement in 2018. He continues to write and lives in the Berkshires of western Massachusetts. More about him can be found at johncrowleyauthor.com.

Samuel R. Delany, sometimes Chip, is a renowned novelist and critic, whose award-winning fiction includes *Dhalgren*, *Babel-17*, *The Mad Man*, *Dark Reflections*, and *Through the Valley of the Nest of Spiders*. In addition to receiving the William Whitehead Memorial Award and the Kessler Award for his lifetime contribution to lesbian and gay writing, Delany was chosen by the *Lambda Book Report* in 1988 as one of the fifty most influential people of the past hundred years to change our conception of queerness. A native New Yorker, Delany teaches English and creative writing at Temple University in Philadelphia, where he lives with his partner. In July of 2002, he was inducted into the Science Fiction Hall of Fame. Visit samueldelany.com for more about him and his work.

Cory Doctorow is an award-winning science fiction author, activist, and journalist. He is the author of numerous books with his most recent novels being *Picks and Shovels*, *The Bezzle*, and *The Lost Cause*, a solarpunk science fiction novel of hope set amid the climate emergency. His most recent nonfiction book is *The Internet Con: How to Seize the Means of Computation*, a Big Tech disassembly manual. He is a MIT Media Lab research affiliate, a visiting professor of computer science at Open University, and a visiting professor of practice at the University of North Carolina's School of Library and Information Science and cofounded the UK Open Rights Group. Born in Toronto, Canada, he now lives in Los Angeles. York University (Canada) made him an Honourary Doctor of Laws; and the Open University (UK) made him an Honourary Doctor of Computer Science. He maintains a daily blog at pluralistic.net.

Meg Elison is an award-winning author of science fiction and horror as well as feminist essays and cultural criticism. She has been published in *McSweeney's, Slate, Fangoria, Fantasy and Science Fiction, Catapult*, and many other places. Her debut novel, *The Book of the Unnamed Midwife*, part of her Road to Nowhere trilogy, won the 2014 Philip K. Dick Award. Her novelette, "The Pill" (from her contribution to the Outspoken Authors series, *Big Girl*) won the 2021 Locus Award. She is a high school dropout and a graduate of UC Berkeley and now resides in Brooklyn. For more information, visit www.megelison.com.

Karen Joy Fowler is the *New York Times* best-selling author of eight novels and five short story collections, including *The Jane Austen Book Club* and *We Are All Completely Beside Ourselves*, which was the winner of the PEN/Faulkner Award and short-listed for the Man Booker Prize. She is the cofounder of the Otherwise Award and a past president of the Clarion Foundation. Fowler and her husband live in Santa Cruz, California. Learn more at karenjoyfowler.com.

Eileen Gunn is a short-story writer, essayist, and editor based in Seattle, Washington, who began publishing in 1978. Her story "Coming to Terms," inspired partly by a friendship with Avram Davidson, won the Nebula Award for Best Short Story in 2004. Several others have been nominated for the Hugo, World Fantasy, Philip K. Dick, and Locus Awards. Gunn was the editor and publisher of the *Infinite Matrix*, an influential online SF magazine. A seasoned SF pro, she is on the board of directors of the Clarion West Writers Workshop and the Locus Foundation. Learn more at eileengunn.com.

Elizabeth Hand flunked out of college a couple of years after seeing Patti Smith perform and subsequently became involved in the nascent punk scenes in DC and New York. From 1979 to 1986 she worked at the Smithsonian's National Air and Space Museum. She eventually returned to university to study cultural anthropology and received her BA. She is the author of many novels, including *Winterlong*, *Waking the Moon*, *Glimmering*, *Mortal Love*, *Illyria*, *Radiant Days*, *Hokuloa Road*, and *A Haunting on the Hill* as well as multiple collections of stories. Her fiction has received the Shirley Jackson, Nebula, World Fantasy, Mythopoeic, Tiptree, and International Horror Guild Awards, and her novels have been chosen as notable books by both *The New York Times* and *The Washington Post*. A regular contributor to the *Washington Post Book World* and the *Magazine of Fantasy and Science Fiction*, she has written for the *Los Angeles Times*, *Salon*, *Boston Review*, and more. She divides her time between London and the coast of Maine. For more info visit www.elizabethhand.com.

Cara Hoffman is the author of three *New York Times* Editors' Choice novels; the most recent, *Running*, was named a Best Book of the Year by *Esquire magazine*. She first received national attention in 2011 with the publication of *So Much Pretty*, which sparked a national dialogue on violence and retribution and was named a Best Novel of the Year by *The New York Times Book Review*. Her second novel, *Be Safe I Love You*, was nominated for a Folio Prize, named one of the Five Best Modern War Novels, and awarded a Sundance Global Filmmaking Award. A MacDowell Fellow and an Edward Albee Fellow, she has lectured at Oxford University's Rhodes Global Scholars Symposium and at the Renewing the Anarchist Tradition Conference. Her work has appeared in *The New York Times*, *Paris Review*, *BOMB*, *Bookforum*, *Rolling Stone*, *Daily Beast*, and on NPR. Hoffman is a founding editor of *The Anarchist Review of Books* and part of the Athens Workshop collective. She lives in New York City and Athens, Greece. You can find out more at carahoffman.net.

Nalo Hopkinson is a superstar of modern fantasy. She was born in Jamaica, grew up there and in Trinidad and Guyana before moving to Canada when she was sixteen. She now lives in Toronto. Her award-winning novels include *Brown Girl in the Ring* (1998), *Midnight Robber* (2000), *The Salt Roads* (2003), and *The*

New Moons Arms (2007). Her short story collection, *Skin Folk* (2001), was the winner of the World Fantasy Award and the Sunburst Award. She has edited and coedited a number of fantasy anthologies and taught at the Clarion workshops and other venues. She is a founding member of the Carl Brandon Society, which exists to further the conversation on race and ethnicity in SF and fantasy. Visit her at nalohopkinson.com.

James Patrick Kelly's short stories are regular favorites in the science fiction magazines and awards lists, having won Hugo, Nebula and Locus Awards. His fiction has been translated into twenty-one languages. He writes a regular column in *Asimov's Science Fiction Magazine*. He was a member of the faculty at the Stonecoast Creative Writing MFA Program from 2005-2018. Appointed by the governor to the New Hampshire State Council on the Arts, he served for eight years, the last two as Chair. After graduating magna cum laude in literature from Notre Dame, James Patrick Kelly burst onto the SF field like a runaway rocket with stories that energized a new generation of readers and introduced him to the top rank of SF pros. He has remained there ever since, adding plays, anthologies, and audio books to array of talents. His work as a teacher and mentor in an MFA program and his audio performances have increased his solid fan base. Learn more at jimkelly.net

John Kessel is the author of the novels *Pride and Prometheus, The Moon and the Other, Good News from Outer Space, Corrupting Dr. Nice*, and in collaboration with James Patrick Kelly, *Freedom Beach*. Kessel's stories have twice received the Nebula Award given by the Science Fiction and Fantasy Writers of America, in addition to the Theodore Sturgeon Memorial Award, the Locus Poll, the James Tiptree Jr. Award. Kessel holds a BA in Physics and English and a PhD in American literature. He helped found and served as the first director of the MFA program in creative writing at North Carolina State University, where he has taught since 1982. He lives and works in Raleigh, NC, with his wife, the author Therese Anne Fowler.

Paul Krassner was the creator of the *Realist*, the legendary underground magazine that many credit as the beginning of the radical "new journalism" of the

1960s as well as a founding member of the Yippies. He was an immoral, revered, and reviled icon of American humor. Wielding satire as a weapon, he began the assault on middle America known today as the "counterculture." Krassner was a contributor to early issues of *Mad* magazine and won awards from *Playboy*, the Feminist Party Media Workshop, and the ACLU. He died in 2019.

Joe R. Lansdale is the author of nearly four dozen novels, including the Edgar Award–winning Hap and Leonard mystery series (*Mucho Mojo, Two Bear Mambo*) and the *New York Times* Notable Book *The Bottoms*. He has received nine Bram Stoker Awards, the American Mystery Award, the British Fantasy Award, and the Grinzane Cavour Prize for Literature. More than two hundred of his stories have appeared in such outlets as *Tales from the Crypt* and *Pulphouse*, and his work has been adapted for *The Twilight Zone* and *Masters of Horror*. His work has been collected in numerous short story collections, and he has edited or coedited over a dozen anthologies. On October 19, 2012, he was inducted into The Texas Literary Hall of Fame. He lives with his family in Nacogdoches, Texas. More about him can be found at joerlansdale.com.

Ursula K. Le Guin was a celebrated author whose body of work includes twenty-three novels, twelve volumes of short stories, eleven volumes of poetry, thirteen children's books, five essay collections, and four works of translation. The breadth and imagination of her work earned her six Nebula Awards, seven Hugo Awards, and SFWA's Grand Master, along with a PEN/Malamud Award and essentially every other major SF and fantasy award. In 2014, she was awarded the National Book Foundation's Medal for Distinguished Contribution to American Letters, a lifetime achievement award. Her acceptance speech, which criticized Amazon as a "profiteer," and praised her fellow authors of fantasy and science fiction, was widely considered the highlight of the ceremony. In 2016, she joined the short list of authors to be published in their lifetimes by the Library of America. She died in 2018, a mentor to two generations of radical feminist and progressive writers. More about her and the continuing impact of her work can be found at ursulakleguin.com.

Jonathan Lethem is the best-selling author of thirteen novels, including *Brooklyn Crime Novel*, *The Feral Detective*, and *Motherless Brooklyn*, winner of the National Book Critics Circle Award. His five story collections include *Men and Cartoons* and *Lucky Alan*, and his short fiction has appeared in the *New Yorker*, *Harper's Magazine*, and the *Paris Review*, among other publications, garnering a Pushcart Prize, a World Fantasy Award, and inclusion in *The Best American Short Stories 2008*. He has taught creative writing at Pomona College since 2011 and lives in Los Angeles and Maine. More about him and his work can be found at jonathanlethem.com.

Ken MacLeod is one of the brightest and most progressive of Britain's new "Hard SF" stars who are navigating exciting new futures, to the delight of a growing legion of fans around the world. His award-winning works combine cutting-edge scientific speculation, socialist and anarchist themes, and a deep humanistic vision. Described by fans and detractors alike as a "techno-utopian socialist," MacLeod delights in engaging recognizable characters in far-flung adventures across the boundaries of space and time. Born in Scotland's legendary Outer Isles, MacLeod graduated from Glasgow University with a degree in zoology and has worked as a computer programmer and written a master's thesis on biomechanics. He is the author of nineteen novels, from *The Star Fraction* (1995) to *Beyond the Light Horizon* (2024), and many articles and short stories. His novels and stories have received three BSFA awards and three Prometheus Awards, and several have been short-listed for the Clarke and Hugo Awards. He is married and has two children and lives in Scotland. More of his work and regular musings on life can be found at kenmacleod.blogspot.com.

Nick Mamatas is an author, anthologist, editor, and bookseller living in Oakland, California. His early nonfiction about digital culture and politics appeared in magazines such as *New Observations*, *Artbyte*, and the *Village Voice*. Nick's first novel, *Move Under Ground* crossed the voice of the Beat movement with the themes of H.P. Lovecraft and became an instant cult classic. His other novels include the radical noir *Love Is the Law*, the satirical science fiction title *Under My Roof*, and the PM Press novel *Sensation*, which both prefigured and predicted the rise and fall of the Occupy movement. Nick's fiction and editorial work has won the Bram Stoker Award and has been nominated for four other Stokers, two World Fantasy awards, two Hugo awards, two Locus Awards, and a Shirley Jackson award. He, with Nisi Shawl, are sharing editorial roles on future titles in the Outspoken Authors series.

Michael Moorcock is a prolific English science fiction and fantasy writer. Born in London and raised on Mars, (or so he claims) he is perhaps the single most important figure in modern Science Fiction, and the most unlikely to get an O.B.E. The author of over seventy novels and countless stories, essays, comics, screeds, and rants such as the Eternal Champion books, including the Elric, Corum, and Hawkmoon series, as well as the literary novel *Mother London*. He lives in Texas. His miscellany can be found at michaelmoorcock.net.

A native of New England with Southern roots, **Paul Park** climaxed his "wanderjahr" in Asia and the Middle East with his Sugar Rain Trilogy, which established him immediately as a writer to watch. His fascinated readers have since followed him into Christian theology, the anatomy of colonialism, and the limits and possibilities of metafictional narrative. His diverse work includes narrations of museum exhibits with artist Steven Vitiello, and lectures on storytelling at Comicon and nonhuman sentience at Berlin's Max Planck Institute. Meanwhile he has taught writing in a thirty-year career at major universities. He lives in western Massachusetts and currently teaches at Williams College.

Gary Phillips has been a community activist, labor organizer, and delivered dog cages. He has published various novels, comics, short stories, and edited several anthologies including *South Central Noir* and the Anthony award-winning *The Obama Inheritance: Fifteen Stories of Conspiracy Noir*. *Violent Spring*, first published in 1994, was named in 2020 one of the essential crime novels of Los Angeles. Recent novels include *One-Shot Harry* and *Matthew Henson and the Ice Temple of Harlem*. He lives with his family in the wilds of Los Angeles. Please visit his website at gdphillips.com.

Marge Piercy is the author of seventeen novels, including the national bestsellers *Gone to Soldiers*, *Braided Lives*, and *Woman on the Edge of Time*, twenty volumes of poetry, and a critically acclaimed memoir, *Sleeping with Cats*. Her work has been translated into twenty-three languages, and she has received many honors and awards. Born in center-city Detroit and educated at the University of Michigan, she has been a key player in many of the major progressive political battles of our time. She lives on Cape Cod with her husband, Ira Wood, the novelist, memoirist, community radio interviewer, and essayist, and their four cats. For more about her visit margepiercy.com.

Rachel Pollack melded the literary, the political, and the spiritual in her own unique way. An award-winning SF and fantasy author (*Unquenchable Fire* and *Godmother Night*), she was also an esteemed Tarot Grand Master with followers and students around the world. A progressive voice in the transgender community and a trusted guide to the ancient traditions of spiritualism, she was for decades a teacher of writing at Goddard College. She died in 2023. Visit her website, www.rachelpollack.com, for much more.

A direct descendant of philosopher G.W. Hegel, **Rudy Rucker** is a mathematician, science author (*The Fourth Dimension*), online editor (*Flurb*), award-winning SF writer (two Philip K. Dick Awards), and confirmed computer geek. He is sometimes referred to as the godfather of cyberpunk and writes SF in a realistic style known as transrealism, often including himself as a character. A native of Kentucky, he lives in the San Francisco Bay Area. For more on him, including a gallery of paintings, please visit rudyrucker.com.

Born in 1952, a Californian through and through, **Kim Stanley Robinson** grew up in Orange County, surfed his way through UC San Diego (writing his doctoral thesis on Philip K. Dick), and now lives in Davis with his family. He spends several weeks a year above 11,500 feet in the High Sierra. He's also a *New York Times* best-selling author of more than twenty books and has won the Hugo, Nebula, and Locus awards. In 2008, he was named a "Hero of the Environment" by *Time* magazine. He lives in Davis, California.

Born in New York, educated on the East Coast, **Carter Scholz** set foot in Berkeley in the 1970s—and never looked back. Considered a "writer's writer" he is perhaps the best-kept secret in SF, with a prophetic voice that points to the future and rarely looks back.

Nisi Shawl is a multiple award-winning African American writer, editor, and journalist. They are best known for their science fiction and fantasy stories and novels dealing with race, gender, and sexual orientation. Even before Shawl's steampunk-flavored alternate history of the "Belgian" Congo, *Everfair*, took the sci-fi world by storm, their short stories had already established them as a cutting-edge black writer whose politically charged fiction is in the grand feminist tradition of Ursula Le Guin, Octavia Butler, and Joanna Russ. More about them and their work can be found at nisishawl.com.

John Shirley is one of the original "Dread Lords" of cyberpunk who brought a new noir sensibility to SF and fantasy in the 1990s. Still associated with his literary compatriots Gibson, Rucker, and Sterling, Shirley has expanded his work into comics, film, TV, and music, bringing his legions of fans along with him. He is the author of numerous books and many, many short stories. His novels include *Bleak History, Crawlers, Demons, In Darkness Waiting*, and seminal cyberpunk works *City Come A-Walkin'* as well as the *A Song Called Youth* trilogy of *Eclipse, Eclipse Penumbra*, and *Eclipse Corona*. His collections include the Bram Stoker and International Horror Guild award-winning *Black Butterflies, Living Shadows: Stories New & Pre-owned*, and *In Extremis: The Most Extreme Short Stories of John Shirley*. He also writes for screen (*The Crow*) and television. As a musician Shirley has fronted his own bands and written lyrics for Blue Öyster Cult and others. Find more strange and wonderful things at john-shirley.com.

Vandana Singh is a writer of speculative fiction and a professor of physics at a small and lively public university near Boston. Her critically acclaimed short stories have been reprinted in numerous best-of-year anthologies, and the collection *Ambiguity Machines and Other Stories* (Small Beer Press and Zubaan, 2018) was a finalist for the Philip K. Dick award. A particle physicist by training, she has been working for a decade on a transdisciplinary, justice-based conceptualization of the climate crisis at the nexus of science, pedagogy, and society. She is a Fellow of the Center for Science and the Imagination at Arizona

State University. She was born and raised in India, where she continues to have multiple entanglements, both personal and professional, and divides her time between New Delhi and the Boston area.

One of the original gang who created science fiction's controversial "New Wave" in the 1960s, New Yorker **Norman Spinrad** is SF's original outlaw, known for his often hilarious and always fearless attacks on the sacred cows of both the right and the left. Alternately censored and celebrated for his novels (including *The Iron Dream* and *Bug Jack Barron*), he has also written for the original *Star Trek* and twice served as president of the Science Fiction Writers of America. He is the author of over twenty novels and many short stories collected in half a dozen volumes. He's an American who makes his home in Paris by choice and citizen of the world by inclination, and sees no contradictions.

PM Press is an independent, radical publisher of critically necessary books for our tumultuous times. Our aim is to deliver bold political ideas and vital stories to all walks of life and arm the dreamers to demand the impossible. Founded in 2007 by a small group of people with decades of publishing, media, and organizing experience, we have sold millions of copies of our books, most often one at a time, face to face. We're old enough to know what we're doing and young enough to know what's at stake. Join us to create a better world.

PM Press
PO Box 23912
Oakland CA 94623
510-703-0327
www.pmpress.org

PM Press in Europe
europe@pmpress.org
www.pmpress.org.uk

FRIENDS OF PM

These are indisputably momentous times—the financial system is melting down globally and the Empire is stumbling. Now more than ever there is a vital need for radical ideas.

In the many years since its founding—and on a mere shoestring—PM Press has risen to the formidable challenge of publishing and distributing knowledge and entertainment for the struggles ahead. With hundreds of releases to date, we have published an impressive and stimulating array of literature, art, music, politics, and culture. Using every available medium, we've succeeded in connecting those hungry for ideas and information to those putting them into practice.

Friends of PM allows you to directly help impact, amplify, and revitalize the discourse and actions of radical writers, filmmakers, and artists. It provides us with a stable foundation from which we can build upon our early successes and provides a much-needed subsidy for the materials that can't necessarily pay their own way. You can help make that happen—and receive every new title automatically delivered to your door once a month—by joining as a Friend of PM Press. And, we'll throw in a free T-shirt when you sign up.

Here are your options:
- **$30 a month** Get all books and pamphlets plus 50% discount on all webstore purchases
- **$40 a month** Get all PM Press releases (including CDs and DVDs) plus 50% discount on all webstore purchases
- **$100 a month** Superstar—Everything plus PM merchandise, free downloads, and 50% discount on all webstore purchases

For those who can't afford $30 or more a month, we have **Sustainer Rates** at $15, $10, and $5. Sustainers get a free PM Press T-shirt and a 50% discount on all purchases from our website.

Your Visa or Mastercard will be billed once a month, until you tell us to stop. Or until our efforts succeed in bringing the revolution around. Or the financial meltdown of Capital makes plastic redundant. Whichever comes first.

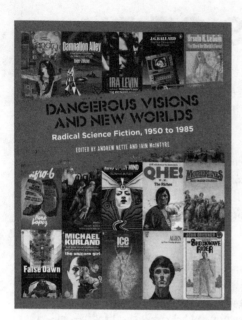

Dangerous Visions and New Worlds

Radical Science Fiction, 1950 to 1985

Edited by Andrew Nette & Iain McIntyre

ISBN: 978-1-62963-883-6 / 978-1-62963-932-1

Paperback / Hardcover

$29.95/ $59.95

8 x 10 • 224 pages

Much has been written about the "long Sixties," the era of the late 1950s through the early 1970s. It was a period of major social change, most graphically illustrated by the emergence of liberatory and resistance movements focused on inequalities of class, race, gender, sexuality, and beyond, whose challenge represented a major shock to the political and social status quo. With its focus on speculation, alternate worlds and the future, science fiction became an ideal vessel for this upsurge of radical protest.

Dangerous Visions and New Worlds: Radical Science Fiction, 1950 to 1985 details, celebrates, and evaluates how science fiction novels and authors depicted, interacted with, and were inspired by these cultural and political movements in America and Great Britain. It starts with progressive authors who rose to prominence in the conservative 1950s, challenging the so-called Golden Age of science fiction and its linear narratives of technological breakthroughs and space-conquering male heroes. The book then moves through the 1960s, when writers, including those in what has been termed the New Wave, shattered existing writing conventions and incorporated contemporary themes such as modern mass media culture, corporate control, growing state surveillance, the Vietnam War, and rising currents of counterculture, ecological awareness, feminism, sexual liberation, and Black Power. The 1970s, when the genre reflected the end of various dreams of the long Sixties and the faltering of the postwar boom, is also explored along with the first half of the 1980s, which gave rise to new subgenres, such as cyberpunk.

Dangerous Visions and New Worlds contains over twenty chapters written by contemporary authors and critics, and hundreds of full-color cover images, including thirteen thematically organised cover selections. New perspectives on key novels and authors, such as Octavia Butler, Ursula K. Le Guin, Philip K. Dick, Harlan Ellison, John Wyndham, Samuel Delany, J.G. Ballard, John Brunner, Judith Merril, Barry Malzberg, Joanna Russ, and many others are presented alongside excavations of topics, works, and writers who have been largely forgotten or undeservedly ignored.

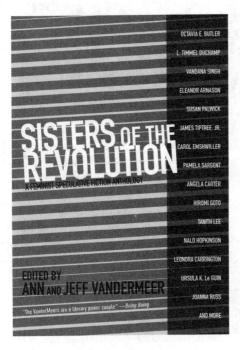

Sisters of the Revolution
A Feminist Speculative Fiction Anthology

Edited by Ann VanderMeer and Jeff VanderMeer

ISBN: 978-1-62963-035-9

$19.95

6 x 9 • 352 pages

Sisters of the Revolution gathers a highly curated selection of feminist speculative fiction (science fiction, fantasy, horror, and more) chosen by one of the most respected editorial teams in speculative literature today, the award-winning Ann and Jeff VanderMeer. Including stories from the 1970s to the present day, the collection seeks to expand the conversation about feminism while engaging the reader in a wealth of imaginative ideas.

From the literary heft of Angela Carter to the searing power of Octavia Butler, Sisters of the Revolution gathers daring examples of speculative fiction's engagement with feminism. Dark, satirical stories such as Eileen Gunn's "Stable Strategies for Middle Management" and the disturbing horror of James Tiptree Jr.'s "The Screwfly Solution" reveal the charged intensity at work in the field. Including new, emerging voices like Nnedi Okorafor and featuring international contributions from Angelica Gorodischer and many more, *Sisters of the Revolution* seeks to expand the ideas of both contemporary fiction and feminism to new fronts. Moving from the fantastic to the futuristic, the subtle to the surreal, these stories will provoke thoughts and emotions about feminism like no other book available today.

Contributors include: Angela Carter, Angelica Gorodischer, Anne Richter, Carol Emshwiller, Catherynne M. Valente, Eileen Gunn, Eleanor Arnason, Elizabeth Vonarburg, Hiromi Goto, James Tiptree Jr., Joanna Russ, Karin Tidbeck, Kelley Eskridge, Kelly Barnhill, Kit Reed, L. Timmel Duchamp, Leena Krohn, Leonora Carrington, Nalo Hopkinson, Nnedi Okorafor, Octavia Butler, Pamela Sargent, Pat Murphy, Rachel Swirsky, Rose Lemberg, Susan Palwick, Tanith Lee, Ursula K. Le Guin, and Vandana Singh.

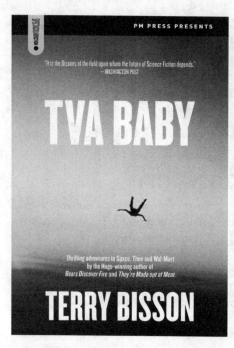

TVA Baby

Terry Bisson

ISBN: 978-1-60486-405-2

$14.95

5 x 8 • 192 pages

Beginning with a harrowing, high-speed ride through the Upper South (a TVA baby is a good ol' boy with a Yankee father and a 12-gauge) and ending in a desperate search through New Orleans graveyards for Darwin's doomsday machine ("Charlie's Angels"), Terry Bisson's newest collection of short stories covers all the territory between—from his droll faux-FAQ's done for Britain's *Science* magazine, to the most seductive of his *Playboy* fantasies ("Private Eye"), to an eerie dreamlike evocation of the 9/11 that might have been ("A Perfect Day"). On the way we meet up with Somali Pirates, a perfect-crime appliance (via PayPal) and a visitor from Atlantis who just wants a burger with fries, please.

Readers who like cigarettes, lost continents, cars, lingerie, or the Future will be delighted. For those who don't, there's always Reality TV.

> "Bisson's work is a fresh, imaginative attempt to confront some of the problems of our time. It is the Bissons of the field upon whom the future if science fiction depends."
> —*Washington Post Book World*

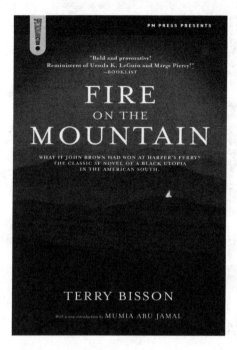

Fire on the Mountain

Terry Bisson
Introduction by Mumia Abu-Jamal

ISBN: 978-1-60486-087-0

$18.95

5 x 8 • 208 pages

It's 1959 in socialist Virginia. The Deep South is an independent Black nation called Nova Africa. The second Mars expedition is about to touch down on the red planet. And a pregnant scientist is climbing the Blue Ridge in search of her great-great grandfather, a teenage slave who fought with John Brown and Harriet Tubman's guerrilla army.

Long unavailable in the US, published in France as *Nova Africa*, *Fire on the Mountain* is the story of what might have happened if John Brown's raid on Harper's Ferry had succeeded—and the Civil War had been started not by the slave owners but the abolitionists.

"History revisioned, turned inside out ... Bisson's wild and wonderful imagination has taken some strange turns to arrive at such a destination."
—Madison Smartt Bell, Anisfield-Wolf Award
winner and author of *Devil's Dream*

"You don't forget Bisson's characters, even well after you've finished his books. His *Fire on the Mountain* does for the Civil War what Philip K. Dick's *The Man in the High Castle* did for World War Two."
—George Alec Effinger, winner of the Hugo and
Nebula awards for *Schrödinger's Kitten*

"A talent for evoking the joyful, vertiginous experiences of a world at fundamental turning points."
—*Publishers Weekly*

Judenstaat

Simone Zelitch

ISBN: 978-1-62963-713-6

$20.00

6 x 9 • 336 pages

It is 1988. Judit Klemmer is a filmmaker who is assembling a fortieth-anniversary official documentary about the birth of Judenstaat, the Jewish homeland surrendered by defeated Germany in 1948. Her work is complicated by Cold War tensions between the competing U.S. and Soviet empires and by internal conflicts among the "black-hat" Orthodox Jews, the far more worldly Bundists, and reactionary Saxon nationalists who are still bent on destroying the new Jewish state.

But Judit's work has far more personal complications. A widow, she has yet to deal with her own heart's terrible loss—the very public assassination of her husband, Hans Klemmer, shot dead while conducting a concert.

Then a shadowy figure slips her a note with new and potentially dangerous information about her famous husband's murder.

> "*Judenstaat* uses the technique of alternate history to offer biting commentary on modern Israel, on the post–Cold War era in which we live, and on religion and nationhood."
> —Cory Doctorow, author of *Little Brother*

> "Zelitch has had the courage, the wit, and the skill to imagine an alternate history of the Jews of Europe after World War II."
> —John Crowley, World Fantasy Award–winning author of *Little, Big*

> "With wit and grace, Simone Zelitch draws the collective grief of the generations living in the shadow of the Holocaust. Part mystery, part ghost story, her smart, politically savvy alternative history explores the growth of a nation and the secrets of the major players involved."
> —Kit Reed, author of *Where*

> "Israel in Europe! What a rich, provocative idea—and what a writer to take it on, with the imagination, heart, and depth it deserves."
> —Terry Bisson, author of *Any Day Now*